ILLUMINATING
THE WORD

THE MAKING OF THE SAINT JOHN'S BIBLE

SECOND EDITION

BY

CHRISTOPHER CALDERHEAD

THE SAINT JOHN'S BIBLE
COLLEGEVILLE, MINNESOTA

HALF TITLE PAGE: Ancient scribal techniques combine with modern artists' methods to produce a contemporary Bible manuscript. On a table next to Donald Jackson's drafting board, quills, brushes and tubes of paint are arrayed within arm's reach.

DEDICATION PAGE: Four details from The Saint John's Bible: *Loaves and Fishes, The Ten Commandments, The Garden of Eden,* and an initial capital from Deuteronomy 4.

TITLE PAGE: A full page illumination from The Saint John's Bible is rendered in gold and color on calf skin. This image is the frontispiece to the Gospel according to John.

A Saint John's Bible Book published by Liturgical Press.

Donald Jackson – *Artistic Director*

www.saintjohnsbible.org

www.litpress.org

Scripture texts in this work are taken from the *New Revised Standard Version Bible: Catholic Edition* © 1989, 1993, Division of Christian Education of the National Council of the Churches of Christ in the United States of America. Used by permission. All rights reserved.

Library of Congress Cataloging-in-Publication Data

Calderhead, Christopher.
  Illuminating the word : the making of the Saint John's Bible / Christopher Calderhead. — 2nd ed.
      pages   cm
  Includes bibliographical references and index.
  ISBN 978-0-8146-9132-8 (alk. paper)
    1. Saint John's Bible.   2. Jackson, Donald, 1938–   3. Manuscripts, English—Minnesota—Collegeville.
  4. Illumination of books and manuscripts—Wales.   I. Title.

  BS191.5.C25 2014
  220.5'20438—dc23   2013035895

To the memory of
Brother Dietrich Reinhart, OSB,
&
Carol Marrin

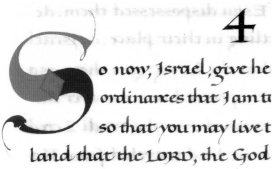

4

So now, Israel, give he
ordinances that I am t
so that you may live t
land that the LORD, the God

CONTENTS

PREFACE TO
THE FIRST EDITION

THIS WHOLE PROJECT is either utter madness or magnificent good fortune. A whole series of chance circumstances have unexpectedly come together to result in the commissioning of an entire Bible copied by hand. For the first time in about five and a half centuries, since Johann Gutenberg began to sell copies of the earliest printed Bibles, an otherwise entirely sane American institution has ordered a new Bible to be made by a process which most people would assume had been rendered obsolete by the invention of printing.

First of all, the setting is a Benedictine monastery. From the beginning, Christian monastic communities have been patrons of art and sponsors of the production of monumental Bibles. The earliest surviving complete Bible in Latin, the huge *Codex Amiatinus*, now in Florence, was made in one of the twin Benedictine houses of Wearmouth or Jarrow in northern England in the early eighth century. The great Carolingian Bibles of the ninth century were almost all prepared in the Benedictine monasteries of Tours. The vast Bury and Winchester Bibles of twelfth-century England were Benedictine commissions, as were many others, such as the Admont and Stavelot Bibles. The custom of creating and using vast manuscript Bibles runs deeply in the ancient Benedictine tradition.

Secondly, Saint John's is a major contemporary university. Books are and always have been at the core of scholarship. Saint John's has a first-rate modern library, its own publisher, and, most famously, the Hill Monastic Manuscript Library, now with some hundred thousand early manuscripts stored by photography and digital technology. It is equipped with the latest scientific techniques of research. In such a context it is reassuring and valuable to modern students to be able to reflect on the methods of communicating all written knowledge at a period when the universities of Europe were in their infancy. The survival and evolution of modern learning has descended directly through a huge epoch of manuscript culture. To those who have never seen a real manuscript, The Saint John's Bible will open a new world. For the experienced historians of books and of the Middle Ages, who cluster around the Hill Monastic Manuscript Library, the Bible will supply answers to countless practical questions on how medieval books were designed and made a thousand or so years ago.

It is chance too that Donald Jackson was prepared to undertake such a project. This should not be underestimated. He is probably the best-known contemporary scribe and illuminator working in Britain or North America. He is an old friend of Saint John's, which he had visited many times before the commission took shape. He has an almost spiritual feeling for parchment and ink and for the written word which fits well with the nature of a Bible. This is probably the most extensive scribal commission in

דברים

Rejoice, Zebulun, in your going out;
  and Issachar, in your tents.
[19] They call peoples to the mountain;
  there they offer the right sacrifices;
  for they suck the affluence of the seas
  and the hidden treasures of the sand.

[20] And of Gad he said:
  Blessed be the enlargement of Gad!
  Gad lives like a lion;
  he tears at arm and scalp.
[21] He chose the best for himself,
  for there a commander's allotment was reserved;
  he came at the head of the people,
  he executed the justice of the LORD,
  and his ordinances for Israel.

[22] And of Dan he said:
  Dan is a lion's whelp
  that leaps forth from Bashan.

[23] And of Naphtali he said:
  O Naphtali, sated with favor,
  full of the blessing of the LORD,
  possess the west and the south.

[24] And of Asher he said:
  Most blessed of sons be Asher;
  may he be the favorite of his brothers,
  and may he dip his foot in oil.
[25] Your bars are iron and bronze;
  and as your days, so is your strength.

[26] There is none like God, O Jeshurun,
  who rides through the heavens to your help,
  majestic through the skies.
[27] He subdues the ancient gods,
  shatters the forces of old;
  he drove out the enemy before you,
  and said, "Destroy!"
[28] So Israel lives in safety,
  untroubled is Jacob's abode
  in a land of grain and wine,
  where the heavens drop down dew.
[29] Happy are you, O Israel! Who is like you,
  a people saved by the LORD,
  the shield of your help,
  and the sword of your triumph!
  Your enemies shall come fawning to you,
  and you shall tread on their backs.

I HAVE LET YOU SEE IT WITH YOUR EYES BUT YOU SHALL NOT CROSS OVER THERE

THEN MOSES THE SERVANT OF THE LORD DIED THERE IN THE LAND OF MOAB AT THE LORD'S COMMAND

The *Death of Moses* appears at the end of the book of Deuteronomy. This illumination was produced by Donald Jackson in collaboration with Aidan Hart.

the western world since the end of the Middle Ages, and it requires an artist of stature with a capacity and a determination for a task of marathon length. It simply happened that this came about at the right moment in the life of the most appropriate scribe.

The timing is also right in a much wider context. We can all see that ancient cultural values are under threat today from secular pressures and from ideological extremism. It is a striking fact that the great Bible commissions of the past have often corresponded with moments when traditional Christianity seemed most at risk. Several huge manuscript Bibles of around 1100 conclude with references to the reassurance of the Scriptures in the time of the First Crusade, proclaimed in 1095. The Dominicans, early champions against heresy and religious deviation, were the principal patrons of orthodox Bibles in the thirteenth century. Even Gutenberg is known to have taken orders for his new printed Bible at the congress in Frankfurt in 1454, convened in response to military advances of the Turks into southeastern Europe. Any manuscript Bible is written slowly. It is almost impossible to study it in haste. If the presence of The Saint John's Bible causes us to pause and to remind ourselves of a life beyond contemporary politics and the daily frenzy of the world, then it will answer a universal need.

Finally, is it complete insanity to make such a book, by such a method? Yes, it probably is, in the sense that it is not necessary to spend so much time and money on something that could be made mechanically in a few moments. It has not happened for a long time. It probably will never happen again. It may be madness or imagination or simply faith that has driven this project, or a combination. Let us be glad that we live in a world where patrons and artists can seize a chance like this to participate in a book, a Bible no less, which will certainly outlive all of us.

CHRISTOPHER DE HAMEL
Gaylord Donnelley Librarian, Parker Library
Corpus Christi College
Cambridge, UK

PREFACE TO THE SECOND EDITION

INCREASINGLY, we live in a world without physical documents, without handwriting. We send e-mails; we tweet. We rarely send postcards—why bother? It's easier to take a photo with our cell phone and post it to a social networking site, even if it means finding an internet café in Kathmandu. Soon, within a matter of years, not decades, newspapers will stop printing and exist only in virtual space. Bookstores—when they exist—are increasingly devoid of books and promote their proprietary electronic book readers instead.

All of this is so new, so rapidly evolving, that we don't know how it will pan out. But there is no question that it is changing the way we read and respond to the written word. Texts are infinitely malleable, always subject to change, editing, and correction. Online texts disappear, go viral, get bowdlerized, or are pirated, edited, and changed beyond recognition.

If we look back at history, this malleability of texts is nothing new. But the speed at which texts have become unstable has sped up.

In the twentieth century, a similar thing happened to the Bible. In the Protestant world, the King James Version remained unchanged and unchallenged for four hundred years. You could pick up your grandmother's well-worn Bible and read the old familiar words. You could commit them to memory. You could recite them before you went to bed. The stability of the text was part of what gave it its authority.

To write the Bible by hand is to step back into an older way of encountering the text.

What does it mean to write the Bible by hand? Is it just an exercise in luxury? Is it an indulgent anachronism? Does it change the text in any way? Does it make you slow down and look at the words? Do you trip over words because they are handwritten, and therefore inherently variable? Or, being unused to reading handwritten text, do you struggle to read? Should you read the Bible as if it is a novel? An e-mail? A tweet?

The Saint John's Bible is a daring experiment. It is a handmade Bible in an era that is rapidly losing the physicality of text. And the making of an entire Bible written by hand suggests that this is not a text like other texts: this is a body of writings that deserves to be read slowly, carefully, pored over. It is not a text that will reveal itself to you with a quick, cursory reading. Instead, it must be pondered, savored, wrestled with.

Writing the Bible by hand also suggests that this is a deeply human text. These words were passed down—in many cases, orally—generation by generation. Over time, they were collected, sifted, redacted, and arranged to make the Bible we have today. And when you read the words in the handwritten book, the human transmission of the text is enacted in a very tangible way. Each word you read was written down by another human being.

THE FIRST EDITION of *Illuminating the Word: The Making of The Saint John's Bible* was published to coincide with the opening of the travelling exhibition that first displayed The Saint John's Bible to the public. Indeed, the book took its main title from that of the exhibition.

When I wrote the first edition, Donald Jackson had completed just three out of the seven volumes that make up the manuscript of The Saint John's Bible. I knew at the time that the first edition was provisional; it would have to be revised once the project was complete. The rest of the story would have to be told.

In May 2012, the last volume of the manuscript, *Letters and Revelation*, was completed and delivered to Saint John's Abbey and University. In the intervening years, another project fundamentally had altered the nature of the project; the Heritage Edition, a full-size reproduction of The Saint John's Bible, went into production in 2006. By 2013, all seven volumes of the manuscript had been published in the printed Heritage Edition. Now The Saint John's Bible exists not simply as one, stand-alone manuscript but as a printed book as well.

Many other changes have taken place since the publication of the first edition of this book. Brother Dietrich Reinhart, president emeritus of Saint John's University and a monk of Saint John's Abbey, who had been such an enthusiastic supporter of the Bible project, died in 2008. Carol Marrin, who had been director of the Bible project, died in 2011. She was a good friend and a wonderful collaborator with me on the first edition.

In addition, The Saint John's Bible has now become fully integrated into the institutional life of the abbey and university. The early improvisatory quality of the project is behind all of us, and now the Bible takes on a new role as a cultural artifact. The pens and brushes and printing presses are still, the artists and scribes have moved on to new projects, and the Bible takes on a life of its own.

In this second, revised edition, we have retained the narrative chapters from the first edition. These stand as a historical document of sorts, recording the beginnings of the project. New chapters have been added to tell the story of the making of each volume in chronological order. We have also added chapters describing the care and handling of the manuscript, examining the scripts in detail, and chronicling the creation of the Heritage Edition. In another new chapter, the artists and scribes who collaborated with Donald Jackson on the project discuss their work on the Bible and its place within their wider careers.

This edition of *Illuminating the Word*, then, describes the making of The Saint John's Bible from its beginning to its end. The project lasted more than fifteen years. I have been honored to have had a role in recording its history as it unfolded.

CHRISTOPHER CALDERHEAD

other side of the sea for us, and get it for us so that we may hear it & observe it?" [14] No, the word is very near to you; it is in your mouth and in your heart for you to observe. ▮ [15] See, I have set before you today life and prosperity, death & adversity. [16] If you obey the commandments of the LORD your God that I am commanding you today, by loving the LORD your God, walking in his ways, and observing his commandments, decrees, and ordinances, then you shall live & become numerous, and the LORD your God will bless you in the land that you are entering to possess. [17] But if your heart turns away and you do not hear, but are led astray to bow down to other gods & serve them, [18] I declare to you today that you shall perish; you shall not live long in the land that you are crossing the Jordan to enter and possess. [19] I call heaven and earth to witness against you today that I have set before you life and death, blessings & curses. Choose life so that you & your descendants may live, [20] loving the LORD your God, obeying him, and holding fast to him; for that means life to you and length of days, so that you may live in the land that the LORD swore to give to your ancestors, to Abraham, to Isaac, and to Jacob.

31

When Moses had finished speaking all these words to all Israel, [2] he said to them: "I am now one hundred twenty years old. I am no longer able to get about, and the LORD has told me, 'You shall not cross over this Jordan.' [3] The LORD your God himself will cross over before you. He will destroy these nations before you, and you shall dispossess them. Joshua also will cross over before you, as the LORD promised. [4] The LORD will do to them as he did to Sihon & Og, the kings of the Amorites, and to their land, when he destroyed them. [5] The LORD will give them over to you and you shall deal with them in full accord with the command that I have given to you. [6] Be strong and bold; have no fear or dread of them, because it is the LORD your God who goes with you; he will not fail you or forsake you." ▮ [7] Then Moses summoned Joshua and said to him in the sight of all Israel: "Be strong and bold, for you are the one who will go with this people into the land that the LORD has sworn to their ancestors to give them; and you will put them in possession of it. [8] It is the LORD who goes before you. He will be with you; he will not fail you or forsake you. Do not fear or be dismayed." ▮ [9] Then Moses wrote down this law, and gave it to the priests, the sons of Levi, who carried the ark of the covenant

Suzanne Moore's special treatment of a text from the Pentateuch appears opposite Deuteronomy 31.

INTRODUCTION

Every scribe who has been trained for the kingdom of heaven is like the master
of a household who brings out of his treasure what is new and what is old.

MATTHEW 13:52 NRSV

YOU ARE HOLDING in your hands a printed book. There is nothing extraordinary in that. We are surrounded by printed books. We assume that books exist in editions—thousands of identical copies. If you should lose this book or if by some mischance you should tear a page, you know that you can always find another somewhere—at a bookshop, at a library or on the internet. This book costs less than dinner and a movie for two at the local mall.

If you have just unpeeled the shrink-wrap from this copy, yours are probably the first human eyes to actually see this page. From its birth on a computer disk, through its journey from printing plant to warehouse to your hands, it has been in the grip of machines. Quality control inspectors have perhaps examined one in every hundred copies to ensure the machines functioned properly, that the ink went down smoothly and didn't streak and that the pages didn't get folded and sewn out of order. But no one has seen the pages of *this* book.

Technology shapes the way we look at books and the way we read them. We tend to treat text as a commodity. We read quickly and efficiently. We rarely pause to examine the book itself.

In the era before printing, every book was unique—and enormously expensive. Reading was slow and deliberate; in the first few centuries of the Common Era, it was almost always done out loud. In a manuscript book, you can tell whether the scribe was rushed or took his time. Sometimes you can see him growing tired, as the script becomes cramped or uneven. Every word you read was written by an actual human being—the act of reading is a moment of contact between you and the scribe.

Medieval scholars and monks would sometimes travel long distances to consult a single book. Important biblical manuscripts, like the Book of Kells or the Lindisfarne Gospels, were elaborately illustrated and decorated. The Winchester Bible is as complex as a gothic cathedral—and, like many cathedrals, it was left unfinished. These books were designed to be pored over, meditated upon, treasured.

ON APRIL 28, 1998, Donald Jackson and Brother Dietrich Reinhart, OSB, signed the contract which officially launched The Saint John's Bible. Donald used a quill pen and brilliant red ink. Together they embarked on a collaboration which would last almost a decade.

The Saint John's Bible is a modern manuscript book. It recaptures the spirit of the great medieval Bibles, yet it grows out of a completely contemporary artistic and theological sensibility.

Donald Jackson, one of the most skilled living calligraphers, is the artistic director of the project. From his Scriptorium in Wales he supervises a team of scribes and illuminators. The Bible is being written with quills on vellum, using hundred-year-old sticks of ink. The illuminations are made with a combination of ancient and modern techniques.

Donald Jackson at the Scriptorium in Wales.

In May 2004 a facsimile of the first volume of The Saint John's Bible was presented to His Holiness, Pope John Paul II, at an audience in Rome, Abbot John Klassen, OSB, Donald Jackson and Dietrich Reinhart, OSB, hold the book, which is opened to the beginning of John's Gospel.

Donald Jackson and Dietrich Reinhart, OSB, sign the contract for The Saint John's Bible.

A committee of scholars and artists guides the work. The Benedictine Abbey of Saint John the Baptist in Minnesota was founded in 1856. It has long been a center for the arts and liturgical renewal. The Saint John's Bible is a reflection of the monastic devotion to the Scriptures. The painstaking work of making the Bible echoes the slow, meditative reading which is a hallmark of Benedictine life and spirituality.

IN THE YEAR 2000 I was asked to begin documenting the making of The Saint John's Bible. For four years I have been interviewing the scribes, artists and scholars involved in the project. I have had the privilege of seeing Donald at work in his Scriptorium and joining the monks in their daily round of prayer at Saint John's. The stories which appear in this book are a distillation of hundreds of hours of interviews. They provide a glimpse of the working process behind the first major illuminated Bible to be produced since the Middle Ages, a Bible for our own times.

CHRISTOPHER CALDERHEAD

New York, 2005

God in the details: a tiny slip of paper with Donald's initials is transformed into a thing of beauty.

Page No	Gathering / folio	Description	Allocation	Time for Text	Date of Text Comp.	No of lines (Text)	No of lines (poetry)	Rubrication & footnotes	Chapter nos & caps. etc	PROOF READ	COMPLETION	Chapter & Verse
						2028	76					
Matthew 25	C1 (h) r.	Text	~~Brian~~	✓ 10 hrs. 30 mins	29.2.'00	102	3	✓ 2 hrs		✓		26:35-75 27:1-5
Matthew 26	C1 (f) v.	Text	~~Brian~~	✓ 9 hrs. 30 mins	2.3.'00	108		✓ "		✓		27:6-56
Matthew 27	C2 (f) r.	Text + decoration	~~Brian~~	✓ 8 hrs.	2.3.'00	65		✓ 1¼ hrs.		✓		27:57-66 28:1-20
Mark frontispiece	C2 (h) v.	Illumination	DJ	✓	—					—		
Mark 1	C3 (h) r.	Incipit + Text	DJ		16.7.'01	30		✓ 1hr.				Mark 1:1-30
Mark 2	C3 (f) v.	Text	~~Brian~~ Sally		28.6.'01	104						1:31-45 2:1-28
Mark 3	C3 (f) r.	Illum. (Sower & Seed) + Text	~~Brian~~ Sally		1.7.'01	76						3:1-35 4:1-4
Mark 4	C3 (h) v.	Text	~~Brian~~ Sally		26.6.'01	102	3					4:5-47 5:1-13
Mark 5	C2 (h) r.	Illum. (two lines) + Text	DJ ~~Brian~~ Sally Benjamin		27.6.'01	69						5:14-43
Mark 6	C2 (f) v.	Illum. (Loaves & Fishes) + Text	DJ Sally		21.04.'02	80		11½ hrs				6:1-34
Mark 7	C1 (f) r.	Illum. " + Text	DJ Sally		08.04.'02	76	∠	10½ hrs				6:35-56 7:1-15
Mark 8	C1 (h) v.	Text + decoration	~~Brian~~	✓	06-05-'00	98		✓ 12½ hrs		✓		7:16-37 8:1-25
Mark 9	D1 (h) r.	Text	✓	✓	10-05-'00	106		✓ 13 hrs		✓		8:26-38 (9:1-32)
Mark 10	D1 (f) v.	Illumination (Transfiguration)	Sue	working/Sue first	—					—		
Mark 11	D2 (f) r.	Text	Sue		22-05-'01	106		8 hrs 30				(9:33-50) 10:1-31
Mark 12	D2 (h) v.	Text	Sue H	✓ 6 hrs. 40	4.3.'00	101	6	✓ 2 hrs				10:32-52 11:1-23
Mark 13	D3 (h) r.	Text + decoration	Sue H	✓ 6 hrs	28.2.'00	86	4	✓ 1¼ hrs				11:24-33 12:1-27
Mark 14	D3 (f) v.	Sp. Treat. + Text	~~Sue~~	working first	25-05-'01	77	3	5 hrs 15				12:28-44 13:1-10
Mark 15	D3 (f) r.	Text	~~Sue~~ — Sue		01-06-'01	100	6	6 hrs 50				13:20-37 14:1-20
Mark 16	D3 (h) v.	Text	Sue H	✓ 6 hrs. 30 mins	29.2.'00	102	3	✓ 1¼ hrs				14:30-72 15:1-7
Mark 17	D2 (h) r.	Text	Sue H	✓ 6 hrs.	18-04-'00	105		✓ 8½ hrs		✓		15:8-47 16:1-8
Mark 18	D2 (f) v.	Text + decoration	DJ Sally	✓ time to be done by Sally	16/03/'01	37		✓		✓		
Mark 19	D1 (f) r.	Decoration	DJ							—		
Luke frontispiece	D1 (h) v.	Luke f. Illumination	DJ							—		

Burial of Christ — 6.4.'01

3758   108

24.10.00 9 completed - 15 to comp.

Pages from the Allocation Book detail each stage a Bible page passes through during production. The columns record the page number, a gathering/folio reference, a description of each page, the scribe allocated, time allowed for writing, chapter numbers, whether the page has been proofread, whether it has been completed and the chapter and verse of each page.

PART 1

THE PROCESS

These opening chapters describe a series of visits I made to Donald Jackson's Scriptorium in Wales between 1999 and 2002. I had the good fortune to be living in Cambridge, England, at the time, and the Scriptorium was a relatively short three-hour journey from my home. I made visits to the Scriptorium every three months or so and was able to see the Bible as it was beginning to take shape. It was a great privilege to be able to spend time wandering through the Scriptorium and enjoying the hospitality of Donald and Mabel Jackson.

These chapters were arranged thematically, explaining how the Scriptorium was organized and how the work flow functioned, describing the tools and materials used, and introducing the main protagonists of the story.

These chapters were originally published in the first edition of Illuminating the Word: The Making of The Saint John's Bible *in 2005. Because they were written during the making of only the first volume, Gospels and Acts, they carry the story through its opening phase. We include them unchanged in this revised edition of* Illuminating the Word *because they evoke that period and stand as a testament of a crucial phase of the project.*

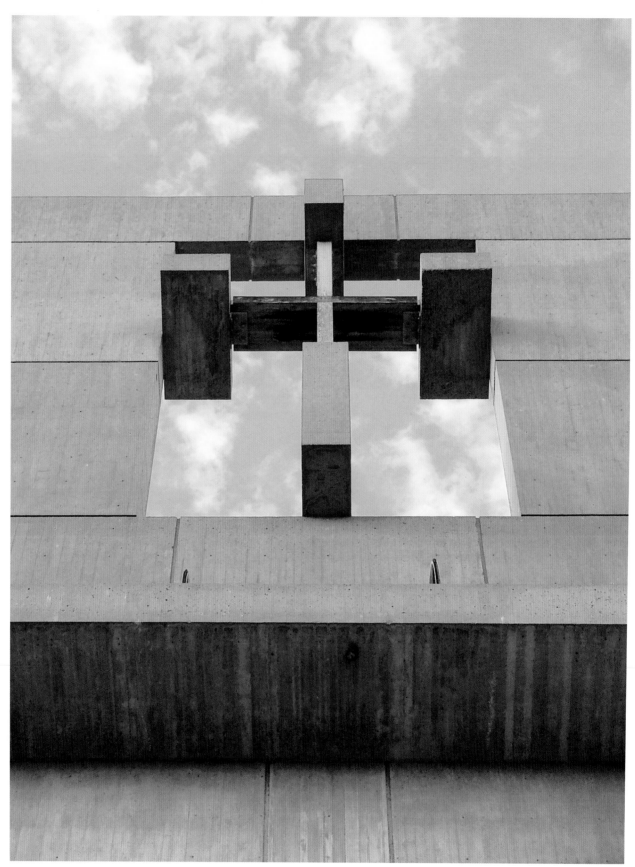

The oak cross fixed in the concrete bell banner in front of the Abbey church was made from wood harvested in Saint John's own managed forests.

CHAPTER 1

LIVING THE WORD

T HE GROUNDS OF Saint John's were perfectly still just before seven in the morning. The monastic and university buildings stood silent sentinel over the green campus. Behind them Lake Sagatagan was glassy-smooth, disturbed only by the tiny black heads of snapping turtles coming up for air. It was an early morning in the spring. The sun had been up for some while; so had many of the monks, but few were stirring beyond the monastic enclosure. A lone man in a black habit walked quietly along the drive in front of the Abbey church.

A bell began to ring out from the Abbey banner, the imposing concrete structure which holds the bells in front of the monastic church. It was the call to prayer.

I had come to Saint John's with many questions. Why had they commissioned Donald Jackson to write and illuminate an entire Bible by hand? In an era when a Gideon Bible is found in every hotel room in America, when biblical Web sites proliferate on the internet, when the Scriptures get carried about in backpacks and underlined with yellow highlighter in subway cars during rush hour, why spend this kind of time, care and attention making a manuscript Bible?

But now was not the time for questions. Carol Marrin, the director of the Bible project, was waiting for me at the door of the Abbey church. We went in and found places in the guest section. An elderly monk clattered past us, his cane tapping an uneven rhythm on the stone floor. Younger monks strode in with all the confidence of men in their prime.

Each seat had its own complement of service books. Carol and I each pulled out three of the binders and turned the pages to find the day's liturgy, arraying our books in order on the small shelf in front of us. Near us a stranger picked out one book, flicked through it, put it back and pulled out another, unsure what to do. An older monk leaned over and with a few whispered words set everything in readiness.

The bell outside sounded again and without a word we all rose in our places.

"Lord, open my lips," the leader said.

We responded, "And my mouth will proclaim your praise."

After singing a hymn, we sat down and began to pray our way through the psalms of the day. Verses sung or chanted by a single voice were followed by verses sung or chanted in unison by all. Some portions were allotted to one side of the church or the other, spoken in dialogue, back and forth across the sanctuary in orderly progression.

The monastic hours of prayer have a distinct pace. The familiar words are not uttered in haste. We paused deliberately after every verse. At the conclusion of each psalm, we kept silence, leaving time for the words to sink down deep.

A reading, a sung canticle and prayers followed in due course and we were done. The community rose and dispersed to every corner of the campus. Our work day had begun.

As Carol and I walked out of the Abbey church, she began to rattle off a list of meetings she'd set up for

The bell banner is silhouetted against a bright morning sky. The cornerstone for Marcel Breuer's Abbey church was laid in 1958. The bold modernism of the church was a confident expression of the monks' commitment to the visual arts. The Saint John's Bible continues that tradition of artistic experimentation.

me through the day. It was 7:30 in the morning and Carol was wide awake and ready to go. There were no gaps in the schedule. Every hour was accounted for. This was the other side of Saint John's—it is not only a place of prayer and silence. It is also a place of very hard work.

We walked to the dining hall while Carol filled me in about the people I would meet, giving brief descriptions of each person, tidbits of monastic politics and pointers about questions I should ask. A squad of ROTC cadets jogged past us, dressed in black T-shirts and shorts. They broke step to walk into the dining hall together. The last cadet held the door for Carol.

Between bites of sausage and egg and toasted Johnnie Bread (a product of the monastery) I made notes. Around us a steady stream of undergraduates were coming into the dining hall. The university was waking up.

Breakfast done, I headed to my first meeting. Carol called after me, "Oh, by the way, Jo White phoned; she's coming by a bit later with some photographs. Come by my office and we can have a look at them." She waved and disappeared down the path.

Holy reading, holy writings

ABBOT JOHN KLASSEN, OSB, is a tall man with a gentle demeanor. I met him in his office. He made me a cup of coffee and we sat near the large, sculptural fireplace. The abbot's office fills a small suite of rooms in the wing of the monastery designed by Marcel Breuer. As I settled into my chair I looked eagerly around the room, enjoying every architectural detail. The interior is a perfectly preserved 1950s modernist interior by one of the great masters. That it is intact is a tribute to Benedictine thrift and good stewardship.

Monks gather in the Abbey church for morning prayer. In his Rule, Saint Benedict organized the monastic day around a regular cycle of prayer. The recitation of the Psalms is the heart of the community's worship.

A monk in the black habit of the Benedictine order walks outside the Abbey church before morning prayer.

Monks are encouraged to develop the habit of reading the Scriptures in a slow, meditative technique referred to as *lectio divina*. The daily practice of *lectio* draws deeply on the imagination as a key to understanding the Bible not only with the mind, but with heart and soul as well.

I asked, "How do you feel The Saint John's Bible connects with the life of the monastery?"

He began with institutional concerns. He spoke of Saint John's commitment to the arts, especially to the book arts, and mentioned some of the other institutions within the community—the Arca Artium collection and the Hill Monastic Manuscript Library—which are part of that commitment.

We chatted back and forth about buildings, staffing, programs. There were many plans for how the Bible might be used. Institutional plans, however, rarely light a fire under anyone. I probed to see what would kindle a flame.

It was peace and justice. The abbot's eyes sparkled. This Bible would be about something new: "It is a retrieval of the Catholic imagination with Scripture. The Word becomes sacramental. It is not just a text. It is like the Eucharist: a visual image of the Word." With his own background in applied ethics and peace studies, he was particularly concerned that The Saint John's Bible should speak for the poor and marginalized. "God's commitment to the poor is embedded in Scripture," he said. "In the prophetic books, in psalmody and throughout the New Testament. The deeper we are drawn into Scripture, the more we will be driven to address these issues in our lives." He hoped the illuminations would be compelling witnesses to "God's own awareness of and his standing with the poor."

Throughout their history, Benedictine monasteries have emphasized the importance of books in the religious life. During the early Middle Ages, they were the most important centers of book production in Western Europe. These nineteenth-century stained glass windows from the former Abbey church reflect the central position of books in the monastic imagination.

He foresaw the Bible moving to exhibitions around the country, engaging people, especially the young, asking them to encounter the Scriptures in a new form. "What happens when you read the Word together? Things come out of the text—new, exciting things." He saw The Saint John's Bible as a way of sharing the Scriptures in a classic Benedictine way: to encourage *lectio divina,* the slow, meditative monastic method of reading the Bible, on a mass scale. That's what he'd like to see Saint John's do with its new Bible; that's what he'd like to see happen in the broader world, when people see the book and pore over it.

After meeting the abbot I walked over to the Hill Museum & Manuscript Library to meet Columba Stewart, OSB. A spare, thin man, he wore black jeans and a short-sleeved clerical shirt, unbuttoned at the collar. His eyes were sharp and intense. He greeted me with a swift, firm handshake.

We sat down and I made small talk.

At the first pause he said, "What do you want to ask me?" He smiled.

I cut the chitchat. "Tell me about *lectio divina.* I want to know more about where it comes from, how it's done."

"It was part of the return to the sources which happened after Vatican II. The Council's statements on monasticism invited the religious communities to reexamine their ways of life. It was often confusing; everything was up for grabs. Should we wear a habit? What hours of prayer should we keep? How are we to translate our worship from Latin into the vernacular?"

The Council forced monasteries to consider afresh the roots of their traditions. Monks and nuns around the world looked at their life with new eyes.

"What does it mean to be a Benedictine, a Trappist, a Franciscan?" he continued. "What are the deep roots of our communities?"

For Benedictine houses like Saint John's, this inevitably meant returning to Saint Benedict's Rule, the very foundation of their tradition. Written in the early sixth century, it presents a simple, balanced life of prayer and work. Steeped in biblical images, much of its text is directly quoted from the Scriptures. It presents a monastic life which is permeated by the Bible. The central practice of the community is the recitation of the psalms, and monks are directed to "listen readily to holy reading" and devote themselves to prayer.*

In the 1970s as the community explored the foundations of its life, it began to recapture a deeply personal, imaginative reading of Scripture. The practice of *lectio* is slow. The earthy image most frequently used to describe it is that of a cow chewing the cud. Ruminating on the Bible rather than analyzing it is the key. The reader pauses whenever a word or phrase strikes him. He sits with that word, letting it sink in. Reading passes into contemplation, which passes into prayer.

Cassian, the fifth-century monastic writer, describes this kind of attentiveness in reading and reciting the psalms. The monk who recites the psalms is like a deer feeding in the pastures of Holy Scripture—

> Being endued, by the strength and succulency of this divine nourishment, with all the affections which are expressed in the psalms, he receives their impression and recites them, as if they were no longer the songs of the Bard of Zion, but his own warm effusions, and that from the depths of a contrite heart, he was really pouring forth his own prayer to God. He believes, at last, that the psalms were made expressly for him, and that the truths they contain were not accomplished in David alone, but are daily accomplished and verified in himself personally. **

A charismatic teacher, Donald Jackson lectures to the participants of the Calligraphy Connection. His bold, fluid writing fills the large panel behind him.

* Rule of Saint Benedict 4:55

** Cassian, *Conferences.* Trans. Father Robert of Mount Saint Bernard's Abbey. London: Thomas Richardson and Son, nineteenth century (no date). Conference 10, Chapter 10, pp. 528–529.

The practice of *lectio*, Father Columba said, was central to the practice of the community. If a monk had trouble with this deliberate, meditative reading of Scripture, then he probably wasn't suited to the monastic life.

I wondered if that wasn't a bit harsh, but I didn't say so. It was certainly a realistic and practical appraisal of the monastic vocation. And Columba struck me as practical to the core. The monks' days are ordered around morning, noon and evening prayer. The Mass is celebrated daily. Monks are expected to build in private time for *lectio divina* every day. They recite and read the Scriptures all day long.

I came away from our meeting with a richer sense of how central the Bible is in monastic life. And a reading list.

Calligraphy at Saint John's

JO WAS WAITING FOR ME in Carol's office. Short, white-haired and feisty, Jo is a force to be reckoned with in the calligraphy world. She'd brought a packet of photos, brochures and journals which illustrated the history of calligraphy at Saint John's.

She greeted me with a warm hug and kiss. Carol pulled out some new prints of Bible pages to show her.

"How's it going?" Jo asked me with her flat Minnesotan vowels.

I gave her a rundown of my visit so far.

"Good, good. Mm-hmm. Yes." Jo likes to keep track of things.

Carol stepped out of the office and Jo reached into her bag and pulled out a box to show me. It held an album of calligraphy samples which she'd been given. All the calligraphy stars were represented—there were pieces by Sheila Waters and her son, Julian, by Donald Jackson and Thomas Ingmire. An exquisite little manuscript by Ann Hechle was tucked into a corner of the box.

The Calligraphy Connection held at Saint John's in 1981 gathered lettering artists from across the world for the first summer calligraphy conference. The Connection spawned a tradition of annual conferences in the United States which has lasted for a quarter century.

"I'm going to show these to Columba," she said, "I want to have them appraised."

Without Jo White there would be no Saint John's Bible. She has promoted calligraphy at Saint John's for more than twenty-five years. As Carol remarked to me after she left, "Jo gets things done. I've seen her stand up in meetings when people are not coming to a decision and say 'Well, who's in charge?'"

Jo organized the Calligraphy Connection at Saint John's in 1981. It was the first conference of its kind, gathering lettering artists from across the United States and Europe for an intense week of practical teaching. The Connection spawned a calligraphy institution, the annual summer conference. Every year since 1981 a conference has been held in a different city in the United States. Saint John's has hosted the annual gathering three times.

In 1988, she collaborated with Jane Borchers to bring a traveling exhibition of Donald Jackson's work to venues across the country. As she likes to say, "Two middle-aged housewives got that show into thirteen cities."

Jo White was also instrumental in planning a symposium entitled *Servi Textus,* designed to initiate a conversation between calligraphers, scholars and collectors. Jo hoped that their deliberations would help create a market for works of calligraphic art, and begin to develop ties between curators and lettering artists.

It was during the planning for *Servi Textus* that the idea of The Saint John's Bible was first proposed.

Once Jo had shown me her lettering samples, she packed them away and headed off the down the hall to see Columba.

A happy group gathers at a diner in St. Joseph, near Saint John's. From left to right, Jo White, Donald and Mabel Jackson, Rebecca Cherry and Jo's husband, Bob.

A Bible is born

WITH A FEW MINUTES before my next appointment, I looked over my notes. The week before, I had phoned Donald Jackson and Eric Hollas, OSB, to ask about the day they first discussed the Bible project.

Memories differ about the details. It was Saturday, November 27, 1995. Father Eric was then in charge of the Hill Museum & Manuscript Library. He was in Chicago with Donald Jackson to promote *Servi Textus.*

Donald remembered, "It was part of the warm up for the conference. Saint John's felt they had to pay court to the calligraphy community. I offered to give a talk at the Newberry Library. It was the first time Eric and I had gone on the boards together. The next day before we went our separate ways we went to the Art Institute to see the Manet exhibition. Lots and lots of haystacks. Afterwards we went out for a late lunch in the Loop. It was a cold day and I bought a fedora at Marshall Fields to keep out the cold."

Eric said, "It was hard to find a place to eat in that neighborhood on a weekend. We went into a little Italian place. It was half empty and dark."

"Eric likes Italian," Donald recalled. "So we ordered pasta and a bottle of red wine. There was a busy lunchtime crowd."

Donald bided his time as they ate their lunch.

"The wine was very good. I waited until we were two-thirds of the way down the bottle and then I popped the question: 'What are you doing to celebrate the millennium?'"

Eric told him Saint John's had no plans in particular.

Donald continued his pitch. "The Archbishop of Canterbury likes to say, 'Whose birthday is it anyway?'"

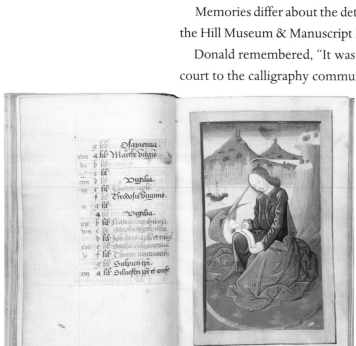

An illumination from a Book of Hours shows John the Evangelist writing with a quill on a small scroll extended across his knee.
Book of Hours. Sarum Use. France (Rouen), end of the fifteenth-century. Manuscript on vellum. Kacmarcik Collection of Arca Artium, Saint John's University.

He suggested to Eric that Saint John's should commission him to write a book of Gospels to mark the two-thousandth anniversary of Christ's birth.

"Donald always says he proposed Gospels," Eric recalled. "I'm sure he said Bible."

Donald sticks to his guns. "I swear to this day I said Gospels. Anyway, Eric, like a good Benedictine, immediately said, 'How much?' I said 'A million dollars.' I wasn't expecting him to ask so I just named a figure."

Eric remembered, "Donald asked me to take the idea back to Saint John's. I thought to myself, 'This will never happen.' But I don't like to say no, so I said I would."

They went their separate ways and Donald went back to the hotel where he and Jo White were staying. She knew he had intended to make his proposal over lunch.

"When I got to the hotel where Jo White and I were staying, she took a two-dollar bill. We wrote the time and date on it and she tore it in half. She handed me one half and she kept the other. She said to me, 'When this project comes off, we'll reunite the two halves.'"

Eric returned to Saint John's and waited to mention the idea to Dietrich Reinhart, OSB, the president of the university.

"It was much later," he recalled. "Dietrich and I were driving one day to the Twin Cities and I had a whole list of items to bring up. When I mentioned my conversation with Donald and the idea of making a Bible, he said immediately, 'We have to do that.' It wasn't a logical response. It came from the gut."

Monasteries make decisions slowly. The men who make up the community have to live with the decisions they make. Brother Dietrich presented the Bible project to the monastic community in 1997. The community debated, argued and wrestled over the idea for a full year. At last they voted yes—the project had the green light. Donald and Jo reunited the two halves of their two-dollar bill.

Jo White's two dollar bill. On the day Donald Jackson first proposed the making of The Saint John's Bible to Eric Hollas, OSB, Jo wrote the date on the bill and tore it in half. The two halves were reunited when the contract was signed.

A celebration of the non-linear

I WANDERED DOWN to my next appointment, lunch with the president of the university.

Dietrich walked me down to the student dining hall. As president of the university, he had been the driving force behind The Saint John's Bible. I'd never met him before although I had seen his picture many times and had spotted him around the campus. His manner was easy-going; he was quick to smile. As we walked through the dining hall he greeted undergraduates and staff as they passed by him. We sat down with our trays and he asked me how my visit was going, about my own career, about the people

Brother Dietrich Reinhart, OSB, the president of the university, chats at a press briefing.

Saint John's University was founded by the monks in 1857, immediately after the Abbey itself was established. Many of the monks teach or work at the university. The ceremonies and rhythms of academic life interweave with those of the monastery.

I'd met. I found myself chatting amiably about my own hopes and fears, my desires for the future, my journey of faith. Twenty minutes into lunch, I suddenly stopped and said, "Wait a minute: you're doing a fantastic job of interviewing me!"

Dietrich smiled back. "It helps me feel at ease," he said and I realized it made us both feel at ease. Our talk felt more like an amiable conversation than an interview.

We began to discuss how the Bible project had come about as well as its impact on the community as a whole. In the midst of this he remarked, "As a historian, I don't want to live in the past." Perhaps that was the key to the whole enterprise for as a historian he has a keen sense of the past. He talked movingly about parts of Saint John's property where you could still make out an Ojibwe burn area, a place where Native Americans had burned away the underbrush to create a better hunting ground. That sense of place was enormously important to him; it was both about knowing what had come before and about having a sense of gratitude for the generations of people who laid foundations to build on. He had a strong feeling that we all "rely on the love of people we never knew. Think of Jesus of Nazareth. People knew him—and they passed it on."

The collections at Saint John's include many important printed and manuscript books. Eric Gill's *The Four Gospels* was printed in England at the Golden Cockerell Press. A convert to Roman Catholicism, Gill tied image and word together into a seamless whole. His design for *The Four Gospels* blends typographic sophistication with a deeply theological sensibility. His refined style was marked by modern simplicity and a keen appreciation for tradition. His work influenced the liturgical arts for more than a generation.

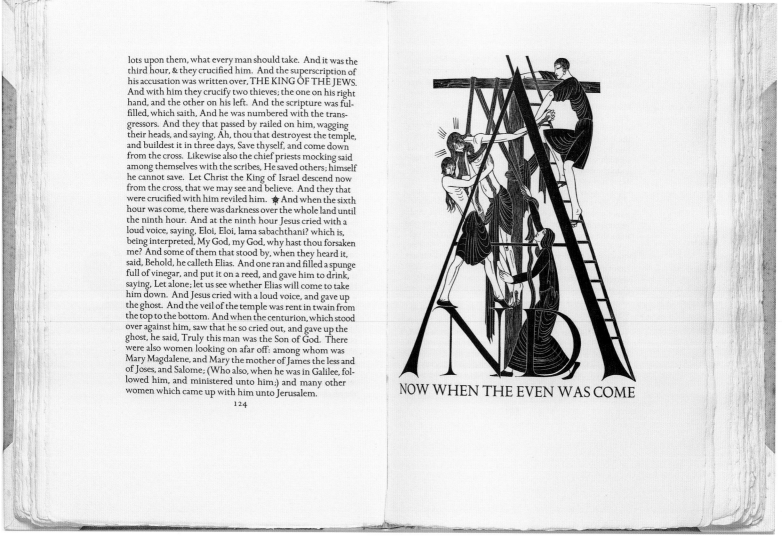

lots upon them, what every man should take. And it was the third hour, & they crucified him. And the superscription of his accusation was written over, THE KING OF THE JEWS. And with him they crucify two thieves; the one on his right hand, and the other on his left. And the scripture was fulfilled, which saith, And he was numbered with the transgressors. And they that passed by railed on him, wagging their heads, and saying, Ah, thou that destroyest the temple, and buildest it in three days, Save thyself, and come down from the cross. Likewise also the chief priests mocking said among themselves with the scribes, He saved others; himself he cannot save. Let Christ the King of Israel descend now from the cross, that we may see and believe. And they that were crucified with him reviled him. ✹ And when the sixth hour was come, there was darkness over the whole land until the ninth hour. And at the ninth hour Jesus cried with a loud voice, saying, Eloi, Eloi, lama sabachthani? which is, being interpreted, My God, my God, why hast thou forsaken me? And some of them that stood by, when they heard it, said, Behold, he calleth Elias. And one ran and filled a spunge full of vinegar, and put it on a reed, and gave him to drink, saying, Let alone; let us see whether Elias will come to take him down. And Jesus cried with a loud voice, and gave up the ghost. And the veil of the temple was rent in twain from the top to the bottom. And when the centurion, which stood over against him, saw that he so cried out, and gave up the ghost, he said, Truly this man was the Son of God. There were also women looking on afar off: among whom was Mary Magdalene, and Mary the mother of James the less and of Joses, and Salome; (Who also, when he was in Galilee, followed him, and ministered unto him;) and many other women which came up with him unto Jerusalem.

124

NOW WHEN THE EVEN WAS COME

Eric Gill. *The Four Gospels.*
Waltham St. Lawrence: The Golden Cockerell Press, 1931.
Kacmarcik Collection of Arca Artium, Saint John's University.

He explained something of the history of Saint John's. "On the 1500th anniversary of Saint Benedict's birth, Cardinal Basil Hume came to Saint John's. He said while he was here, 'I have studied medieval monasteries; I think this is the first living one I've visited.' I think what Hume was sensing was that Saint John's, like so many medieval monasteries, had determined the pattern of settlement for the whole area."

Dietrich described how the German monks who had built the monastery had served local parishes in this area of Minnesota and how the place names themselves reflected the German Catholic piety of those founding monks. Then he explained that the founding vision had given way to a new vision. In the 1940s with the entrance of the first African American monks and with the growing importance of the monastery as a center for liturgical revival and ecumenical and interfaith activities, Saint John's began to see itself as a cutting-edge place. By the 1960s, there were more than four hundred monks. The new, modernist church designed by Marcel Breuer reflected the optimism of that time.

This strong legacy had built a large and important complex of buildings; it had given rise to a host of other institutions, the university foremost among these, which were grouped around the monastery. But the legacy also had its shadow side. The liturgical renewal which Saint John's had helped pioneer had borne fruit. This was a good thing, but it meant Saint John's no longer had a cutting-edge position. The Church at large had adopted the reforms and changes the monastery had advocated. The late sixties also saw the decline of monastic vocations and the departure of quite a few monks. Perhaps, Dietrich suggested, the institution had been grieving. And perhaps not all that grieving was resolved. Was there a way of finding a project which would give Saint John's a new vision, something which would refocus its energies, excite people and shift the focus toward the future?

The original Abbey church was built by the monks themselves using bricks made at the monastery. When Breuer's modern Abbey church was built, the spires of the old building were removed and it was converted for use as the Great Hall. It is seen here through the parabolic arch of the bell banner.

When The Saint John's Bible was first mentioned to him he thought perhaps this was something they could rally around.

"If it was an anachronism, I wouldn't be interested," he said. He wasn't going to live in the past. This project with very old roots just like Saint John's—or the monastic tradition itself—could be a way to light a new fire.

"It wouldn't work if it was clichéd or if it was some project out there in cloud cuckoo land. No. It had to be great art. It had to be about the real world today. It had to resonate with Catholic tradition but not in a dogmatic way. It had to connect to the curriculum."

He began to describe all the ways a project like this could involve different parts of the community, how it could engage the imaginations of people over a period of many years.

Ultimately the project was about huge issues. "What would happen if we took seriously when we say, 'I can treat every person I meet as Christ.' If we took that literally, think how transforming it would be. Each person I meet has a word of salvation for me." He paused to let that thought sink in.

"But the thing is, we're *guys*. We're living a middle-class lifestyle. We're part of a mainline tradition. So we don't like to wear our faith on our sleeves. We need props. We need vestments and an altar to say sacred words. We need a curriculum to discuss ethics. We need roles to allow people to open up and ask advice. But when you look at the discussions which take place around The Saint John's Bible, people allow themselves to say they were moved. People who aren't ordained find themselves talking about Christ. Very practical, down-to-earth people ask, 'What about religious art?'" It was just that potential which had made Dietrich such a strong advocate of the project.

"The Saint John's Bible is a celebration of the non-linear," he said with a broad smile.

Scope of the project

"SO TAKE ME THROUGH STEP BY STEP," I said to Carol back in her office. "What goes in to making The Saint John's Bible?"

"The aim of the project," she said, "is to ignite the spiritual imagination. We want to develop programs around the Bible in spirituality, art and education." These programs will continue to grow long after the Bible is finished.

The thick binders on her shelves are filled with documents relating to the Bible project. She took one out and placed it on the table in front of us.

"Certain values guide The Saint John's Bible," she said, pointing to one of the sections in the book. Bold face headings listed a set of goals.

"We set these values down at the very beginning of the project. Some of them are self-explanatory: ignite the imagination; glorify God's Word; foster the arts. Others are more complex, like this one." She pointed to the words "Revive tradition."

She explained, "Monasteries of the Middle Ages were places where books were made. In some periods of history they were the only centers of book production." Since printing took over the book trade this tradition of hand-written manuscripts has been almost entirely absent from the Christian world. The Saint John's Bible revives the link between monastic communities and the hand-made book.

"Here's another one: Discover history. Who has made a manuscript book of this scale in the last five hundred years? We hope that the experience of writing out The Saint John's Bible will throw light on workshop practices and craft techniques."

"What about 'Give voice?'" I asked. "What do you mean by that?"

"The Scriptures speak forcefully for the excluded and underprivileged. We hope that The Saint John's Bible will be a voice for the marginalized in the true spirit of Christianity. The subjects which have been selected for illumination emphasize this important theme throughout the Bible."

Carol went on to explain that the Bible would be composed of seven volumes—Pentateuch, Historical Books, Wisdom Literature, Psalms, Prophets, Gospels and Acts, and Letters and Revelation.

"Are they being made in that order?" I wondered.

"No. Donald began with Gospels and Acts, which is the most heavily illuminated volume. Then he wrote Pentateuch and Psalms. In fact the making of each volume overlaps with the making of the others. The production schedule is complex to say the least."

The choice of translation was up to Saint John's. They selected the New Revised Standard Version (NRSV) as the most up-to-date, scholarly translation available. The order of the books reflects the Roman Catholic canon. The "Deuterocanonical" books, which Protestants refer to as the "Apocrypha," are included among the other writings in the Old Testament.

"Donald is the Artistic Director of the project," she continued. "He's gathered a team of scribes and illuminators to help him complete the manuscript. He could never have made the entire book by himself. He is creating most of the illuminations but he often collaborates with other artists. Quite a few illuminations are done by guest artists working under his direction and most of the text is written by the scribal team using a script Donald has designed with them."

The robust physicality of early books is beautifully expressed in this Latin printed Bible of 1491. A small, thick book in an *octavo* format, its tooled leather cover is ornamented with metal detailing and clasps. When The Saint John's Bible is completed in 2007, it will be bound between stout oak boards. The large vellum pages will recapture the physical grandeur of early books.

Bible. Latin Version.
Basel: Johann Froben, 1491.
Sixteenth-century stamped pigskin binding with clasps and metalwork (dated 1536).
Kacmarcik Collection of Arca Artium, Saint John's University.

The Gospel of Saint John.
Wenner Manuscript: Eth. Ms. 1.
Ethiopia, 1918.
Parchment bound with wooden boards,
in a two-part leather case. Hill Museum &
Manuscript Library, Saint John's University.

In some cultures the tradition of writing Bibles by hand has survived into the modern era. This small Ethiopian manuscript of John's Gospel, made in the early twentieth century, was designed to be carried in a small leather pouch.

"And how does Saint John's contribute to the design process?" I asked.

"Two monks, David Cotter, OSB, and Michael Patella, OSB, worked up something we call the 'schema.' It lists the passages which will be illuminated in the Bible and it sets out major themes in each volume. It functions as the master plan for the project."

The schema provided an outline for the detailed theological briefs which were then written for each illumination.

"The Committee on Illumination and Text was formed to work with Donald. Father Michael is the chair and the members are drawn from the wider Saint John's community. Many of them are monks from the monastery. Others are scholars connected to the university. It's an interesting group. There are both academics and artists on the committee. They wrote the briefs and they see Donald's working sketches. They give him feedback and direction as he works."

There will only be one copy of The Saint John's Bible; that's the nature of a manuscript book. It is a singular object. I asked Carol how people would be able to see the Bible.

She answered, "It will be on display here at Saint John's. We will also be publishing an expensive, full-size facsimile of the manuscript. There will be a smaller trade edition as well so people can have a copy at home. Right now we're planning for an exhibition at The Minneapolis Institute of Art."

"The project isn't finished though, is it?"

"Not yet. We have the first three volumes which will be shown in the exhibition. Donald is still working on the last four volumes. The whole Bible will be finished in 2007."

"But that's just the beginning, isn't it?"

"Oh yes. Once the Bible itself is finished, then it will take on a life of its own—The Saint John's Bible will be here long after we're gone."

I looked at my watch. It was time for my next appointment.

Taking tea

A CLUE TO THE ETHOS of Saint John's can be found at the pottery studio Richard Bresnahan maintains in the basement of Saint Joseph Hall. Trained in Japan, Richard has imported the tradition of taking tea in the workshop each afternoon with his apprentices, students and guests. A hearth stands near the front end of the studio. Surrounded on four sides by a low wall topped with beautifully finished wood, the center is a hollow filled with sand. A single gas ring supports the iron kettle.

Richard greeted me at the door. His head was wrapped in a printed bandana; he wore practical work clothes. He shook my hand warmly.

"Do you know Sister Johanna?" he said.

"Oh yes, we've met," I answered turning to her and shaking her hand.

Johanna Becker, OSB, has been Richard's great mentor through the years. Her academic field is East Asian art, specializing in ceramics. When he finished his undergraduate degree at Saint John's, she helped arrange his two-year Japanese apprenticeship. When he built the largest wood fired kiln in North America, which stands across the road, he named it after her.

Sister Johanna had brought a friend of hers, a priest, who filled out our party. Richard turned to his apprentice, a young man with a beard and a ponytail, and instructed him to fetch Johanna a comfortable chair. The rest of us sat on stools while Richard made the tea. The tea pot, water jug and cups were all products of his studio. We chatted as the water boiled softly on the gas ring.

Richard established his pottery on campus in 1979. The ethos of the studio combines Benedictine values of sustainability and self-sufficiency with Japanese workshop practices.

"In America, we're making up our culture," he commented. "Some of the things I do here would never happen in Japan." He showed us a tea pot with an elegant woven reed handle. "I work with the weaver to make these pots." In conversation with the weaver, he creates new ceramic forms which complement the exquisitely twining handles. He explained that in Japan the pottery traditions are more fixed. Each region produces its own varieties of pottery based on local materials and centuries of workshop practice. In America, by contrast, the field is more open; there is no tradition to guide—or limit—his work.

Richard is creating a new tradition at his studio. He uses local materials and sustainable methods. His clay comes from a site nearby; he has enough clay in store to last the rest of his and several other lifetimes. Many of the glazes are made of agricultural byproducts from farms in the region.

"I couldn't do this at an ordinary university," he said. "We fire the Johanna kiln once every twelve months. Who's going to wait twelve months for a grade?" It isn't economical in the narrow sense of turning a quick profit. To run a pottery like this one has to take the long view. Like the monastery the pottery is designed around distant time frames longer than any one person's lifespan. The forest which surrounds Saint John's is managed in a sustainable fashion; the buildings are meant to last. The land is husbanded rather than simply exploited.

Conversation turned to lighter topics. Tea cups were filled and refilled. Soon it was time for Johanna to go; her ride was waiting to take her back to Saint Benedict's, her monastic home in St. Joseph. We all rose to say goodbye.

When the other guests had left, Richard gave me a tour of the studio. Opening a large vat he plunged his hand in and brought up a handful of wet, grey mud.

Benedictine crosses decorate windows on the towers of the old Abbey church, now the Great Hall.

The imagery of The Saint John's Bible makes reference to many world traditions. The Arabic Bible shown here was printed in Italy in 1590–91. It is an example of a cross-cultural Bible from the European Renaissance made for Christian communities in the Middle East.
Evangelium Sanctum Domini Nostri Iesu Christi Conscriptum A Quatuor Evangelistis Sanctis.
Rome: Typographia Medicea, 1590–91. Saint John's Rare Books, Alcuin Library, Saint John's University.

"The glazes we use are all natural."

I reached my hand in and felt the fine silt between my fingers. It was cold and smooth.

"I've been to so many funerals of my peers. When we were students no one told us not to plunge our hands into the chemical glazes—yellow cadmium and cobalt blue."

"Heavy metals," I said, making the connection.

"Exactly. I've been experimenting with glazes made from local materials. This is made from navy bean straw."

We walked down to the Johanna kiln across the road. Richard's apprentice followed close behind. Housed in a large shed, the kiln was cold, empty. The shed is built over a steep part of a hill; the kiln rises in three large chambers, each with its own set of flues and doors for stoking the fires. Along the vaulted top of the central chamber, a series of small holes with lids can be opened in a precise sequence during the firing.

The bricks were recycled from demolished buildings at the monastery. "The monks made all these bricks by hand on site."

A deep appreciation for the land, for the work of those who have come before and for future generations informs Richard's working practice. We went back up the hill to his studio where he showed me some of his wares.

The Stella Maris chapel, built during World War I, stands on a rocky outcrop jutting into Lake Sagatagan. It can be seen from the lakeshore behind the Abbey church.

The Abbey church in the snow.

"The ceramics which survive are those which find multiple uses," he said. He tries to make forms which can be adapted to many functions—the best hope that his work will continue to be used and valued far into the future.

It brought to mind something Eric had said to me: "The Saint John's Bible could last longer than any of the buildings at the monastery. Think about the great manuscripts of the past. They have survived long after the monasteries which produced them have disappeared."

I took my leave of Richard and walked up the grassy hill to the Abbey church. Undergraduates were playing catch on the lawns around their dorms. The bell rang out six p.m.

The close of day

AT NINE O'CLOCK the bell does not ring for Compline, the service of night prayer. The Abbey church is dark. A small group of ten or twelve monks walks silently into a pool of light around the altar. They form a wide semi-circle and begin to sing.

> Lord, now you let your servant go in peace;
> your word has been fulfilled.
> My own eyes have seen the salvation
> which you have prepared in the sight of every people,
> the light to reveal you to the nations
> and the glory of your people, Israel.

The day is ended. The monks disperse to their rooms and to bed.

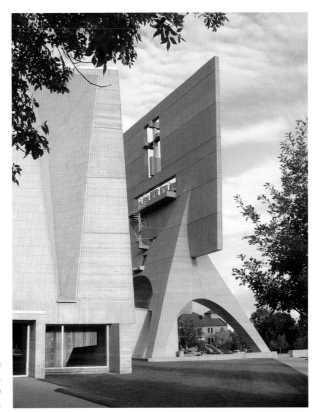

The bold, sculptural forms of the Abbey church dominate the monastery and university grounds. The bell banner looming above the entrance can be seen for miles around.

THE SAINT JOHN'S BIBLE

PENTATEUCH

158 pages

Genesis

Exodus

Leviticus

Numbers

Deuteronomy

HISTORICAL BOOKS

319 pages

Joshua

Judges

Ruth

1 Samuel

2 Samuel

1 Kings

2 Kings

1 Chronicles

2 Chronicles

Ezra

Nehemiah

Tobit

Judith

Esther

1 Maccabees

2 Maccabees

WISDOM LITERATURE

102 pages

Job

Proverbs

Ecclesiastes

The Song of Songs

The Wisdom of Solomon

Sirach (Ecclesiasticus)

PSALMS

80 pages

PROPHETS

272 pages

Isaiah

Jeremiah

Lamentations

Baruch

Ezekiel

Daniel

Hosea

Joel

Amos

Obadiah

Jonah

Micah

Nahum

Habakkuk

Zephaniah

Haggai

Zechariah

Malachi

GOSPELS AND ACTS

136 pages

Matthew

Mark

Luke

John

Acts of the Apostles

LETTERS AND REVELATION

93 pages

Romans

1 Corinthians

2 Corinthians

Galatians

Ephesians

Philippians

Colossians

1 Thessalonians

2 Thessalonians

1 Timothy

2 Timothy

Titus

Philemon

Hebrews

James

1 Peter

2 Peter

1 John

2 John

3 John

Jude

Revelation

Sketches for the *Loaves and Fishes* illumination are spread out on a table. Early Christian mosaic fish, Native American baskets and Islamic filigree patterns combine to form a dense, interwoven texture, reflecting the diversity of images incorporated into The Saint John's Bible.

CHAPTER 2

A VISIT TO THE SCRIPTORIUM

O N February 24, 2000, I looked out the window of a train heading westward across England. The landscape was bare, brown and grey in the soft winter daylight. We passed villages with ancient church towers. Electric pylons marched across the countryside. At one point the train stopped right next to a huge industrial site. Great concrete cooling towers loomed over us. A few miles on, in the distance I could make out a prehistoric chalk carving in the side of a hill: a huge white horse. The people next to me on the train were talking about university admissions. I was on my way to Wales to visit Donald Jackson's Scriptorium. The train ride provided a clue of what I would find: something completely modern with roots in something very old indeed.

Mabel, who is married to Donald, picked me up at the station. We trundled my bags into the back of her old, beat up Volvo and headed off to The Hendre Hall.

"It's been quite a week!" Mabel said and then laughed. A team of four calligraphers had arrived and begun the work of writing pages for the Bible. Only two of them were still there; the other two had decided this project wasn't for them. As we drove on, Mabel told me about the ups and downs of managing a household full of people. The Saint John's Bible is the collaborative effort of a whole team. Sally Mae Joseph is in charge of running the studio. She is Donald's only in-house scribe and illuminator. There is the team of scribes, a computer consultant, an office manager, and a whole cast of characters including the gardener, the cleaning lady, and various members of Donald's extended family. Mabel helps keep this team together by managing the household and logistics. She does it with great humor and patience.

As we traveled through the Welsh countryside, we left behind the bleak industrial landscape surrounding Newport and began to move up through hills and valleys. Soon we were deep in the countryside. The landscape is rugged and the road hugs the contours of the hills. Centuries of cultivation have left their mark on the land. We came to a crossroads where we waited for a single passing car so we could cross over. "Oh, there's traffic," Mabel said to herself.

I was arriving in the midst of a drama. Production was shifting into high gear. The preliminary design work was finished, and now Donald was training his group of scribes to begin writing out each page of the actual manuscript. The number of people working on the project was growing, and what had been a small and rather intimate process was now becoming a humming industry. The mood at The Hendre was changing as new people and new personalities were added to the team.

Mabel continued her story. Four calligraphers had come to The Hendre to take up the work. They were all professionals with great skill, but The Saint John's Bible is not like any calligraphic project any of them had worked on before. The sheer size of the project and the demands of working in a team had proved quite a challenge.

Mabel said, "One of the calligraphers actually disappeared at one point—we had to ring the police!"

"The police? Why?" I asked.

"Well, it was very worrying. He just went off one day and no one knew where he'd gone. He was struggling, I think, with the writing."

What had happened was this: the calligraphers had arrived several weeks before. Originally Donald had intended to train them for a week and then immediately set them to writing full pages of the manuscript. It had proved difficult to get the team ready to work so fast. Their different personalities had to mesh. They had to adapt quickly, not only to using new tools and materials but also to the script Donald had devised. One week of training became two and the scribes were still mastering Donald's technique. This was much more complex than anyone had thought. Not only was there the question of a large leap in skills but also the scribes were being asked to practice their craft in a collaborative workshop setting. None of the team had ever worked in a major scriptorium like this. In fact, there are no scriptoria like this—and there haven't been since the invention of movable type revolutionized book production in the fifteenth and early sixteenth centuries.

One calligrapher decided to opt out early on. Another scribe was working hard to master the script but was finding the whole set up difficult. This task was not suited to everyone's temperament and abilities. So one day he decided to take a walk, perhaps to think things through.

An hour passed and no one took much notice. Then two hours passed. The rest of the team began to get concerned. Finally, everyone set off on a search-and-find expedition and the police were called.

"He showed up hours later," Mabel said. "In the end, it was nothing; he'd just taken himself off for a walk and a breath of fresh air. We were very relieved."

He too decided to leave the project. Suddenly I knew why Donald had said to me on the phone, "You're writing about the setting of the Scriptorium? The real story is what's going on here with the calligraphers." I was to hear much more about this drama in the days which followed.

The Hendre Hall where Donald Jackson lives and works is nestled in a hollow in the Welsh countryside near Monmouth. Across the road from the Hall is a compound of working buildings where The Saint John's Bible is being made.

An industrious household

THE CAR PULLED into the house at The Hendre Hall. Donald and Mabel live in a converted village hall, a rambling half-timbered building, beautiful against the hills which surround it. Donald keeps his own office in a wing of the Hall. Across the small road there is a group of small sheds and outbuildings, loosely grouped around a gravel courtyard and a grassy lawn. The main building is the Schoolroom, a converted mechanics' shed, which has been renovated to make a fine scriptorium. It is full of natural light with a row of desks for the scribal team. In the back are a kitchen and the space where Sally works. There is also a little room where visitors can stay.

Across from the Schoolroom stands the Black Iron Shed, built, as its name implies, of corrugated metal. It serves as a storage area. In one corner of the shed, there is a small electric griddle, filled with sand: a place to cure quills. Across the lawn, the New Shed serves as a place to prepare vellum skins for writing.

The Hendre Hall was originally part of the Rolls estate—that's the Rolls as in Rolls Royce. In the old paternalistic days of large estates, the building had been built to serve as the village hall. The people of the village lived in houses belonging to the estate. In the 1970s, before they bought and converted it, Donald and Mabel remember going to the Hall for village events, for fêtes and pantomimes. When the estate was still thriving, the outbuildings across the yard had served as sheds for mechanics who tinkered with cars. This old paternalistic world has now passed away and the estate has been broken up and sold off.

The Hendre Hall is a huge Tudor revival style building. The main space—the Hall itself—has been transformed into a large and comfortable living room. All around there remains evidence of the communal life The Hendre Hall had once hosted. Huge wooden rafters in dark wood support the tall ceiling. Small heraldic shields are carved into the woodwork. At one end there is a large raised platform to serve as a stage. All around are large windows which admit the constantly changing sunlight. The stair rails are worn smooth by decades of hands, coming and going to village events. In its present incarnation the

Donald Jackson and Sally Mae Joseph walk in the woods behind the Schoolroom. The delicate iron bridge in the foreground crosses a small brook.

room is filled with couches, tables and comfortable chairs. It is a lush environment and I wanted to wander through and look at all the collections which were displayed on every surface. A set of old inkpots in cut glass caught my eye; but it was time to put down my bags in my upstairs room and head over to see The Saint John's Bible in the making.

I walked into the Schoolroom, where I found two scribes writing at their desks. The room was hushed, filled with that silence which comes of people sitting together in total concentration. Over the shoulders of the calligraphers, I could just glimpse fine columns of beautiful writing, even and clear and black against the off-white vellum.

Donald beckoned silently to me to follow him over to the New Shed, where Sally was preparing a vellum skin. It's messy work. The skins have to be sanded with several grades of sandpaper and the dust gets everywhere. Sally wore work gloves and a mask as she labored over a large calfskin. Donald's brother, who is a furniture maker, was jury-rigging a fan device to catch the flying dust. We stopped the fan.

"What do you call this process?" I asked.

"It's called 'scrutching,'" came the answer, and they all laughed. "Scrutching"* will not be found in any dictionary, but it is a perfect word to describe the scratchy, sweaty job.

Donald's eye suddenly shifted to the skin Sally was preparing. Chatting amiably one moment, he stopped. There was something amiss about the skin on the table. Sally stood aside as he picked it up.

"I think a hole is developing in the skin," he said.

He picked up the skin, running his large hands across the surface.

"Yes, I think there must have been a particle of dust underneath; there's a small flaw. You'll have to be careful of that spot."

He looked at the surface of the formica table on which Sally was working. A fine layer of dust had accumulated on the tabletop. Perhaps indeed a small lump of vellum dust had sat under the surface and the sanding had thinned the skin a trifle too much.

"Every skin is just a bit different," Donald said. "It's a living thing. It's not like this table top." He tapped the formica surface. "This is the kind of perfection we're used to, mechanical, cold, flawless." He continued drumming his fingers along the tabletop. "We can't achieve that here. It's not what we're about."

"Perfection is not an option," Sally said and everyone laughed. This had become their watchword. The perfection of the craftsman is something we're not used to anymore, living in a formica world.

The Bible is being written in the ancient manner on calf skins. These come to The Hendre uncut: large, flat skins with rough edges. They never sit perfectly flat, but always retain just a bit of flexibility. Part of Sally's job is to select a skin for each folio of the book. All of the skins are of the highest quality available, smooth, off-white and without blemishes, holes or markings. The thickness of the vellum can vary, both between skins and even within each skin. Sally selects thicker skins to take large illuminations; the thicker skins are more stable and able to withstand paint and gilding better. Each skin has to be sanded to raise the fiber a bit, giving the skin a soft, almost velvety nap. This gives the scribe a surface with some 'tooth' to aid the writing. Areas which will be illuminated need less of this nap and are sanded more delicately.

Unlike a printed book in which a kind of slick perfection is sought after, a manuscript begins with a material which is organic, variable and has a life of its own. Over time, once The Saint John's Bible is bound, the vellum pages will slowly mold to each other, creating a gently undulating regularity. Making

* "Scrutch" rhymes with "butch."

Brian Simpson, one of the scribes, writes in the Schoolroom. The desks are carefully positioned to receive natural light from the scribe's left so his writing hand will not cast a shadow on his work.

Sally Mae Joseph uses a small knife in her left hand to hold the undulating vellum down as she writes. A small sheet of paper under her hand protects the writing surface as she works.

the Bible is more like gardening than engineering; it is about working with materials which have personalities of their own. Donald's task is to work with these natural materials, to make them work in harmony, just as he has to pull his team of scribes into a kind of harmony.

At lunchtime I went up to the Hall to eat with Donald and the family while the scribal team ate down at the Schoolroom. The kitchen at the Hall, like the living room, is filled with objects. His daughter Carmen has painted an inscription along the top of the walls in an art nouveau style listing various English foods. Mabel laid out a simple lunch of soup, bread and cheese. It felt very—as the English would say—homely. As we chatted over lunch, I could sense how special this place was. There are not many households like this one anymore, in which work and family, labor and meals hold together as an organic whole.

Creating a contemporary Scriptorium

AFTER LUNCH, I asked Donald to tell me more about the work with his scribal team. His cheeks puffed slightly as he let out a long, steady stream of air.

"The thing is," he explained to me, "calligraphers aren't trained for this kind of work. Who are the great calligraphers? Thomas Ingmire, Denis Brown. Great personalities, unique personalities. But here on this project I want people to understand, 'It is not my idiosyncrasies which are valued, but my consistency and the group harmonic.'"

Donald compared the task at hand to the work of professional musicians. If you are hired to be part of a band, you know how to pick up your instrument and join in. You adjust to the rhythms of the group and you're ready to play on an afternoon's notice.

Donald Jackson and Sally Mae Joseph examine a small computer printout of the first volume. Visual references and sketches for the illuminations are spread out on the table in front of them.

During the design process small-scale mock-ups of each volume help Donald Jackson and his team make visual decisions and keep track of production. During the design process this printout of *Gospels and Acts* was pinned to the studio wall. It was used for the allocation and distribution of guest artists' work and then served as a visual record of the completion of written pages and illuminations.

The *Gospels and Acts* studio working dummy, a large printout arranged in folios and gatherings, was used to guide the selection and ruling up of skins, and recording finished capitals, chapter numbers and running headlines. It is decorated with a photocopy of Aidan Hart's sketch for *The Sower and the Seed* and a tiny image of a monk reading. Donald Jackson has splashed Sally Mae Joseph's name across the top in a spontaneous and vigorous italic hand.

Calligraphers by contrast usually work by themselves. Their training is often based on a careful, detailed analysis of the letterforms they are trying to use. This leads to a great deal of examination of pen angle, the width of the strokes, the shapes of the arches and all the minutiae which make up a well thought-through calligraphic script.

"I am also looking for a team which can be responsive to me. They need to show a willingness to empty themselves, so I can take them where we need to go together."

Donald turned to the working habits he wanted people to develop in the Scriptorium.

"All movements have to be efficient. I watched some of them at the beginning. They put their ink over there," he said, gesturing to his left. "Then they would pick up their pen and brush, lean over to put the brush in the ink, readjust themselves in front of their writing, load their pen and then begin to write." His body became more and more contorted as he acted this out; his back and shoulders swayed back and forth as he mimed this complicated set of movements.

"That's three or four steps before you even begin writing. Instead, I asked them to put their ink right near by where they could dip the pen in a single gesture and carry on writing."

I had seen the arrangement he'd made for himself at one of the desks. It was a small chair with two cardboard boxes, one duct-taped to the seat and the other to the back of the chair. Elegant it was not; but it was very, very practical. There is another kind of elegance which comes of a craftsman setting up an efficient workspace. It was sturdy and it held everything he needed to write with. Everything was within arm's reach, without the writer having to move from a writing position.

Donald turned to the attitudinal shift he was trying to develop in his team.

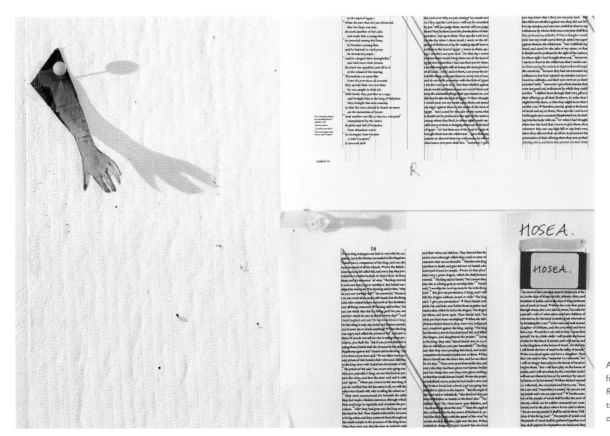

A tiny drawn hand, left over from the rough drawings for the *Resurrection* illumination, is pinned to the wall near a computer print-out of the books of the Prophets.

"I'm looking for a deeper perfection. Not superficial perfection. They have to let go of what makes them feel safe," Donald said. We were back to the subject he'd mentioned while drumming on the Formica table in the New Shed. The fact is we are so used to mechanical perfection, the flawless regularity of the machine age, that we have to reaccustom ourselves to working in a pre-industrial manner.

"I would watch people go back into an analytical mode. It's just not appropriate here," Donald said. The analytical approach in which most English calligraphers are trained has a lot to do with trying to achieve a mechanical kind of perfection.

Donald continued, "The problem is, you can't sustain the analytical approach over time. When you have a whole page to write, you can't continue analyzing what you're doing. Sometimes the vellum skins are dodgy; they have rough parts and smooth parts, and you just have to keep going."

One of the problems in setting up this Scriptorium is that there isn't a large pool of people to draw from. This has a lot to do with the difficulty of earning a living at calligraphy. Without a large, sustainable market for the work, people aren't used to functioning in this kind of sustained way. Donald is one of the few scribes who have pushed their craft far enough—and who have brought enough business savvy to the enterprise—to be able to make a career of it.

"Calligraphers simply aren't paid enough for what they do," he said. He was right. The average calligrapher barely makes a living at professional lettering. It is often treated as a passionate vocation rather than as a profession.

Donald continued, "As a result, it's very hard for most calligraphers to sit down and turn out the work." They are used to taking a long time over projects, doing it as much for the love of the craft as for any hope of being paid for it. Calligraphers on the whole work alone in a studio at home. This makes it particularly hard for them to come in and immediately slip into the collective work of a major scriptorium. The Saint John's Bible demands a kind of collaborative effort which just doesn't happen elsewhere.

I wandered back down to the Schoolroom. Chattering came from the back kitchen, where the scribes were taking a break with Olivia Edwards, who was the office manager at the time. Sally made me a cup of tea and I sat down at the table. Sue Hufton, one of the scribes, plopped a bag of dried figs onto the table along with a bag of dried sunflower seeds. A box of liquorice appeared and made the rounds. Brian Simpson, the other scribe, joined us. The room was full of happy energy, a well-earned break from the intense concentration of several hours of writing.

"How's it been going?" I asked.

"It's not perfect, but we just have to keep going," Sue said.

Olivia from the office added, "I think we all have to. I hit a moment about two weeks ago when I really needed reassurance."

"I know," said Sally. "I just felt totally useless."

"Well, I'm the only one who *is* totally useless!" Brian chimed in and everyone laughed. Brian is much older than the rest of the team and brings a lifetime of craftsmanship and good sense to the job. He often drops the right remark into a conversation to lighten the tone and set people at ease.

We began to talk about how the work had progressed.

Sue said, "It's not easy to be put back into a student role when you've been working for a long time. I noticed when we got here that Donald slipped automatically into the teacher mode, and I think some of us had a hard time with that; but we had to be receptive to Donald and what he was doing."

The tiny desiccated body of a newt rests atop Chris Tomlin's sketchbook and a sheaf of writing samples.

Originally all the scribes were to have been given a sample of the script to look at before they arrived. Ten days before the team arrived at The Hendre everyone had been given a paragraph of writing to study but Donald had said, "This isn't resolved. It's not an exemplar." Donald had been designing the script as he went along; it was not fixed, but evolving. This fluidity in the script had given a lot of the team a hard time.

"But Donald is very forgiving of mistakes. He gave each of us a lot of rope; but he also always left the door open," Sue commented.

When the team had arrived to begin its training, some of the scribes had tried to analyze the hand, but it was inconsistent. The writing varied, with different shapes of arches, different strokes at the end of the letters, and all sorts of variants. I could see on a table the study sheets he had worked out with them. They were a mass of small fragments of letters, mere notations of a living practice of writing.

And yet, looking at sample pages Donald had written, I saw the texture of the script was remarkably even, while the writing remained incredibly alive, fluent and spontaneous. I could see how hard it would be for the calligraphers on the team to capture this spirit. Learning to write in this way was about learning to follow Donald's adage: "Thinking doesn't happen from the neck up." I remembered what he had said to me: "It's not about pen angle, nib width or the structure of arches. It's about achieving a certain feeling." In a lively mixed metaphor, he said, "In a hundred years, when they look at the manuscript, it's the feeling they're going to hear."

That night Donald and Mabel took everyone out to the pub for dinner. The name of the local pub is "The Halfway House," which sounds rather dire, until you realize that it is halfway between Monmouth and Abergavenny. We gathered around the log fire and had drinks before dinner. We sat down to a simple and hearty meal, and talked about everything but the Bible.

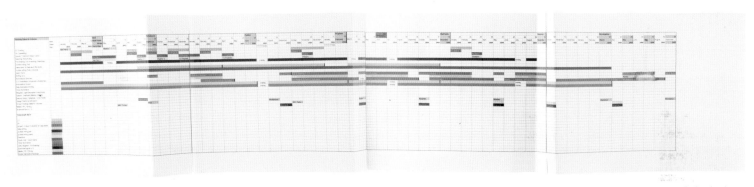

With the precision of a battle plan, a flow chart details the various stages of production for the entire Bible project.

Perfection is not an option

THE NEXT MORNING, I wandered around the Schoolroom as everyone worked, watching the scribes writing, examining the finished pages and reading through some of the theological briefs for the illuminations prepared by the Committee on Illumination and Text at Saint John's. Glancing up from these, I saw that each person sitting at their desk had their own body language. Brian sat absolutely still, perfectly calm, with a relaxed but concentrated expression on his face. Sue looked serious, deeply pensive and her body seemed ever so slightly tense as she wrote. And Donald—how can I describe it?—although he was sitting in the same position as the others, his eyes intent on his work, he exuded a physicality I didn't sense in the others. His large hands seemed to caress the vellum. From time to time he would stop and run his hands across the skin. I could see, looking at him, that he wasn't thinking "from the neck up." Years ago, he described to me writing with a quill on vellum as having the feeling of "running the flat of your fingernail softly down a baby's back." And here he was, doing just that—gently working the quill across the skin with enormous control and equal vitality, bringing this Bible to birth.

Not wanting to disturb the work which was going on, I sat down in the kitchen of the Schoolroom, made myself a cup of tea, and spent some time looking at the computer layout pages and the theological briefs which set out themes for the illuminations. The computer printouts were interesting. Most calligraphic books in this day and age are fairly simple affairs, and once the basic formats have been determined, the writing can be done without further planning. In the case of The Saint John's Bible, because it is such a huge undertaking, the layout for every page has to be determined before any writing can take place.

Another record book holds details of the folios taken away by scribes after each visit to work on in their own studios.

One reason for this careful formatting is the set of exacting requirements demanded by the committee which holds the copyright of the New Revised Standard Version (NRSV). They set stringent guidelines for layout which have to be respected, even in this unique hand-made book. Formats need to be prepared and proofread to make sure all the NRSV requirements have been met on each page.

There is another reason formatting has to be done first on the computer. In order to parcel out pages to individual scribes on the team, the text has to be fixed, down to each line break. This also allows pages to be written out of sequence. Once the team had mastered the script, they would begin taking pages home with them; the bulk of the writing would be done on their own and they would return at intervals to compare and examine their work and to pick up fresh sheets of vellum. The layout had to be completely fixed beforehand.

"Vin" Godier is the computer expert who produces the layout pages. He uses Sanvito, a multiple master typeface, which very closely approximates the spacing of the manuscript hand. Twenty-first century technology serves the ancient art of writing by hand.

So I settled in to look at these computer printouts, comparing them to finished pages of the book. As I sat there over my cup of tea, Sally and Donald quietly came into the room and went over to Sally's desk. They put a page of the manuscript onto the desk, and began discussing what they saw. They talked in hushed tones for about half an hour before I noticed something was amiss.

"That's right," Sally said.

"Yes, but this is about a centimeter out of line," replied Donald.

Sally frowned without saying a word. Donald was very calm but it was clear something had gone wrong. I watched from the kitchen table, not wanting to interrupt. I slowly realized that Donald had written a whole page, only to have Sally discover that she had ruled the columns ever so slightly off square.

Silence fills the Schoolroom as scribes write at their desks with complete concentration.

The lines themselves were perfectly square and true. But the columns, which are long, weren't quite at ninety degree angles to the straight lines of writing. The cumulative mistake meant that while the columns lined up at the top, they were five to ten millimeters from where they should be at the bottom. Visually, this was so minor that it was hardly noticeable, except that the pages had to be ruled up on the opposite side. Vellum being slightly translucent, any writing shows through slightly; this would highlight the fact that columns on either side of this sheet didn't line up properly.

Because vellum is a natural material, it never sits completely flat. Any turning of the page means it settles on the desk differently. Ruling up such a supple material is almost as subtle and difficult as ruling up a piece of fabric—it just doesn't stay still. Moisture also affects the skins, which swell and stretch in high humidity and shrink in dry weather. Even if a skin were perfectly ruled one day, by the next it might have slightly moved.

Computer printouts on the wall of the Schoolroom show the layout of the first volume at a glance. Each row of sheets is a single book from the volume—Matthew, Mark, Luke, John and Acts of the Apostles. Blank spaces indicate where the illuminations will appear in the finished manuscript. Small colored rectangles mark the position of small decorative details.

Sue came in after a while and pointed out that, having spent the better part of an hour and a half discussing the problem, perhaps it would be better just to re-rule a sheet and do the page over. I noticed no one took her up on this offer. After a bit Donald went back up to the main house. He wasn't angry; he knew this was simply part of the learning curve.

Sue might have repeated the mantra "Perfection is not an option," but probably thought better of it under the circumstances.

Sally came over to the table, clearly not pleased with what had happened.

"I suppose it was good that it happened to one of Donald's sheets rather than to Sue or Brian. That would have been worse," I said.

"You're telling me," Sally answered, as she reached for a rice cake. She munched on it silently as the rest of us chatted about other things.

Later, at lunchtime, Sally waited for Sue and Brian to be out of the room and she went from desk to desk, measuring the line ruling on everyone's pages. There were slight variations in their columns, but none were as far out of square as those on the page Donald had finished. Sally's relief was palpable—it was she who was responsible for the ruling up of all the pages.

Treasures

An ivory-handled erasing knife sits next to a small jar containing a sample of Japanese sumi ink. If his supply of antique ink sticks ran out, Donald Jackson would have been obliged to find a modern ink to complete his seven volumes.

LATER THAT AFTERNOON, I asked to talk with Donald about the tools and materials he was using. I had seen the skins, but I was curious about the quills and the inks. In particular I was curious about the precious ink sticks with fine gold Chinese writing stamped on them.

Donald unwrapped a clean, black stick of ink. These needed to be ground in water in a slate inkstone

Donald Jackson works at his tilted desk in the Schoolroom.

to make each day's portion of writing ink. Donald had more than one hundred of these, from a shop in Camden Town, London, called Roberson's.

Donald told me, "Roberson's were old-fashioned artist's colormen whose shop had been open since 1810. They supplied famous Victorian artists like Lord Leighton (the academic painter). In fact Lord Leighton's palette, which he had signed and given to the shop, still hung over the counter."

When Donald shopped there in the sixties and seventies, the proprietor was already old. The sticks had been brought over from China by sail with shipments of tea in the time of his father. Donald bought a large supply of ink sticks at two shillings apiece.

Once the project was underway, it became clear there would not be enough ink sticks to complete all seven volumes. Donald had some research done. The ink sticks turned out to be extremely valuable collectors' items. There was no way they could afford to buy more.

During one of Sally Mae's Bible presentations, she showed a picture of the stick ink and talked about its unique qualities and the problems of supply. From the back of the room a voice spoke up "I think I have some of those sticks." It was the voice of a calligrapher who had worked with Donald some years before. He had given her a quantity of the sticks but she had never used them. So she donated them to the project.

Later two other calligraphers to whom Donald had given ink sticks donated theirs as well. Those sticks sat in drawers around the world waiting to come home to complete The Saint John's Bible—a valuable gift to the project.

The vermilion Donald uses comes from another artist's supplier. The firm which manufactured the vermilion cakes closed in 1867, and the shopkeeper who had this rare supply was wary of parting with too many at a time.

"I used to go in and buy just enough not to arouse his suspicion. Then I'd send one of my friends in to buy some. But then you had to wait a decent time before going in again, or he would refuse to sell you any." Eventually, when the shop was to close, Donald offered to buy the lot at seven-and-six per cake (which is seven shillings, sixpence in the predecimal English coin) and was refused. After the shop closed Donald tracked down the whereabouts of the remaining stock to find that the old man had been hoarding over two-thousand cakes of the precious color and he was able to buy the lot for a fraction of the original cost.

These cakes were exquisite. Brilliantly red-orange, they were pressed into molds and were as clean and shiny as mint coins. Each was carefully wrapped in paper. Donald has enough in reserve to last him the remainder of his professional life.

Breaking the tension

BRIAN AND SUE went home in mid-afternoon on Friday. They would return the following Monday to continue work. The last event of my visit was the Friday afternoon planning meeting with Olivia, Sally and Donald.

As we settled into comfortable chairs in The Hendre Hall, everyone was relaxed and there was a lot of laughter in the room. Olivia led the meeting, raising the various subjects for discussion and decision. There were many logistical issues to resolve. Donald was preparing to go to America for a major promotional tour—how was he going to balance that with the need to spend time working on the project itself? They discussed ways to handle the film crew which was about to descend on them to shoot a documentary. As they worked out a plan for the American tour, they also discussed the progress report they would file with Saint John's that afternoon.

The conversation began to wander from the agenda. Someone mentioned that the illumination of the Baptism of Christ included a full-length portrait of John the Baptist—how would Donald handle the image, they wondered?

"I bet he was thin," someone said. "He was probably in pretty good shape, with his healthy, outdoor lifestyle."

Someone else pointed out that his hair shirt was probably a rather slinky number. This idea of John the Baptist as a New Testament Leonardo DiCaprio set Olivia and Sally off and everyone laughed. It was good for them to break the tension of the morning and put the problem of the slightly skewed columns behind them.

In the two days I spent at The Hendre, Donald introduced me to a community of people who were being molded into a team to produce a work of great craftsmanship. They are using all the resources available to make something which is grounded in the ancient tradition of calligraphy, yet which is also entirely up-to-date. There's nothing at all nostalgic about it—it's hard work, with production schedules, computers, visiting television crews and tight deadlines. And yet it is also a place where they are rediscovering the techniques of the medieval scriptorium. It is a place of quills, vellum, rare vermilion and hundred-year-old sticks of ink. What better setting could there be to create a twenty-first century, living Bible?

A light moment at the Scriptorium. Team members assemble for a group shot, holding a folded printout of one of the Bible volumes.

A hanging flower basket stands out against the grey stone wall of the Schoolroom.

The technique of manufacturing vellum has remained almost unchanged since the Middle Ages. All of the great medieval manuscripts—the Book of Kells, the Lindisfarne Gospels or the Winchester Bible, for example—were written on such skins. In our modern era, there is still no better surface for fine writing. This room at William Cowley Parchment and Vellum Works in Newport Pagnell, England, is filled with hundreds of finely prepared skins.

CHAPTER 3

IN SEARCH OF
THE PERFECT WRITING SURFACE

I ASKED Donald why he chose to write The Saint John's Bible on vellum.

"I've thought of all the possibilities," he said. "I considered setting the whole thing in type and letting the hard, metal letters press sculpturally into soft paper. Or writing on mylar plastic—I've done it; it takes writing beautifully."

So why vellum? Some calligraphers use vellum because of the sheer weight of tradition. Vellum has always been considered the most exquisite writing material. Others choose vellum because of their arts and crafts movement convictions. It is an anti-industrial statement. It harks back to a simpler time of individual scribes using organic tools and materials in a holistic way. It connects them to something foundational in the western tradition and evokes a kind of spirituality of work.

For Donald the question is more open. What effects does he want to achieve, and what material will let him do those things best? If this means a return to the most traditional of writing surfaces, he needs to know it is because that surface can do things no other surface can. Deeply imbued with the ethos of the working craftsman, Donald needs, nonetheless, as a contemporary artist, to use whatever means he can find to make work of his own era. This means that despite years of working on vellum, he still had to explore the question of why this particular surface was right for The Saint John's Bible.

I remember talking to Donald once after he'd done a large manuscript book on paper. "I have a new respect for calligraphers who work on paper," he said. "Paper is so much more demanding— scary, even. If you make a mistake, you're finished." Paper, with its more fragile surface, can withstand only the gentlest of corrections; erasures leave rough patches, which can only be smoothed with painstaking effort. Its clean, hard finish leaves the letters isolated against the background. The surface itself, lacking any variation of tone, gives no visual anchor for the text which sits on it. Paper can also raise problems of sharpness, especially with small writing. The natural absorbency of paper resists the scribe's efforts to produce perfectly sharp, crisp stroke endings.

Vellum, by contrast, while it is a most demanding material, responds as no other surface can to the ministrations of the pen. The quill and ink cut gently into the fine, raised nap of the prepared vellum surface, allowing the writing to be sharp and subtle. In its own way, vellum guides the movement of the pen in the scribe's hand. It allows just a hint of writing to show through from one side to the other, creating a gentle grid which lightly ghosts through from one page to the next. At the same time, it is enormously strong, and able to withstand the work of many hands. What sheet of paper could take the kind of labor expended on a single page of The Saint John's Bible? Many hands work their way across the surface of every page, writing text, adding marginal notes and small colored capitals, illuminating and gilding.

Vellum comes in many varieties. Heavier skins are useful for bookbinding, while thinner skins are best for making the pages of books. The Saint John's Bible required very large unblemished skins. Donald Jackson tried the products of several makers before he found the best source.

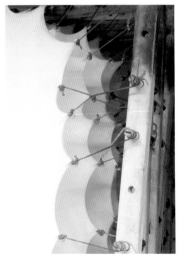

Skins stretched on frames dry taut at Cowley's.

Paper would require enormous care not to be creased or discolored in the process of passing through the hands of so many craftspeople. On vellum, mistakes can be erased with a sharp knife, leaving a surface only marginally different from surrounding areas and which can still take fine writing.

Vellum as a material is also beautiful in its own right. Its soft, variable surface is to paper as alabaster is to frosted glass. Every sheet of vellum has its own character, its own quirks, its own slight variations in tone and thickness. The incredible translucency of vellum catches the light. This is not a hard, mechanical surface but an organic substance which gives richness to the page no other material can reproduce.

Donald turned the options over in his mind. The durability of vellum is unquestioned—every major medieval manuscript is written on it. But most importantly no other material could have given him the surface qualities he needed for the book he was creating. "I've been there. I know all the disadvantages. But just like a cabinet-maker who chooses to work in elm—the grain goes crazy, and it's hard to work but he does it anyway—I choose to work in vellum. I do it for the way it responds to my hands or the work of my hands and to my senses. That's it. That's why I do it."

It is one thing to decide to use vellum; it is another thing altogether to find a reliable supply. Having settled on vellum as his material, Donald set out on a search which would put him in contact with vellum makers in Israel, Canada and Ireland before he finally found a supplier in England who was able to produce what he needed. "It's like looking for the Holy Grail," Donald says, reflecting on his quest for just the right kind of vellum for the Bible.

The manufacture of vellum

IT IS MANY YEARS, even many centuries since vellum has been produced in the vast quantities needed for the writing of a major book like The Saint John's Bible. Even in the Middle Ages, it was no small thing to get appropriate skins. The craft of making vellum requires great skill and is very labor intensive. It requires vast amounts of water and a large supply of animal skins. Slowly but surely, the commercial suppliers of vellum and parchment have been disappearing, along with centuries of insight into the niceties of preparing skins by hand. The economics of vellum manufacturing become more tenuous every year as commercial uses of the product disappear. There was a time when legal documents throughout the western world were written or printed on vellum. Many musical instruments, especially drums, had vellum components. Gradually paper and plastics have reduced the need for the material, leaving fewer and fewer commercial outlets to suppliers. Perhaps most importantly, in a world which values economic efficiency over every other value, there is less and less room for a traditional craft which is entirely based on the one-to-one relationship between a maker and his material.

Vellum is made of the skins of calves. Any animal skin may be used—I have seen examples made of kangaroo and even ostrich. Some very fine small Books of Hours in the Middle Ages may even have been produced with squirrel skins, which could be why they are so thin and fine in texture. In contemporary practice, the most common animal skins are calf, goat and sheep. Most calligraphers today reserve the term vellum (related to the word veal) for calf skins, using the word parchment for other skins, especially those of sheep. In common practice the words vellum and parchment are often interchangeable, as a quick peek in the Oxford English Dictionary will demonstrate.

The basic technique of making vellum has remained unchanged for almost two thousand years. Some illuminated medieval manuscripts contain beautiful illustrations of the vellum making process which

The translucency of vellum is one of its great appeals. In a manuscript book, the writing shows slightly through the page. In printed books, this would be considered a fault. In manuscripts, the show-through creates a light shadow which calligraphers value.

Donald Jackson prepares a skin using sand paper. A deep sensitivity to the qualities of the skin is essential. Every skin is unique and careful attention is required not to crease or damage it.

remain recognizable today. Today's makers may wear jeans and Wellington boots to work and they may have tattoos on their forearms but they still use essentially the same tools and materials that their forebears did a thousand years ago. The medieval illustrations show us exactly what still takes place.

The process starts with skins soaked in a solution of lime and water for up to two weeks.[*] The hair mostly falls off; what remains is scraped from the surface. They are then reimmersed in the lime solution for another fortnight. After this treatment the skins are stretched on a wooden frame. These frames are large and rectangular with pegs around all four sides. The skin is suspended in space with little cords which join the frame's pegs to small gatherings around the edges of the skin. As the skin dries, it stretches taut and flat. It is treated with pumice and water and is carefully scraped with a special knife called a *lunellum*. This knife (as the name suggests) has a crescent-shaped blade; its handle is set at ninety degrees to the plane of the blade. If the blade nicks the surface of the skin, a small hole will open up; in some manuscripts, like the Book of Kells, the scribes simply wrote around the holes. If a blood vessel has burst during the soaking process, the skin can become blotched with a deep purple bloom. Many skins bear the maker's marks of the person who scraped them. Breaking off the tines of a fork to produce a unique pattern, the maker pokes his distinct mark into the edge of the skin.

The aim of the vellum maker is to drain the skin of grease and to prepare the surface for writing. Vellum, unlike leather, loses its suppleness and becomes taut and stiff. Depending on the thickness of the skin, its stiffness can vary. Thick skins are as unyielding as cardboard; thin skins fold and bend easily.

When the skin has been repeatedly scraped, wet down and dried out, it is cut from the frame. Skins are sorted by color, weight and size. They are stacked or rolled and put into storage.

The finished skins have two distinct sides: the hair side and the flesh side. The hair side, from the exterior of the animal, has a fine, slightly slick texture and generally a soft cream-color. If any markings from the animal remain, they sometimes show on this side either as a network of very fine black dots or as soft,

[*] For the technique of manufacturing vellum, I have drawn on Christopher de Hamel's, *Illuminated Manuscripts* and on Sam Somerville's article "Parchment and Vellum" in *The Calligrapher's Handbook*.

When handled properly, vellum is enormously strong. Donald Jackson erases multiple lines from a Bible page using a sharp knife. He literally scrapes away the surface. After an erasure has been made, the skin is prepared again and new writing can be added. Paper would not easily stand up to such intrusive treatment.

cloud-like areas of light brown or grey. The flesh side has a somewhat rougher texture and is generally a purer white than the hair side. Good skins for writing are slightly velvety to the touch; the issue of "raising the nap" of the skin is of crucial importance to the scribe. The vellum manufacturers prepare the skin to various degrees, some offering skins almost ready for writing, others leaving the finish, especially on the hair side, slightly greasy and slick, allowing for the calligrapher to make his or her own adjustments.

The skins in their rough-cut state retain the overall shape of the animal. To a calligrapher with a trained eye, the roughly rectangular shape betrays the places where neck, tail and limbs once extended from the hide. Along the spine the skin is often slightly thicker; sometimes slight stretch marks indicate the underbelly. The skin is also subtly variable in its thickness from one end to the other; the shoulder end is generally thicker than the tail end. Along the edge of the rough-cut skin, the margins can become almost translucent. This horn-like area is useless for writing and must be trimmed from the final page.

Among its quirks as a material for writing, vellum is very susceptible to moisture. In dry weather it shrinks, becoming hard and stiff, even brittle. In damp weather it expands, becoming soft and supple. When soaked in water, it returns to its original state as a completely limp, flexible hide; it needs to be restretched if the calligrapher wants a flat writing surface. Because it reacts so strongly to moisture, it needs to be stored in rooms with stable humidity and the calligrapher has to be very careful about the amount of liquid which comes into contact with the page. This is a particular concern when illuminations or gilding are called for.

When using vellum, the calligrapher needs to know the material intimately with all its strengths and weaknesses. As the scribe writes, he or she becomes involved closely with the surface, aware of its every shift in thickness and texture. The pen glides across rough areas and smooth. It reacts differently on either side of the skin. Every skin is unique, individual. The calligrapher learns over time to react to each idiosyncrasy of the page and to accept the inevitable variations which the surface dictates in their writing.

The raw skins are soaked in a solution of lime and water for several weeks. The hair falls off and fat is drawn out of the skin.

The search for vellum makers

BEFORE HE COULD BEGIN The Saint John's Bible, Donald needed to find a reliable source for large amounts of vellum. For the ordinary scribal job the task of finding the right skin is simple. Going through the available skins, the calligrapher usually only needs to find a single sheet which meets the task. But this job was different. Donald needed to supply his Scriptorium with a huge number of skins, all of which had to be of a matching standard. There were to be no markings on the hair side. All the skins had to be even in texture, thickness and color. There could be no holes in the skins (despite the example of the Book of Kells!). In addition, Donald had decided on a huge page size—fifteen and seven-eighths inches wide by twenty-four-and-a-half inches tall. This meant that the skins had to be at least twenty-seven-and-a-half inches by thirty-five inches in order to allow each sheet to be folded once, as well as allowing a small working margin of one-and-a-half inches all around. This large measurement put Donald's requirements right at the outer limit of available skins. But it was not simply a question of finding the right number of skins or of finding skins of the right size. More pressing was to find a supplier who was still making skins which were acceptable for writing at all.

A sodden skin is completely pliable.

"What about the Irish source?" I asked Donald in a conversation at The Hendre. I knew there was a maker in Ireland who was very popular with students at the Roehampton Institute, one of the few places which exist to train professional calligraphers.

"I'm afraid they're basically making vellum for musical instruments; it's hit or miss when it comes to writing. They don't think like calligraphers at all. The students like them, but that's because they're not experienced enough."

Donald continued, "I tried a source in Canada as well. I have to say, he made some of the finest skins I've seen since my student days."

"Why didn't you go with him?"

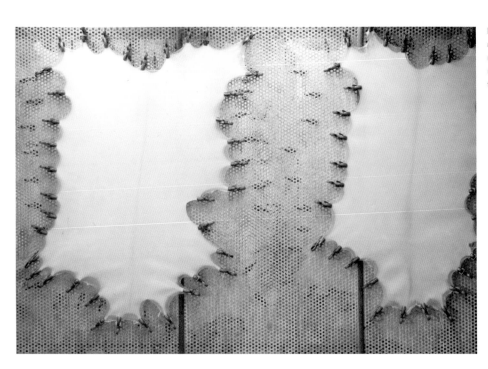

Even when the hair has been removed and the skins are ready to be scraped they recall the shape of the calf from which they came.

The skins are stretched onto wooden frames before scraping. Tiny balls of vellum off-cuts or newspaper are wrapped into gatherings made at the edges of the skin. These are then tied to the adjustable pegs lining the frame. Care is taken to ensure the tension across the skin is even so it dries perfectly flat.

"He does it in his spare time and I just wasn't sure he could produce skins in the quantity I needed them."

While the writing quality of the Canadian skins had been excellent, the samples that he'd been sent weren't quite the right size. He needed to consider other makers, people who could produce two-hundred-fifty skins of uniform quality at the large size required.

The next logical step was Israel.

Israeli Jews produce a massive amount of vellum to satisfy the religious market; Judaism requires the use of vellum for a huge range of ritual goods. The Torah must be written by hand on scrolls of vellum, as must the tiny *mezuzot* which hang on the doors of observant Jewish homes. Tiny inscriptions on vellum are wrapped in the phylacteries used for prayer. With this religiously sanctioned tradition in place, Jewish artists also produce wedding contracts and other Judaica on fine skins. There is a massive demand for calligraphy on vellum, and a working, living tradition of the *soferim*—ritual scribes[*]—to meet this demand. In addition to the *soferim* who work within the religious community under the strictest guidelines, there is a wider community of Israeli artists in Jerusalem who draw inspiration from the formal calligraphic tradition and use vellum in painting, drawing and lettering.

Donald went to Jerusalem where he was guided around the calligraphic scene by Izzy Pludwinski, a *sofer* in his own right. Together they went to the religious neighborhood of Mea Shearim. Located within walking distance of the Old City, its streets are narrow and not very clean. The buildings are mostly less than a hundred years old. Sometimes it is hard to believe you are still in Jerusalem; the streets could almost be in Crown Heights in New York or in any dusty, gritty Levantine city. And yet there is a very unusual air about the place. Large signs posted about the streets ask women to dress modestly out of respect for the religious views of the people of the neighborhood. Most of the women in the street are dressed in dark clothing, their hair carefully covered even in the heat of Jerusalem. The men, from various sects of Eastern European Jewry, wear long beards and wide-brimmed black hats. Their curly forelocks dance as they rush down the streets. Their coats come in many forms, from long black formal coats, reaching mid-calf, to robes of striped grey, almost like dressing gowns. The streets are filled with specialist shops, mostly tiny and dark, selling religious books and supplies. Ritual silver and beautiful prayer shawls are for sale. Heavy tomes for Talmudic scholars fill shop windows. If you are a man without a *kippeh*, or yalmulke, and you enter one of the small shops, small children may come and stare.

Everywhere you turn, there are the *yeshivot*—schools for studying Torah according to the various traditions of the neighborhood. Earnest men can be seen through the windows, poring over scrolls and massive copies of the Talmud. Mea Shearim is a place where religious observance is the dominating fact of life, a place for a people who have set themselves apart in order to pursue their particular understanding of what life should be.

Izzy led Donald into this foreign world, taking him to two of the more important parchment outlets of Mea Shearim. As they arrived at one outlet, so did Izzy's friend Mala, an artist who often works on vellum herself. They walked into the first of the outlets, and Donald was amazed at the scene.

"Here was a living tradition," Donald said. "Shelves were stocked with turkey quills, and there were rolls and rolls of vellum around. It fitted. I felt like I was at home. Calligraphers were scurrying in and out, paying for their supplies. Unlike going to western art shops or vellum suppliers, here I felt there was a real understanding of what I, as a scribe, was looking for. The skins looked right; they had an authentic

[*]The singular of the Hebrew word for scribe is *sofer*; the plural is *soferim*.

feel; they looked like the old manuscripts. There's also the whole question of secularity. I go to a western vellum supplier, and he says to me, 'I'm making this for cricket bat handles.' By contrast I go to Israel and here people are saying, 'In God's name, I'm asking you for this; it will be a Torah.' It felt more comfortable, more like what I'm after."

Izzy introduced Donald to the owner. The shop was a family business and several generations worked together there. Mala spoke up and wanted the owner to know that this was a very important western scribe he was dealing with. Speaking in Hebrew, she laid it on thick, playing up Donald's many commissions for the Queen of England. The old man behind the counter was unimpressed. "So?" he said, "Okay, I'll give him two chairs to sit on!"

These preliminaries done with, they quickly set to business. Skins were pulled from the shelves. They were very fine. The Israeli skins are prepared for writing on only one side, on the flesh side, but the parchment dealers said they could prepare both sides if need be. They could also arrange for skins large enough for Donald's needs.

"Where do the skins come from?" Donald asked.

"From Chicago," came the answer. The Israeli vellum makers import the raw skins from the huge abattoirs of the American Midwest; local supplies are too meager for their needs. The untanned skins arrive from Chicago, packed in brine and ready for processing.

The conversation was fruitful and the parchmenters[*] were very helpful but Donald had some qualms about what he saw. Many of the skins on offer were so specifically made for their Jewish context that they wouldn't work in the way Donald needed them to. Israelis design their vellum with the *sofer* market in mind. They even supply some skins pre-scored for mezuzot—saving the sofer time in ruling up.

"In the end, though I liked the skins, I couldn't use them," Donald said to me months later. "They are culturally specific. They don't give me the qualities I need in a skin. They seemed too rough on the flesh side and too absorbent on the hair side."

He continued, "The Israeli vellum is sanded in one direction. This matches the strong horizontal stroke of Hebrew calligraphy. The nap runs in a single direction and you are writing against the nap."

"The most serious problem was that the parchmenter told me the skins couldn't take any moisture; moisture leads to extreme cockling. When I got home and we tried it, it was true. The skins reacted strongly to the painting and cockled. Gilding worried me most. I suspected it would just pop off the skins."

In the Jewish religious tradition these parchmenters served, there is no need for decoration. The skins simply aren't prepared with the idea of illumination and gilding in mind. Donald suggested that the Israeli skins were stretched more tightly than the western skins and thus when they were exposed to moisture, they reacted more strongly.

"Also you must remember," Donald told me, "that there is a relationship between quill, ink and vellum. These three elements have to work together. The Israeli skins were designed to work with Israeli ink. Working on the flesh side of the skin with its heavy nap, they use an ink with a high gum content. The viscosity of that particular ink works well on skins with a strong nap.

"I also had two questions about the Israeli ink. One was very basic: is this archival? Is it acid? I couldn't guarantee that it wouldn't eat into the skins over time. The second question was aesthetic. The sofer ink is shiny, and it dries raised; it doesn't lie flat on the page. It wasn't the look I wanted to achieve."

So Donald was back to square one.

[*] "Parchmenter" is an old English term for a person who deals in vellum and parchment; it is the primary term Donald used to describe the vellum dealers of Mea Shearim. Interestingly, when talking of his English suppliers, Donald rarely uses the term. The traditional scribal atmosphere of the shops in Mea Shearim evokes that lost world of stationers who once supplied western calligraphers and scriveners with vellum. By contrast the more industrial world of western vellum makers seems one step removed from scribal lore and practice.

The next logical place to try was also the closest to home: Cowley's in Newport Pagnell, a three-hour drive from Wales. They had the largest available selection of skins prepared in the western manner Donald was accustomed to. Having made the decision to go with Cowley's, Donald had to consider very carefully what kinds of skins he needed. This wasn't just a scouting expedition; it was time to get very particular about the skins that would be chosen.

"I rang them up and told them what we were looking for," Donald told me. His first concern was the size of the available skins. At the large size he was looking for it was hard to find skins that were thin and supple enough; large skins come from large animals and they tend to be thicker and tougher. Then the skins had to be free of markings on the hair side and without structural weaknesses; there had to be no evidence of overstretching or any thin patches in the skin.

Donald and Sally made two visits to Cowley's. In order to speed up the selection, they brought with them a flat wooden frame which they used as a template. The frame was several inches larger than the trimmed page size of the finished book. Fine threads stretched inside the frame indicated the trim margins. Laying the frame on top of each skin, they could see immediately whether it had the right dimensions. They could also see if any flaws in the skin appeared within the trim area. They were especially concerned that none of the "horny" areas of skin would intrude; these areas, besides standing out with their different texture and color, also absorb moisture differently. If they are included within the final trimmed area, they produce a structural weakness in the book. As the rest of the page expands and contracts with changes in humidity, these areas remain stubbornly unyielding, leading to a progressive cockling in the page over time. They also looked to make sure that the two thin patches which tend to develop near the neck would not be included; these tend not to lie as flat as other parts of the skin.

"On our first visit, it became clear we hadn't been selective enough. We went through quite a few

The stretchers are taken
to a heated room where
the skins dry drum-tight on
their frames.

skins and made our selection but when we brought them back to the Scriptorium, we saw all sorts of little details we hadn't seen at Cowley's." The showroom at Cowley's—if one can call it that—is simply a space attached to the vellum factory; the light is not strong and sometimes it is hard to see every detail of the skins. On their second visit he was able to go through about one hundred skins. He chose thirty skins. Of these thirty, seven had to be sent back later.

"We were fortunate to be able to have so many skins to look at," Donald told me. Cowley's produces vellum for the British Parliament which prints a vellum copy of every law as it becomes official. In a bid for modernization, the Labor government had been looking into printing the official statutes on paper and had put all the vellum orders on hold. This gave Donald a rare opportunity to select from a huge backlog of skins. Now that Parliament has decided to continue printing its laws on vellum sheets, Donald faces stiff competition for the available skins.

It could be frustrating. "The best skins always seemed to be just a quarter inch too small," Donald said. Still, one by one the skins piled up and he had a good selection of skins with which to begin the book.

The art of scrutching

BACK AT THE SCRIPTORIUM, with a sheaf of skins to work with, the hard job of preparation had to begin. Skins come from the vellum factory prepared to a certain extent, but it's up to the calligrapher to do a final preparation before beginning to write. This stage has traditionally been called "pouncing" and involves rubbing down the skin with a mixture of abrasives to create the appropriate texture for writing. Old law scriveners used to keep a pouncing bag at their desks. This contained a mixture of powdered pumice (an abrasive), whiting (a slaked chalk which absorbs any remaining grease) and sandarac (which repels water, helping control ink flow and preventing the letters from bleeding into the skin). Dusting down the skin with this mixture, they would rub it in before starting to write. In Donald's Scriptorium, modern materials have replaced some of these elements but the principle remains the same.

The special knife used to scrape the skins is referred to as a *lunellum*. The crescent-shaped blade is set at a ninety-degree angle to the handle. Scraping the skin is highly skilled work. A small mistake in the use of the *lunellum* can tear or cut the skin, ruining it. Exactly the same process is illustrated in medieval manuscripts.

Each skin is carefully examined and assigned a particular position in the book. As the pages are folded, each opening has to match—that is, hair side must be opposite hair side, flesh side opposite flesh side. Illuminations should be on slightly thicker parts of the skin than areas of pure writing; the extra thickness supports paint better. Since the vellum tends to be thicker at the neck and shoulder area and thinner at the tail end, the skins can be positioned within the manuscript to make sure that full page illuminations appear on the thicker parts of the skins. Areas to be illuminated need less preparation, while areas to receive writing require more sensitive preparation.

In the middle of our interview, Donald turned to me suddenly and said, "You know, if you're going to write about this, I think you need to experience what it's like to actually write on the vellum we're using. It's the only way to really understand what we're after." He took out a large practice sheet and prepared different areas of the skin in various ways so I could feel for myself how the writing worked. The sheet of vellum in front of me seemed huge, a full page. Just physically managing such a large skin was an issue in itself. I had to be careful not to crease it as I leaned forward to write. He prepared several areas, and encouraged me to try the hair side first, then try the flesh side. Some of the areas were carefully prepared; some over-prepared; some left almost as they came from Cowley's.

The aim of the preparation is to create a soft, raised surface. Before it has been prepared, the skin can be too slick and shiny; the pen can get no purchase on the skin. If an area is prepared too much, however, the writing becomes difficult; the pen drags and the letters break up. Donald handed me a quill and prepared a little pool of ink, and walked off, leaving me alone to see what I could discover.

I began on a slick, horny part of the skin right at the edge. The pen had no purchase on the surface; it slid around and every quaver of my hand produced little glitches in the edges of my letters. As my pen skittered across the page the ink refused to adhere properly.

On a more thoroughly prepared section, Donald put gum sandarac on one part and left it off another part. Where the gum sandarac had been rubbed in gently, the writing was beautiful. I could feel the quill bite gently into the raised nap of the skin, slowing my hand just enough to give me control over the writing. In the area without the sandarac, the pen again skidded around and felt too loose against the surface. In one area the sandarac was purposely applied too thickly. Here, though the writing felt good, the ink didn't sit properly on the page. As it dried, a tiny white hairline appeared down the center of each stroke of the pen. The sandarac, which repels water, wouldn't allow the ink to settle in the tiny channel created by the pen.

It's an extremely delicate balance to achieve. The skin has to be sanded to raise just the right amount of nap; if it is sanded too much, the skin begins to break up, becoming too fibrous for the writing. The sandarac has to be added in just the right quantity to give a bit more tooth to the page and to keep the writing crisp and sharp. But if too much sandarac is used, the letters break up. Add to this subtle balance the fact that the skins are of different textures on hair and flesh sides and that they are also variable from one end of the skin to the other and you have an incredibly subtle and delicate job on your hands.

That delicate job went first to Sally. Later other assistants took over the work of preparing skins. Working in the scrutching shed,[*] the scrutcher first examines the whole surface of each skin. Every sheet

* The term "scrutching" describes the act of rubbing down a skin in preparation for writing. The word was invented by Donald's brother, Barry.

A mortar and pestle are used to grind the sandarac "pounce," a fine powder which is dusted onto the skins during their preparation at the Scriptorium. The little cloth pouch holds the pounce, which sifts evenly through the mesh of the fabric.

of vellum is from an individual calf and it must be held up to the light to see where the skin is thick and where it is thin. The light shows through any tiny pin-prick holes which are already in the vellum. Then it is examined in raking light. This shows how much the nap is already raised. Are there places where the skin is "breaking up"; that is to say, are there places where the surface is already so textured that further preparation would be unwise?

The skin is then placed flesh side up on the smooth table. It is rubbed with a relatively heavy grade of sand paper (grade 240 silicone carbide), using a good deal of elbow grease. The action is very much like that of planing a piece of wood—an infinitesimally fine layer of the skin is rasped off. This raises the nap and removes any trace of sheen or chalkiness from the skin. The scrutcher checks her work as she goes, running her thumb along the surface and bending down repeatedly to see how the finish is developing. Turning the skin over to work on the hair side, she repeats the process, but this time a bit more gently.

The next step is the addition of gum sandarac. This resin has been ground with a mortar and pestle and sits to one side, wrapped in a fine-weave cloth bag. Dusting the surface with the bag causes the tiny grains to sift evenly across the surface. With a finer grade of sandpaper (grade 400 silicone carbide), she gently rubs the skin down again, this time using a circular motion. This is delicate work and she pauses more and more often to check the result. The skin should take on a soft, velvety finish. If particles of the sandarac build up, they can sometimes leave scratch marks. As the work proceeds, the rubbing becomes ever gentler, until the skin is absolutely ready for the scribes.

Sarah Harris at work in the scrutching shed. She works at a formica table and sands the skins with progressively finer grades of sandpaper. The mask she wears protects her from inhaling fine particles of vellum dust.

As the project continues, this process is being slowly refined. Donald feels that the sandarac should not be rubbed in with sandpaper, while the scribal team has asked on occasion for a heavier dose of sandarac. Slowly as a team they are working out the details. It may well be that each volume will be treated somewhat differently, as the best practice develops through trial, error and growing experience.

The search for the perfect writing surface is perhaps less like looking for the Holy Grail than it is an attempt to find a series of balances. Donald and his team of scribes are trying to realize an ideal. It is only when the pen begins its slow dance across the page that human skill is united to its chosen tools and materials in a way which produces something truly splendid, wondrous and yes, even holy.

The suppleness of the vellum page is apparent in this detail from an early design proposal. Properly cared for, a vellum manuscript will last for centuries.

out of the mouth that defiles." [12] Then the disciple approached and said to him, "Do you know that the Pharisees took offense when they heard what you said?" [13] He answered, "Every plant that m heavenly Father has not planted will be uproote [14] Let them alone; they are blind guides of the blin[d] And if one blind person guides another, both wil fall into a pit." [15] But Peter said to him, "Explai this parable to us." [16] Then he said, "Are you als still without understanding? [17] Do you not see tha whatever goes into the mouth enters the stomac and goes out into the sewer? [18] But what comes ou of the mouth proceeds from the heart, and this i what defiles. [19] For out of the heart come evil inte ions, murder, adultery, fornication, theft, fals witness, slander. [20] These are what defile a persor out to eat with unwashed hands does not defile

CHAPTER 4

THE WORD TAKES FLESH

ORGET OLD Hollywood historical dramas and their floppy ostrich plume pens. That's not how it works. Turkeys, geese and swans provide the raw material. The barbs of the feather have to go first. All you need is the clean shaft of the quill. Nothing must interfere with the writing. Then you take a sharp quill knife and make a scooping cut on the underside of the quill. Cut the slit; cut each side; slice the end to its proper shape. Finally, cut the very tip off absolutely straight, leaving yourself a chisel-edged end. The chisel edge is the key to the whole enterprise.

Your pen doesn't look like much. It's about the size of the average pencil. It's the color of your fingernails. It weighs next to nothing. But with that clean-cut chisel-edge, you can make the most subtle and satisfying letters. Holding the quill naturally in the right hand, the writing flows with grace and ease: thick stroke, thin stroke, sliding back to thick. Undulating, modulated lines compose themselves into letters and words and sentences, knitting the page together. The words text and textile share a common root—the Latin *texere*, to weave.

A practice of writing

I HAVE IN FRONT OF ME a sheaf of photocopies from the Scriptorium. They are covered with variants of the text, attempts to define the characteristics of the script. More than at any point in this project, Donald was very reticent when I tried to get him to talk about the design of the writing. Perhaps this is where the process of design is most elusive. The expectation is that he will produce a script like a type-face: something you can put a name to, something you can analyze and take apart and perhaps even license and sell. Donald just doesn't work that way. Not with script. It is not about putting a formula in a machine and producing page after page of standard output. It is about an organic process building a team and setting in motion something which in the end, will result in a script. It is a practice of writing, not a branded, saleable typeface. Donald's reticence was a protection of the space where that practice could grow and develop.

It is fashionable these days to co-opt the counterculture to sell things. Fancy brands of sneakers try to be bearers of counterculture, just as national chains try to reproduce beatnik espresso bars on a vast world-dominating scale. But the practice of writing which the scribes have joined is, in fact, really countercultural, setting all of our assumptions about script on their head. The script of The Saint John's Bible is emerging from a process of collaboration and consultation in which the scribes are recreating the ethos of an ancient scriptorium. Under Donald's leadership and tutelage, they are watching the script evolve together. Donald shapes the evolution; he doesn't have a fixed end-point. It's a setup that would make a systems analyst have a coronary. But it may be the best way for a script to take on a life of its own. That liveliness shows in the final product.

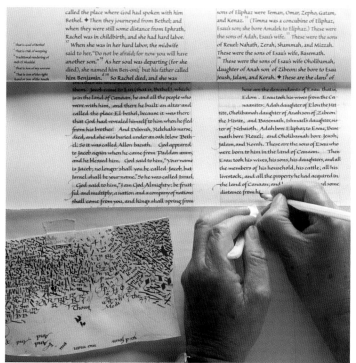

Quills stand at the ready, arrayed on a shelf in front of sketches for the script. The large blue capitals are prototypes for the initial letters which mark the beginnings of chapters. On the wall behind is an article on healthy posture for calligraphers.

As the scribe writes a Bible page with a carefully cut quill, the vellum page is held down with a knife or a bone tool held in the left hand. The computer printout above provides the scribe with his text. The green sections on the printout indicate which lines have been squeezed to fit the column width; the scribe must condense his text accordingly as he writes. A guard sheet under the writer's hands protects the vellum. The little scratch sheet on the left allows the scribe to test his ink flow before writing on the actual page.

Building a scribal vocabulary

CALLIGRAPHY, like every trade or craft, has its own vocabulary. Anyone who has taken an evening calligraphy class will be familiar with the names of the various styles of writing offered—italic, roundhand, carolingian and so on. A professional calligrapher will not usually call these *styles* of writing, still less *fonts*, a purely typographic term whose misuse has been popularized by the computer. The professional will refer to them as *scripts* or *hands*. A professional also knows that these seemingly distinct scripts are actually variations on a theme. There are infinite varieties of italic, just as there are multiplicities of roundhands or gothics. And the distinction between the hands is not sharp either. A particular italic hand can slide into a gothic with only small variations of pen handling and letter shape. The names of various scripts serve, then, as shorthand descriptions rather than closed classifications.

All of this reflects the history of writing. Edged-pen calligraphy is based on the writing practices of Western Europe between about 300 and 1500 AD. In that period, scripts were in constant flux. Thousands of people writing documents over a period of centuries produced a living tradition which grew and developed with time. For grand books like Bibles, there were formal, carefully written scripts; for quick letters between friends, there were cursive ("running") scripts. With time, cursive elements would creep into formal writing, and formal writing would decay into a quicker cursive form. Over a thousand years, this flow back and forth between formal and informal writing produced innumerable variations on the basic scripts in use. Add to that shifts in taste and fashion, and you have a complex and rich tradition of writing.

When we come back to look at all these varieties of script, we inevitably begin to spot certain key landmarks: the rigidly parallel lines of a high gothic script with its strong, diamond-shaped terminations; the round and lush forms of the Book of Kells, referred to in the trade as an "insular semi-uncial;" the elegant flow of a Renaissance italic. These are just the highpoints of a tradition largely without boundaries. And the more deeply you explore the history of western writing, the more it becomes clear that few of these scripts have clean endings or beginnings. The shift from the round and open carolingian script to the angular and compressed gothic took place in four hundred years of small incremental steps.

To talk intelligently about a script, then, calligraphers need more precise words to describe the act of writing. The terminology can become very technical. The most basic term is pen angle, an often elusive concept for beginning students. Imagine a page of lined paper. You hold an edged pen in your hand. You place the pen on the page. If you drag it in one direction, you will get a thick line, using the full width of the chisel edge. If you drag it in another direction, you get a perfectly thin, fine line. The thicks and thins of the writing emerge from the edge of the pen held at a constant angle to the baseline on which the letters sit. This is the pen angle. The italic hand is usually described as a script written at forty-five degrees; roundhand is described as having a thirty degree pen angle.

Were it so simple. Pen angle is rarely as fixed as it seems. Pen manipulation is the practice of twisting the pen during the act of writing, varying the pen angle within the letters themselves. In point of fact, everyone manipulates the pen slightly. It's not humanly possible to hold the pen at a mechanically constant angle to the page, even if it were desirable. But there are certainly scripts which seem to keep a relatively consistent pen angle and others which require twists and turns of the pen.

Slope describes the angle of the upright strokes of your script. Look at the **h** or the **d**. Does it lean forward, anticipating the movement of the script? It can be described as having a slight forward slope. Usually this is no more than about three to five degrees off the vertical, a gentle tilting of the letters. This is often barely conscious on the part of the writer; it is a natural tendency to lean the letters in the direction of the writing. Left-to-right scripts tend to lean to the right, while right-to-left scripts like Hebrew or Arabic tend to lean to the left. To the untrained eye the slope may not be apparent until ruler and compass are used to check the uprights. Slope affects pen angle as well.

Weight describes how dark a line of writing appears to be. A gothic hand, for instance, is considerably darker and "weightier" than your average italic. It's easy to see the difference between the two but it is very difficult to master all the variables that give the writer control over the weight.

In addition letters have parts. The top of the **h** which breaks above the rest is an ascender. The long tail of **y** which drops below the line is a descender. Letters like **e** and **g** have closed circular shapes called bowls, while the **n** and **m** are capped with neat arches. Some strokes end with little wedges or thin terminations called serifs.

This is the vocabulary of the trade. Donald's team came ready to use this language in thinking about the script. How wrong they were.

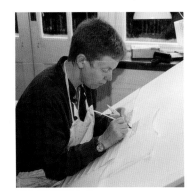

Sue Hufton practices the Bible script.

Starts and false starts

I LAID OUT MY PHOTOCOPIES of the writing on a coffee table before Donald. Light scripts and dark scripts, spiky ones and round ones covered the table. All of them were in the standard column format he had chosen. It was obvious from the samples that small changes in the shape or size of the script had an enormous effect on the appearance of the columns.

Donald pointed to one of the samples. "The problem is retaining the line-ness of the line of writing; if the script is too open, the linear quality goes."

He pointed to a column of handsome script. It was a tall italic. "Look," he said, "it becomes visual mush." He waved his hand up and down, showing me how the lines of text were too light to make a contrast to the interlinear white spaces. The result: a tall column with an even grey texture. Mush.

His trials to develop a Bible script were guided by an interlocking matrix of factors. One basic issue was creating a script which would sit properly within the two-column format he'd worked out. It had to be weighty enough to produce that "line-ness" he was looking for. Like any book script the Bible hand needed to be fairly formal as well as relatively simple in construction. Legibility and ease of writing were both important. Because of the huge amount of text, the writing would have to be small. Those were the technical concerns. Other, less easily defined issues also guided Donald's thinking. The script had to feel worthy of the sacred texts it was being used to transmit. And while it might draw from the tradition, it could not look antiquarian. It had to be a script of today.

One large sample stood out from the rest. It was a page of large letters made with a felt tip marker. In the middle of the page the words "speed flexibility—juice" summed up their lively personality. Lower down on the page, the serifs of some of the letters were circled, as though he had been explaining different ways of ending strokes of the pen. Labelled in Donald's flowing handwriting "Demonstration to prod. Committee" it was dated March 1999.

"This is lively. What were you trying to do here?" I asked.

"I was looking at the Cnut Charter," he said. This famous manuscript was written in the year 1018 and is kept in the British Library (Stow Charter 38). The script is full of interesting idiosyncrasies involving pen manipulation. It is elegant and highly legible. Like any historical script, it could only provide a starting point for a modern script. For one thing it doesn't include all the modern English letters, being written in medieval Latin. For another it's full of obsolete forms and conventions. "I discarded it because it didn't modernize." No matter how he tried to adapt his model, it retained its "archaic aura." "The Cnut hand has to disavow its antiquity," Donald said. "In any case, it's too jumpy for the two column format."

The Winchester Bible had also provided a possible model. Produced in the twelfth century at the monastery connected to Winchester Cathedral, it remains in the Cathedral library to this day. It is one of the most splendid medieval manuscript Bibles and would prove a major source for Donald as he designed the pages of The Saint John's Bible.

On the table in front of us there were some handsome samples of Donald's version of the Winchester script. One thing immediately leapt out from these samples: the Winchester Bible—in Latin—benefits from the even texture of that language. The same script used for our own language becomes much more spiky, the smooth ms and ns of the Latin giving way to the staccato hs, fs and ys of English. Where Latin creates a naturally flowing rhythm, English breaks the line more, throwing many more ascenders and

Three kinds of quills are used in the Bible—swan, goose and turkey. Only the foremost flight feathers are used for making quills for writing. All the scribes use goose quills for writing the main body of text. Feathers for making quills come from domestic geese from the United States and Wales and from wild Canada geese from Minnesota and New England. Turkey and swan feathers are used for heavier letterforms, such as the capitals and chapter numbers.

descenders into those interlinear spaces above and below the lines of writing. But that wasn't what killed it. "It defies modernization." There's no more to say.

We looked at the spiky italic again. "Much of this writing was designed with the computer in mind. I was trying to get a word count—a consistent number of letters per line." All the time he was designing a script for his team of calligraphers, Donald was also aware that it was on the computer that the final layouts would be made. His script had to have enough consistency to allow the computer to process the text in preparation for the work of writing. It was an unusual process for a hand-written Bible, made necessary by the complexity and size of the project.

"But this italic isn't just a response to the computer, is it?" I asked.

"It's trying to do something more consciously modern," Donald replied. "But I thought it was too pared down. It would be cloying over a long period, like eating nothing but frosting."

The sketches from 1998 and 1999 were extremely varied. By 2000, the script had begun to settle into shape. Its basic weight and scale were set, and it had even acquired a name: "Jacksonian #2." By now, too, people were beginning to be invited to be part of the scribal team. The script would have to be resolved and soon.

Collaboration

WHEN THE FIRST TEAM of scribes met at The Hendre, they arrived at the Scriptorium to find a script in development, a work in flux.

This was not just an omission. There was a method in it. The next stage of development couldn't happen without the team in place. The calligraphers' initial visit in February 2000 has been dubbed "the master class." The rest of the project was put to one side as Donald and his scribes studied the script together. The whole process of writing was examined, tested, pulled apart and put back together again. The script would gel along with the group.

"It's not a question of copying a shape," Donald said, "but adopting a shape as your own child—nurturing it—making it your own. It should be open for the scribes to do what they'd hoped they'd do with it."

The challenge he was setting them was enormous. What was this script he presented to them? It was a complex creation.

Brian Simpson described the hand. "It was more different from other scripts than I thought. I looked at it at first and said, 'Oh, it's a rounded italic.' But it's not. It is difficult."

Sue Hufton had a stab at describing it. "It is not conventional. Not roundhand, italic or foundational. I got myself in a muddle early on with these terms. It's not even a mixture of these terms. It's not easily defined. It's to do with the movement of the pen. It's rounded, but not a wide round. It's based on an oval rather than on a circle. The action is similar to round letterforms and to cursive, italic, whatever."

This was a script which challenged the easy classification the scribes might have been used to. I asked Sally Mae to describe it: what was the pen angle? what were the proportions?

"It's not to do with that. No pen angle, no x-height, no exemplars. At the end of the day, I had to throw all that out the window. You have to trust yourself, and you have to trust DJ."

Sue echoed Sally: "I was presented with a script that in a funny kind of way made me set aside everything I knew about letter forms, the relationships between letters—put to one side all my preconceptions about letterforms. And yet this is the thing—I needed every scrap of knowledge and experience I could draw from."

Before it can be cut, a quill must be soaked and softened in water. It is then cured in hot sand in order to harden the shaft. Sarah Harris works in the Black Iron Shed with an electric skillet. With a spoon she pours hot sand into the cavity of the quill, which she then plunges into the sandy skillet.

The notes for the master class found their way into my sheaf of photocopies titled "The script as it was explained to the calligraphers." A block of eighteen lines of Bible script appears at the top of the first page. It is a loose, even casual version of the script. It is dotted with small annotations. Below this, enlarged letters and parts of letters give evidence of a detailed discussion of the Bible script. These, too, are marked with small checks and **x**s. This is not an exemplar. It looks like the kind of thing you see on a blackboard in school after a long and complicated lecture. Donald told me he had to stop doing the large demonstration writing; it altered the motion of the pen, so it didn't reflect the subtleties of the writing at the smaller scale of the actual text.

Sue remarked, "I would not have done it this way. This is what I am required to do. But then it becomes my own." She paused for a moment before correcting herself. "No. It becomes ours."

The team aspect quickly became important. Sue said, "When we go down to The Hendre, we feel part of a team, even if we haven't met all the team members—especially the illuminators. We refine the script together. Donald doesn't have any one set way. You want the security of an exemplar. But it's good we never had one. The evolution has been allowed to happen."

Now that they had been writing for the better part of two years, Brian said to me, "Two years in, and we're just beginning to understand the script. It feels better, it looks better." Sue agreed. "It amazed me how much we've been pushed to our limits."

The scribes

IN AN ENTERPRISE like this, then, the members of the team are all important. The script took shape in an atmosphere of learning and cooperation where personalities could come to the fore. So who were the scribes?

Brian Simpson studied at the Central School of Arts and Crafts in London at the same time as Donald. Bearded and avuncular, his manner is gentle and self-effacing. As Sally says, "Steady Brian. Honest. Steady. Reliable. His whole heart is in it. Lots of care goes into his work. Very careful he—he's not a reckless man, I don't think. Brian picked up the script right away."

At the Central School he had two days a week of calligraphy, one with Irene Wellington, the other with M.C. Oliver. Unlike his classmate Donald, who had moved to London to go to the school, Brian

commuted down from his native Leicester. He worked three days a week doing commercial lettering—"brush work for printing"—to pay for two days of calligraphy class. He said to me, "Sue and Sally trained together. It shows. I think their writing is similar. Donald and I studied together. Our writing is similar."

"What makes your writing similar, do you think?" I asked.

He thought for a moment before answering. "I think it's pen manipulation. We use the corner of the pen more. When the pen lifts [off the page], it tends to go on to the corner. Sue and Sally, perhaps they use the flat of the pen more."

"Do you think this has to do with how you were trained?"

"Maybe it was. Irene always wanted you to come up with a project of your own, and she'd let you loose. Then she made gentle suggestions—well, not gentle. But she didn't say this is an **A** and this is the way it's done. She encouraged you to think for yourself."

"How was that different from M.C. Oliver?" I asked.

"Perhaps it says something that we called her Irene, and him Mr. Oliver. He was more dogmatic. This is the way to do it. And that's what you did." His tone changed when he spoke of Irene. "Irene was an excellent teacher, sympathetic. She took it to heart. She was sensitive to people."

I wondered how he felt working with Donald. "I've worked with him a lot over the years. It's helped me knowing Donald so long. As a youngster, he was just the same as now." He chuckled a bit. "He can be frustrating." This last word he drew out in his Leicester accent: froos-trat-ting. "That's Donald. But he comes up with the goods, gets the results. That's what matters in the end. Donald does it by the seat of his pants. It harks back to Irene."

"How was it when you began the writing of the Bible?" I wondered.

"On the first page I wrote I started three-fourths of the page down the first column, so the shaky, tentative writing would not be right at the top."

"I notice you retouch your work sometimes."

"Yes, sometimes. On the tails of the **y**s, sometimes the two ends of the nib catch. I scrape it clean. The counters of the **e**s also fill in. When that happens I make a little tick mark in the margin, and come back and fix it later. With the knife."

The quill is an exquisitely precise tool working in concert with the vellum surface. Unlike a metal pen it is supple and allows the ink to flow freely, producing fine hairlines at the end of strokes. The raised nap of the vellum with its velvety texture gives the page some "tooth." Note the tiny scale of the writing.

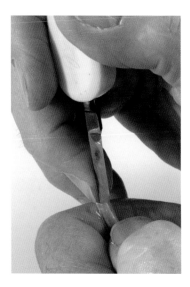
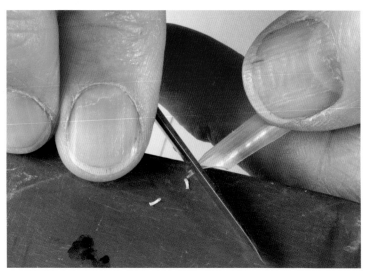

In the hands of a master, a quill is quickly cut. The quill knife must be razor sharp. The barbs on each side of the quill are removed first. A simple sequence of cuts produces a pointed end with evenly curved sides. A slit is then made at the tip. The final step, the "nibbing," produces a chisel-edge shape ready for writing.

This sample of script was used in the "dummy" Donald Jackson presented to Saint John's. Executed in 1997, it uses the King James translation. After many trials, Donald would eventually come full circle; the final script has a character very much like this first trial.

saith unto her, I that speak unto thee am he And upon this came his disciples, & marvelled n that he talked with the woman : yet no man said what seekest thou ? or, Why talkest thou with her ? The woman then left her waterpot, and went

A self-consciously modern vertical compressed italic from 1998. Donald Jackson felt there was not enough substance or complexity in the script to sustain the message over a thousand pages.

15
16
17

18

19

20

21

22
23

nor in Jerusalem. You worship what you do not know; we worship what we know, for salvation is from the Jews. Jesus said to her, "Go, call your husband, and come back". The woman answered him, "I have no husband." Jesus said to her, "You are right in saying 'I have no husband'; for you have had five husbands, and the one you have now is not your husband. What you have said is true." The woman said to him, "Sir, I see you are a prophet. Our ancestors worshiped on this mountain, but you say that the place where people must worship is in Jerusalem." Jesus said to her, "Woman, believe me, the hour is coming when you will worship the Father neither on this mountain nor in Jerusalem. You worship what you do not know; we worship what we know, for salvation is from the Jews. Jesus said to her, "Go, call your husband, and come back". The woman answered him, "I have no husband". Jesus said to her, "You are right in saying 'I have no husband'; for you have had five husbands, and the one you have now is not your husband. What you have said is true." The woman said to him, "Sir, I see you are a prophet. Our

Now there was a Pharisee named Nicodemus, a leader of the Jews. He came to Jesus by night and said to him, "Rabbi, we know that you are a teacher who has come from God; for no one can do these signs that you do apart from the presence of God." Jesus answered him, "Very truly, I tell you, n no one can see the presence of God without being born from above · Nicodemus said unto him, How can anyone be born after growing old ? Can one enter again a second time into the mothers womb and be born ?" Jesus Answered "Very truly, I tell you, no one can enter the kingdom of God without being born of water and Spirit."

Another script from 1998 with a strongly vertical quality. The column width was still undecided at this stage. Donald Jackson describes this sample as "mush." Rather than achieving a pattern of dense lines with clear interlinear channels of white, the letters blend into a solid grey mass.

R R who is close to the fathers heart?"

R who is close to the eire the

This is the testimony given by John Jews sent priests and Levites from Je ask him, Who are you? He confess not deny it but confessed, I am not And they asked him, What then ? Elijah ? He said, I am not. Are you He answered, No. Then they said are you ? Let us have an answer for sent us. What do you say about yo He said: I am the one voice of cry the wilderness, Make straight of the Lord as the prophet Isaiah s

Donald Jackson flirted with a script based on the Cnut Charter, an English document of the early eleventh century. This, too, he rejected. The writing could not be purged of its archaic flavor.

5

When Jesus saw the crowds, he went up the mountain: and after he sat down, his disciples came to him. ¶ Then he began to speak, and taught them, saying : ¶ "Blessed are the poor in spirit, for theirs is the kingdom of heaven. ¶ "Blessed are those who mourn, for they will be comforted. ¶ "Blessed are the meek, for they will inherit the earth. ¶ "Blessed are those who hunger and thirst for righteousness, for they will be filled. ¶ "Blessed are the merciful, for they will receive mercy. ¶ "Blessed are the pure in heart, for they will see God. ¶ "Blessed are the peacemakers, for they will be called children of God. ¶ "Blessed are those who are persecuted for righteousness sake, for theirs is the kingdom of heaven. r

A sample from January 2000. "This is getting there," Donald Jackson said. "It has a classic feel. The spaces between lines and letters are as important for harmony as the letters themselves." This sample became an important model for the scribes.

> claiming a baptism of repentance for the forgiveness
> of sins, 4 as it is written in the book of the words of
> the prophet Isaiah,
>
> "The voice of one crying out in the wilderness:
>   'Prepare the way of the Lord,
>   make his paths straight'.
> 5 Every valley shall be filled,
>   and every mountain and hill shall be made low,
>   and the crooked shall be made straight,
>   and the rough ways made smooth;
> 6 and all flesh shall see the salvation of God.'"
>
> 7 ▌ John said to the crowds that came out to be bap-
> tized by him, "You brood of vipers! Who warned
> you to flee from the wrath to come? 8 Bear fruits
> worthy of repentance. Do not begin to say to your-
> selves, 'We have Abraham as our ancestor'; for I tell

If you look at his pages, you will see some of the tails of the ys carefully scratched along their edges to make neat, clean flourishes.

Brian knows his trade. And he knows how to get out of a tough spot. "That's what makes a good craftsman," he said. "It's not that you don't make mistakes. It's knowing how to get out of a mess."

Sue is as lean and precise as her work. There is an air of seriousness about her. She weighs her words before she speaks. "My background emphasis was on drawn, painted and carved letters. I didn't like calligraphy. I felt a bit of a fraud when I was asked to be part of the team." This, she explained, had everything to do with her tools. She was writing with metal pens on paper. But the Bible was a completely different thing—writing on vellum with quill pens was a pleasure. The pleasure had not come, however, without significant struggle. The mastery of the quill was a huge issue. "The script itself is very nice to write now. You do relax: but I have to say relaxing does not mean speeding up. I've actually been trying to slow down. Brian takes twelve to thirteen hours to write a page. I do it in almost half the time: I'll take seven hours."

I wondered if it began to flow more easily as she gained practice. No. It didn't. The writing is demanding. "I am always thinking about how to get the line to fit into its space. Vin (the computer layout technician) is getting a lot better with the typesetting of the computer drafts for the scribes; he's becoming a better judge of the spacing. Sometimes you have a line with fifty-five characters to fit in, followed by a line of forty-five characters. You have to make the lines look the same on the page, have the same color and consistency."

I asked her, "Now that you have really internalized the script, how would you describe your writing?"

"I keep a more consistent pen angle than the others. I do not do manipulations easily. At Roehampton, I wrote the Cnut Charter hand without pen manipulation."

I expressed surprise—at the Roehampton Institute, where we both trained, the study of the Cnut Charter hand was almost entirely designed to teach us about pen manipulation. "I know, I know," she said. "It just came out differently. That's all. It was a different thing."

"Do you think there's a difference in the way each of you write?" I wondered.

"It's less obvious now. Brian and Donald write similarly. Sally and I write similarly. It's to do with our training. Or maybe it's the time when we trained. We trained at different times with different tutors; perhaps that's what makes the difference."

Some things, however, did not come down to training. "Brian does a lot more pen manipulation. Sally does, too."

The first group of scribes gathered in February 2000 to begin writing Bible pages. Instead of being handed an exemplar to copy, they were plunged into a detailed examination of the evolving Bible script. These jottings are a record of that conversation showing different strategies for making the letters.

I asked Sally Mae if her writing was similar to Sue's.

"No, it's not," she said definitively. "Sue wasn't even doing calligraphy: she came more out of drawn and painted letters." There was a hint of fire in what she said. Sally is energetic and enthusiastic, ready to get stuck into a project, with more than a touch of a wild streak. She is quick-eyed, with a wicked laugh. As the studio manager she was involved in the project long before the other two. Unlike Brian and Sue, who do most of their work at home, Sally is at the Scriptorium all the time. She moved to Wales to take up the job. Although she was involved in the design stages of the script, she didn't start writing Bible pages until well after the other two had begun.

"I've been involved in so many aspects of the Bible," she said, listing all the tasks she'd done or overseen. The reality of meetings, devising work

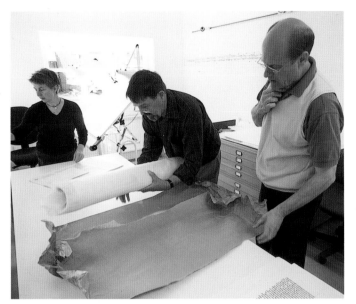

Brian Simpson, Sue Hufton, Donald Jackson and Sally Mae Joseph examine and discuss finished Bible pages. The four scribes who work away from the Scriptorium write most of the pages at home, returning at regular intervals to The Hendre. Working in isolation, the scribes find that their writing gradually deviates from the standard script. By meeting together with Donald and Sally Mae they continue to bond as a team and bring their writing back into harmony.

Brian Simpson unrolls the pages he has written at his home in Leicester.

schedules, keeping everyone and everything moving along, as well as being involved in vellum preparation and illumination, means that she doesn't have the chance to write as much as the other two.

"I rarely get the chance to sit and write smoothly and without interruption." But she knows the script. "Even though I started later on the writing, I was part of the master class and the development of the thing. So I picked it up faster."

She also had experience doing peerages—the legal documents Donald produces for the Crown Office at the House of Lords. She was used to writing Donald's house style. It wasn't a far leap into Bible script.

In October 2002 two new scribes joined the team: Susie Leiper and Angela Swan. Unlike the first calligraphers, who were involved with the creation of the script, the two new scribes were learning to adapt to something which had already taken form.

Susie Leiper laughed when I asked her where she had trained. "I came into this sideways," she said. "I didn't go to Roehampton. My very first western calligraphy teacher was in Hong Kong where I was living at the time. Sally tells me it's an advantage coming from a different background."

When she arrived for her first week at The Hendre, there were three other newcomers. Their training lasted five weeks: three weeks at the Scriptorium, interspersed with two weeks at home to practice on their own.

"The very first thing we learned was how to sit properly," she said. "We divided the day up, with a bit of quill cutting every day. The days just disappeared!"

At the end of the third week, two of the four were selected to continue with the project. "It did become quite tense," she said. "There was that awful moment when Donald said, 'Two of you are ready.' And he named them. I was surprised to be one of them."

When she began to write actual Bible pages, she found it daunting. "I felt so unsure. I have never shaken so much in my whole life. But the earthquake subsided into simple fear after the first line or so."

Soon she settled into a rhythm. She remarked, "I disappear into another world. It's an otherworldly experience." She usually writes for about three-and-a-half hours at a stretch, preferably in the mornings.

Dozens of practice vellum
pages document the growing
confidence of the scribes as
they master the Bible script.

"I shut myself off from the rest of the world. If it's a Bible morning, I look forward to it."

The other newcomer was Angela Swan who had studied at Roehampton and who had, in fact, worked as Donald's studio assistant from 1988 to 1991. This project was very different from her previous experience at The Hendre. Back then, "I was filling in lots of certificates." Good, skilled calligraphic grunt work. The Bible is a much more intense and involved project.

Mastering the quill had challenged her. "This is the first time I've come to grips with cutting the quills. I have good days and bad days. But at least now I know which is a bad quill day and which is just a bad day."

Some of the recent batch of quills have gone soft very quickly; all the scribes have remarked on the change. The earlier quills were harder and easier to use. "My fourth quill was a little beauty," she crooned. "I wrote twenty-four pages with it. I've kept it hanging in my workshop with a little label: "Best Quill—24 pages." It kept its edge; it never split; it never misbehaved."

Like the other scribes, Angela struggles to maintain a consistent script while working at home.

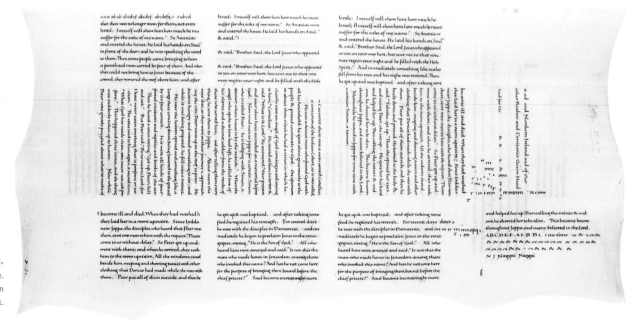

No scrap of the precious vellum is allowed to go to waste.
This practice sheet has been
used front and back.

"You can lose the goalposts," she said. "I have a little square example of script of about twelve lines. It has the right weight and was okayed by Donald. But even when I'm using this sample, I can stand up and look at what I've written, and say 'Oh no! It's smaller and lighter.' It may only be off by a hair's breadth, but over a whole page it makes a great difference."

The camaraderie of the team has helped a great deal. "We have such a lot of laughs. We understand what one another have been going through. We share the joy of doing it as well. There's a lot of mutual respect and understanding. Because it isn't easy."

And then, as Sally likes to say, there is "The Man," Donald himself. His main preoccupation is the illumination; compared to the others, he has written relatively few whole pages.

Sue remarked, "It's a consensus. It is not purely Donald's script. All he gave us was the starting point of an idea—all four of us have developed and changed." At the same time, the script is not decided by committee. She continued, "He's still in charge. He's got the responsibility." She pauses for effect: "He's the man who said 'yes.'"

Brian was of a similar mind. "Donald's style has shifted as well. We've all fed off one another during this project. For instance, my **g**s. Donald saw them and said, 'I like that. I'll do that.' It's an ensemble. It has to be. No one could work for long under other conditions." Still, "Donald is the master. Happy for us to make suggestions. But he is the linchpin."

The Man who said "yes" had a lot to say about the act of writing: "It's very physical. It's not about "what alphabet?" but instead it's about the way of sitting, the alignment of the desk, breathing, position. This doesn't come up unless you say you're going to write for many years in a team."

Donald looked at a page of writing. "I see wayward sheep: a healthy development? Or do they betray a lack of understanding?" Their first pages, he told them, were "Wonderfully good enough: you will get better."

Touchstone

A MEDIEVAL MONASTIC SCRIPTORIUM was made up of people who lived, ate, prayed and worked together. Their writing naturally held together because they rubbed shoulders day by day. After the master class, Donald's scribes scattered. Sally and Donald stayed at The Hendre, but Sue took her pages back to Sussex and Brian took his back to Leicester. In order to keep the team together, the scribes must meet at The Hendre at regular intervals. Given the organic approach of script-building Donald had opted for, regular meetings are the only way to keep wayward sheep from striking out on their own.

Sue told me, "Donald doesn't define things at all. His is the so-called 'intuitive approach'—definition is not easy for him. When you don't pin it down, it changes easily. And anyway, we all need someone to look and say, 'Come on, what can you see?' If you don't have that you can't progress, develop. Each time Donald picks out aspects of form: What am I doing? Why? The point is not to be slipshod in any way. Tiny things: how the serif goes at the bottom of **f**."

How often did they meet?

"It varies," Sue said. "We last met back in October: That's about three months ago. Normally, it's about every six to eight weeks. And now it's stretched out. We're scheduled to go back in three months' time."

Chinese ink sticks are ground in an ink stone with distilled water. The scribe has complete control over the density of the black and the viscosity of the ink. The quill is dipped into the well of the ink stone. A small lid covers the liquid ink to prevent evaporation when the scribe steps away from her or his desk.

While most of the text is written with black Chinese stick ink, a few elements are written using vermillion. This paint is mixed with egg yolk and water and is of a thicker consistency than the stick ink. A brush is used to load it onto the quill.

Susan Leiper, who joined the project as a scribe in 2002, writes at a desk in the Schoolroom.

Angela Swan also joined the project as a scribe in 2002.

Brian mentioned the pitfalls of working so far apart. "With Sue and I working away from the Scriptorium, it's hard. That's why it sometimes goes in different directions. Gradual changes creep in. As soon as we unrolled our pages at the Scriptorium, I was horrified with mine. It struck me immediately—a big change. I've lived with mine for weeks. You get used to your own writing. Yesterday, we were laboring away to produce a small sample, just half a dozen lines to take back with us." A touchstone.

Sue said much the same thing. "You think you've got it, but if you're slightly off, each page degrades. From page to page there is a slow shift. We're searching for some kind of standard: there isn't one."

Brian continued, "You do one page and you like it. Then you do another and you compare it to the first. It may have gotten just a bit lighter in weight. Then you do a third page and compare it to the second. It's slightly lighter but not enough to jump out at you. If you do that for enough pages, and you come back to your first page, then you're shocked to see how far you've come from your original page."

"There are so many variables, quill, light, ink," said Sue. "This time we looked at weight—the pattern on the page. Not form. We've looked at forms. When the weight goes, then the linear quality goes.

"Donald photocopied pages from three months ago and from a year ago, and blew them up," Sue continued. "The change was remarkable."

"How so?"

"My writing is consistent in size and shape and form."

"So what had changed?"

"It's about flow. Sally 'knits' the script. It's about the way the **t** and **r** join in, about ligatures and overlapping. It's to do with the way one letter leads into another, especially along the top of the line. There are elements of cursive in it: then you get a good strong line."

When they looked at Brian's writing, they saw his too had changed. Why?

"Is it the slope?" Sue asked. "The pen angle?"

They debated the possibilities. It didn't seem to be any obvious thing. Sue said, "We thought perhaps it was the angle at which he had cut the right oblique edge of his nib: a slight change in angle produces a change in the movement of the quill, which changes the dynamic of the writing." Exquisite nuance of tone: this is the level at which the team is working.

Sally said the conversation had revolved around the organic "feel" of the script. Donald drew a contrast between a "medieval" quality of a line of writing and a "Renaissance" sensibility. The medieval line, it seemed to him, had that strong "knittedness, and richness." The Renaissance tendency was, he said, "more like a copy book or a printed page: it was typographical." He wanted the calligraphers to aim more for the rich, organic feel of the medieval line and move away from the rigidities of the Renaissance.

Sally said, "Brian's writing is closer to the medieval look, but it's gotten smaller and lighter in weight." Perhaps this had to do with the change in the vellum. As the studio assistant Sarah Harris gets more expert at preparing vellum, the writing sharpens up. The thins are better, and so Brian ends up with more fine lines. It shifts the balance of the writing in a lighter direction.

The variables are endless. The conversation goes on. The writing shifts back and forth within the narrow range Donald has set. The personalities shine through, yet the whole book holds together. "Marvelously good enough?" Better than that.

Brian said in January 2002, "It got quite exciting—we laid our pages all out like a book—we could see

A computer sheet with annotations provides the fully prepared text for the scribe. In the upper left, the note "DJ text" indicates that Donald Jackson will be writing this page. The faded rubber stamp of a cherub in the upper right shows that this is a calligrapher's copy sheet. The three roughly written lines in the top left column indicate a passage to be written in free capital letters used for the beginning of each Gospel. In the bottom left, the code "A1 (F) V" refers to the Allocation Book. The same reference appears at the bottom of each vellum sheet. The scribe is responsible to check that he or she is writing the text on the correct sheet. The code lists the folio number (A1), and specifies that the script appears on the flesh side of the skin (F). The page is on the left-hand side of an opening—in scribal terms, the "verso" (V).

Notations on each finished sheet record who did the writing, how long it took and where the page will fit within the finished manuscript book. These small notes will be cut from the sheets at the end of the project when all seven volumes are trimmed and bound.

the thing as a whole. It came to life. The weight, texture, appearance of the script all held together. It was all from the same book. Personality is important. It does not stifle personality. It's a harmony. The individual struggles fade away."

When they step back from their work they can enjoy what they have made. I asked him about how the ink sat on the page. "The ink dries well. It's almost shiny. You can see that it stands just proud on the vellum." He paused for a moment. "It's a lovely thing," he said with a sigh.

The two-column format of The Saint John's Bible gives structure to the page. Strong enough to stand up against the bold illuminations the columns provide a stable grid which allows for many variations in writing styles and weights. Certain books begin with a dense texture of large capitals. The lush interplay of letter-forms makes full use of the flexibility of the quill pen. No metal pen could match the versatility of this supple tool.

THE GOSPEL ACCORDING TO JOHN

IN THE BEGINNING WAS THE WORD AND THE WORD WAS WITH GOD, AND THE WORD WAS GOD. HE WAS IN THE BEGINNING WITH GOD. ALL THINGS CAME INTO BEING THROUGH HIM, AND WITHOUT HIM NOT ONE THING CAME INTO BEING. WHAT HAS COME INTO BEING IN HIM WAS LIFE, AND THE LIFE WAS THE LIGHT OF ALL PEOPLE. THE LIGHT SHINES IN THE DARKNESS, AND THE DARKNESS DID NOT OVERCOME IT. THERE WAS A MAN SENT FROM GOD, WHOSE NAME WAS JOHN. HE CAME AS A WITNESS TO TESTIFY TO THE LIGHT, SO THAT ALL MIGHT BELIEVE THROUGH HIM. HE HIMSELF WAS NOT THE LIGHT, BUT HE CAME TO TESTIFY TO THE LIGHT. THE TRUE LIGHT, WHICH ENLIGHTENS EVERYONE, WAS COMING INTO THE WORLD. HE WAS IN THE WORLD, AND THE WORLD CAME INTO BEING THROUGH HIM; YET THE WORLD DID NOT

KNOW HIM. HE CAME TO WHAT WAS HIS OWN, & HIS OWN PEOPLE DID NOT ACCEPT HIM. BUT TO ALL WHO RECEIVED HIM, WHO BELIEVED IN HIS NAME, HE GAVE POWER TO BECOME CHILDREN OF GOD, WHO WERE BORN, NOT OF BLOOD OR OF THE WILL OF THE FLESH OR OF THE WILL OF MAN, BUT OF GOD. AND THE WORD BECAME FLESH & LIVED AMONG US, AND WE HAVE SEEN HIS GLORY, THE GLORY AS OF A FATHER'S ONLY SON, FULL OF GRACE AND TRUTH.

15 (John testified to him and cried out, "This was he of whom I said, 'He who comes after me ranks ahead of me because he was before me.'") 16 From his fullness we have all received grace upon grace. 17 The law indeed was given through Moses; grace and truth came through Jesus Christ. 18 No one has ever seen God. It is God the only Son, who is close to the Father's heart, who has made him known.

19 This is the testimony given by John when the Jews sent priests and Levites from Jerusalem to ask him, "Who are you?" 20 He confessed & did not deny it, but confessed, "I am not the Messiah." 21 And they asked him, "What then? Are you Elijah?" He said, "I am not." "Are you the prophet?" He answered, "No." 22 Then they said to him, "Who are you? Let us have an answer for those who sent us. What do you say about yourself?" 23 He said,

"I am the voice of one crying out in the wilderness, 'Make straight the way of the Lord,'"

24 as the prophet Isaiah said. Now they had been sent from the Pharisees. 25 They asked him, "Why then are you baptizing if you are neither the Messiah, nor Elijah, nor the prophet?" 26 John answered them, "I baptize with water. Among you stands one whom you do not know, 27 the one who is coming after me; I am not worthy to untie the thong of his sandal." 28 This took place in Bethany across the Jordan where

29 John was baptizing The next day he saw Jesus coming toward him & declared, "Here is the Lamb of God who takes away the sin of the world! 30 This

a or through him. And with out him not one thing came into being. What has come into being b or He was the true light that enlightens everyone coming into the world c or to his own home d or the Father's only Son e other ancient authorities read: It is an only Son, God, or, It is the only Son f Gk bosom g or the Christ h or the Christ

CHAPTER 5

THE ARCHITECTURE
OF THE PAGE

THERE IS A WELL-WORN paperback book which sits near Donald's writing desk. It is about the Winchester Bible, one of the great medieval manuscript Bibles. It is full of notes and measurements written in the margins. On the inside back cover in Donald's handwriting these words have been quickly jotted down:

ignition · spark · divinity · divine harmonic · pure quality · all this happens to [an] intellectual but that is quality of an idea · grasps or strives to produce an idea · the artist creates a thing

The writing is rapid, the lines jumbled, word jostling against word. What was Donald trying to work out? I went and asked him.

The Winchester Bible, a twelfth-century manuscript, came from a highly developed scribal culture. The elements of the page work together to produce the kind of flow—the spark—which Donald wanted to achieve in his manuscript Bible. Looking at the reproductions in his book, Donald was convinced there was a "visual harmonic" operating—but what was it? What were the components of that underlying harmony he could see on the page?

"I took out a ruler and I began to measure the proportions," he said. "I felt there was something there, some system underlying the whole book." Was there some practical method, now lost to us, that gave the book page its inherent order and its "divine harmonic"? Donald measured the page, the text area, the spaces between lines of writing, the gutter between the columns. He was looking for some repetitive element, some recurring relationship between the components of the page.

"Was there some proportion which would crop up in other permutations? I was looking for a common denominator measurement. I was switching between measuring in inches and centimeters. Oddly enough, in centimeters it began to have more sense—more coincidences than when I measured in inches. I seem to remember that some pattern of thirty-three millimeters recurring, something to do with the gutter."

He tried to tease out the system—but there was no system, no magic formula which he could apply. In the end, the artist is left with the problem of making an object. The scholar seeks an explanation, a mathematical relationship. For the artist, there is simply the fact of the thing.

"In the last line of those jotted notes, I was thinking of Edward Johnston, how he talked about making a thing," said Donald. Johnston, the founder of the twentieth-century calligraphy movement in Britain, always talked about the importance of practical work for the scribe. Theoretical debate and analysis have their place. Rough drafts and samples of writing also have their place. But in the end, "practicing," Johnston said, "teaches you to practice." In his foundational work on calligraphy, *Writing & Illuminating & Lettering,* first published in 1906, he advised his students: "Only an attempt to do practical work will raise practical problems, and therefore *useful practice is the making of real or definite things.*"*

The cryptic notes on the flyleaf of a book in the studio point to a realization. Donald would not find the answers he was looking for in a theoretical system; he would not try to impose an external notion of order or harmony on the book. Instead, the answers would grow out of the problem of working with matter in front of him: the ink, vellum, paint and gold. His ideas, unlike those of the scholar or theoretician, would emerge from an engagement with the physical reality of the thing. Following the lead of his hand, eye and instinct, and guided by his training and knowledge of the manuscript tradition, he would give shape to the Bible in the craftsman-artist's way: the artist creates a thing.

A vision

IN 1996 DONALD was at a conference at Saint John's. Entitled *Servi Textus,* it brought together scholars working on manuscripts, people who made books and patrons interested in the book arts. Donald says, "I remember the defining moment of the conference for me. There was a ceremony in the Abbey church—perhaps a funeral or a solemn profession; I don't actually remember. In the middle of the ceremony, a monk carried a large book down into the congregation. He read from it, and then I saw him hold it up, and say, 'This is the Word of God.'" In the midst of a conference about books and artists, here was a book which was unlike all others. In the conference hall they were talking about books. In the church, they were actually using a book. For just a moment during a long ceremony that book became the focal point of a living belief, a meeting point of the human and the divine. The book as an object had to be a thing of sufficient dignity and beauty to live up to its high purpose; the form of the book had to grow out of its role as the expression of belief. For an artist who makes books, here is the heart of the craft: how do you make an object which can embody this living tradition?

"I always had an idea that The Saint John's Bible would be used in ceremonies," Donald says. "It would be a ceremonial object, not simply a utilitarian thing. I have little knowledge of liturgy. The symbolism attracts me—a book like this is about the importance of the words and of the object which holds them. Making The Saint John's Bible is a restatement of the value we place in the words themselves. It's not just about reading the words. These are special words: and it's worthwhile to sweat and to labor to make the words go down on the page."

For Donald there has always been a dual purpose in making The Saint John's Bible. On the one hand the book will be read from in public liturgies. On the other hand it is designed for display as well, to communicate by its size and scale and by its nature as a hand-made object, that this is a unique text: it contains the Word of God.

To say that such a project is unusual is to understate the case. We are so used to printed editions of the Bible and so far removed from the manuscript tradition that there are few guideposts along the way for the craftsman. When I asked him about printed Bibles, Donald sniffed. The Bible translation Saint John's has chosen is the New Revised Standard Version (NRSV) and he has to work closely within the parameters set by the NRSV committee. These are designed solely with printed editions in mind. He said to me, "Some editions of the NRSV are actually anti-aesthetic—it's almost with pride that they are not aesthetic. It's as if they are saying, 'We cannot concern ourselves with the look of the thing.' Con-

A book from Saint John's collection illustrates the simple beauty of well-proportioned design. In this fifteenth-century printed Bible, a band of commentary surrounds two columns of scripture. The initial capitals were added by hand with tremendous flair.

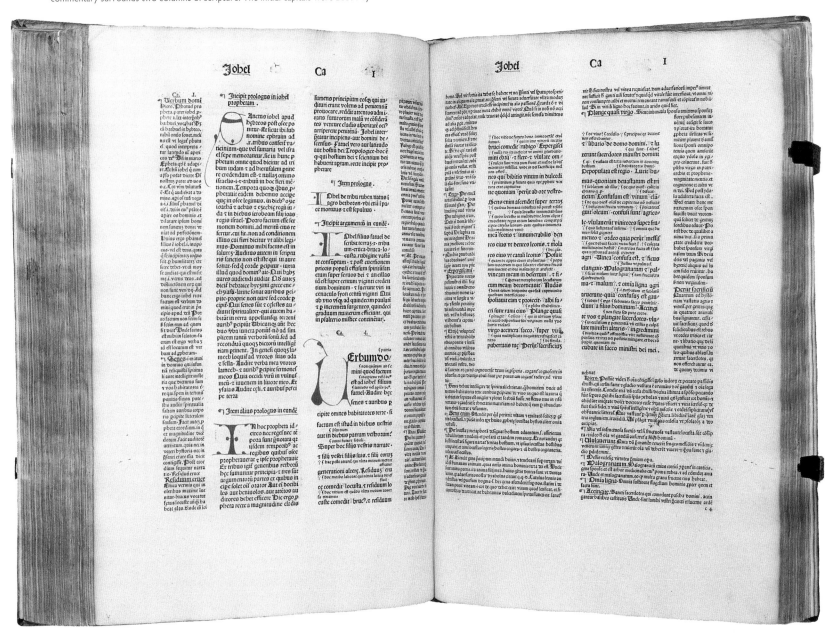

Strasbourg Bible.
Bible in Latin (Vulgate) with Glossa ordinaria. Strasbourg: Adolf Rusch for Anton Koberger of Nuremberg, 1481. Kacmarcik Collection of Arca Artium, Saint John's University.

temporary printed Bibles are a kind of spur to me, a validation of the whole enterprise of writing out the Bible by hand. Look at the self-congratulatory ugliness of the printed editions." Donald smiled slightly, enjoying the words as he said them. "Compare that with the early printed Bibles—Gutenberg and others. They were printing in gothic type faces and faced the first challenge of mass-producing what had been a written tradition. And they stand on the shoulders of the handmade Bibles which had come before." Modern printed versions rarely live up to Gutenberg. "This is the Word of God: therefore it should be goodly, which is to say, Godly."

A small rectangular title panel marks the beginning of each biblical book. Within the structure of this simple format there is room for improvisation. The smaller Hebrew titles appear above the title panels throughout the Old Testament. They were written by Izzy Pludwinski.

בראשית

שמות

במדבר

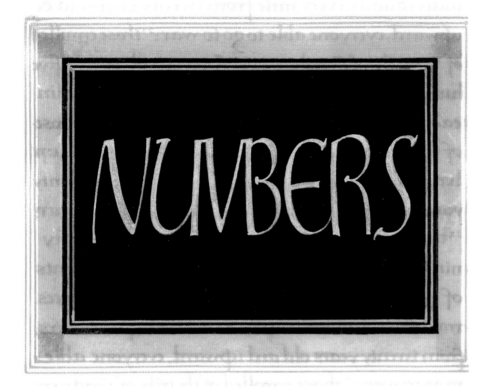

דברים

The initial capitals are written by Donald Jackson with a quill using color and occasionally gold. These are the final page elements to be added to each volume after all the other work has been finished. The lively variety of their shapes is a playful counterpoint to the strong columns of regular text.

* Otto Pacht, *Book Illumination in the Middle Ages*. (London: Harvey Miller Publishers, 1984) pp. 18 & 46.

** Ibid., p. 18.

The page takes form

WHAT SHAPE would give The Saint John's Bible that goodly form? Donald's quest would send him back to the hand-written tradition to rediscover the sources from which our printed Bibles ultimately derive. There is a variety of manuscripts to choose from. Hand-written Bibles have come down to us in a large range of sizes and shapes. Only a limited number of these manuscripts are valuable as guides to the making of The Saint John's Bible. The oldest manuscripts—the biblical books found amongst the Dead Sea Scrolls, for example—are in a different format. The Saint John's Bible is a codex, the book form most contemporary people would identify as a book. It has pages bound along a spine, sewn together and contained within stout covers. So as beautiful and ancient as the Dead Sea Scrolls may be, they have little to offer as models for this project. Other early manuscripts survive as small fragments written on papyrus. Some, like the Stonyhurst Gospel, which was found in the coffin of St. Cuthbert and dates to the seventh century, are small, portable books designed for private reading. Most biblical manuscripts, in fact, only contain portions of the Bible. Psalters and Gospel books are probably the most common types of these. Some of the most famous books from before the era of printing—such as the Book of Kells or the Lindisfarne Gospels—only contain a small part of the New Testament. Donald was searching out pandects—books which contain all the canonical books of scripture in a single collection. This limited his choice of models.

The British Library is probably the best place in the world to make such a study. Their collection includes some of the earliest pandect Bibles which have survived largely intact. The Codex Sinaiticus and the Codex Alexandrinus, of the fourth and fifth centuries respectively,* give us elegant examples of manuscripts from the early days of the Church after Constantine and are used by biblical scholars as important evidence in establishing the most accurate biblical text. These have a squarish, squat page format, without illuminations or illustrations. Sinaiticus is written in a four-column format, perhaps reflecting the narrow columns of the smaller books from which it may have been copied, or perhaps aping the format of a scroll. The large, square pages create a very wide, horizontal double-page spread with four columns on either side of the center and certainly evoke the horizontality of the scroll. The visual relationship to the scroll may have served to give the Codex Sinaiticus a kind of authority by evoking the older tradition.**

Donald's search took him deeper into the heart of the Middle Ages. He wanted to see books which represented the manuscript tradition in full flower. His idea that The Saint John's Bible should have a kind of monumentality and architectural scale guided him to some of the largest manuscripts in the collection.

Donald said, "On the one hand, books like the Book of Kells are really very dainty in size. Most calligraphic manuscripts are of a scale which is extraordinarily personal: they are books to be held in the hand, or in one's lap. The communion between the reader and the object is private. I think that's a key word. It is a private experience. By contrast, our Bible is public. That's where the monumentality comes in." At the same time the encounter between the reader and the text remains personal. The design problem is to find the right "scale of marks within the overall drama of its size—it's about an intimacy of scale within a larger scale."

The librarians pulled out one large manuscript after another. One of these was the Moutier-Grandval

Bible, a Carolingian book from about 835 AD, copied out at a monastery in Tours in northern France.[*] It is a large book, with pages measuring 19¾ x 14½ inches (50 x 37cm). There are two columns on each page, each composed of fifty lines of text (although in the book of Psalms, a fifty-two line column is used). Much of the manuscript is in a pristine state, the vellum seeming as fresh and clean as the day on which it was written.

Donald looked at the weight and size of the book. It was beautiful, and yet he was disquieted by what he saw: "The vellum is milk white and thin. But the book is just too big: it is a danger to itself. It would be so easy to crease the pages when turning them. I used to go look at it when it was at the British Museum in its case. The skins were so thin and fine but in the dryness of the air, they began to curl. Grandval convinced me that the weight of our vellum had to be heavier, so the book could bear its own weight. It also showed me that the book had to be split into several volumes." He envisaged a book of monumental scale, of an architectural scale, which would suit its setting within the monastic community at Saint John's. He had also imagined it as a work spanning several volumes. The Moutier-Grandval Bible confirmed this instinct. "I saw our book as a collection of seven volumes—it was both a practical and a visual idea. I imagined what it would look like on display, with one volume in the center, flanked by three on each side. The manuscript book, displayed open, is like a peacock opening its tail. But this will be a series of peacocks instead of just one." Later when Donald would present the idea of a many-volume Bible to the community at Saint John's, the committee in charge naturally came up with a seven-volume division of the text. This they did for theological and scriptural reasons and it fit neatly with Donald's practical concerns and his visual concept. So the project began to take form in a way which was beginning to make all the varying ideas converge. The "thing" was beginning to take concrete shape.

A medieval mentor: the Winchester Bible

DONALD NOW TURNED BACK to the manuscript Bible which seemed best to embody the kind of monumentality he was looking for—the Winchester Bible. "I chose it," he said, "because it was the high point of twelfth-century Bibles."[**] Written in a monastic scriptorium and made for a monastic community, it was an apt choice as a model. It remains today at Winchester Cathedral, in the library attached to the south transept. It seems never to have left the place where it was made, with two brief exceptions—once during the English Civil War and then during World War II when it was removed for safety from bombing raids. Otherwise it has stayed put, surviving the Reformation and the destruction of the monastic community which had once served the Cathedral.

The Winchester Bible is a large manuscript, even larger than Moutier-Grandval, with a page size of 23 x 15¾ inches (58 x 39.5cm). It was written by a single scribe with minor alterations and corrections by a different hand. The writing alone probably took about four years. It is lavishly illustrated in color and in gold. For calligraphers and for art historians it is particularly interesting since its illustrations were left unfinished. Leafing through, one can find examples of every stage of the process of illumination. On some pages only the faint pen-made underdrawing was completed; on others one can see the gesso laid, ready to receive its gold; on others still, fully finished illuminations dazzle with their skill and refinement. Most of the Bible is intact although some initials and pages have been cut out by thieves. One particularly fine page, known as the "Morgan Leaf," was detached long ago from the manuscript.

*British Library Additional Ms 10546; reproduced in Stan Knight, *Historical Scripts*, 2nd ed. (New Castle, Delaware: Oak Knoll Press, 1998) p. 6.

** I am indebted to Claire Donovan's excellent short book, *The Winchester Bible*, for the following description of the Winchester Bible and its making (London and Winchester: The British library and Winchester Cathedral Enterprises, Ltd., 1993).

A selection of
the initial capitals
written by Donald Jackson.

Again he en
was there
watched
cure him on the sab
him.³ And he said to
hand, "Come forwa

Now a certo
any, the v
Martha
ed the Lord with perf
her hair; her brother
sent a message to Je

But on the first
they came to th
they had prep
rolled away from the to
they did not find the b
plexed about this, sud
clothes stood beside th

mained in the valley

So now, Israel,
ordinances tha
so that you ma
land that the LORD, th
giving you.² You must

publicly to Israel.

2

In those days a decree
Augustus that all the wo
² This was the first regi
while Quirinius was govern
to their own towns to be reg

tell you,
taste de
in his ki

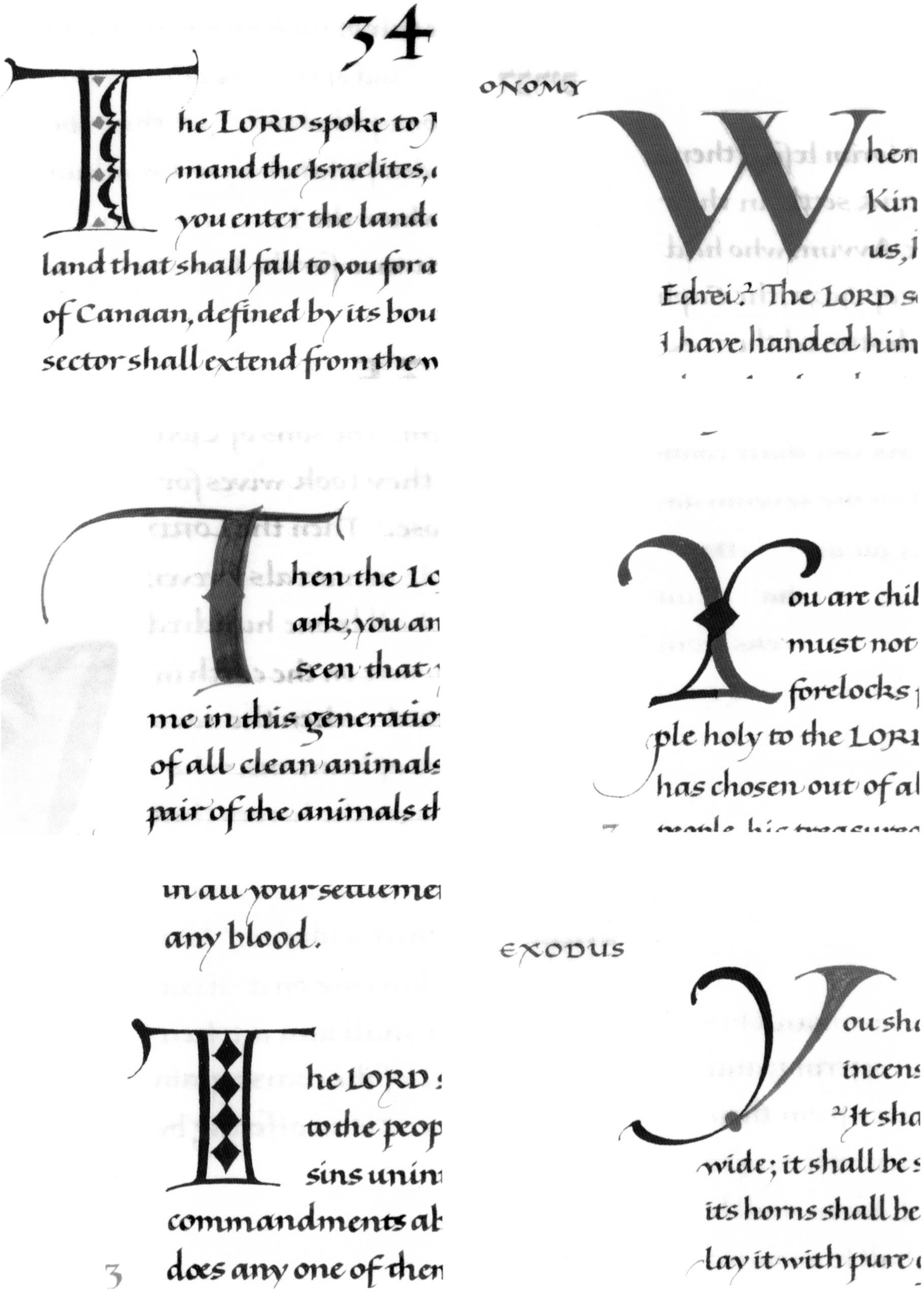

34

The LORD spoke to ¹
mand the Israelites, ᵃ
you enter the land ᵃ
land that shall fall to you for a
of Canaan, defined by its bou
sector shall extend from the w

onomy **W**hen
Kin
us, ᵃ
Edrei.² The LORD s
I have handed him

Then the Lᵒ
ark, you an
seen that ᵃ
me in this generatiᵒ
of all clean animals
pair of the animals t⁴

in all your settlemeᵗ
any blood.

You are chil
must not
forelocks ¹
ple holy to the LORᵈ
has chosen out of aˡ

exodus **Y**ou shᵃ
incens
²It shᵃ
wide; it shall be s
its horns shall be
lay it with pure ᵍ

The LORD ᵈ
to the peop
sins unin
commandments aᵇ
3   does any one of them

Book headings appear at the top of each spread. In the Old Testament they are written in Hebrew and English. In the New Testament only the English headings are used.

Poetry is written in a slightly smaller variant of the main Bible script. This allows a slightly longer word count per line and avoids broken lines.

Marginalia decorate the edges of many pages. These butterflies, native to Minnesota, were executed in acrylic by Chris Tomlin.

GENESIS

and they sewed fig leaves together and made loincloths for themselves. ¶ They heard the sound of the LORD God walking in the garden at the time of the evening breeze; and the man and his wife hid themselves from the presence of the LORD God among the trees of the garden. ⁹ But the LORD God called to the man, and said to him, "Where are you?" ¹⁰ He said, "I heard the sound of you in the garden, and I was afraid, because I was naked; and I hid myself." ¹¹ He said, "Who told you that you were naked? Have you eaten from the tree of which I commanded you not to eat?" ¹² The man said, "The woman whom you gave to be with me, she gave me fruit from the tree, and I ate." ¹³ Then the LORD God said to the woman, "What is this that you have done?" The woman said, "The serpent tricked me, and I ate." ¹⁴ The LORD God said to the serpent,

"Because you have done this,
    cursed are you among all animals
    and among all wild creatures;
upon your belly you shall go,
    and dust you shall eat
    all the days of your life.
¹⁵ I will put enmity between you and the woman,
    and between your offspring and hers;
he will strike your head,
    and you will strike his heel."

¹⁶ To the woman he said,
"I will greatly increase your pangs in childbearing;
    in pain you shall bring forth children,
yet your desire shall be for your husband,
    and he shall rule over you."

¹⁷ And to the man he said,
"Because you have listened to the voice of your wife,
    and have eaten of the tree
    about which I commanded you,
    'You shall not eat of it,'
cursed is the ground because of you;
    in toil you shall eat of it all the days of your life;
¹⁸ thorns and thistles it shall bring forth for you;
    and you shall eat the plants of the field.
¹⁹ By the sweat of your face
    you shall eat bread
until you return to the ground,
    for out of it you were taken;
you are dust,
    and to dust you shall return."

¹ Or to Adam
ᵐ In Heb Eve resembles the word for living
ⁿ Or for Adam
ᵒ The verb in Heb resembles the word for Cain
ᵖ Sam Gk Syr Compare Vg: MT lacks Let us go out to the field
ᵍ Gk Syr Vg: Heb Therefore
ʳ That is Wandering

²⁰ The man named his wife Eve, because she was the mother of all living. ²¹ And the LORD God made garments of skins for the man and for his wife, and clothed them. ²² Then the LORD God said, "See, the man has become like one of us, knowing good and evil; and now, he might reach out his hand & take also from the tree of life, and eat, and live for-

ever" ²³ therefore the LORD God sent him forth from the garden of Eden, to till the ground from which he was taken. ²⁴ He drove out the man; and at the east of the garden of Eden he placed the cherubim, and a sword flaming and turning to guard the way to the tree of life.

4

Now the man knew his wife Eve, and she conceived and bore Cain, saying, "I have produced a man with the help of the LORD." ² Next she bore his brother Abel. Now Abel was a keeper of sheep, and Cain a tiller of the ground. ³ In the course of time Cain brought to the LORD an offering of the fruit of the ground, ⁴ and Abel for his part brought of the firstlings of his flock, their fat portions. And the LORD had regard for Abel & his offering, ⁵ but for Cain and his offering he had no regard. So Cain was very angry, and his countenance fell. ⁶ The LORD said to Cain, "Why are you angry, and why has your countenance fallen? ⁷ If you do well, will you not be accepted? And if you do not do well, sin is lurking at the door; its desire is for you, but you must master it." ¶ Cain said to his brother Abel, "Let us go out to the field." And when they were in the field, Cain rose up against his brother Abel, and killed him. ⁹ Then the LORD said to Cain, "Where is your brother Abel?" He said, "I do not know; am I my brother's keeper?" ¹⁰ And the LORD said, "What have you done? Listen; your brother's blood is crying out to me from the ground! ¹¹ And now you are cursed from the ground, which has opened its mouth to receive your brother's blood from your hand. ¹² When you till the ground, it will no longer yield to you its strength; you will be a fugitive and a wanderer on the earth." ¹³ Cain said to the LORD, "My punishment is greater than I can bear! ¹⁴ Today you have driven me away from the soil, and I shall be hidden from your face; I shall be a fugitive & a wanderer on the earth, and anyone who meets me may kill me." ¹⁵ Then the LORD said to him, "Not so! Whoever kills Cain will suffer a sevenfold vengeance." And the LORD put a mark on Cain, so that no one who came upon him would kill him. ¹⁶ Then Cain went away from the presence of the LORD, and settled in the land of Nod, east of Eden. ¶ Cain knew his wife, and she conceived and bore Enoch; and he built a city, and named it Enoch after his son Enoch. ¹⁸ To Enoch was born Irad; and Irad was the father of Mehujael, and Mehujael the father of Methushael, and Methushael the father of Lamech. ¹⁹ Lamech took two wives; the name of the one was Adah, and the name of the other Zil-

Each double-page spread is written by a single scribe to ensure an even texture. Calligraphers define the size of a text by its "x-height": the height of a small letter x. The Bible script has a two-millimeter x-height.

ברא שית

lah.²⁰ Adah bore Jabal; he was the ancestor of those
who live in tents & have livestock.²¹ His brother's
name was Jubal; he was the ancestor of all those
who play the lyre and pipe.²² Zillah bore Tubal-
cain, who made all kinds of bronze and iron tools.
23 The sister of Tubal-cain was Naamah. ¶ Lamech
said to his wives:
"Adah and Zillah, hear my voice;
you wives of Lamech, listen to what I say:
I have killed a man for wounding me,
a young man for striking me.
²⁴ If Cain is avenged sevenfold,
truly Lamech seventy-sevenfold."
25 ¶ Adam knew his wife again, and she bore a son &
named him Seth, for she said, "God has appointed
for me another child instead of Abel, because Cain
killed him."²⁶ To Seth also a son was born, and he
named him Enosh. At that time people began to
invoke the name of the LORD.

5

This is the list of the descendants of Adam.
When God created humankind, he made
them in the likeness of God.² Male and
female he created them, and he blessed them and
named them "Humankind" when they were created.
3 ¶ When Adam had lived one hundred thirty years,
he became the father of a son in his likeness, according to his image, and named him Seth.⁴ The days
of Adam after he became the father of Seth were
eight hundred years; and he had other sons and
daughters.⁵ Thus all the days that Adam lived were
6 nine hundred thirty years; and he died. ¶ When
Seth had lived one hundred five years, he became
the father of Enosh.⁷ Seth lived after the birth of
Enosh eight hundred seven years, and had other
sons & daughters.⁸ Thus all the days of Seth were
9 nine hundred twelve years; and he died. ¶ When
Enosh had lived ninety years, he became the father
of Kenan.¹⁰ Enosh lived after the birth of Kenan
eight hundred fifteen years, and had other sons
and daughters.¹¹ Thus all the days of Enosh were
12 nine hundred five years; and he died. ¶ When
Kenan had lived seventy years, he became the father of Mahalalel.¹³ Kenan lived after the birth of
Mahalalel eight hundred and forty years, and had
other sons and daughters.¹⁴ Thus all the days of
Kenan were nine hundred and ten years; and he
15 died. ¶ When Mahalalel had lived sixty five years,
he became the father of Jared.¹⁶ Mahalalel lived
after the birth of Jared eight hundred thirty years,
and had other sons and daughters.¹⁷ Thus all the
days of Mahalalel were eight hundred ninety five

18 years; and he died. ¶ When Jared had lived one
hundred sixty two years he became the father of
Enoch.¹⁹ Jared lived after the birth of Enoch eight
hundred years, and had other sons and daughters.
²⁰ Thus all the days of Jared were nine hundred
21 sixty two years; and he died. ¶ When Enoch had
lived sixty five years, he became the father of Me-
thuselah.²² Enoch walked with God after the birth
of Methuselah three hundred years, and had other
sons and daughters.²³ Thus all the days of Enoch
were three hundred sixty five years.²⁴ Enoch walked
with God; then he was no more, because God took
25 him. ¶ When Methuselah had lived one hundred
eighty seven years, he became the father of Lamech.
²⁶ Methuselah lived after the birth of Lamech seven
hundred eighty two years, and had other sons and
daughters.²⁷ Thus all the days of Methuselah were
28 nine hundred sixty nine years; and he died. ¶ When
Lamech had lived one hundred eighty two years,
he became the father of a son;²⁹ he named him
Noah, saying, "Out of the ground that the LORD has
cursed this one shall bring us relief from our work
and from the toil of our hands."³⁰ Lamech lived
after the birth of Noah five hundred ninety five
years, and had other sons and daughters.³¹ Thus
all the days of Lamech were seven hundred seventy
32 seven years; and he died. ¶ After Noah was five
hundred years old, Noah became the father of Shem,
Ham, and Japheth.

6

When people began to multiply on the
face of the ground, and daughters
were born to them,² the sons of God
saw that they were fair; and they took wives for
themselves of all that they chose.³ Then the LORD
said, "My spirit shall not abide in mortals forever;
for they are flesh; their days shall be one hundred
twenty years."⁴ The Nephilim were on the earth in
those days—and also afterward—when the sons
of God went in to the daughters of humans, who
bore children to them. These were the heroes that
were of old, warriors of renown. ¶ The LORD saw
5 that the wickedness of humankind was great in the
earth, and that every inclination of the thoughts
of their hearts was only evil continually.⁶ And the
LORD was sorry that he had made humankind on
the earth, and it grieved him to his heart.⁷ So the
LORD said, "I will blot out from the earth the human
beings I have created—people together with animals
& creeping things & birds of the air; for I am sorry
that I have made them."⁸ But Noah found favor in
9 the sight of the LORD. ¶ These are the descendants

ᵇ The verb in Heb resembles
the word for Seth.
ᶜ Heb adam
ᵈ Heb him
ᵉ Heb adam
ᶠ Meaning of Heb
uncertain

Small pen-made "bullets" written in color mark
paragraphs. The verse numbers for paragraphs
appear in the margins while the remaining verse
numbers appear within the body of text.

Initial capitals in color usually come at the
start of each chapter. These are the final
page elements added to each volume.
Donald Jackson writes them with a quill.

Chapter numbers are written as large
numerals separating major portions of
the text.

Notes for the New Revised Standard
Version appear in the lower margins of
each page. The small superscript letters
within the text refer to these notes.

Marginalia fill many of the borders and empty spaces within columns. Many of these small paintings depict insects and plants native to the Minnesota woods surrounding Saint John's or to the Welsh countryside near The Hendre. These ground the Bible in a particular place and time.

The butterflies are by Chris Tomlin.

It is in the collection of the Pierpont-Morgan Library in New York and represents one of the finest examples of Romanesque illumination. The survival of such a massive work with so few losses is nothing short of remarkable.

The Winchester Bible has been rebound twice. Originally it was a two-volume work. In the nineteenth century, the quires were broken into three volumes and then in 1948 it was bound into its present configuration of four volumes. In its original setting the Winchester Bible would probably have been kept in the chapter room of the monastery attached to the Cathedral where it would serve the community and be read from on a regular basis.

Donald's main reason for turning to the Winchester Bible was what he called its "architectural scale." The writing is dense and dark in a transitional hand, midway between a Carolingian minuscule and a Gothic. Each page is arranged in two columns of fifty-four lines each. The two-column format and the visual strength of the writing create a powerful grid which can act as an armature for a wide variety of illuminations. Because the columns are so strong, they can stand up to the force of full-page illuminations; they also allow illustrations of different shapes and sizes to react to the grid they establish.

The trick was how to translate the strength of the Winchester Bible into a format for the modern Saint John's Bible. In order to do that a whole series of elements had to be brought into the right balance. It is not at all a question of copying the medieval manuscript. Donald's task was to learn from his example and to express what he learned within the very different requirements and limitations of a contemporary book. Copying the format of the Winchester Bible was never an option. In the first place, a straight copy would be nothing more than an antiquarian exercise and not in line with his main aim: to make a book for our own time. His illuminations are much looser and more painterly than the tightly controlled Romanesque illuminations of Winchester.

Secondly, even if he were to copy the format literally, he would never achieve the same texture and balance. The simple act of shifting from the Latin text of the Vulgate, the text used at Winchester, to the English of the NRSV, would immediately alter the look of the book. Latin has fewer ascenders and descenders than does English and it leaves a cleaner channel of white space between each line. The texture of a line of English writing always breaks into this clean channel of white more aggressively. The Winchester copyist also had the luxury of breaking words and abbreviating them as he needed in order to achieve an even right-hand margin. In English word breaks have to be made according to more stringent rules and abbreviations within texts in prose are not possible. Even if he had wanted to, Donald could not have written an English Bible in the same manner as his medieval model and produce the same texture on the page.

The point in any case is not to be a copyist. As Edward Johnston observed, it is legitimate to copy a method but not a style. The modern calligraphy movement has always stressed learning from the workshop methods of the medieval scriptoria in order to understand how things were made by people who were writing with certain tools and materials. They stand as masters because they were imbued with the ethos of making things by hand. We look to them in order to make manuscripts according to methods they developed to such a high degree and we do so to make things by hand for our own generation and our own time. Donald said, "We have a long backward look. We can examine a medieval book, and say to ourselves, 'Here is a codex which functions sweetly and reasonably.' We can benefit from the hundreds of years of experience represented by these books. The Saint John's Bible is modern precisely

A sample box of insects was used in Chris Tomlin's research for his marginal illustrations.

A paste-up sketch for the end of Mark's Gospel shows the cumulative process of building up a page. The different page elements—writing, headings, illustration and abstract patterning—are each created by a different artist or scribe. Many hands combine to form a satisfying whole.

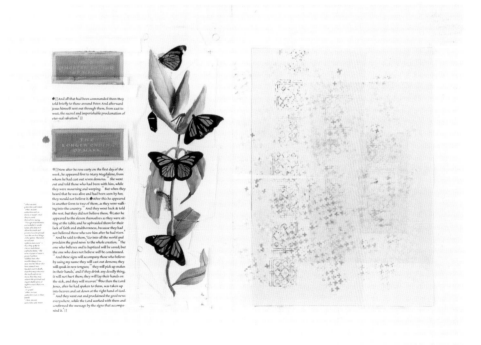

Chris Tomlin, a specialist in botanical and nature illustration, went to Minnesota to research the butterflies and plants which decorate the margins of the Bible.

because it understands the medieval tradition. It's like a man plastering a wall with a trowel or a man laying bricks. You can do modern things with bricks. It's not a tradition. It's a function." Looking at the Winchester Bible, Donald had found a kind of weight and texture which would suit his needs. He now had the difficult task of rendering this pattern using an English text.

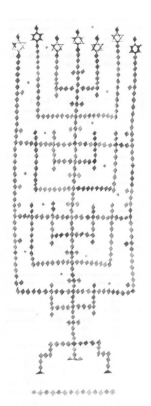

Sally Mae Joseph

Aidan Hart

* Jan Tshichold, *The Form of the Book*, trans. Hajo Hadeler. (Point Roberts, Washington: Hartley & Marks, 1991) pp. 36–64.

The perfect column

IN ORDER TO ACHIEVE the best texture of writing, a wide set of variables had to be brought into play. The various elements needed to be subtly shifted in size and weight until they began to hum together in that visual harmonic Donald was searching for. Over and over he returned to this idea of architecture, of the power of his columns of writing. When he talks about the layout of the page and he describes these ideal columns, he reaches out his right hand and inscribes a tall column in the air. All the decisions he took were designed to give these columns the strong character they needed to give structure to his book.

Many visual elements had to be considered as Donald began to create these strong text columns. The page size had to be finalized. The size and proportion of the columns themselves had to be determined. The number of lines per column and the size of the writing needed to be brought into the mix. Once these basic factors had been fixed, all the other graphic elements had to be considered to make sure the whole format worked in harmony.

If listing the elements like this conjures up a pilot doing his pre-flight checklist, then I have failed to describe it properly. Watching Donald at work, it becomes clear that it was more like a composer scoring an orchestral piece: the overarching vision is there but the composer slowly has to bring all the parts into the right relationship. If the horns play too loudly, the violins are drowned out. Even then the piece doesn't come to life until the orchestra plays. Donald knew that a hand-made book is not just a "design" executed by a machine. What he was doing was to lay a foundation on which others—the calligraphic team—would build. As they built, they would subtly influence the shape of the whole. Like a Gothic cathedral, the Bible would change as it passed through various phases; one volume would differ subtly from the one which preceded it. Everything would grow out of a workshop acting together. Knowing this, he still had some decisions to make.

The page size he chose was larger than either Moutier-Grandval or Winchester. He opted for a page 25 x 15⅞ inches. This varied somewhat as the design progressed; the final page size is just a half inch shorter, giving him a page of 24½ x 15⅞ inches (622 x 403mm). "The half inch," Donald explained, "is the measure of reality." The skins available were just that much too small.

The next question was how to position the columns of text on the page and how to break the columns into lines of writing. Sally, Donald's principal assistant, tried designing a format using Jan Tschichold's diagram for determining the size of the text area in relationship to the page.* She told me, "When I began talking that way—" she paused. "Well, it's just not the way Donald thinks." It was too cold and analytical and it didn't produce the tall columns he was aiming at. The squat columns indicated by the diagram would not have had the strength of height he needed; he couldn't break them up with illustrations and still have a strong underlying structure. Donald's approach, as always, relied more on intuition than on theory. Sally remarked, "Designing on the hoof, I think that's what they call it."

The design of the columns had to happen in relation to the developing script as well. For the calligrapher, a long line length is ideal, for this helps the writing hit and maintain its rhythm. Line breaks which come too often only break the flow of writing. At the same time, Donald knew that calligraphy, being a bit less legible to the modern eye than type, required relatively short lines, or the reader would tire quickly. One can't read more than about ten words to a line with ease. Furthermore, in order to get a consistent line length in English requires a certain minimum number of letters per line; the more words on a line, the easier it is to get an even right hand margin. In addition, the interlinear space comes into play. Lines to be with him, and to be sent out to proclaim the message, [15] and to have authority to cast out demons. [16] So he appointed the twelve: Simon [to whom he gave the name Peter]; [17] James son of Zebedee and John the brother of James [to whom he gave the name Boanerges, that is, Sons of Thunder]; [18] and Andrew, and Philip, and Bartholomew, and Matthew, and Thomas, and James son of Alphaeus, & Thaddaeus, and Simon the Cananaean, [19] and Judas Iscariot, who betrayed him. ■ Then he went home; [20] and the crowd came together again, so that they went out to restrain him, for people were saying, "He has gone out of his mind." [22] And the scribes who came down from Jerusalem said, "He has Beelzebul, and by the ruler of the demons he casts out demons." [23] And he called them to him, and spoke to them in parables," How can Satan cast out Satan? [24] If a kingdom is divided against itself, that kingdom cannot stand. [25] And if a house is divided against itself, that house will not be able to stand. [26] And if Satan has risen up against himself and is divided, he cannot stand, but his end has come. [27] But no one can enter a strong man's house & plunder his prop

could not even eat. [21] When his family heard it, they

Occasional skipped lines are an occupational hazard for the scribes. Sometimes mistakes must be erased by scraping with a knife. When a whole line has been accidentally left out, it is written in the bottom margin with this notation. This sample is reproduced at actual size.

further apart aid legibility as the eye is guided by the broader channel of white between the lines. Move the lines very far apart and the column becomes too light in its overall color, as the balance of black writing and white spaces is thrown out of balance. Move the lines too close together and the column loses its texture composed of distinct lines of writing and becomes a solid grey mass. All these factors had to be borne in mind.

While he played with these delicate balances of visual elements, Donald began to think more and more about the relationship between the texture of writing on the page and textiles. "This is another thread, so to speak, running through the Bible," he said. The texture of the column was meant to be like a subtly woven fabric. The viewer was meant to see the overall shape of the column as a large unit made up of the subtle variation of dense writing and clean interlinear spaces; he didn't want the components to disappear but instead to sit on the page together, rather like a herringbone weave. In the illuminations he has picked up the textile theme by using bits of lace, inked with a roller, to print patterns underneath and through his larger designs. "For me," he said, "textiles are deeply symbolic of interconnectivity. Intertwining threads join to make a wonderful whole." The textile theme also helps him achieve one of the aims of The Saint John's Bible: that of reflecting all the world's societies. "Textiles are, after all, common to almost all the world's cultures."

The computer came into its own in this phase of the design. Using a typeface which approximated the weight and spacing of his hand-written text, he and his computer assistant, Vin Godier, began to produce layouts. Varying the line spacing, they tried out different proportional relationships. They could also see how their decisions would affect the length of each volume. Each layout could be used as a template to "flow in" the text on the computer, giving Donald a very precise measure of how many pages the book would be with a given line spacing and column width.

Eventually the writing and columns began to come together, only taking their final form as the first team of calligraphers arrived to be trained. The computer was put to good use as each and every page could be laid out to the grid. At the last minute, Donald had decided that the right-hand margin should be justified, rather than left ragged. Only a hard right margin gave him the visual strength he needed for his columns. The computer helped him enormously by allowing all the decisions about line breaks to be made in advance.

Donald noted happily that the final design had exactly the same number of lines per column as the Winchester Bible—he had circled around, looking for the right solution and returned to his starting point. The script itself was very far removed from that of his medieval mentor, but the columns had achieved the right balance of weight and texture.

The elements of the page

HAVING WORKED LONG AND HARD to find a point of fixed reference within his design, Donald was suddenly free to begin playing with the balance of other elements on the page. The play was restricted, however, by the stringent rules laid down by the NRSV. All editions of the NRSV, including this manuscript version, must abide by established guidelines. This applies not simply to following the text faithfully, but also has important implications for how it sits on the page. Paragraphing and spacing between paragraphs are all integral parts of the translation. There is even a special dictionary which establishes how words are to be broken. There are rules about the arrangement of poetry passages, as well as guidelines about foot-

"YOU SHALL
LOVE THE
LORD YOUR
GOD WITH
ALL YOUR
HEART AND
WITH ALL
YOUR SOUL
AND WITH
ALL YOUR
STRENGTH
AND WITH
ALL YOUR
MIND: &YOUR
NEIGHBOR
AS YOURSELF"

A text from Luke 10
by Hazel Dolby.

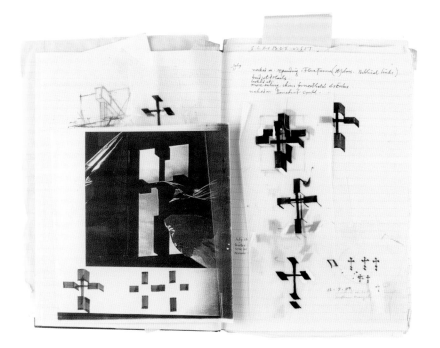

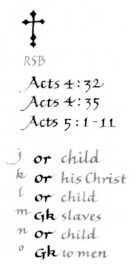

RSB

Acts 4:32
Acts 4:35
Acts 5:1-11

ʲ *or* child
ᵏ *or* his Christ
ˡ *or* child
ᵐ Gk slaves
ⁿ *or* child
ᵒ Gk to men

A small pen-made cross, based on the cross which stands in the bell banner in front of the Abbey church, marks passages which are quoted in the Rule of Saint Benedict. This small visual cue is a reminder of the way in which the Benedictine life has been shaped through the centuries by its encounter with the Bible. Donald Jackson's sketches show the process of abstracting the bell banner cross from a photograph.

notes. Working with the Committee on Illumination and Text (CIT) as well as with the NRSV guidelines, Donald had quite a few people looking over his shoulder at this stage of the design.

The most important thing was to guard the integrity of the columns. Donald tried breaking paragraphs much as one would in a printed text—but this left large gaps of various lengths in the right-hand margin every time a paragraph ended. He opted instead for a system of small colored bullets within the text block to indicate paragraph breaks. This left the columns solid and uninterrupted. Donald had to negotiate a special permission with the NRSV committee to use these bullets. Most verse numbers are placed within the text, written with a smaller pen, while the verse numbers corresponding to the beginnings of new paragraphs dance in the margins.

The primary divisions in the text break each volume into its constituent books. Each book begins with an illuminated title, fitting largely within the grid of the columns. These are lush and colorful and many have raised and burnished gold letters.

The secondary divisions of the text were made at the chapters. Two or three blank lines between each chapter separate the sections (depending on the length of the "widow," or short line at the end of the preceding paragraph). A large chapter number appears in this space and a three-line drop capital marks the beginning of the new chapter. Every now and again, chapters break in the middle of continuous text or chapters begin right next to illuminations; in these cases the chapter numbers appear in the outer margins.

All the footnotes to the text appear in the outermost margins of each page. The titles of the books appear in "running heads" in the upper left-hand corner of the page; in the Old Testament these are mirrored on the upper right corner by their Hebrew equivalents.

Poetry has to be treated very carefully. The NRSV requires a system of indentations which specifies where each line must begin. There are four different levels of indentation. In order to fit poetry into the format of the column, Donald chose to have it written slightly smaller, which allows many lines to appear in full without having to run into a second line.

A text from Luke 1 by Donald Jackson.

Rubber stamps and stencils were used to make the *Tree of Life* carpet page based on an Indian quilt. The stamps were hand cut. Lino ink was rolled out on a glass plate and used to print the pattern. Two mirror-image stamps were cut allowing for the gentle curve of the branches.

Carpet pages appear at the end of each Gospel, serving two functions: they provide a visual pause between each book and cover the show-through of the full-page illumination on the following page. Sally Mae Joseph created this page with its *Tree of Life* theme.

The effect of all these carefully orchestrated elements is to enliven the margins and the text with a host of minor themes all carefully balanced to play off the solidity of the great columns of writing.

There are, interestingly, no elaborately illuminated initial letters (in the traditional sense) in The Saint John's Bible. The CIT pointed out that these have relatively little function in an English book. In Latin many of the initial words of sentences are significant, thus illuminating and decorating the first word of a passage often serves as a device to highlight the content of the text. In English where the first word is so often "the" or "a" or "there," these markers lose their significance.

Carpet pages

THE CARPET PAGES are purely decorative pages appearing at the end of each Gospel. They have a dual function. They create a visual pause between one book and the next. They also veil the back of full-page illuminations. The vellum pages are gently translucent, and show-through can become an unsightly problem to modern eyes when a heavy illustration is placed on the back of a blank page.

There is ample precedent for these illuminations in the medieval tradition. The term "carpet page" is used by contemporary scholars to describe certain full-page illuminations in insular manuscripts like the Lindisfarne Gospels and the Book of Kells. It aptly describes the dense, interwoven texture of crosses and linked animal forms which is the distinguishing feature of these pages. Donald's concept for the carpet pages was inspired by textile patterns of the Middle East, India and Pakistan. His brief to Sally Mae Joseph was to create carpet pages that would incorporate the sense of loosely woven fabric.

Sally began by thinking through how she could achieve the "veiled" background. After many days experimenting, she was having difficulty finding a way. "A friend of mine suggested I experiment with a pattern of interlocking crosses. I made a grid and started coloring in the squares," she said.

These patterns suggested the use of a stencil. "Donald liked that idea, so I made a stencil and using a very dry brush, I covered the whole surface with white Plaka paint. It made a lacy background which was quite neutral."

Sally Mae Joseph then began to create the Tree of Life carpet page at the end of Luke's Gospel.

"Donald gave me a photograph of a bedspread his daughter had bought back from India; he wanted me to replicate the design using rubber stamps," she remembered. "I said to him, 'I'm not sure I can.'" Her voice dropped pitch. "'You have to,' he said. And so I did."

She cut two rubber stamps, one for the branches on the right side, the other for those on the left. The difficulty was getting the right amount of curve to enable the subtle shape of the branches to flow "naturally." Rolling out lino ink on a glass plate, she printed the design onto the background she had made. The trunk was added using a hand-cut paper stencil and a very dry brush.

"It was all a very new experience," she reflected. "It was a steep learning curve. Lino ink, rubber stamps, stencils—they were all new to me."

Special treatments

CERTAIN PASSAGES are selected to be handled as "special treatments." These are portions of the text which are written in a larger size and decorated with gold and color. They highlight biblical texts which are used regularly in worship, such as the Lord's Prayer, or key texts within the Judeo-Christian tradition, such as the command to love one's neighbor.

46 ❧ AND MARY SAID,

My soul magnifies the Lord,
and my spirit rejoices in God my Savior,
47 for he has looked with favor
on the lowliness of his servant.
Surely, from now on all generations
will call me blessed;
48 for the Mighty One has done
great things for me,
and holy is his name.
49 His mercy is for those who fear him
from generation to generation.
50 He has shown strength with his arm;
he has scattered the proud
in the thoughts of their hearts.
51 He has brought down the
powerful from their thrones,
and lifted up the lowly;
52 he has filled the hungry with good things,
and sent the rich away empty.
53 He has helped his servant Israel,
in remembrance of his mercy,
54 according to the promise he
made to our ancestors,
55 to Abraham & to his descendants forever.

56 ❧ And Mary remained with her about three months
and then returned to her home. ❧ Now the time
57 came for Elizabeth to give birth, and she bore a son.
58 Her neighbors and relatives heard that the Lord
had shown his great mercy to her, and they rejoiced
59 with her. ❧ On the eighth day they came to circumcise the child, and they were going to name him
Zechariah after his father. 60 But his mother said,
"No; he is to be called John." 61 They said to her, "None
of your relatives has this name." 62 Then they began
motioning to his father to find out what name he
wanted to give him. 63 He asked for a writing tablet
& wrote, "His name is John." And all of them were
amazed. 64 Immediately his mouth was opened &
his tongue freed, and he began to speak, praising
God. 65 Fear came over all their neighbors, and all
these things were talked about throughout the entire hill country of Judea. 66 All who heard them
pondered them & said, "What then will this child
become?" For, indeed, the hand of the Lord was
67 with him. ❧ Then his father Zechariah was filled
with the Holy Spirit and spoke this prophecy:

Blessed be the Lord God of Israel,
for he has looked favorably
on his people and redeemed them.
He has raised up a mighty savior for us
in the house of his servant David,
as he spoke through the mouth
of his holy prophets from of old,
that we would be saved from our
enemies and from the hand
of all who hate us.
Thus he has shown the mercy
promised to our ancestors,
& has remembered his holy covenant,
the oath that he swore

Three special treatments appear
on a single spread in the Gospel
according to Luke. These were
created by Sally Mae Joseph.
The texts are the *Magnificat*, the
Virgin Mary's canticle of joy, the
Benedictus, Zechariah's song, and
the *Gloria in Excelsis*, the song of
the angels in Bethlehem.

to our ancestor Abraham,
to grant us 74 that we, being rescued
from the hands of our enemies,
might serve him without fear, 75 in holiness & righteousness
before him all our days.
76 And you, child, will be called the
prophet of the Most High;
for you will go before the Lord
to prepare his ways,
77 to give knowledge of salvation
to his people
by the forgiveness of their sins.
78 By the tender mercy of our God,
the dawn from on high
will break upon us,
79 to give light to those who sit in
darkness & in the shadow of death,
to guide our feet
into the way of peace."

80 ❧ The child grew and became strong in spirit, and
he was in the wilderness until the day he appeared
publicly to Israel.

2

I n those days a decree went out from Emperor
Augustus that all the world should be registered.
2 This was the first registration and was taken
while Quirinius was governor of Syria. 3 All went
to their own towns to be registered. 4 Joseph also
went from the town of Nazareth in Galilee to Judea,
to the city of David called Bethlehem, because he

was descended from the house and family of David.
5 He went to be registered with Mary, to whom he
was engaged and who was expecting a child. 6 While
they were there, the time came for her to deliver
her child. 7 And she gave birth to her firstborn son
and wrapped him in bands of cloth, and laid him
in a manger, because there was no place for them
8 in the inn. ❧ In that region there were shepherds
living in the fields, keeping watch over their flock
by night. 9 Then an angel of the Lord stood before
them, and the glory of the Lord shone around them,
and they were terrified. 10 But the angel said to them,
"Do not be afraid; for see—I am bringing you good
news of great joy for all the people: 11 to you is born
this day in the city of David a Savior, who is the Mes
siah, the Lord. 12 This will be a sign for you: you will
find a child wrapped in bands of cloth and lying in
a manger." 13 And suddenly there was with the angel
a multitude of the heavenly host, praising God & saying,

14
GLORY TO GOD IN
THE HIGHEST HEAVEN
& ON EARTH PEACE
AMONG THOSE
WHOM HE FAVORS!"

15 ❧ When the angels had left them & gone into heav
en, the shepherds said to one another, "Let us go
now to Bethlehem and see this thing that has taken
place, which the Lord has made known to us." 16 So
they went with haste and found Mary and Joseph,
and the child lying in the manger. 17 When they saw
this, they made known what had been told them
about this child; 18 and all who heard it were amazed
at what the shepherds told them. 19 But Mary trea
sured all these words and pondered them in her
heart. 20 The shepherds returned, glorifying and
praising God for all they had heard and seen, as it
21 had been told them. ❧ After eight days had passed,
it was time to circumcise the child; and he was called
Jesus, the name given by the angel before he was
22 conceived in the womb. ❧ When the time came for
their purification according to the law of Moses,
they brought him up to Jerusalem to present him
to the Lord 23 [as it is written in the law of the Lord,
"Every firstborn male shall be designated as holy
to the Lord"], 24 and they offered a sacrifice accord
ing to what is stated in the law of the Lord, "a pair
25 of turtledoves or two young pigeons." ❧ Now there
was a man in Jerusalem whose name was Simeon;
this man was righteous and devout, looking for
ward to the consolation of Israel, and the Holy Spirit

f Other ancient authorities
read Elizabeth.
g Gk a horn of salvation
h Other ancient authorities
read has broken upon
i Or the Christ
j Gk army
k Other ancient authorities
read peace, goodwill
among people
l Gk Symeon

When Donald began the Bible, he intended all these special treatments to be continuous parts of the text and so in the first volume they appear within the body of the writing. He quickly discovered the limitations of this approach. If the special treatments were embedded within the text, their placement on the page was difficult to adjust—they fell randomly on the page. He was also obliged to follow the NRSV strictures for layout. In the first volume he wrestled with these limitations. In later volumes, he opted to treat them as separate illustrations, leaving the text uninterrupted. Special treatments became illuminations in their right, which gave him much greater flexibility in their positioning and allowed him to play with the shapes of the words.

A single opening from the Gospel of Luke illustrates the variety and sumptuousness of these special treatments. Luke's account of the birth of Christ contains a number of key texts which have worked their way into the liturgical life of the Church through the centuries. The Magnificat, Mary's song of joy, the Benedictus, Zechariah's canticle, and the Gloria in Excelsis, the song of the angels to the shepherds of Bethlehem, all stand out from the text in color and gold.

Sally was responsible for many of these special treatments. She explained, "Donald had done a rough of the text with a gothic script, which had helped him see how much space to reserve at the planning stage when working on layout with Vin Godier. He'd also done a version with a pointed, free italic. I had to use that as my starting point. He liked the free italic and said he wanted gold on a colored background. I had never used a colored background in my work. I spent days with paper and paint doing experiments."

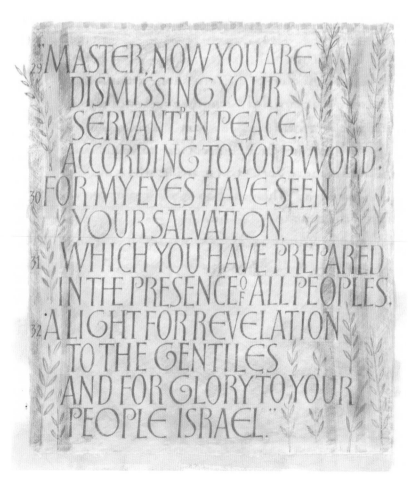

A special treatment by Hazel Dolby. Each artist brings a unique sensibility to the special treatments he or she creates. This text has been treated with great delicacy and refinement in Hazel's signature style.

Blue was selected as a background color for the *Magnificat*, a logical choice as blue has always been associated with the Virgin Mary. Sally remarked, "Brown just seemed right for Zechariah. For the *Gloria in Excelsis*, Donald suggested I look at the work of Paul Klee."

The backgrounds were laid with a wide decorator's brush. Rubbed down with sandpaper, they acquired a pleasingly distressed finish. The letters were added in gold—raised and burnished gold on a gesso ground for the *Magnificat* and *Benedictus* and shell gold, a finely ground gold in a gum medium, for the *Gloria in Excelsis*.

"This was the first gilding I did in the studio. I wasn't doing it the way Donald did. In the end I used his method; he was worried that the gesso would dry out too much and not take the gold properly if I did it my way. It was January and we had to keep the heat off so the humidity would stay high in the studio."

The special treatments stand somewhere between text and illumination. The strong architecture of the page is designed to create a powerful armature against which the illustrations and marginalia can dance and play freely. The layout has enough variability in itself to support page after page of continuous text without becoming dull and enough consistency and weight to stand up against the visual demands of the illuminations.

A sketch by Donald Jackson for the *Magnificat* in a vigorous gothic script provided a point of reference for Sally Mae Joseph as she worked on her special treatment of the text.

THE WORK OF THE C·I·T

I was at Saint John's to meet members of the Committee on Illumination and Text (CIT), and I was five minutes behind schedule. When I burst into the room which had been set up for interviews, breathless from running across the campus, Johanna Becker, OSB, was waiting for me.

"I'm sorry I'm late."

"That's all right. You have forty-five minutes. I have another appointment right after this one."

Out came my pad and she launched straight in. Sister Johanna talked with intensity and purpose, barely pausing to take a breath. I wrote furiously, trying to keep up with her stream of thought. Exactly forty-five minutes later, she rose, thanked me and was on her way.

In June 2002, I interviewed four members of the Committee on Illumination and Text, the CIT. These are busy people with impressive academic and career credentials. The chairman of the committee, Michael Patella, OSB, had just left for his sabbatical. Johanna Becker, OSB, Susan Wood, SCL, Alan Reed, OSB, and Nathanael Hauser, OSB, took time to talk with me about the work of the group.

Their different temperaments reflected some of the diversity of the committee. Sister Johanna was as soft-spoken as she was formidable. Sister Susan was quiet, thoughtful, perhaps even guarded. A wry smile sometimes lit her face as she talked. Brother Alan, shifting back and forth to ease his back pain, had an air of world-weariness about him, generous and cynical by turns. Father Nathanael was enthusiastic, leaning forward eagerly in his chair, his eyes dancing as he talked. As they spoke of the work of the committee, they talked with great humility, acknowledging their own limits, giving lots of credit and always wary to criticize others.

The CIT is the key committee on The Saint John's Bible project. Its main work has been to write detailed briefs for each illumination in the Bible. It reviews Donald's sketches and works with him as the illuminations develop. It formally accepts Donald's work. With such a pivotal role, the CIT is a flashpoint for tensions. Its members have a responsibility to the Saint John's community to guide the Bible through its making; they are also responsible to work creatively with Donald. They form a microcosm of community life, working slowly and sometimes painfully to find the best ways of moving the project forward.

Susan said, "This committee's had a rocky history, both internally and with Donald. There have been personality conflicts and ideological differences." There were disagreements about the role of artistic freedom and tensions over deadlines. Susan remarked, "Originally the group was called the Production Committee." This caused problems, suggesting that the committee was responsible for delivering a product on time. With a change of name, the committee's role was more clearly defined as a thoughtful steering group.

Nathanael, who has been on the CIT since its inception, told me, "I was at the first meeting before the committee began. Donald was there. I could see his eyes." Nathanael's own eyes grew wide as he re-imagined the scene. He could see Donald's dawning realization: "These people are going to be direct-ing me."

Susan said, "The CIT is a communal activity. This is a multifaceted project. Did anyone foresee the complexity?"

She continued, "Donald might have thought he could have done the whole thing by himself." Yet clearly he needed direction as he worked. He knew he would need help with the artistic side. "So he assembled an atelier of artisans. That was clear to him from the beginning: he needed to create an artistic commu-nity." Similarly he needed a monastic, scholarly community to inform and shape the work.

These intersecting communities, artistic and monastic, reflect the Benedictine setting of The Saint John's Bible. In the Middle Ages many of the great Bibles, like many great cathedrals, were the product of monastic houses. They reflected the shared wisdom of the communities which produced them. The Winchester Bible, which has influenced Donald deeply in his design for The Saint John's Bible, came out of a monastic setting. The whole book was imbued with a collaborative spirit with artists and scholar-monks working side by side. Everything, from the text itself to the illuminations which brought it to life, grew out of a deep contemplation on the Bible and its themes. Scholars labored to provide the best, most correct text and they defined themes and subjects for illumination. The illustrations often made links between passages of the Bible, drawing out the story of redemption in its fullness. The life and prayer of the community shaped the images that were being created. Artists and scribes brought form to these ideas, shaping them to the glory of God. The Saint John's Bible does this for our own time. The CIT was formed to give expression to the communal genesis of the project.

In September 2004, Donald Jackson traveled to Saint John's to deliver Psalms. Here he presents pages from the finished manuscript as Michael Patella, OSB, looks over his shoulder.

Donald Jackson comments on design decisions within the Psalms as Alan Reed, OSB, Nathanael Hauser, OSB, Michael Patella, OSB, and Johanna Becker, OSB, look on.

Scholars and artists

MOST OF the CIT members are Benedictines. Members of other orders and secular scholars round out the membership. They are highly educated people with impressive lists of multiple higher degrees. And yet, as Susan reminded me, "This isn't a group of highly charged Scripture scholars doing meticulous academic work. It's a diverse group of people: artists, art historians, medieval historians and theologians. Columba Stewart, OSB, represents Monastic Studies, Irene Nowell, OSB, the Old Testament, and Michael, the New Testament."

During the course of the project, committee members have come and gone. While many of them have been on the committee from the beginning, there has been a steady addition of new faces to replace those who have left. At the very start of the project, David Cotter, OSB, and Michael worked together to decide which passages would be illuminated. They produced a document called the "schema" which would guide Donald and the committee. At various times, Jerome Tupa, OSB, was on the committee, as was Rosanne Keller, and Ellen Joyce. Members were chosen to form a balanced group which reflected the broad range of skills needed for a project of this complexity. Their own stories mirror the complexity of monastic life today.

Rebecca Cherry, accompanied him to Saint John's to deliver the Psalms. Here she chats with Nathanael Hauser, OSB.

Nathanael, who recently celebrated his twenty-fifth year jubilee as a priest, is typical of the group. He teaches art history at the university and has worked at the Hill Monastic Manuscript Library (HMML) and at the prep school.

In the past twenty-five years, "the community has gotten smaller and older," he said. There is a great challenge balancing the spiritual, communal life with a heavy teaching load. With fewer people to do the work, monks have to be careful to defend and nurture their spiritual lives. In some ways this intentionality has deepened their spirituality.

"These days, I have more sense of people talking on a deeper level of spirituality than before. There is a sense of being here for a purpose," he said. "With smaller numbers, we have the same workload. There are some tensions keeping a monastic life. You have to fight for space. Sometimes you have to say, 'This is as far as I can go; I need my time.' We have to take lots of personal responsibility."

The mesh of organizations which makes up Saint John's could easily overwhelm the monastery which is at the heart of the community. "We want to be a monastery which is running a university, not the other way around." As education becomes more complicated, maintaining that equilibrium takes work. At the turn of the century, it was much more straightforward. "Bring a pig, we'll teach your kids—that was the tuition!" Those days are long gone.

Alan was blunt. "I got conscripted onto the committee. I came in the middle of the thing." An artist and designer, as well as curator of the monastery and university art collections, he was quick to point out he had no scriptural qualifications.

"I came to Saint John's as a young man to study architecture," he said. "My vocation to the monastic community was artistic as much as spiritual. I never had a theology course as a young monk. I had one class in Old Testament and one class in New Testament; I don't remember either one. It didn't teach me to love the Old Testament. Working on the committee helped me love the Old Testament."

He wanted to know whom I would interview after him.

"Who's next?" he asked.

"Susan Wood."

"Oooooh. These are such great people."

Susan described herself as coming to the committee both as an insider and an outsider. "I'm not a monastic. I am a Sister of Charity. My community is in Leavenworth, Kansas. Ours is not a monastic but an apostolic, Vincentian spirituality." I asked her to explain the difference.

"It is based on the work of Saint Vincent de Paul," she said. She smiled at the irony of where she has ended up. "Here I am in the rural Midwest. I've been at Saint John's for ten years. I work as the Associate Dean of the School of Theology. I am a systematic theologian, not a Scripture scholar or an artist. I came as an observer of the text."

Johanna also made her disclaimer. "I'm not a biblical scholar. I pray the psalter daily. I'm not a theologian. I am a lifelong artist. Later, in art history, I went in for Asia; I didn't like the Renaissance." She described her contribution to the committee. "I bring visualizations to the CIT. I don't bring a Bible with me. Columba would bring a well-worn Greek Bible, and would translate straight from the text. I want to think what I see: I don't want to have a text in front of me."

There are certain themes which she is eager to see prominently featured in the Bible project. "I'm here to put forward the feminine, artists and non-Christians." Her work with the World Parliament of Religions and the Monastic Interreligious Dialogue reflects her passion for Eastern religion.

"Non-professionally, but personally, I'm interested in how the universe came to be, in cosmology." She noted with a certain pride, "I was the one who sent Donald the NASA URL for the image from the Hubbell Space Telescope," which was included in one of the illuminations.

The committee with all its variety of expertise and opinion, has embarked on a scriptural conversation which has grown and matured over the years. That conversation has guided the making of The Saint John's Bible from its outset.

Working together

"OUR WORK is sort of like a prayer service with lots of laughter," Alan said. "We're close friends doing communal *lectio divina*."

Nathanael echoed Alan. "We describe it as communal lectio divina. We have a good time."

Lectio divina—holy reading—is an ancient monastic tradition of careful, prayerful reading. Nathanael explained, "Doing *lectio* is very strongly emphasized in the monastic house. Most people try to get in an hour at least every day."

"Is it a specific technique?" I asked him.

"No. It's not a technique thing. It's more about entering into a psychologically more receptive state: 'This is *lectio* time.'"

Lectio time is qualitatively different from ordinary time. It is not a time to study the Scriptures in an academic way. It speaks to a different part of the psyche. "I get into a meditative state," Nathanael said. "The key is to read slowly enough—to be comfortable stopping when a word or phrase catches my attention, and then allowing it to speak throughout my day. It's like a cow chewing the cud."

The practice of *lectio* requires a certain discipline, he said. "At times it takes mental gymnastics to get away from scholarly issues. It's like the way medievals read Scripture. You begin to see underneath the literal word."

Digital artistry reunites the members of the Committee on Illumination and Text for a promotional group portrait taken in 2001. Back row: Johanna Becker, OSB, Michael Patella, OSB, chair, Nathanael Hauser, OSB, Alan Reed, OSB. Front row: Irene Nowell, OSB, Ellen Joyce, Susan Wood, SCL, and Columba Stewart, OSB. The image of Ellen Joyce was electronically imported into the portrait.

Other members of the broader Saint John's community have served at various times on the Committee on Illumination and Text including Rosanne Keller and David Cotter, OSB.

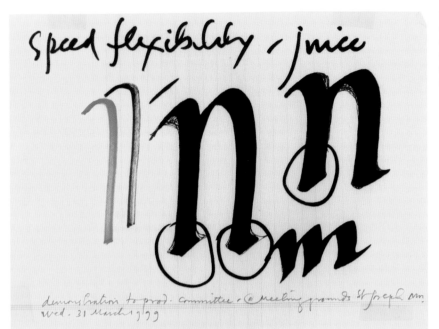

In an early meeting with the Committee on Illumination and Text, Donald Jackson described the vitality he sought for the Bible script. Using the tools he had at hand, he gave an impromptu demonstration.

With the emphasis on *lectio* within the monastic community, there has been a growing appreciation for non-linear, associative reading of Scripture. "The language is starting to come back. It's so different from when I started doing theology," Nathanael remarked.

Communal *lectio divina* clarifies the themes which will inform the making of the book "so Donald is not just drawing on his own resources. He is not an artist working in isolation." His work is drawn into this communal, prayerful exploration of the meanings of the text.

The twice monthly meetings of the committee usually last an hour and a half. In that time the group first looks at images Donald has sent and then turns to a particular illumination.

Before each meeting, Michael sends out a memo describing what the committee will be doing. "So theoretically," Nathanael told me, laughing, "everyone has read what we're going to work on."

Alan described his first meeting. "I was surrounded by people who knew every word of the Bible. I brought my Bible with me, opened it and the spine went crack. It was so humiliating!"

The group humored him—"Oh, you brought your good Bible, not the one you read!"

The committee is almost equally divided between what Nathanael describes as "artistic and theology types." They've worked hard to learn each others' language. He said, "A theologian will give an introductory talk, just to bring us into it. It's like first sitting down and starting to read: it focuses our attention. At the early meetings we had to work through it. People were talking theology—the artist types were nodding off. Now we flow back and forth."

The back-and-forth dialogue has opened up the Bible for many on the committee. Nathanael described the pleasure of listening to "a person with real expertise." It would be exciting if the Bible project spawned other groups who could work creatively with the Scriptures in the way the committee has learned to do.

"My personal vision of the Bible has been deepened by talking about it. It's made my own reading of Scripture more exciting," said Nathanael.

After one of the scholars has talked about the Scripture passage before them, there is an open discussion. Sometimes this begins with a hush. Nathanael described it as a kind of pause; he stared into space for a moment, then snapped his fingers. "Then someone will bring up a topic. People begin bringing up images. It's allowed to be free flowing."

Susan said, "The artists have taught us how to see, to think in images. It hasn't always come naturally. As a systematic theologian, I'm linear and verbal. Johanna's great gift is to sit and imagine. We toss out various possibilities, getting into the text, imagining our way in graphically. Johanna does that best. Alan likes abstract art. He images very differently from Johanna. Johanna does it more concretely. Alan, more abstractly."

"The theologians have good visual insights," Alan said. He gives Sister Irene credit for the way she brought her enthusiasm to their meetings. "I even went out and bought her book—and it doesn't even have pictures in it!"

As they discuss a passage, the group begins to select which images "work" and which ones don't. Nathanael said, "We talk around an image someone has in mind. Then if it becomes clear it's not what we like, it gets edited out." The best images and ideas make it into the briefs.

Susan said, "Most conversation is free association—How does this text relate to other texts?" They might look at particular images, and see what parallels emerge. For instance, a garden image might be in

The members of the Committee on Illumination and Text describe their work as "communal *lectio divina*." They discuss scholarly aspects of each text and then allow their imaginations free rein to explore new dimensions of meaning.

the text. What does that conjure up? People begin listing passages which occur to them—Creation, Eden, Gethsemane, the Song of Songs.

"We pick up motifs," she continued. "We look for references to Christ and we note passages in the liturgical life of the Church. For example, the Joel passage used on Ash Wednesday. We pull that out of our communal recollection of life. A passage from Sirach came up: 'Spread your fragrance like incense.' I asked, 'Isn't that used on the feast of Saint Benedict?' The others didn't recall."

She added, "The briefs are not academically researched. The footnotes in the Oxford study edition will influence us and The Collegeville Bible Commentary of the New American Bible is also available at the meetings." The aim, after all, is not to produce a detailed commentary, but to open a conversation which will inform Donald's working process. It is intentionally open-ended.

Susan said, "We sit until we have nothing left to say."

Johanna remarked, "After one and a half hours, you lose focus. It's so intense." She added, "We have an excellent secretary. She attends the meetings and she makes a tape recording that she can take away." All the spontaneous reactions are typed into briefs under headings. "She gets them concretized. We get the minutes electronically and have input."

The editing of the briefs is an important stage in the process. The committee wants to share their thoughts with Donald, not box him in. Nathanael said it was important to communicate to him that "these were our thoughts. On paper, it sounds like a directive of sorts. So we put it in the subjunctive somehow. Unless we're saying, 'It's theologically important that you do or don't do this,' the rest is suggestion. It stokes the engines, gets them going."

Johanna added, "What are the benefits of CIT? It's non-judgmental: a concrete validation of the importance of free thinking. We're not evaluating—it's a free discussion. We never arrive at an idea by ourselves; there is a creative interplay of concepts with no limits."

The group enjoys these intense discussions. Nathanael said, "It's the only committee where you leave feeling refreshed, excited. Johanna echoed him: "I'm on a lot of committees. I look forward to this one."

New directions

ON MEMORIAL DAY weekend 2002 the CIT made a breakthrough. Having worked together for several years, they had built a working relationship with each other and with Donald. Michael was about to leave for his sabbatical and so they took themselves away to a retreat center in Chaska, outside Minneapolis. In an intense three-day weekend, they did an entire year's worth of work. The briefs for Psalms, Prophets and Historical Books had to be created. Nathanael told me, "We went through a metamorphosis with Psalms."

Alan said, "At this three-day meeting, there was no minute stuff, no review of images. We just hunkered down with Scripture. 'Bible camp' we called it. It was wonderfully intense. Michael is the most disciplined person I know. Our sessions lasted from eight-thirty in the morning until noon, and two forty-five in the afternoon until six—sitting in a room, hours on end."

The Psalter is at the core of the monastic life. It is also a book of poetry. They decided to throw out earlier ideas and address the psalms from scratch.

Alan said, "The Psalms are easier for me to deal with. The Psalms you know." His face rumpled, and

The theological briefs created by the Committee on Illumination and Text guide Donald Jackson as he works out visual interpretations of the chosen Bible texts. Freely responding to the ideas in the brief, he begins to work up a sketch. Michael Patella, OSB, remarked, "The illuminations are not illustrations. They are spiritual meditations on a text. It is a very Catholic approach to the Scriptures. It says, 'look at this.' It is rich, decorative, colorful."

The sketch process develops as gold and color begin to define the details. Once a rough has reached a certain point, Donald Jackson sends it via the Internet to the Committee on Illumination and Text for comments.

A rough paste-up demonstrates the relationship of the illumination to the page of writing which it faces. All the essential elements have come into place, balanced around the central gold shaft of divine light. The scale of the drawing has become more refined and delicate, better suited to the scale of the whole.

Photocopies, acetate overlays and painted figures are taped into place as the design is slowly resolved. A vigorous bull based on a Stone Age painting from the cave in Lascaux, France, has taken a prominent place in the composition. Donald Jackson remarked, "The bull expresses the vitality and power of earthly life, as well as the humble circumstances of Christ's birth. It contrasts with the ethereal wonder of the flying angels and heavenly light descending into the world."

he added, "That's affected—you can plan your whole day while saying psalms and not miss a word!" But since working on the briefs, "I've started noticing the Psalms."

The committee as a whole was more familiar with the Psalter than with other biblical books. By now it was also more familiar with Donald and his working process. Nathanael described how this affected their work: "With psalms, we now know visually how Donald works. We are veering around to thinking, 'How can we help Donald play to his strengths?' This only came with working through various things. On the psalms, we got almost giddy with what Donald could do with this. That worry—will it work?—has gone away now. At first it was like the New Testament—should every page have something on it? Then we asked ourselves, 'How would Donald feel?'" They imagined him using different styles to express subtle theological ideas. "It's an exciting process—deeply theological—how do we put that on a page? It will all be calligraphically done as far as we can see—a real change from the way we first thought of it."

Nathanael felt that the group had changed. It was "spiritually deepened." He laughed and said, "I think I know what happened. Talking to scholars, the scholastic part of it came to life." He put his hands out in front of him, far apart. "This was the creative side," he said, looking to one hand, "and this was the scholarly." He brought his hands together. "Now, they are integrated much more: I've seen it in the others. For me, I feel that there isn't that kind of break between the scholarly and the creative. It's a kind of prayer experience when you're done."

He added, "I've run study groups: 'we must be serious now.' For us we just go right at it. We make jokes, get angry. It's a whole different experience."

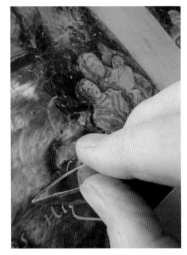

In a last-minute correction, Donald Jackson erases a passage of text from the *Nativity* illumination using a sharp knife. When the finished work was brought to Saint John's, it became clear that the text which had been written over the left side of the image referred not to Christ but to John the Baptist. Donald made the correction on the spot, first erasing the erroneous text and replacing it with free brushwork.

"The Psalms will be the most beautiful book," Alan predicted. "There will be small keys to highlight psalms used in the daily office, or passages quoted by Christ. Maybe it won't have any gold in it!" In an aside, he added, "Gold is like the computer—click a button. 'Oh wow, that's cool!' Gold is like that. When you don't know what else to do, add gold." Gold, to Alan, is "splashy"—not the kindest adjective in his lexicon.

Nathanael is delighted with the gold. "It's a pity that no reproduction will ever stand up to the original. Most people will see reproductions. But they won't have the visceral experience of gold on the page."

Susan said, "The Psalms brief is architectural rather than illustrational." The committee looked at the Psalter and its division into five books. "'Amens' and 'Alleluias' indicate the end of each book." They imagined Donald exploring these textual breaks as a way of building his design. The result is a brief which is much more calligraphic than illustrational. "We didn't want Bambi leaping through the Psalms like a deer. The Psalms are not in narrative form."

Nathanael added. "I can't wait to see what Donald does with the Psalms."

The briefs are just one part of the CIT's work. Reviewing and commenting on Donald's sketches take up a good deal of their time. With this task the artists on the committee naturally come to the fore. As Susan said, "The artists have the language."

Nathanael explained this stage of their working procedure. Sketches are photographed with a digital camera at the Scriptorium and relayed to Saint John's electronically. At first "we tried showing them on the wall—that worked pretty well. Now we print out color copies for everybody; it's easier. These are sent out before our meeting. We go through our own reactions, then process them and come to the meeting. Now pretty much everybody knows what the others will say. When there are disagreements, they are usually on minor points. There is no huge divergence of opinion."

Susan expressed the difficulty of working long distance. "It's a challenge," she said, "to work across an ocean, meeting with Donald several times a year face-to-face. Communication has gotten better, but Donald is ninety-nine percent visual in his orientation. We are communicating verbally." There is a lot of room for misunderstanding.

If the briefs are open-ended expressions of a process, so are the sketches. Nathanael said, "When Donald sends the images we have to do the same thing: remind ourselves, 'These are just sketches.' It took a while for both sides to become comfortable with that."

The scholars and the artists naturally approached the question differently. Nathanael told me, "On the committee, the theologians were looking at the images and parsing them like a text. The artists were asking themselves, 'What would I do if I were doing it?'"

Johanna said, "Some things I look at and think, 'I wish I'd thought of that.' Like the Bull of Lascaux which appears in the Nativity illumination." The cave at Lascaux in France contains some of the oldest representational paintings in Europe.

"It's hard as an artist not to have a specific image in mind," Alan said, reflecting on the feeling of sending out the briefs. "It's like a teaching assignment. Different stuff comes back and you think, 'These are pretty good.' It's hard not to see colors, patterns, images. For instance, the historical books are full of references to Jerusalem. I'm thinking, 'How do you express the huge sense of a people struggling to discover God in the midst of political and natural disasters?' I start to imagine patterns, contrasting colors."

When the images come back from Donald, there is the shock of another artist's reaction to the brief— "Oh, wow—ooph, I never thought of that."

Alan pulled no punches. "When Donald did one sketch and I didn't see my idea, I thought to myself, 'No, this will never do.'"

It takes a certain distance for an artist to stand back and let another artist work in freedom. Nathanael said, "I remind myself that I am trying to sense his vision, not my vision. In spirit, bringing Donald in."

The process has changed the briefs as well. Alan said, "It's moved from, 'Here's what we're thinking of' to, 'Here are the issues.'"

Speaking for the scholars on the committee, Susan said, "We all share—we share as individuals, not out of our expertise." This applies to the imagery as well as to the briefs.

Susan said, "The working relationship with Donald has been sensitive. There has been tension between the oversight that comes with patronage versus artistic freedom. Where is Donald free to do his own thing?"

There has been a question about the committee's role: what sort of oversight do they have? Do they have to formally approve each sketch? Susan said, "Donald is delighted when he presents us with something we haven't seen." Johanna told me that sometimes when they review a sketch, "Donald has already moved on." Did this pose a problem, I wondered? "No problem." But it does cause tension.

Even within the committee there is a variety of opinion about the degree of freedom Donald should enjoy as an artist. Some have argued for his complete artistic freedom, while others have wanted the committee to be more directive. Slowly, as they have worked with Donald, they have built a working relationship.

The Committee on Illumination and Text is not the only constituency which demands Donald Jackson's time. Here he presents his work at a media briefing on May 26, 2004, at the Centro Russia Ecumenica in Vatican City. Dietrich Reinhart, OSB, and Abbot John Klassen, OSB, sit on the left while Donald addresses the crowd.

Johanna said, "Donald is a very interpersonal, sensitive person. I wasn't able to attend the presentation when Donald brought the first pages back to Saint John's. He came up to me twice to say he was sorry I wasn't there. Then he arranged a special showing and went through the whole thing, page by page. My impression is that it's far exceeded our expectations."

She feels the relationship has matured. "It's taken a long time. We were finding out what we were about; at the start, we were very directive. There is a whole bunch of prima donnas on this committee, people used to being in charge."

Sometimes, however, the committee did have to express reservations about sketches. Johanna recounted, "It was painful for both sides when we rejected something Donald did." That led to questions: "What kinds of contribution does the CIT make? How should Donald take the CIT's input?"

Susan said, "We sometimes want to say 'Stop! It's great!' He adds detail. We think he's at his best when he's more abstract, free, suggestive. Sometimes he loses fluidity and freedom and movement."

A growing trust has helped both Donald and the committee. Susan continued, "As he sees the product, he relaxes. He gets better. He has the sensitivity of an artist and a lot of pride." She caught herself, and began to laugh. "How do I say this diplomatically? He needs his independence. The committee can't tell him what he should draw but it takes an outside eye to tell an artist when he achieves the most. It remains delicate, but it's gotten better."

Johanna knows the heart of the artist. "Donald is a great showman, a great demonstrator. We were doing verbal things. He was doing visual. We said to him once, "Leave all your tools behind when we meet next. He brought the briefs which he had highlighted and filled with marginal notes. We saw for the first time how he used the briefs. We saw it was all being used."

Others are less sure how helpful Donald finds the briefs. Susan told me, "The question to ask Donald is, how do you use the briefs? I think he throws up his hands. It's the very fact that Donald envisions the whole process schematically and pictorially." And yet, "He couldn't illuminate what he illuminates without interiorizing the concept: the *Raising of Lazarus* illumination is so gripping. He resonates with the text in a deep way. It does not come out in pious language."

Controversy and debate

CERTAIN ASPECTS of the project have occasioned deep conversations, even controversy, between Donald and the committee. Aidan Hart's work with its traditional iconographic visual language has sparked a strong debate.

Alan said, "Aidan's work really sticks out."

Nathanael also had concerns. "The Byzantine images. I'm an iconographer myself. I'm still ambivalent about them. I love the tradition. I love making icons. He's a very good iconographer as well. But it's not my vision of how the Bible is going to look."

Some of the concern stemmed from the traditional look of the imagery: did it fit a contemporary Bible? Other concerns had to do with the mixing of different styles and techniques within the volume.

Nathanael felt in the end "different styles are okay, but they have to be throughout the whole book, not willy nilly."

Susan was satisfied that the images had been negotiated successfully. "The whole worked. It will appeal to a variety of tastes. The borders which Sally Mae added around Aidan's illuminations are fluid; the work escapes the border. The borders around the iconography result in a mixed style, less rigid."

Another issue was the use of imagery from other faith traditions. The committee reflected a variety of opinions.

Johanna, who is particularly concerned with interfaith dialogue, argued for the inclusion of images from other traditions. She was also concerned that these not be misinterpreted. She said, "We were very sensitive to not be offensive to the Jewish tradition." The menorah at the opening of Matthew's Gospel went through many versions. "A member of the committee talked to a rabbi, discussing the mixture of images—the menorah, the tree of life, the genealogy of Christ. He gave the okay."

She mentioned other images she had contributed. "I suggested the stamped images from the Koran: lacy medallions in the margins." She was pleased with "some Zen symbols and the Navajo baskets in the Loaves and Fishes illumination. They give depth and relationship—the inter-time spanning reality of this phenomenon."

Nathanael expressed his concerns. "There have been objections to the marginalia, both artistic and theological. For example, we discussed the use of Islamic calligraphic imagery. How worldwide do we want to be? How Catholic? It brought up issues for us—what about Buddhist images? This is a Catholic Bible for a Catholic community. The images have to fit that." He was also sensitive to the use of Jewish images. "Some illuminations could be taken as critical of Judaism; a supercessionist interpretation is possible. The Scripture scholars were particularly attuned to this. People looking at certain images could object to them." He felt one of the committee's tasks was to make sure these images were used with sensitivity.

The fruits of their labor

THEY EACH HAD their favorite illuminations.

Alan said, "I like the special treatments better than the illustrations. They are more inherently part of the writing." He clasped his hands together, fingers intertwined. "It meshes more for me." He was also partial to the *Loaves and Fishes* illumination, running around the edges of the page. It could have been an illustration of "a cute little mountainside, people munching on fish sticks." Instead the illumination exploded into the margins, evoking and not illustrating the scene. "I really, really like this one."

Johanna agreed with him. "I am so pleased with the concept of the loaves and fishes—so much better than pictures of people carrying loads of baskets. And I like the Navajo baskets, spreading through age and time and space symbolically."

Susan thought the *Raising of Lazarus* was stunning. The little figure at the end of a dark tunnel captivated her imagination. "The tunnel is in greater proportion to the figure—the figure is not dominant. The illustration is more about concept of 'raising' than on Lazarus as an individual. I love the enormous contrast between light and dark."

Johanna remembered, "An image we worked with a lot was the *Birth of Christ*. I've never lost the sense of wonder at that. Donald is working with images done for two thousand years, and he's coming up with something fresh. The face of Mary is remarkable in its wonder and tenderness. I'm personally fascinated with the bull from Lascaux—this is getting to the significant meaning of the event rather than doing something which would be illustrative."

Nathanael also recalled working on the *Birth of Christ* which was the first major illumination Donald and the committee worked on together. "I know all the pressures, the various evolutions. It was very frightening for everybody: is this going to work?" He was pleased. It had.

Susan and Alan agreed that the full-page illumination of the *Life of Paul* was successful. Susan said, "Donald is best when he's free. He has an ability to meld abstract form with content. The image of Saint Paul is embedded in a background of overlapping, interlinking churches and buildings." Alan remarked, "Saint Paul: the world and the church, with modern cities in the background, evoking how Paul took the message and spread it. It's a message for the world, against a background of houses and tenements. Donald was not drawing pictures of shipwrecks and jails."

Johanna reflected on the difficulty of creating this kind of imagery today. "There are centuries and centuries of artistic tradition. How do you do this so there's a new door, a new dimension? Every century, the Scriptures take a new dimension as human culture changes and develops." Describing the work Donald and the committee have put in, she said, "Shocking is okay. Errors you want to avoid."

She summed up the role of the committee by saying, "I'm not here to like or dislike. I'm here to perceive, to put the illuminations into context. It relieves Donald of the burden of being everything, knowing everything."

Nathanael expressed the joy of seeing the CIT's labors realized. When he first heard of The Saint John's Bible he thought, "That's serendipity! What a neat thing to do. But I never thought it would happen. There was a big discussion in the community: where does this fit in? What do we do with it afterwards?"

And yet there was "the excitement of doing something which reaches into the Benedictine past. It's deep in the bones. That excited people. And it fits our mission as Benedictines in education. The arts and education are more than vocational tech—it's about more than just getting a job.

"When I saw the first volume, I was excited. I was getting breathless at points." Did he have a favorite illumination? "No. We discuss all of them so much. We feel, 'This is my image.' It's like asking 'Which child is your favorite child?'"

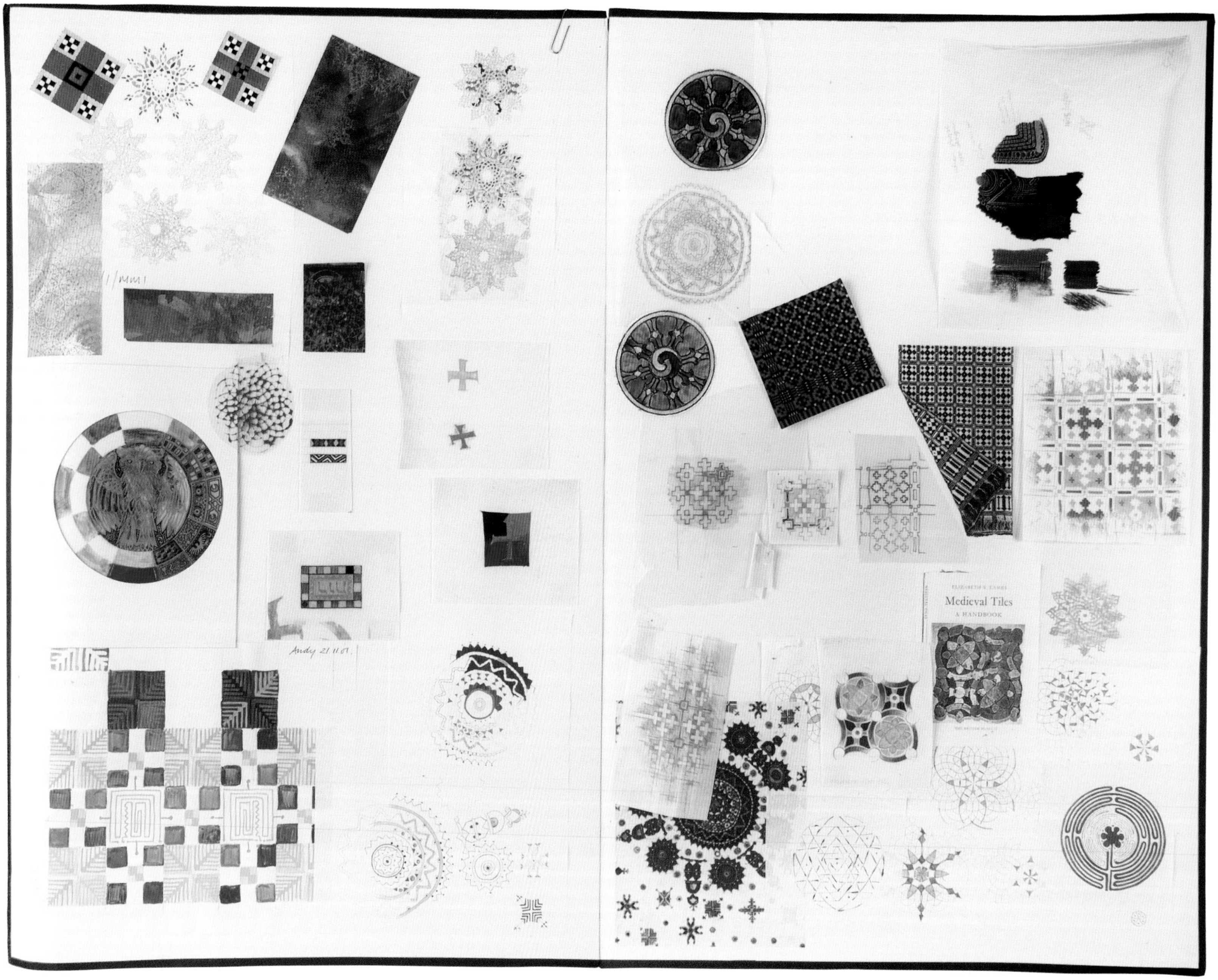

A collection of design studies exploring decorative ideas for marginal illustrations and carpet pages.

CHAPTER 7

THE PAGE COMES TO LIFE

L IKE the monastery in Collegeville, the Scriptorium is a community. It has its own rhythms and crises. Its life reflects the passing of seasons and the cycles of the countryside. It is a calm place, but there are also moments of tension and division. Creating the illuminations, in particular, began to put strain on this little community.

The end of the beginning

DONALD AND I walked into the Scriptorium. His working area had changed completely since my previous visit. Before when he had been mostly concerned with the Bible script, his corner had been uncluttered. He needed little more than pen, ink and quill knife.

Now it was different. The desk itself had not changed: it was still the calm eye of the storm, a clean, open space. But now it was surrounded by a tempest of tools and books and scraps of paper and vellum, a cacophony of colors and textures vying for attention. To one side in place of the small chair which had stood to his right hand there was now a large table covered with tubes of paint, burnishers, powdered pigments in small ceramic dishes, brushes, water pots, knives—a whole array of materials at his fingertips. Behind his chair a large flat table stood prepared for gilding and burnishing.

There was a bookshelf to his left under the window. As Donald wandered off to chat with Mark, his studio assistant at the time, I bent down and looked to see what visual sources Donald was using. The bookshelf was crammed to overflowing. Some of these were old. I picked up an exhibition catalog, *An Illustrated Souvenir of the Exhibition of Persian Art:* Burlington House, 1931. It still had a price on its cover: "Five shillings, net." It jostled against books on alchemy, angels and sacred dance. Other volumes included books on Hebrew, Islamic and medieval Christian illumination, Indian textiles, and Palestinian costume. Most of the books were full of little torn slips of paper serving as bookmarks. A glance at the rough drawings on the walls showed that he'd used his books extensively.

Donald joined me at his desk. He was subdued. It was just six weeks since he had made a trip to Saint John's to unveil the first finished pages. He had talked, entertained and politicked. To cap it off, he had walked down the central aisle of the Abbey church with his wife Mabel carrying his *Death of Christ* and *Road to Emmaus* illuminations for a grand ceremony of celebration. For the first time, he had seen his work used liturgically. The assembled crowd had gasped when they saw the page coming down the aisle. For Donald, it was confirmation that all his efforts were coming to fruition: this is why he had wanted to write a Bible. Now it was over. He was physically and emotionally wiped out. Those who see him on stage, in action, know him as a consummate performer, a delightful speaker and a perfect showman. Those who work with him behind scenes know how much he is drained by these performances.

There was more, however, to Donald's fatigue. The ceremony marked a turning point. The opening phase was done. Now the freshness had worn off. From now on it would be a long haul, keeping the pace—keeping it up, page by page, volume by volume.

In purely technical terms, the design problems posed by the Bible had entered a new phase as well. In the opening stages, the most demanding decisions had been essentially about issues of craftsmanship—where to get vellum, how to prepare it, what the script should look like, how to get a team of scribes up and running to produce pages of text. Donald had spent months answering these questions and, with the help of Sally Mae, devising systems for his team to follow. The illuminations he had created during this phase had been relatively few and must have seemed like welcomed breaks after the strain of putting his systems into operation. Now with the text more or less settled, Donald's attention had shifted almost entirely to the illuminations. More than any part of the project, these have challenged Donald to expand his range and to push his abilities. Each illustration is a small design problem of its own. This is the ultimate test because with the major illuminations, the pressure is on Donald the artist. Not the art director, the scribe or the business manager—not even the showman. The artist now came to the fore.

The artist and his client

WHILE HE PUSHED HIMSELF artistically, Donald was also more directly engaging in a dialogue with his client. The illuminations were the product of negotiation, a back and forth conversation between The Hendre and Collegeville. No wonder Donald looked a bit worn. Sitting in front of his desk, Donald said, "The process of design is different from medieval illuminated manuscripts. It's more of a dialogue; and never forget, I'm being briefed by a committee."

He showed me emails that had gone back and forth between him and Michael. Over one illumination there had been discussions, debates, points of clarification, reactions. Donald was trying to work with a whole body of people looking over his shoulder—committees, finance people, the documentarians who want to record the process and perhaps worst of all, the demons of his own hopes and dreams and expectations for himself.

I asked him to tell me more about how the illuminations were made.

"The illuminations . . . yes," he said softly, wondering where to begin. His mind wanders. You can almost see it working as he tries to think a way in, a way to explain what he's trying to do. He looked at the table: sheaves of emails and computer roughs lay there.

"The thing . . . the thing about the illuminations . . . is that I have to lay out this book perhaps years before illuminating it. Look at the steps it has to go through—computer, layout, proofreading, the scribes—all before it comes to me." He paused.

"I've been relatively conservative in my layouts," he said. His eyes hardened somewhat. "You can bet your bottom dollar that the Winchester Bible was a copy of something that already existed. It was a product of generations of continuous tradition."

He picked up a book full of images from the famous manuscript. "Look, look," he said, flipping past pages. "Look at the way this initial fits into a space. They knew what they were doing. They knew what was coming. I'm looking at a computer screen."

If the artist had to come to the front row, he needed to vent his frustrations a bit beforehand. The bril-

One of Donald Jackson's notebooks contains a spontaneous watercolor of a blue heron on the shore of Lake Sagatagan at Saint John's.

Marked and annotated books provide visual stimulus during the design process. Other images are found on the World Wide Web.

Donald Jackson unpeels layers of his
sketch for the *Baptism of Christ* to
show how the image developed.

liant showman in Donald could handle the client just fine, but the artist wanted space—space to experiment, to be free. He looked at the computer layouts.

"I am designing the book and *guessing* at spaces. I am graphically hindered. The text is largely passive.
'Why isn't he doing exciting things with the layout of the text?'" Donald's over-the-shoulder demons
were speaking again. "It's because the pages have to be laid out so long in advance. So the text has got to
be a foil. In this book the dialogue between text and illustration is relatively staid."

Pointing to one place where he'd been able to play a bit with the page layouts, he said, "At least the
Raising of Lazarus breaks the columns." On the whole, however, the layouts do have to be kept fairly
simple. Donald has to commit himself very early on to a layout for each page so the scribes can keep
churning out their quota of pages. He makes these decisions long before he can embark on the illuminations or even begin sketching out ideas.

His eyes jumped to the rough layout for the Book of Judges. Here he was more positive: "But then in
Judges I picked up the idea of the five disparate stories which the CIT gave me. I left five spaces, which
will have the five stories, like a ribbon or thread running through the whole book. All this chaos—these
stories about God being far from the people, all come together at the end of the book. God is there, but
in the spaces in between, in the apparent chaos of these violent stories."

Donald began to describe how he works through CIT's commentary. The sequence of illuminations
was defined by a small team at Saint John's at the very beginning of the project. Michael and David

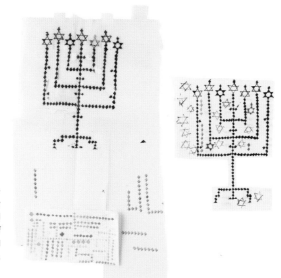

Small pen-made menorah patterns were executed by Sally Mae Joseph as an ornamental counterpoint for the end of the books of Genesis and Deuteronomy.

worked out the schema, a list of passages which would be illuminated. The schema was circulated, refined and presented to Donald with short commentaries. Donald responded, asking for more detail. On one of his copies of the schema he wrote: "By being more expansive you are not tying me down or muddling me: you are feeding me."

The CIT came back to Donald with much more comprehensive theological briefs. In these each illumination is explored at length. The first section of each brief exegetes the passage, which is to say that it explains or comments on it from the perspective of contemporary biblical criticism. The second section contains scriptural cross-references for the passage. The third section, probably the most visually helpful, is a free association in which the committee brainstorms, suggesting a huge variety of images and themes. For some illuminations the schema goes on for several pages. It is not always easy for Donald to take in all this information. "The Nativity scene—twenty-seven different ideas I'm given. I have to please a committee," he said, perhaps forgetting he'd asked to be fed more detail.

Sometimes it is not the quantity of ideas which stymies Donald, but the impenetrability of the prose. The committee sometimes slips into the technical language of its own disciplines, forgetting it is addressing an artist. At times he is utterly perplexed by what he reads: "Here we have a realized eschatology, the 'divine-man,' and yet we must be cautious for this Gospel was indeed redacted to refute Gnosticism." Illuminate that. After you've deciphered it.

Most of the time, however, briefs are more straightforward. Donald ponders the briefs and begins

A small accordion-fold mock-up of *Letters and Revelation* helps Donald Jackson visualize the flow of illuminations within the text.

to develop his ideas. When he presents his sketches, it is the CIT's turn to interpret what they've been given. Both sides of the negotiation have had to learn how to work together. All the sketches Donald prepares are sent to Saint John's for comment and feedback from the CIT. This has been a sensitive issue. The committee is not always sure how to interpret his sketches or to manage the working schedule. In the early days of the project, when the committee was first formed, they had tried functioning as a group responsible for riding herd on their artist. As Donald describes it, they felt responsible to produce the Bible to schedule. Their brief was refined. The group now saw itself in more of an advisory role. Still, how were they to interpret the drawings and collages they were presented by Donald? And what kind of approvals or comments would they be invited to make? Even now, the relationship was continuing to develop. Each new illumination opened new issues of control and freedom, direction and trust.

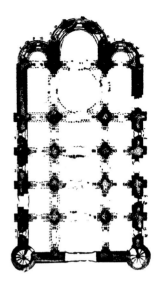

Very early in the process, Donald had produced a half size mock-up using computer type and scanned imagery to suggest the balance of image and text in the book. The imagery itself was drawn from all kinds of sources and included non-Christian religious images. The committee, quite naturally, reacted to the detailed content of the imagery, which, for Donald, was only used to indicate the scale, color and weight of the illustrations he was proposing: their content was largely beside the point. Donald presented his mock-up. The committee looked at it and wanted to know what the Buddha was doing there—a classic example of a visual artist appropriating the visual impact of a selection of images, while the more literal, verbally oriented client reacted to the detailed content of the images.

Later in the process he presented a sketch which incorporated some photocopied images. He had used the photocopier to adjust the size and scale of certain visual elements; because he had photocopied them, they'd ended up in black and white in his presentation sketch. The committee reacted by saying, "We particularly like Donald's use of grey in the image." Once again what they had seen was very different from what Donald had envisaged.

With time, the committee began to see that the images sent from the Scriptorium were rough sketches. They were loose renditions which might shift in tone, scale and color. The task of the committee was to shape and guide the content of the illumination, leaving room for Donald to work visually. Donald and the CIT began to clarify each other's roles.

Despite the CIT's need to see drawings and approve them, Donald knew he needed the flexibility to shift and change his compositions, both for his own artistic integrity, and simply in order to retain some sense of spontaneous joy in the making. In effect he would have to say, "This is a sketch. Now trust me."

With one of the early illuminations Sally Mae recalled, "Donald had done a detailed rough, and then he had to copy it." An almost impossible task especially for an artist like Donald who has always thrived on the spontaneous moment.

"He wasn't being free and expressive anymore," Sally said. "He did struggle with that."

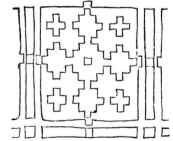

In all his work, even in very precise legal documents for the Queen's signature, he tries to have some moment on the page when he is able to throw himself in and "wing it." Even in his most formal work there is usually a flourish, a tiny detail, a dab of color, which adds a spark of freshness and vitality to the page. Without it, not only would the page be less vigorous, less lively, but Donald's own interest would be dimmed: he needs to feel that slight sense of danger which comes from every encounter with the page. Plan everything ahead and the result dies. It becomes sterile.

Rubber stamps of designs from many sources are used in illuminations and carpet pages throughout The Saint John's Bible. These small designs are a *leitmotif* which runs through the book.

Process and product

"SO WHERE DO YOU START with your sketches?" I asked him, pointing at the cluttered collage-like rough on his desk.

"The first question in most of my sketches is: What are the light and dark relationships? Where is there gold?"

Aidan Hart confers with Donald Jackson. He works as a traditional Orthodox icon painter. In The Saint John's Bible he uses an ancient technique in surprising ways. He and Donald have worked together on several illuminations which blend Orthodox and contemporary modes of expression within the same painting. Donald commented, "People are shocked when they hear I erased and worked over parts of Aidan's image. It's a true collaboration in which we are all working to make something bigger than any of us."

Donald sketches with a large brush, using whatever colors are at hand. Dark and light areas are quickly painted in. Great swaths of inexpensive gold paint fill in for the gold leaf. From then on, Donald's sketches become collages. He pastes and tapes things in place. He adds bits and pieces photocopied from his source books; he draws or paints or writes over the emerging composition. Often, he uses acetate overlays to add elements without obliterating what is below. Sometimes he tapes in real plants: a twig, a leaf, a dried frond of plant from outside the Scriptorium door. Frequently, because the page is large, he starts with big, bold figures; these, he quickly realizes, are too large, too crude. The image gets reduced on the photocopier. The scale gets smaller and smaller, more and more precise as he circles into the composition. He picks up smaller brushes and begins adding finer detail.

We looked at the sketch of the *Nativity* page, and Donald talked about his working process. "It's very intuitive. This animal has to have its feet in shit," he said. He works with any materials he finds at hand—anything that will get his ideas down onto the page. The sketches often remain in work for months, changing in only tiny increments.

Donald stands over the work and squints. He moves a small piece of acetate left or right, often only few millimeters. He stares, breathes and moves it back again. Several rough sketches are in process at any one time. And then in a sudden attack, a rough which has hardly changed in weeks will be radically shifted, moved about, changed and come together. The circadian rhythm of the artist doesn't always match the regular meeting pattern of the CIT. There are times when an illustration goes to Collegeville for the committee to look at, only to be transformed the next day by some new intuition on Donald's part. There are times when working directly on the skin on the final illustration he continues to develop his ideas and makes changes. In Collegeville, he had pointed to a "finished" illumination and said to me, "The colors need adjusting in the small panels." He is always looking at ways to improve and develop the work.

Donald Jackson and Chris Tomlin examine flora and fauna from around Saint John's. In addition to his marginal illustrations, Chris has collaborated with Donald on illuminations such as *Jacob's Ladder* and *The Garden of Eden*.

I asked him about his sources. The illuminations are quite modern. They feel loose, free and contemporary with their generous brushstrokes, broadly abstracted figures and overlapping, juxtaposed imagery. He surprised me by pulling a book from his bookshelf on Carolingian illumination—a historic style of the ninth and tenth centuries. Turning to a page from the Gospels of Saint Medard, a fine Carolingian manuscript, he pointed to the loose brushwork and freely drawn imagery. Even the color sense echoes his own work; the violets and pinks echoed the colors of his *Road to Emmaus* illumination. He turned to another page: the Vienna Genesis. This uncial manuscript is written gold on purple-stained vellum—an opulent and rich manuscript. The illustrations, unbound by boxes or borders, populate the bottom margins of the manuscript. The relationship of figure to ground in the manuscript is closely related to Donald's free illuminations, always bursting their bounds, exploring and engaging the open space in the margins. It is striking that Donald did not invoke the Winchester Bible for the illuminations—that craftsmanlike manuscript of the Romanesque period had served him well as a model for the craftwork of the page. It could not help him with the free artistry of the illumination. It is also striking that Donald could ground his contemporary sensibility in one of the richest parts of the manuscript tradition, exploring an entirely new dimension of these ninth-century paintings.

The transition from rough sketch to final illumination is difficult. Donald, like many artists, prefers to keep his ideas loose even when he begins to attack the final illustration. As he discovered in the *Nativity* scene, if the rough is too tightly resolved the artist is left having to recreate or worse, to copy the rough. In that case the artist feels the working process as a sequence of two distinct campaigns: in the first, he resolves the design, in the second he executes it. Follow it too closely and the final version can simply

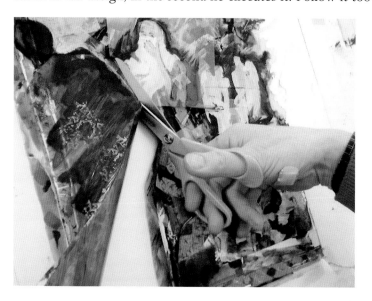 

die on him, losing all the vitality and spark of the rough. Graced with a clean sheet of white vellum and a fully resolved rough drawing, the artist feels, though he may not say it, that he is done. Why do it again?

The best working process is a seamless progress, not a two-step campaign. The rough sketch does not resolve every artistic question and close every creative door; it simply provides a strong guideline. The artist comes to the moment when he transfers his exploration from sketch to final surface, hopefully not breaking the ongoing feeling of problem-solving and pushing forward. The image continues its unbroken chain of development, but the scene of the battle shifts from rough to finished page.

Certain technical issues make the seamless artistic process hard to achieve. Traditional medieval illumination was usually made in a predictable order. The underdrawing was made in light ink with a pointed pen. Then areas to be gilded would receive their gesso ground. Once this was dry, the gold would be laid and burnished. All other areas of color were then painted in, beginning with large areas and ending with delicate highlights in white or powdered gold paint. The underdrawing was usually extremely precise and it provided distinct boundaries for each color. The illuminator simply colored in the drawing, albeit with great grace and finesse. When the painter departed from the sketch, it was only within certain accepted bounds. Donald's free and loose approach to the illustrations makes this mode of working impossible; his overlapping images and his painterly technique with gold force him to attack the problem differently.

Once his rough sketch is ready to be transferred to the vellum page, the steps are worked out in stages. The vellum skin needs to be prepared for the rough treatment it will receive. Gold is a demanding medium and dictates much of the order in which the components come together.

Hazel Dolby talks with Donald Jackson at The Hendre. Hazel is responsible for special treatments and illuminations in several volumes of The Saint John's Bible.

Making an illumination

THE FIRST HURDLE is the preparation of the vellum skin. Because of its absorbent nature, vellum needs to be readied to receive large coats of wet pigment. It has to be stretched and its edges pinned to a board so that Donald can use as much moisture as he needs. A stretched skin will take this moisture, expand and then contract back into position. An unstretched skin would become more and more distorted in shape as it twisted and contorted itself under successive coats of gesso and paint.

In order to stretch the skin out, the vellum sheet is left in the scrutching shed overnight. The moisture of the damp shed causes the vellum sheet to expand very gently. No extra moisture is added—only the moisture which can be picked up from the atmosphere. The next morning the sheet is pulled flat on a large composite board covered with Formica. It is not pulled too hard, just enough to smooth the wrinkles. It is then stapled to the board along its outermost margin (which will be trimmed off during the binding) and masking tape is applied all around. This tape, too, is applied only to areas which will be cut away. The stretched and mounted vellum sheet is then left in the schoolroom. As it dries it shrinks slowly; the page becomes taut and flat. This procedure may sound rather risky. It is. The skin must not be over-stretched. Pulled too tight, the page will go out of square, distorting the regular grid of the book. If there is writing on the sheet, it must not get smudged. It's delicate work.

Even before they are stretched, areas for illumination are treated differently than other parts of the page. Most of the skins are prepared with writing in mind. The final stage of an ordinary skin's preparation involves a final rubbing down with gum sandarac (a substance not unlike the rosin baseball pitchers keep on the pitcher's mound). The liquid-resistant properties of the gum help writing stay clean, crisp and sharp by discouraging the spreading or feathering of the ink. In areas of illumination, where large areas of wet pigment have to be laid onto the page, the water resistance would not be a help but a barrier. On these pages the final sanding of the skin is left out. The skin is therefore left in a slightly smoother, more slick state. Before an illumination can be added to the page, the surface has to be examined: has it been sanded a bit too enthusiastically? If so, it needs to be gently burnished down to flatten it.

Once the skin is stretched and fully dried out, it is ready for Donald to begin working. He makes a tight sketch of the basic elements of his composition, which he transfers to the vellum page. This compositional underdrawing sometimes needs to be transferred to the vellum page repeatedly, as elements disappear under layers of gold and color. He keeps his tracing paper drawing throughout the process. Sometimes Donald uses a kind of white carbon paper sold in the United States for dress pattern making. Donald pulled out two boxes of the transfer paper to show me. Both were a good twenty years old, bought in New York on a trip in the late seventies or eighties. The logo reads "Saral" in a jaunty, old-fashioned commercial script popular in the late fifties.

"Look," he said, holding out the paper for me to look at and to feel. "See how thin and fine that is? The thinner the paper, the better the tracing. This paper is perfectly suited to its task. But then look at this one." He turned around and grabbed the other box. The design of the box had changed slightly; it had been bought a year or two later.

"Feel that—the paper's gotten thicker. The white coating is coarser, too." Indeed it was. I reached forward and felt the two sheets. "They're making this for home dressmakers, and to them it doesn't matter. But it does matter to me. The newer paper is just slightly thicker, slightly coarser. It doesn't transfer the

Thomas Ingmire, one of the illuminators, at work at the Scriptorium.

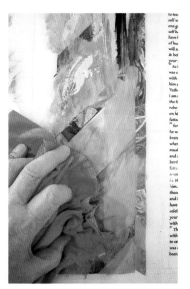

Donald Jackson places a piece of raw silk on top of an illumination in progress. He used the cloth as a model for the dress Mary of Bethany wears in the *Luke Anthology* illumination.

A sketch and its finished version. In the intermediate photograph the background had been laid down; Saral carbon paper, made for dressmakers, has been used to trace down the outlines of the letters, which were then painted in with shell gold using a sable brush.

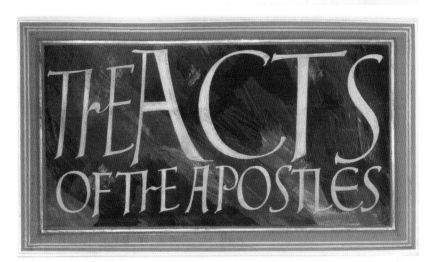

drawings with as much delicacy and detail. Anything new is problematic." As a craftsman he relies on the properties of his tools and materials. When they change he has to change his practices—and he doesn't like it. So he guards this ancient box of Saral transfer paper, because he knows of nothing like it on the market today.

The challenge of working in gold

THE BLANK SHEET of vellum stands ready to receive its design. What comes first? As in ancient manuscripts, it is often the gold which determines the order of the work. Now there are three types of gold which are used in The Saint John's Bible. Each of these is made of real gold; fake gold paint is only for roughs. The first kind of gold is powder gold, sometimes called "shell gold" because it was once sold in containers made of discarded mussel shells. This is a fine dust of gold, ground fine. Donald buys this in small tablets in which the grains are pre-mixed with a binding agent. He prefers to add his own binding agent so he soaks the tablets in water, dissolving the gum or glue. Three changes of water are needed to wash out every impurity. He then adds a tiny amount of fish glue—just enough to keep the gold from flaking off. As with other powdered colors, gold becomes dull and lifeless if it is drowning in glue; the master craftsman knows just how much binder is needed to keep the gold or pigment on the page without losing its luster. Powder gold is relatively easy to use: it is painted on with a brush. It is lustrous and rich. It can be rubbed with a burnisher to take on a high sheen, although "Beware," Donald warns. "Too much looks tawdry." The granular nature of the gold makes for a gently rough surface which catches light in a complex way. It never takes on the lucid brightness of gold leaf. Its finish is flatter, darker.

The other two types of gold—acrylic medium and gesso gilding—are technically more demanding. These involve use of gold leaf: sheets of gold which have been hammered out to an incredible thinness. Gold leaf is unbelievably delicate. The least puff of wind sends it flying through the air. Windows must be shut, and even a careless breath on the part of the gilder can send his precious gold sheet scurrying across the room. The tools used for gilding have to be spotlessly clean: the gold leaf sticks to any surface that has even the tiniest residue of grease. And yet it is a stubborn material as well and will not stick evenly to any surface that hasn't been properly prepared. In order to apply gold leaf to the page, a special ground needs to be laid first. Different grounds create different finishes. For a fairly flat, matte effect, Donald uses an acrylic medium diluted with rain water. This is painted on the surface, allowed to dry and then covered with sheets of gold leaf. The inherent stickiness of the material, even when dry, acts as a firm binding agent for the gold.

By far the most demanding—and most spectacular—gilding is the laying of gold leaf on gesso ground. Donald is justly famous for his gesso gilding. He wrote the entry on it in The Calligrapher's Handbook.* The gesso recipe varies but it usually includes dental-grade plaster, white lead, sugar, fish glue and a tiny amount of powdered color. Craft calligraphers can debate for hours about the properties of each of these ingredients, about the necessity for the sugar and about acceptable variations and substitutions in the recipe. The gesso must be prepared long in advance; small dried cakes of it made by Sam Somerville, Thomas Ingmire, Donald and Sally Mae are kept at the Scriptorium.

Donald uses the gesso like any cake of watercolor paint, tempering it—that is to say, wetting it—with glair, a liquid drained from beaten egg whites. The gesso, with its plaster and lead ingredients, lies thickly on the page. It adds a third dimension to the gilding and dries both hard and flexible. Donald exploits this third dimension, scratching into the wet gesso before it dries, sculpting the surface. He lays the gesso with a specially cut quill or with a brush; at times, he has been known to use his finger to push the gesso around the page. The laying of the gesso is an exacting craft. The consistency has to be just right or gesso sets poorly. There can be no bubbles or lumps. Once it is dry, it can be sanded or scraped, if needed. Once the

Donald Jackson uses a sharp knife to break the outer membrane of the yolk of an egg. A tiny drop of egg yolk added to vermillion both binds the pigment to the page and brightens its tone.

* *The Calligrapher's Handbook.* London: A&C Black, 1985. Ed: Heather Child. Donald's article on gilding appears on pages 176–197.

The gesso letters are written with a quill.

The dry gesso letters are scraped with a sharp knife to produce a smooth cushion to receive the gold.

The shavings here will be vacuumed with a tiny dust buster. Since gesso contains poisonous white lead, extreme caution must be taken not to inhale particles of the fine dust.

The suede gilder's cushion provides a surface on which to position a leaf of 24-carat gold. The leaf is cut into small, manageable pieces. The gilding knife must be kept scrupulously clean; any hint of grease will make the gold stick to the knife.

A GESSO RECIPE

slaked plaster	16 parts
white lead	6 parts
sugar	2 parts
fish glue	1 part
Armenian bole	
(enough to color the mixture pink)	

The ingredients are carefully blended. The liquid mixture is allowed to dry, forming a small cake of gesso.

In order to use the gesso, glair (a liquid made from egg whites) and water are added to the dry cake to create a paint with the consistency of heavy cream.

Speed is of the essence when gilding. As Sally Mae Joseph holds the bamboo tube in her mouth, breathing over one tiny section of the piece, she holds a tiny sliver of gold leaf on her left index finger. When the gesso is sufficiently moist, she will gently rest the gold leaf onto the gesso surface. A cloth in her right hand will be used to press the gold down.

Sally Mae Joseph transfers a sheet of gold leaf to the surface of her gilding cushion. The delicate leaves of gold are kept between the pages of a little paper booklet.

Once the gold has been pressed in place, it is burnished onto the surface. Here it has formed a bond with the gesso and has taken on a bright sheen. Although a delicate sense of touch is essential, a surprising amount of pressure can be used when burnishing.

Holding a burnishing tool in her right hand and piece of gold leaf in her left, Sally Mae Joseph breathes gently through a bamboo tube onto the gesso ground. The moisture of her breath activates the glue binding agent in the gesso, until it is sticky enough to bond with the gold leaf.

gold is laid, every flaw and variation in the surface will show. Donald has been working with gesso for more than forty years, and he handles it with an ease few can match. He knows all its properties intimately, and knows how to push it to achieve a whole range of effects. He produces a crisp, smooth surface which will react well to its metallic golden overcoat.

Once the gesso ground has been prepared to Donald's satisfaction, he lays the gold leaf. Cutting the leaf to size on a small gilder's cushion with his gilder's knife, he picks it up with the tip of his finger. The normal grease of skin attracts the gold like a magnet. His hand hangs in midair, the wispy gold surface dangling gently in the still room. He blows softly on the gesso, warming and moistening it slightly with his breath; this brings the gesso to life. It becomes slightly sticky to the touch. As soon as Donald is satisfied that the gesso is ready to receive gold, then—bam!—down goes the gold. He covers the area with a silk cloth and burnishes the gold hard. This process is repeated until the entire gesso area is covered with gold. A final burnishing is done after the gesso has dried and become perfectly hard again. Sometimes he varies the final effect by pressing a piece of silk into the malleable gesso surface after he has laid the gold. This leaves a gentle fabric imprint which catches the light very differently from cleanly burnished, flat areas of gold.

Gesso gilding results in a thin skin of gold that looks bright and metallic, as though an actual chunk of gold were laid onto the manuscript page. Because the gesso creates a raised surface, its edges curving gently to meet the page, its contours reflect the light in a constantly changing display. Raised and burnished gold captures every tiny bit of available light around it; as the page is turned the highlights flutter across the gold surfaces. Why is it called manuscript "illumination"? Turn a gold-bespecked page in a dim room and you will see. The page will flash to life.

All of this gold is just one stage of the process, of course. Powder gold can be added at any stage in the process of creating a finished illumination; the areas of gold leaf are more demanding. Donald described his working order to me. "The gesso is usually the first to go down; otherwise the gold sticks to paints exactly where you don't want it." The implication of this is that any painted areas need to be added after the gold, so no errant gold flecks stick to adjacent areas of color.

"The traditional method has always been to lay gesso first, then gold, then paint all around," Donald said.

"But is there any way to avoid this?" I asked. "What if your design made it hard to lay the gold first?"

"You can get away, to some extent, with gilding near paint by adding a dusting of French chalk over the places where you don't want the gold to stick, but this is a stopgap and not the ideal way of working."

There are other technical concerns. Donald continued, "Gesso doesn't readily adhere to acrylic." In some illuminations in the Bible, Donald has wanted a figure in raised and burnished gold to sit in the middle of an area of matte gold. "The Crucifixion, for example, uses gesso over powder gold." He pointed to the illumination, lying on a table in front of us. His hands inscribed broad arcs across the page. "I used neat glair—undiluted with water—in the gesso. Neat glair is tricky. When it's dry, it becomes almost waterproof which makes it hard to lay the gold leaf." He went quiet, his eyes making wide sweeps across the page. It's always a balancing act, pushing the materials, seeing what he can get away with, trying to make the composition work, both technically and visually.

A silk cloth is used to remove excess leaf. In some areas, the gold may stick to the vellum itself. These stubborn patches of gold are removed with an erasing pencil.

Tiny areas where the gold has not bonded properly are touched up.

Adding color

ONCE THE GOLD is in place then the rest of the painting and drawing can be done. We turned to look at the cluttered table beside his work desk. Tubes of watercolor and gouache were jostling against small pots of casein-based paints. There were pigments in small jars and tubes of acrylic medium. Printmaking rollers, brushes and quills sat side by side.

Donald began to get impatient as I asked him about all these materials. His answers were less forthcoming. They came in short staccato bursts, not in the lush, reflective manner he adopted when talking about the artistic process. Technique seemed to bore him; talking about it seemed frustrating. I wasn't sure whether he was protecting his trade secrets or if he'd simply spent so long with these tools and techniques that they were second nature to him. I tried my best to pump him for information.

"What kind of water do you use?" I ventured.

"I use rainwater for this: it comes off the roof and I ladle it out of the water-barrel by the door," he said.

I picked up a small, beautiful nineteenth century tablet of red color. "Stick vermillion," he said, "mercuric sulphide, bound together with glue. Add egg yolk (just a drop) and water; it glows." The egg yolk helps bind the color to the page. "What you put down should stay on the side of the page where you put it."

"And the roller?"

"The roller is for the water-based printing ink. You can lay the color pretty dry; there's less moisture. That's better for the skin."

"You have a lot of different kinds of paint here," I said.

"Yes, these cost me a lot of money. How much did we spend on the paints? Two hundred, three hundred pounds? I'll ask Mark to check the receipts." Later in the day, Mark would unearth the receipt—£295, or more than $500, for tubes of gouache and watercolor.

"I use casein for its glazing potential," Donald said, explaining that, unlike gouache, the casein would take many layers of paint. "There's no oil paint of course . . . the oils would stain through the vellum. Aidan (the Orthodox icon painter who has painted some of the illuminations) glazes his icons after a year or so." His face brightened. "Apparently they use boiled down beer in Russia. Clearly we can't do that."

"And what about the powdered pigments? How do you use those?"

"Sometimes I add them to gouache. They give more grit." The gritty texture is better to work with.

"Can they be used on their own?" I asked. Donald's brow furrowed. We launched into a conversation about binding agents, pigments and gilding. "Acacia gum as a binding agent will darken the color and become brittle over time. Isinglass, a gelatine of great purity, is made from the flotation bladder of the sturgeon and gives you the purest color. Ordinary fish glue is any old thing: heads, guts, tails. Old sign writers used to use the gelatine pill capsules you could buy through chemists for their glass gilding."

He quickly veered off this topic. The point was something different. It wasn't about the materials, about giving out recipes for using powder pigments. It was about something entirely other, about the feel of the thing. He changed tack: "Arabic calligraphers used particular reeds from a particular place. Marsh Arabs had the best reeds. It is said these improved if they were left in dung for six months. The way of handling materials is different. It's not like the way we talk about technology but about having a feel for their materials."

Details from Psalm 1 in various stages of completion. The tracing above was used to transfer the lettering design to the vellum page. Below the gesso has been laid. Its contours are still rough and will require gentle scraping. The image on the facing page shows the gold glistening in light. The three dimensional contours of the letters refract light in every direction.

I was quiet for a moment. As I was about to prod him further about the materials in front of us, he said, "In all the talk about materials, there is a great problem of getting too arcane about everything versus getting it done." Lancashire practicality trumped clever questions about medieval and modern pigments. "It's about feel and integrity. Not about cookery!"

We stood in silence for a time and then began to talk about the rubber stamps he uses in his designs. We chatted about the ways he distresses his paintings with sandpaper, breaking up the colored surfaces. In the middle of our conversation he suddenly said, "Come here, look at this."

He took me outside and pointed up under the Scriptorium eave. There, hanging from an old rusty nail, was a wasp, just beginning to build her paper-thin nest. She had just a few strands in place and patiently, patiently moved back and forth, trying to establish herself and her brood.

"She's been at it since yesterday but isn't showing much progress," he said.

I could see that the place she needed to attach her next paper segment was on the painted rafter into which the rusty nail had been hammered. The paint was too smooth, too new. It didn't give her any purchase and try as she might, she could not get her thin paper walls to stick. We watched her for a while, chatting about the craftsmanship of the wasp, her patience and the danger she faced if she didn't make progress soon. His irritation with the discussion on materials evaporated. As we stood and watched this tiny wasp struggle on with her task, it was as if we were watching ourselves. Her struggle was to make a nest with the materials she had available to her; Donald's is to make a manuscript Bible. The wasp, the Marsh Arabs, the feel of gold under his burnisher—they were all of a piece. It was all about a quality of encounter with the world around us, about living with a kind of sensitivity to the physical realities of life. That's what Donald's Bible illuminations are about. That's what he's about.

Sally Mae once said to me, "Everything he does has to be taken on board, looked at, thought about, touched and smelled." Watching the wasp with Donald, I saw it was so.

Quills and artists' colors lie on a table next to a fragment of illumination from the Gospel according to Matthew. Donald Jackson uses tools and materials of every description in the making of The Saint John's Bible. The red vermillion cakes were made in the 1870s and are used for the red bullets and footnotes throughout the Bible.

CHAPTER 8

TOOLS OF THE TRADE

EVERY TOOL has its place. Every tool has its purpose. "I use a lot of adhesive tape," Donald said to me. "It keeps the things on my desk from moving around. If I didn't have my heavy metal tape dispenser, I don't know what I'd do. It's cast iron and stays put."

The Saint John's Bible is made with tools as simple and mundane as adhesive tape and with tools as up-to-date and technological as computers. Some of the tools you can buy in any stationery store; others have to be custom-made by hand. Some are precious objects, passed down from scribe to scribe over the years; others are used up and chucked away without a second thought.

The only test of a tool is whether it works.

Tools for thinking

PERHAPS THE MOST SURPRISING tool used in the project is the computer. I asked Donald whether he had taken on the computer gladly, or was it a more grudging acceptance?

"I took to the computer avidly," he said. "I was completely enthusiastic. You know, a number of years ago I was at a conference at Oxford. It was sponsored by the Crafts Council. We were looking at the future of the graphic arts—but there weren't any computers there. Calligrapher Ann Hechle and I both said 'Where are the computers?' I was dying to get my hands on a mouse and see what could be done."

The computer organizes the project in fundamental ways. In Donald's hands it is also an expressive, experimental tool. I asked Vin Godier, the project's graphic designer/typesetter, about the technology.

"In early days doing roughs, the computer was used to create mock-ups for Saint John's. We could create instant visuals. Very early on we produced a whole book of the Gospels, including sample illustrations, to give Saint John's a better feel of what the finished book would be like. If we hadn't had the computer, how many pages would Donald have been able to produce by hand—ten, twelve pages?" The computer gave Donald the freedom to visualize whole books at a time.

It also helped him refine his design more quickly than he could by hand.

"The computer helped Donald decide on the proportions of the text column, the x-height of the letters and the line spacing. It was the very best way of using the computer: Donald could see things very quickly. He had lots of elasticity. He could try anything he fancied. It was almost instant. We used the computer to do all the variations, churning out column after column."

The hardware consists of a PowerMac G3 with an upgraded memory capacity, a Umax PowerLook 3 flatbed scanner, and an Epson Stylus Color 3000 printer.

"The printer is a big beastie. It was the biggest printer we could get," Vin said. "We're printing out sheets of A2"—large sheets in the European A-series of standard paper sizes. "They have even bigger printers now, but it's still large."

A tube of water-based lino ink bears the marks of frequent use.

A Victorian erasing knife is perfectly shaped for its task. The exquisitely sharp edges of the hollow-ground blade do not need frequent resharp-ening. The bone handle fits comfortably in the hand.

Rare nineteenth-century Chinese ink comes in solid form. This stick is used to make the dense black ink used throughout the Bible. The thin layer of gold which decorates the outside of the stick does not affect the black-ness of the ink when the stick is ground in water.

The software includes Quark Xpress 4.1 and Photoshop 6.

"We've been through several upgrades of Quark Xpress—we must have started with 3.3."

I wondered how it felt to use computer technology on a project like this. Calligraphy is a very intimate thing; it's all about a personal encounter with the writing. The computer seems rather cold by comparison. I asked Vin if there was a personal dimension to working with a computer.

"A personal dimension?" he said. "I suppose the only thing that makes it personal is the way you design your own style sheets; you build the software around you. But then, you can share style sheets so it's not that personal.

"The one thing we did produce which was unique was the font. We created it ourselves, built from Adobe multiple master fonts. The 'font creator' is a kind of mini-program with little flag bars: you slide the bars and it will change the weight and the optical size of the type. It's literally an elastic type."

This special font of type was designed to mimic the weight and spacing of Donald's Bible script.

"Donald wrote a block of text and all the characters in the Bible script. Manipulating a typeface called Sanvito on the computer, I did lots of samples and printed them out. Through trial and error we got it to match Donald's writing."

"How close did it come? When you look at the Sanvito in the printouts, it doesn't really look like Donald's writing," I said.

"It was a case of getting as close as possible. We achieved the best compromise we could using an electronic font."

An old vial holds a small amount of ground blue artists' pigment which can be mixed with gum, egg yolk or glair.

And indeed it spaces out in a way which is very like the Bible script. Using it, Vin can create a perfect layout; the written Bible will match it line for line. The master layouts are printed in multiples. Originally he printed two copies at the full size (15⅞ x 24½ inches or 403 x 622mm); one for the scribe, one for the proofreader—now only one copy is used for both purposes. Five sets, reduced to standard European letterhead size (A4), are bound as books; two of these stay at the Scriptorium, three go to Saint John's. These are used for day-to-day reference. The last set, reduced even further, is posted on the studio wall in a long strip to serve as a visual diagram for an entire volume. Vin's master layout allows people scattered in sites across two continents to work simultaneously on all the varied processes involved in production, from proofreading to fine writing to illumination. When Vin says, "It's a very useful tool to have," he is understating the case considerably.

Vin takes the raw digital text of the New Revised Standard Version and flows it into the text boxes. Chapter headings, drop caps, and paragraph bullets are added. All the hyphens and em-dashes have to be changed; the default settings of these are wider than the Bible script version. Any blocks of text which are to receive special treatments are marked in color so they stand out. Now the raw columns of text are ready to be justified. This is where things get interesting, because the layout is not a piece of formal typesetting; it is a guide for writing by hand. He breaks all sorts of typographic rules and conventions to produce a master layout for the scribes. The broken rules begin with the type itself.

Donald Jackson uses casein-based paints extensively in the Bible. The lids are color coded for easy recognition.

"We decided on 19.4 point type on 22.572 point leading."

"What a bizarre measurement," I said. "A typesetter would never choose such an odd size."

"It is purely to make it match the Bible script visually—in the end this isn't a computer job. It's replicating calligraphy. That means the job has some strange aspects. I'm not producing neat, clean, tidy typesetting as

Rollers can be used to spread a thin film of water-based lino ink on the vellum. The ink's low moisture content allows it to be used to lay down large areas of transparent color. Rollers and lino ink are also used for printing with rubber stamps. A glass sheet provides a perfectly smooth surface for the preparation and mixing of the ink.

you would in a printed book, for example. I'm producing a layout in type which is a guide for the scribes' spacing—it's different from typography.

"For example, I leave no space at all near some punctuation, particularly quotation marks. The proofreaders often mark this as wrong. But most punctuation in calligraphy tucks in tighter. Set electronically, it overhangs far too much."

The result is a computer layout which is incorrect typographically precisely because it is used as a carefully calibrated guide to calligraphic spacing. The automatic settings on the computer would leave holes and gaps in the writing. So Vin spaces out every line by hand, bearing in mind the way the Bible script sits on the page.

Although the columns are justified, with clean, even margins both left and right, Vin instructs the computer to align the text flush left. Through his own hand adjustment, he draws out or squeezes the lines into alignment on the right-hand side. It is extremely labor intensive as he works his way through the text line by line.

"I use tracking to squeeze the words, then I have a coding when the tracking is extremely tight. I color a line green if it's at maximum tracking of –7. That alerts the calligraphers on very tight lines. The text doesn't fall in easily. People think you're using a computer, so it's automatic. It's not. Every single line has to be hand done. The way I approach it the computer is completely serving the calligraphy. On screen it bears no resemblance to good typography."

Once the justification of the text is done, Vin and Donald sit together to decide where the illuminations will sit in the text. This is a creative time.

"When Donald is planning spaces for illustrations, he'll explore various spaces that could be used. He can see what the placement of an illumination does to the chapters which follow on. Sometimes we find it's advantageous to add a few lines to an illustration to avoid awkward breaks. It also lets Donald see different variations from the creative point of view. He can explore the layouts electronically before they're set in stone, if you will. It's given Donald flexibility in creativity; an opportunity to try things out, to have a look."

The marriage between calligrapher and computer is not always smooth. I asked Donald about the computer as a creative tool.

"There is an absolute meeting point," Donald said, "which shows the relationship problem between the scribe and the computer which underlines the limitations of it."

He described to me how he had come to work on the opening passage of the Gospel according to John. This was to be treated as what they are calling an "incipit," a portion of text at the beginning of a biblical book which is given prominence by being written larger and with elements in color and gold. The John incipit poses some delicate design problems. It appears opposite a full page illumination. The name of the book—the Gospel according to John—appears in a box above it. Blocks of text in ordinary Bible script hedge it in at the bottom.

"I sketched that out two years ago," Donald said, "before we had even finalized the choice of translation. It was a rough sketch. I estimated the amount of space I had to do it in. I said to Vin, 'This is how it will look. Let's do a font that imitates my caps.' He flowed it in; it looked reasonable. The line breaks were okay. It looked okay on the computer. The computer is good at organizing text. Then fast forward: it is two years later. All the text is written, the illumination on the opposite full page is progressing, and I come back to the incipit.

Pen in hand, Donald was ready to execute the design. But the computer layout had to be translated into actual pen lettering.

"Now I'm not so sure I like this; it's too squashed." He paused for effect to let this sink in.

"This is where a switch in your head takes place. I start trying to write it. The counter spaces were too big. It was too flimsy. There is too little text and too big a hole."

Fine writing is all about the balance of weight and proportion. In Donald's hands, it is an extremely subtle visual language. The progress of the pen across the page is like a dance, and he was alone on a very large dance floor. The balance was all off.

"There is that subtle point calligraphers look for where the whole thing holds together. You don't want light blasting through the letters from behind. You don't want the line to disintegrate like an old piece of lace."

He went back to Vin; they continued to re-jig the layout on the computer, using what Donald had learned with the pen. Donald's studio assistant had to re-rule the page three times as the layout changed and changed again.

In the end, Donald said, "The computer has to follow the pen: that's a key understanding. It's a tool, not a magic thing."

Tools for vellum

WHILE THE COMPUTER has become an ordinary part of our post-industrial officescape, the other tools in the Scriptorium are more specialized. The preparation, ruling up and storage of the vellum require a host of tools and skills which are more unusual.

Donald and Sally Mae Joseph established a pattern of preparation for the vellum which has been carried on with minor refinements ever since. Mark L'Argent, who was the studio assistant for two years beginning in June 2000, told me they had discovered that "preparing the vellum in the driest season of the year is best; the skins are more stable. They're easier to prepare, easier to write on. On the flesh side, they aren't so coarse." He paused a moment. "The only thing coarse in the studio is my language."

The raw skins are cut to working size using a wooden template, like a picture frame. After they have been scrutched, they are ready for ruling up. This is done at a large drafting table with an attached parallel motion set-square. The columns are marked with little prick marks. These are made either with a burin or with a pin held in a pencil-shaped device called a pin-vice. The lines on the hair side are ruled first, using a 2H pencil. Measurements permanently attached to the table give the proper alignment for the ruling up.

Ruling the flesh side is more problematic. The skins never entirely forget their original animal contours and never lie quite flat. When the skin is turned over, it will never lie in perfect geometric alignment to the ruling guides. But the lines ruled on the flesh side must register perfectly with those on the hair side.

"You're moving the surface of the skin as you rule up," Mark explained. The three-foot-long metal rule he uses to rule up shifts the skin every time he lays it down. He can see the lines showing through, which give him a guide. The pricked marks for the columns also give him a fixed point.

"I have to do it all by eyeball. There's lots of manipulating the pencil to get the lines to marry-up with the lines on the other side of the page. You have to keep your wits about you, really." Skins get handled again and again during the making. Sometimes, inevitably, tiny creases get made in them.

Different brushes serve varied functions. From left to right: a flat sable
brush for laying down washes; a coarse,
round decorators' bristle brush for
gestural, textured marks; a short mixing
brush; two stiff brushes for use
with casein and gouache; a stenciling
brush; and another mixing brush.

A dry brush may be used to loosen excess
gold after a gesso design has been gilded.

"I use a bone folder for extracting the creases I've made in my haste," Mark said. Bone folders are small tools, usually about five to eight inches long, which look a bit like tongue depressors. Made from real animal bone, they have gentle contours. They are often rounded at one end and gently pointed at the other. Placing a bit of soft card under the crease to act as a cushion, Mark uses the bone folder to gently flatten and push it down.

"Donald takes out creases with his thumbnail," Mark said. It's tricky. "You have to get the tension right."

He demonstrated how Donald would gently pull the skin with one hand, while carefully rubbing the crease out with his thumbnail. The principle is the same: a hard, flattish edge gradually pressing the skin into position—organic tool against organic surface, not too hard, not too rough, coaxing the skin rather than forcing it.

Another tool which is important for the vellum is the hygrometer. Sally Mae explained to me what this tool was for. "The hygrometer measures relative humidity in the atmosphere. We're becoming more aware of humidity and how it affects the skins. We were particularly concerned about some of the skins which had been worked on and which were beginning to show a lot of movement. We had Chris Clarkson, the binder and conservator, come in."

Clarkson is one of the most distinguished book conservators in the world. He has visited the Scriptorium at intervals to give advice about handling vellum and about how the book binding should influence design decisions. Shifts in humidity are a major concern.

"He's discussed with us the idea of getting an air conditioning unit for the studio. Right now, we keep the vellum in the plan chest:* it's a fairly constant fifty percent humidity in there. We were relieved that he wasn't too worried about it."

Sally continued, "I brought in a greenhouse hygrometer. It was really, really basic. I wanted to check the humidity when I was gilding." Gilding requires very moist conditions and works best on really damp days.

"Chris Clarkson was being all technical and asking all sorts of questions like, 'Does your hygrometer have a filament inside?'"

Sally began to laugh as she talked.

"He works in conservancy—it's a very high-tech business, and they're used to these really specialized tools. I was embarrassed by our little greenhouse hygrometer. I brought it out to show him. I mean it doesn't even have measurements on it: it just says 'DAMP' on one side and 'DRY' on the other."

Big laugh. "Clarkson was amused."

Two new high-tech hygrometers now keep watch over the Scriptorium, one in each room of the studio.

Donald told me, "They're quite hypnotic: we rush from one to the other, comparing the readings. This will give us solid information about the ideal humidity for the Bible skins. Because we know how a skin should look, we can tell when it is either too dry or too wet. We'll come up with a definitive ideal humidity for the place where the Bible is eventually kept."

Tools for writing

THERE WAS A TIME not that long ago when you could walk into a stationers' shop and simply buy a quill.

Donald told me, "We have Victorian price lists. They had seven or eight grades of quills on offer, ranging from pennies to several shillings. I'm still using Victorian quills I was given over thirty years ago."

These days quills are harder to find. The shops no longer stock them and the birds themselves are different. Most people don't even know what to look for.

"I was lucky. I know what a quill should look like. I was around at just the right time. My teacher, M.C. Oliver, didn't have to think about it—he just went into a shop and bought them."

*Sally uses the term plan chest to describe what Americans usually call a flat file. It is a chest of shallow drawers large enough to accommodate large sheets of paper or vellum without folding or rolling them.

Donald Jackson holds a condor feather in one hand and part of a goose wing in the other as he gives an impromptu lecture on the identification and selection of feathers for quills to a visiting museum curator and designer.

Jars filled with goose and
swan feathers await
selection and curing.

Donald does have to think about it.

"I'm not interested in the cookery side of calligraphy," he said. But he has had to take an interest in his tools and how they are made because he is one of the few people who have seen, touched and used the old traditional tools. When he set out on his scribal career, there were still little pockets of trade left over from the Victorian era and the tools and materials which were available reflected a different level of craftsmanship. He is not romantic about it; these tools were well made because they had a job to do. And now that there is no significant demand for quills, it is no wonder they are hard to come by. Donald is poised between his teachers' generation, which took good quills for granted, and a younger generation which has never seen or used the real thing. He knows what he is looking for. The trick is finding it.

"Like cooking, the key is in the ingredients," Donald said. "Most geese are produced for the table." The result is a young bird with underdeveloped flight feathers. "I am looking for feathers from mature birds. Any hunter would know this: the gander that leads the skein is completely different from the neophyte who brings up the rear. There's a vast difference—pounds of difference in weight." Their feathers, too, are different.

"I found a swan's wings under a power line. The whole carcass was there. It must have flown into the power line; if a fox had killed it, it would have eaten the feathers. I brought back the wings, which were intact."

I asked if chance encounters with dead birds were the only way to find feathers.

"No, not at all. Last Easter we were given quills by Scott Cleland who collected them in Minnesota.

They were top quality, mature Canada goose flight feathers." He'd picked them up from a field the geese frequented.

The feathers for quill-making come from the leading edge of the wing—the first three flight feathers at the very end of each wing. Ideally, flight feathers from the left wing are used by right handed scribes; the gentle curve of the quill sits comfortably in the hand.

"What kinds of birds provide the best quills?" I asked.

"Turkey, swan and goose."

"Can you describe the different properties of the birds? What is a turkey quill like?"

"Turkey is more rigid than the other two. It can be quite big. The barrel wall of the quill is thicker, not as pliable, not so generous with ink flow. It can be like writing with a stick. So you have to make a larger slit and longer shape to the end of the pen. The 'shoulder' of the cut quill starts further back—but this then adds its own structural problems."

"And swan?"

"Swan and goose are from the same family. They're 'gallinaceous.' The swan is larger than goose. Turkey is from a different family of bird altogether." Donald's impatience began to rise. "The best and most important thing you can say is that a mature bird gives you a strong and not overly pliable quill." It is not about three 'brands' of bird which give you differing quills; it is about knowing how to cut a quill with sensitivity. Donald looks for certain qualities in a pen. He wants a quill which combines strength and suppleness in a very subtle balance. When he cuts the quill, he does not follow a formula. He adjusts the length of the various cuts he makes to the hardness and suppleness of the feather in his hand. He literally feels his way along. He can do that because he knows exactly what the ideal tool feels like in the hand.

Before quills can be cut, however, they have to be prepared. Raw quills are too supple and go soft when kept wet—as, for instance, when subjected to several hours of dipping in wet ink. The curing is a hardening process, like tempering steel. It involves plunging the barrel of the quill in hot sand. Mark does much of the curing.

"We started with ninety-four quills at last curing," Mark told me. "Donald selected, graded and discarded. He got rid of quills with oval-section barrels (quills are best with round barrels). He also rejected soft ones and quills with thin barrel walls. This whittled them down to perhaps fifty. After we cured these, Donald figured about five were just right. Donald calculated his time, Sally's time, my time—it worked out to £45 (or about $75) a quill!"

Donald said to me, "The key problem was this: the ingredients themselves were of poor quality. The goose quills were borderline in the first place because they were from young birds." Perhaps they were lucky to get even five out of the lot.

I asked Mark to take me through the curing process.

"First I cut the end off with quill knife and leave the quills to soak in water for twenty-four hours. The next day I take out the little internal membrane, and warm up the sand in a frying pan on an electric stove."

The traditional method involves quickly filling the empty barrel of the quill with hot sand, and then plunging the barrel into the sand in the skillet.

"We no longer plunge quills in sand; there was no visual control doing it that way. So now, I fill them first, then pour sand over the quill while rotating it. I can watch the color of the barrel change."

Small fragments of lace mounted on cardboard are used to make stamped designs. Their delicate patterns enliven the margins and backgrounds of some of the illuminations.

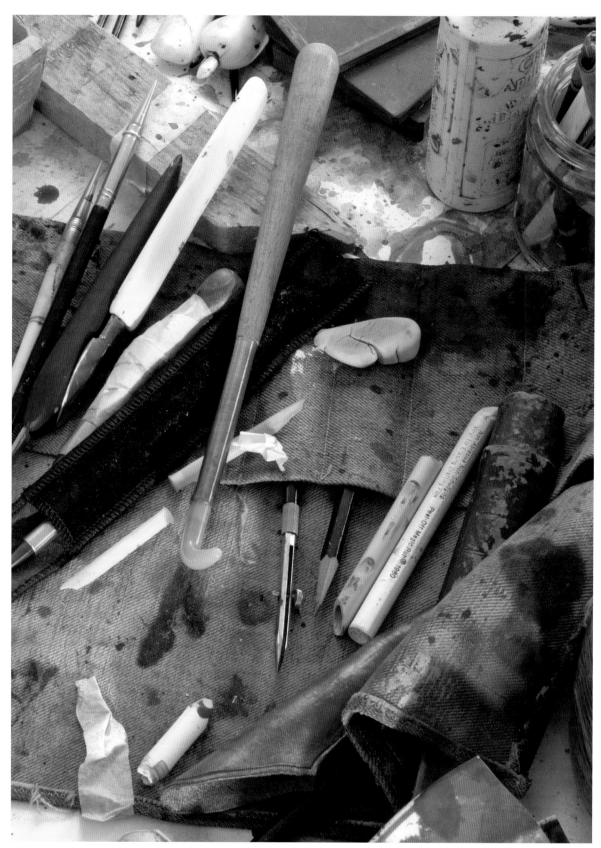

Well-worn tools reflect the hand of the craftsman. Donald Jackson has used many of these burnishers and knives for decades. He sharpens his own knives, carefully honing the edge to achieve exactly the sharpness needed. His burnishers are likewise shaped precisely to serve their intended function.

The hematite burnisher in the foreground was made by Donald Jackson forty years ago. The shape of the tool conforms to a pattern favored by the early twentieth-century master gilder, Graily Hewitt.

"What are you looking for?" I asked.

"I'm waiting for it to go from milky to clear. It gives me real control of what I'm doing. This way I don't leave it too long in the hot sand. It cuts down on quills cracking and going brittle."

The cured quills are stored in a jar. When the time comes for Donald to cut them, Mark cuts the feathery end off. He trims away the long barbs on one side, leaving the shorter barbs from the leading edge of the wing.

I asked Donald if he himself cut all the quills.

"Originally I cut them all so I could determine if they were good quills. So the scribes were provided with hand-cut quills. Now they're so good at cutting and keeping quills in shape, theoretically they could keep the same quill for months and months."

"Doesn't the end get blunt? Don't they have to recut their quills?" I asked.

"The biggest misapprehension is that you would keep changing your quill: you get the hang of one quill and you don't want to change it in any way. You get in a rhythm and relationship to a quill. Each quill has an individual personality—hardness, the way it lies in the hand—the slit needs to run clean and true, but when you know how to take care of your quill, there's very little you need to do to keep it sharp and crisp. First you might take two or three slivers off the underside. Then later you might take a sliver off each side and a shaving off the tip. You only recut them when you have to."

Later, Donald would reflect that he had underestimated the challenge the scribes would face as they tried keeping their quills in good condition. "That 'very little' they have to do," he said, "is like the 'very little' a heart surgeon has to do when making an aortic incision!"

The quill is not the only writing instrument used in The Saint John's Bible. Sally Mae told me about other tools the team uses.

"We have steel nibs for the footnotes," she said. "These are old pointed school nibs. Donald ground them down so they have a slight chisel edge. He gave a pair of these to me, Brian and Sue. There's a smaller one for red footnotes and a larger one for black notes."

These, too, need resharpening from time to time. They get freshened up by being gently rubbed against crocus cloth, a very fine sanding paper.

"They came out of a box in a plan chest in the studio," she said.

I asked Donald how old they were.

"They're just ordinary metal nibs from the 1950s," he told me. "They were making superb pen nibs in Britain well into the 1960s and 70s. Then the school market dried up. And the nibs were too good. Calligraphers were the only ones left buying nibs but they didn't buy enough. So this pattern has been discontinued."

Perhaps the most precious writing implement used on the project is also the most humble: a cut reed. This simple tool has a fine provenance. I'll let Sally tell the story herself. It begins at the house of Heather Child, editor of The Calligrapher's Handbook, and one of the most prominent English scribes of her generation.

"I went to visit Heather Child not long before she died. She loved the video I had made on gilding techniques. She sat and watched it through—all two and a half hours of it. Afterwards, she took me across to her studio. She pulled out a box containing about a dozen cut reed pens. She handed me three

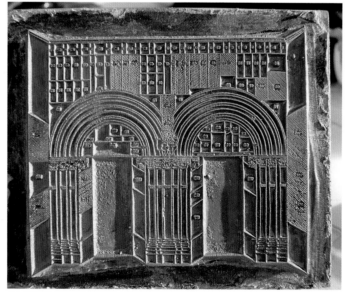

Rubber stamps are a modern addition to the illuminator's tool kit.

of them. She said to me, 'These were cut by Edward Johnston.' It was one of those awesome moments. You can't quite believe it's happening. I looked down at them and I thought, 'Blimey. Wow.'"

Edward Johnston founded the twentieth-century British calligraphy movement. His book *Writing & Illuminating & Lettering* is the foundational text of our tradition. Sally was holding his reed pens in her hand. Heather Child was giving them to her.

"It was so moving. I couldn't believe it."

She saved them for something special.

"I used them for the roughs of the *Magnificat* in Luke's Gospel. I wanted the effect of the pen not being completely and utterly sharp. I sanded off the edges slightly. It gave me a different feeling to a quill."

There's a wonderful practicality in that. Yes, these were Johnston's reed pens. But if they needed to be sanded to give the proper effect, then so be it. It is moving to be part of a calligraphic tradition and to use pens cut by our scribal forebears—but the real living tradition is to use the pens without fear and without being precious about them. So Sally sanded them to get the right shape. In a final irony, they weren't used on the actual Bible page.

"It was too bad. But I couldn't use the reed pen on the colored background: it lifted up the paint underneath. So I was going to use it, but in the end I used a slightly blunted quill."

Craftsmanship trumps romanticism every time.

Tools for cutting and scraping

"OUR QUILL KNIVES come from George Yanagita in America," Mark said to me as he handed me a sharp knife. It was delicately balanced. The wooden handle with its gentle curves sat comfortably in my palm.

"Everybody in the studio gets one. You have to sharpen and take care of them: Donald's and Sally's are well-lived in. Mine is sort of virgin. All of them are numbered." I looked at the number. George keeps a strict accounting of his work; every knife is recorded.

The quill knife is designed specifically for the cutting of quills. The edge of its blade is perfectly straight. One side of the blade is flat; the other is softly curved. In calligraphy circles there's a good deal of mystique surrounding these knives. I asked Donald why that was.

"The quill knife has a very particular shape. You need the curve on one side in order to help you make the curved cuts when shaping a quill. A perfectly straight blade, like a scalpel or X-acto blade, would want to slice in a straight line. In a quill, we're looking for that soft curve."

As Donald described the action, he made a curved motion with his hand, not unlike the motion one might make when peeling a potato with a small paring knife. I could see how the curve on the blade's side echoed the motion of the hand.

This very specialized knife blade is not easy to find. Over the years, Donald has had to teach people to grind and shape commercially available knives to the right shape.

"The nearest I could find was a German brand of wood chipping knife. But these were shaped like an X-acto knife—both sides of the knife were flat. I had to teach people to grind the blade down, to shape it and sharpen it. That was the only way I could provide the right kinds of knives. The curve is crucial; it helps you, it guides you."

George Yanagita now makes knives which, as Donald puts it, "fit the bill." But, like all craftsman's tools, they need to be taken care of.

"You can buy a sharp tool," Donald said. "But if you want to keep it that way you have to take responsibility for doing it. Every time you re-sharpen it, you have to be aware of what you are doing. I strop the blade with a polishing paper jewelers use."

"Is it a problem maintaining the blade?" I asked.

"Mostly stropping the blade is enough to keep it sharp. But when you strop it, you tend to round the flat side. From time to time, you need to grind it and reshape it."

George's knives, as fine as they are, lack one feature which the Victorians used in theirs: the Victorians had hollow-ground blades. Both sides of the Victorian blade were curved. The outer side was convex. The inner side was concave. The edge of the blade, therefore, had an even more acute angle than the edge of George's modern version. The result? The blade didn't blunt as quickly.

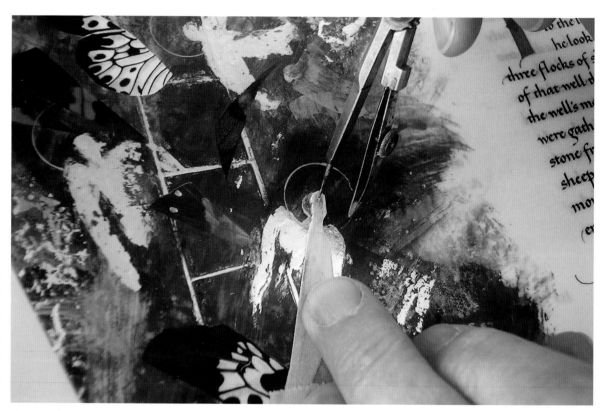

Donald Jackson uses an antique compass to mark a halo around the head of an angel. A small sliver of vellum holds the pointed end, protecting the vellum page underneath from puncture marks. The gold paint he uses is shell gold—pure gold ground to a fine powder and suspended in a gum or fish glue medium.

Nevertheless, George's knives are superbly honed tools. Donald described the absolute sharpness required of a quill knife.

"Cutting a quill, you want almost no burr on the knife. You can tell when a knife is perfectly sharp. It leaves a glassy edge on the quill barrel. Any roughness leaves a chalky edge."

You know you are talking to a craftsman when you reflect that the edge Donald is describing is only hundredths of a millimeter thick.

"When scraping vellum to erase mistakes, you need more tooth. That's why it's best not to erase with a quill knife," he added.

"Sally erases with hers," I countered.

"I know," he said, making no further comment.

Every craftsman has his or her own approach to the craft. I asked Sally to describe how she used the quill knife.

"I use it to cut quills—and to mend small mistakes, mistakes of just one or two letters. The secret to getting out mistakes is having a really sharp quill knife. That may seem obvious, but it's one of the things I had to learn. I didn't understand it until I had a really sharp knife. If you use a slightly dull knife, it leaves a slightly rough, textured surface. You can burnish it down but it's never the same. You have to keep the knife razor sharp."

The ideal tool for erasing is not the quill knife but an erasing knife. Donald has a fine old Victorian knife which he uses. It has a straight handle, terminating in a symmetrical, two-sided blade. The shield shape of the blade provides a perfect curvature for erasing mistakes. Its blade is also larger than that of a quill knife, so it is better suited to erasing large areas. (For large painted surfaces, simple sandpaper is used.)

"Donald has been trying to develop an erasing knife. It's sort of on the back burner," Mark told me. "Donald goes just so far with it, puts it down, then picks it up again."

I looked at the prototype blades at the Scriptorium—seven beautifully shaped samples by George Yanagita. They varied in size and shape. Some of them had blades tilted up from their handles; others were designed flush with their handles. Looking at them reminded me of displays of halberds in medieval armories: a fugue of variations in knife blades.

Donald wasn't so sure about any of these designs. He picked each up, feeling it in his hand. He fretted about how the handle might interfere with seeing the page. He toyed with different ways of holding the blade. I could see his hesitation.

"Then out of the blue," Sally said, "we received these new knives. All of a sudden they landed on the doorstep. They were George's idea."

The new erasing knives were based on a radically different design. Taking the vellum maker's specialist knife, the *lunellum*, as an example, George produced an erasing knife blade positioned like that of a hoe or an old-fashioned safety razor. The blade sits at ninety degrees to its handle.

"We weren't so sure about them at first. They were so different from what we were used to. But I started using mine. I got used to the way it handled. With it you can erase two lines of writing at a time. This knife has a flat area and curved area. You have to be careful using it; you can catch the corner and slice into the vellum. But I've got used to it, and it works rather well."

Donald, too, has begun using Yanagita's scraper and has been taken with it. For a man who claims no interest in "cookery," he gave a pretty good account of George's practices.

"George is using steel. Now when steel is too hard, it snaps. When it is too soft, it doesn't retain its edge. It's the age-old balance of flexibility and strength. In Japan, for example, when they made a traditional chisel, they tempered the first inch but the shank was left untempered. So when you hit it hard, the softer steel absorbed the blow without snapping."

Donald said he was glad to have George working on these knives. "I don't like making tools. George Yanagita adores making tools."

Tools for rubbing

A WELL-MADE BURNISHER is a beauty to behold. Shaped from agate or hematite, they come in different shapes and sizes suited to different tasks. Donald has a long flat agate burnisher which ends in a straight edge. He has others made of hematite and shaped like lipsticks. Sally has a set of antique agate burnishers which are long, thin and pointed, set into fine handles. Donald has even seen a burnisher made from an actual dog's tooth. Burnishers are used for rubbing the nap of the vellum down, smoothing rough patches of skin. They are used for gilding, pressing gold leaf into a gesso or acrylic medium, rubbing it down so it adheres to every contour of the support. They are used to polish and shape areas of gold, pressing hard on certain areas to make them shine or gently impressing shapes into the gold.

Like quill knives, good burnishers are not easily come by.

"When I was a student at the Central School of Arts and Crafts," Donald said, "I learned about an old gentleman, Victor Hughes, who had been a kind of technical assistant to Graily Hewitt."

Graily Hewitt, one of Edward Johnston's pupils, was particularly famous for his gilding. Through Victor Hughes, Donald was touching one of the great masters of the craft.

"He once made a burnisher for another student in M.C. Oliver's class. When I saw it, I told him I'd like to buy one as well. His response was to say, 'Go and find some hematite.'"

There was wisdom in that. He could have simply given Donald a price and produced a finished tool. Instead, he sent Donald on a quest. "I looked in rock shops. There were all sorts of hematite. I realized I didn't have any idea what I was looking for. When I went back to him, he showed me different unfinished pieces of stone. It gave me an understanding of what I needed for a burnisher. He did me a great favor."

That understanding would benefit Donald years later.

"I was gilding one day in the bathroom (as you do for the high humidity) and I dropped the burnisher in the iron bath. It chipped. But because he had led me through the process, I knew how to reshape it."

Donald has passed that knowledge on to his own students, continuing the transmission of skill and craft from one generation to the next.

"One hematite burnisher I made thirty years ago became a prototype for a lot of what followed. In the States years ago, Louis Strick took a lost-wax cast of my burnisher. He sent the cast to Germany, to a maker for the dental market. They copied it and Louis offered it for sale.

"Lou is an incredibly important part of the last three decades in the story of contemporary calligraphy in the United States. His Pentalic Corporation stocked tools, materials, books, everything. He was a pioneer—he supplied all of America with calligraphers' materials in the seventies and eighties. Back in 1973, I included his address in teaching notes I gave out in California. Someone picked his name up from the notes and he made it into the second *Whole Earth Catalog*."

I pictured Graily Hewitt, the former barrister turned master calligrapher and gilder, working quietly in his rooms in Gray's Inn in London before the First World War. Could he ever have conceived of his work rippling out across the world through a medium as brash as the *Whole Earth Catalog* seventy years later?

Tools for gold

BESIDES BURNISHERS there are a host of tools used for gilding. Quills and brushes to lay gesso, gilding cushions and knives to cut the gold leaf, pieces of silk through which to press it into position—all the various tools of the gilder's trade have their place. Donald and Sally have both done gilding in the Bible. I asked Sally if they used any unusual tools.

"We use what's called 'Peel-off Magic Rub,'" she said, breaking into a loud laugh. "Sounds quite erotic, that! What does it say on the package? 'Non abrasive, non-smudging vinyl for erasing.' We use it for cleaning off unwanted gold. Sometimes gold adheres in spots where you don't want it. It's especially useful when gilding on watercolor backgrounds. The gold tends to stick to areas of color. It came from America. Mark had to track down someone who sold it; they were in Minneapolis as it turned out."

Donald said, "Diane von Arx Anderson went to a great deal of trouble to go and pick it up and ship it to us. Be sure to mention her."

Sometimes the use of tools has been a bone of contention. I asked Sally to describe how she used the gilders' cushion and knife and stumbled onto a clash of wills.

"At first, I didn't use it. I used scissors to cut the gold leaf, using the little piece of paper which comes interleaved with the gold as a support. This intensely irritated Donald. There were little bits of paper flying all over the studio, and he worried about the length of time it was taking for me to lay the gold."

As she told the story, she started to sputter a bit, hunting for the right words to describe what had happened.

"So I took his advice . . . No, he showed me how . . . No." She began laughing again.

"This grated on him so much. I decided . . . No. He made me . . . I'm struggling here." Now she was laughing hard.

"See, I did learn. I did. The method I was using took a bit longer. I'd never done such large areas of gilding. And time is crucial when you're laying gold. With a whole panel of gold to lay, Donald was worried that the gesso at the bottom was drying out. Cutting on a gilder's cushion, I could get the gold on the gesso faster. He showed me how."

She thought that over. "Of course, I knew how; I was just doing it a different way. But I did learn. I now have a more developed technique of laying gold."

Strong wills battled it out over the gilded *Magnificat*. In the end, Donald's way prevailed.

"I cut the gold on the gilders' cushion and pick it up by the corner with my finger like Donald does." The natural greasiness of the human finger acts like a magnet to gold.

"Immediately after I've breathed on the gesso, to moisten it and activate it, I can place the leaf. I have a silk handkerchief, which I can lay over the gold. I rub the burnisher straight onto the silk. Sometimes you get the silk pattern transferring onto the gold. It makes a beautiful texture. If on the other hand you don't want that, you can take a burnisher and rub it out again."

The tiny remnants of gold leaf left over from gilding are carefully saved. They can be ground into a powder and used in painting.

A utilitarian miscellany

I ASKED DONALD, Sally and Mark to name all the tools we'd missed—the answers came back fast and furious.

"I like china mixing palettes," Donald said. "And erasers—I prefer green ones. The more plastic ones leave shiny surface. They smear. The old typing eraser is better. It's actual rubber."

Sally mentioned her mortar and pestle. "I grind my own gum sandarac. I prefer a large mortar and pestle; you can see what you're doing. It gives you better control. And then there's the little linen bag to hold the sandarac. I use an old hankie tied up with masking tape." Tapping this little sandarac bag against the vellum dusts the surface with a small, even amount of the rosin-like powder.

"Don't leave out the Optivisor for cutting quills," Sally added, referring to a set of magnifying goggles. "Donald's and my eyes are getting old: we need it to see the detail. Mark thought he could do it without the Optivisor. Now he uses it too. We all need it; we're cutting very fine quills with a slightly oblique cut."

Mark said, "The sharpening stones are important. They're made of artificial diamond in a honeycomb grid. They're so incredibly powerful—you just literally run the blade across once or twice. The surface stays truer than a traditional whetstone."

More tools—rubber rollers, ink stones, scalpels, self-healing cutting mats, sand paper, Frisket for masking areas of color.

Sally Mae brought up the lamps: were they tools, or furniture?

"Lamps with daylight bulbs are crucial as well. They are absolutely essential for fine work, like cutting quills. I always have the lamp on when cutting quills. Donald discourages use of desk lamps when working on vellum, because of the heat they generate."

Donald described brushes of all kinds and shapes. Hog's hair for large areas, sable brushes for finer work. "It's probably libelous to say so, but the quality of sable brushes is not what it used to be. I'm convinced they've changed."

More tools—face masks to protect the scrutchers from vellum particles in the air. Paper towels, scissors and bits of old lace for printing. The photocopier. A little disk, like a slide rule, Donald uses to calculate percentages of reduction and enlargement. This was a gift from a retired Pittsburgh lettering artist. New tools, old tools, rare tools, common tools.

Sometimes tools take on a life of their own.

Sally said, "We make designs for rubber stamps, and send them to a firm in Cardiff where they make them for us. They scan the designs on a computer, make a mould and produce our stamps. Sometimes we cut our own out of Mars plastic erasers using surgical scalpels. I did that for the *Tree of Life* at the end of Luke."

The illuminators who work away from the Scriptorium have taken to the idea.

"We gave Thomas Ingmire one of the geometrical stamps. But then we had a page come back from Suzanne Moore with the same stamp. We spotted it and did a double-take—wasn't that Thomas' stamp?"

"What was going on?" I asked.

"Suzanne saw some of Thomas' work and liked the shape of the stamp. Thomas sent her an impression and she had one made for herself. When she sent her work to us, we recognized the stamp. It feels like they're being cloned all over North America."

"It's Donald's 'spiritual arithmetic' in action, isn't it?" I said. Exponential grace, multiplying across the continents in the form of a simple rubber stamp.

PART 2

THE PRODUCT

In part 2, we turn to a chronological history of the making of The Saint John's Bible. *The volumes are discussed here in the order they were written. Those who are familiar with the text of the Bible will immediately recognize that the volumes of* The Saint John's Bible *were not written in the same order in which they appear in the canon.*

Gospels and Acts *was the first volume to be produced. It not only is the most heavily illuminated of the seven volumes but also holds a central place in the liturgical and devotional life of the church. For the client, it was important to begin the project with this most important of biblical texts.*

In each chapter of this section, I note important variations in the format and layout of each volume. Key illuminations are discussed in detail.

CHAPTER 9

GOSPELS AND ACTS

Delivered in May 2002

THE THING ABOUT the beginning of the project was that there was no beginning, at least not for Donald Jackson. This may come as a surprise—after all, the Bible project was announced to the public in a series of highly choreographed events, each of which seemed to mark a splashy, exciting start to this major undertaking. But put yourself in Donald's shoes. I have already described in chapter 1 how he wooed his client, opening a conversation that ended in a signed contract. But that is just the broadest overview of what actually happened. By the time Donald actually set to work on the Bible itself, he had been working on it for several years, producing proposals, attending conferences, schmoozing, talking to important players in the monastic and university community, meeting potential donors, and creating schedules and draft layouts. It's hard to set a date for when the project formally "began." Instead, the process was a deepening relationship between artist and client, a gradual establishment of trust, and a growing commitment to collaboration on the part of both parties.

Everyone knew there was significant risk involved. This project would cost money. Serious money. And that would have to be raised from new donors, since the project had to be self-supporting. It would commit both artist and client to a major time commitment, lasting many years. And it would be a defining project for both Saint John's and Donald Jackson. Reputations were on the line. As a result, Donald and Saint John's were prudent and tested the waters. The monastic community continued to discuss and debate the project, and Donald continued to present ideas about what it might look like and what kind of work—and budget—it might entail.

In the end, talk can go only so far. There came a moment when the Saint John's community had to commit some funds to explore the feasibility of moving forward. In 1997, the University and Abbey provided a seed grant so Donald could produce sketches, samples of the text script, and Psalms openings. Donald hired Vin Godier as his graphics and computer expert and purchased Macintosh computers, a large-format printer, and design software. This is when Donald first felt the project was actually getting underway. The project was still in its developmental stage, as there was still no contract to actually make the Bible, but the seed money represented a first step toward an ongoing working relationship. Saint John's had now committed real funds to the project, and Donald began to reconfigure his Scriptorium to make room for it.

Once the sketches were produced, Saint John's decided to move ahead, and contract negotiations began. This was a busy time for Donald. "You have to remember," he said to me, "in the period of 1997 to 1998, I had a business, the Calligraphy Centre, that employed between five and seven people. I needed to begin winding down the business." In addition, he was serving at that time as Master of the Scrivener's Company, one of the historic Guilds of the City of London. "I still had official duties in the City," he said. All of this made for a busy period as he shifted gears and prepared to take on the largest project he had ever tackled.

In April 1998, Saint John's University and Abbey signed a contract with Donald to create The Saint John's Bible. The contract envisioned a project lasting six years and costing one million pounds. The signing took

The Beatitudes illumination from Matthew
was created by Thomas Ingmire.

place at Saint John's, and Donald used a large, theatrical quill to sign the document. This was the first public event that announced the beginning of the project, the culmination of three years of negotiations.

Was this the beginning? It was a major turning point. But so much had gone before that perhaps we should quote Churchill and say it was the end of the beginning. Now the actual book would be made. Little did they know at the time that the manuscript would eventually take thirteen years to bring to completion.

It was decided from the outset that the Bible would be produced in seven volumes, using the Roman Catholic canon, which includes the Apocryphal books and a slightly different ordering from Protestant Bibles. Saint John's asked Donald to begin, not with Genesis, but with Gospels and Acts, the most ambitious and most heavily illuminated volume.

The making of that first volume was, then, doubly complicated: the format, styles of writing, and techniques of illumination all had to be worked out as the first volume was being created. Decisions made now would have to be carried through the rest of the project. And Donald and Saint John's had to learn the hard way how they would work together. It's nice to toss around words like collaboration and community, but anyone who has ever tried to work in collaboration or to create a community-based project knows that conflict and tension are natural parts of the process. A good community is not one without conflict; rather, it is one that knows how to work through disagreement and misunderstanding to build a better relationship.

The Saint John's Bible was not simply one man's vision of the Bible; it was not made by Donald working alone. It was, instead, created through a process that involved people bringing their insights and talents to the common task. Groups at Saint John's worked to articulate the main themes that should be addressed in the design and to provide scholarly background about the biblical text. On the artistic side of the project, Donald chose a group of scribes to write the text and a group of artists to work with him to create the illuminations. At the center of all these groups, Donald as artistic director pulled together all the different contributions, making sure that the final manuscript cohered, held together.

Decisions

NOW THAT THE PROJECT was underway, Donald and his client had to decide how they would organize their collaboration. The sketches he had produced were theoretical, not finished designs set in stone. It had to be decided who would function as Donald's contact people at Saint John's and how he and they would work together. The original structure Saint John's set up was a Production Committee with Michael Patella, OSB, as chair. The first director of the Production Committee was Valerie Kolarik. She stayed for a year, after which Carol Marrin was appointed as the overall director. This structure would evolve significantly over the course of the project.

In addition, Donald sought guidance from his client on what parts of the text would be illuminated. Fr. Michael Patella and Fr. David Cotter created a document known as the "schema." Going through the whole Bible, from Genesis to Revelation, the schema identified all the topics for the illuminations, and it specified a size for each one: full page, third page, or quarter page. This document gave structure to the enterprise and indicated how Donald should begin laying out the pages. It also suggested the way that certain key stories and passages held more weight for the Saint John's community than others.

It was at this stage that certain principles began to be applied to the design of the Bible. The pictures in the book were quite consciously referred to as *heavy illuminations,* indicating that they would not be merely literalistic illustrations but stand as interpretive visual meditations on the text. The distinction was important: Donald's evocative, collaged style of image making meshed beautifully with the monastic community's practice of *lectio divina,* in which a slow reading of Scripture produces a body of associations, rather than a single closed reading of the text.

The selection of images in the schema also demonstrated that The Saint John's Bible would not simply be a rehash of tradition. Many familiar stories were, in fact, not selected for illumination, and some passages infrequently treated in the history of Christian art were given a prominent position in the schema. Noah's ark and the Tower of Babel did not make the cut, for example, while the female figure of Wisdom, or Sophia, who appears in Ecclesiastes and the Wisdom of Solomon, was to appear prominently.

The schema also had financial connotations. Donald said, "The schema was tailored to the budget. The budget was based on my average earnings from calligraphy and graphic design at the time and my estimated operating costs." Donald provided a formula that laid out how much time (and therefore money) would be needed for each size of illumination. A full page was allotted twenty days; a third page, fifteen days; a quarter page, ten days. The schema broke that budget down into a specific list. Another category of illumination was referred to as *medium* and meant for text enhancement. (These later became known as special treatments.) A quarter-page medium would be two and a half days; a third page, seven and a half

The Calming of the Storm, by Suzanne Moore, spreads across the fold at Matthew 9.

days. Finally, there was an allowance for *light*, additional decoration. At this stage there was no time allotted for chapter capitals or book headings. As he explained, "The question they were asking was, 'How much illumination will this budget buy us?'"

The illuminations were subject to an approval process; Donald was asked to provide sketches for each illumination as it took shape, working in concert with his client. As the project developed, this would be a subject of some tension, as artist and client learned to work together.

In addition to illuminations, certain biblical passages were selected as deserving of greater visual elaboration. These are referred to as "special treatments." The intention of the special treatments is to celebrate specific passages by writing them larger than the main text and selecting a unique script for each one. The special treatments often include gilding and colored backgrounds. They are not, however, as elaborate as full-scale illuminations and do not involve pictorial elements. They are always intended to be legible. Unlike the illuminations, special treatments were not subject to detailed guidance or approvals from the client, and Donald was free to create them as he wished.

The frontispiece of the Gospel according to Mark shows John the Baptist in the foreground. Behind him, the drama of Jesus' temptation in the wilderness unfolds. This is the only place in The Saint John's Bible where the Baptist, the patron of the monastery, appears.

In addition to illuminations and special treatments, marginal illustrations were to be another crucial visual addition to the Bible pages. Chris Tomlin, a natural history artist with a crisp, photorealist style, would be selected in 1999 to add the illustrations of plants and animals that ornament the margins.

In September 1998, Donald and Mabel Jackson flew to Collegeville for a formal blessing ceremony in the Great Hall. This was another highly public celebration of the inception of the project. And it was reminder that this was a very unusual project for our times—a collaboration between artist and patron to produce a Bible on a magnificent scale and the product of a functioning religious community.

Now many things had to come together very rapidly. Donald set out immediately to begin sourcing the vellum, selecting William Cowley, a British manufacturer, after a global search for suppliers. Donald began deciding on the page size and format and started to get his head around who he might ask to collaborate with him artistically.

Publicity

BUT NOW I have to interrupt. Yes, this is a story about an artist at work, and we should be talking about tools and vellum and gold going onto the page. But *Smithsonian Magazine* needs Donald for an interview. A potential donor is waiting in his corner office high above the streets of Minneapolis, and he wants to meet the artist. NBC would like to book Donald for a morning newscast. It will be brief, won't take any time at all. Can he be at the studio at five o'clock in the morning for makeup?

It is so tempting to think an artist sits in his studio and thinks deep thoughts while giving his full attention to the sketch in front of him. And many days, life in the Scriptorium was like that. But the reality was that the project could not go forward without generating a buzz in the press and spending time cultivating the donors who would be so generous and help fund the Bible.

Press releases are wonderful things, and they serve an important function, but in the end, a lot of people wanted and needed face time with Donald. And many of those people were not in Wales but in the United States.

Donald told me, "I had to be open to doing publicity. Fortunately I have had to 'sell' calligraphy and its role as a unique means of communication all my working life."

An artist who did not know how to handle the media could have made major missteps. Donald said, "There was concern on the part of the Saint John's people about how the media would view the project. I was concerned too, because I know the media thrives on controversy. It's easy to say the wrong thing. But in fifteen years I have experienced nothing but genuine interest and enthusiasm across the board for the project."

The media interest often happened in short, intense bursts, especially on Donald's trips to the States. And it took a toll on the production of the Bible. Donald commented, "It did break up the work. It affected our rhythm and productivity."

It could also be exhausting. "I've sometimes sat down and given five different angles to five different newspapers or TV stations in one day. Each one wants their own story." After each trip to the States, Donald needed several days to recover. He couldn't simply fly home, show up in the Scriptorium, and set to work a day later.

This aspect of the making of the Bible is actually a crucial part of the story. From the inception of the project, both Donald and Saint John's knew that Donald would have to be pulled away from the drawing board to travel and promote the project. And they budgeted funds to pay for these trips. What neither party had calculated, however, was that as the interest spread these interruptions would be as extensive as they were and that they would quickly begin to have an impact on the production schedule itself. They slowed the project down.

The first illumination

IN EARLY 1999, Donald was still working by himself at the Scriptorium. Even though the page size was not fully fixed and the layout of the book was in its early, tentative stages, he was asked to create the very first full-page illumination, the *Genealogy of Christ* that appears as the frontispiece to the Gospel according to Matthew. This would be unveiled publicly in Minnesota and New York in March 1999.

I asked him how he felt when he first began to make the actual manuscript. Was he full of excitement? Exhilaration? "What I most often felt was dread," he answered. "I needed to generate a level of nervous energy, as a kind of fuel for action. So much of the preparation is internal. The marks themselves are often drawn from a combination of desperation and passion."

The guidance Donald received from the client was, at this stage, rather minimal. "It came straight from the schema," Donald said. "Other than some early face-to-face discussion with the Production Committee at Saint John's, there was no detailed brief at that stage. Just a five-line description, beginning: 'The genealogy contains the whole sweep of Jewish history. . . . Abraham, David, Tamar, Bathsheba, and Ruth should be highlighted.'"

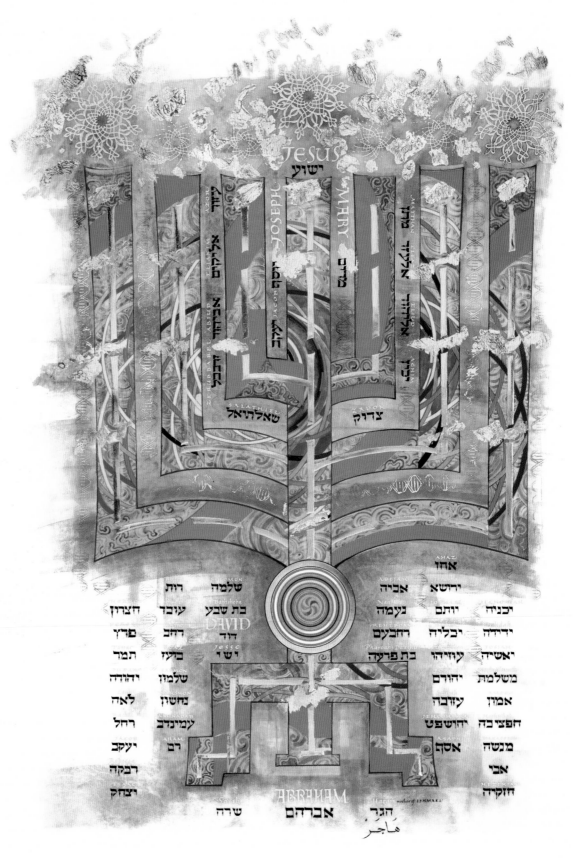

The *Genealogy of Christ* appears as the frontispiece to Matthew's Gospel. This was the first illumination made for The Saint John's Bible.

The first chapter of Matthew's Gospel traces the lineage of Jesus back through David to Abraham. The schema highlights this chapter as a sign of continuity, rooting the Gospel in the traditions of the Old Testament. In Donald's illumination, the names of Christ's ancestors appear in Hebrew sprinkled across the page.

"I was on my own—I had to work it out," Donald recalls. "My idea was to suggest a bridge between the Old Testament and the New, so I used the menorah as a foundation of the design to acknowledge Christianity's Jewish roots."

Donald viewed this family tree as an "invocation of the idea of a family of all people, including your family and mine." He included small DNA helixes as symbols of life passed from one generation to another. And he envisioned the menorah here as a tree of life: "It has a springing point, a circle: the core from which all life comes."

He incorporated imagery from other, non-Christian cultures into the illumination. The illumination "implies a kinship with other spiritual teachers—that's why I introduced Islamic roundel motifs and mandala fragments from the Buddhist visual tradition. A tiny word written in Arabic quietly emphasizes Hagar, Ishmael's mother." This makes a quiet visual link to the third great Abrahamic faith, Islam.

Donald said his ultimate aim was to suggest the "connectedness of all seekers of enlightenment. All paths lead to God."

The illumination completed, Donald prepared to fly to Minneapolis, where it was to be shown to the public at an event at the Minneapolis Institute of Arts. He said, "This unveiling was a major turning point both for Saint John's and for me."

At the last minute, however, there was a sudden flurry of concern: Would the image prove offensive to the Jewish community? Would they see the use of the menorah as an act of appropriation? It was even suggested that perhaps he create something else—ditch this illumination and replace it in a matter of days. Or perhaps he could cover the menorah with leaves, to make it into more of a tree.

Cooler heads prevailed. Donald brought the illumination, unchanged, to Minnesota. "We showed the page to Evan Mauer who was at that time the director of the MIA and was a great supporter of the project from the start. He is also a devout Jew. He turned to Brother Dietrich [the president of the University] and said, 'We are all men of the book. We must have The Saint John's Bible on exhibit here.'"

Everyone was relieved. And this moment proved to be an important hurdle. Seeing the positive reaction, both Saint John's and Donald could see that they were on the right course and that they could trust one another. Donald said the unveiling demonstrated that "there was a public acceptance of what I was doing. It was striking the right note. And there was a new level of acceptance from my client as well. They saw that people were reacting positively to the work."

After the successful unveiling in Minneapolis, Donald took the illumination to New York, where it was shown at the New York Public Library. There it was greeted with a similarly warm reception. The project was up and running and in the public eye.

Staffing

IN 1999, the Scriptorium began to hum with activity. Donald now had to begin finding staff for an operation that was rapidly growing. This included hiring managers for his studio and his office and looking for scribes to help him write the text and artists to collaborate with him on illustrations. It was clear he was not going to produce the book entirely alone but would pull together a team that would create it with him.

This sketch closely resembles the finished illumination. The tightly drawn menorah on the upper left would later become much more abstract and the piece would become more layered. The basic elements of the design have, however, been resolved.

He was at the helm as artistic director, and he would produce most of the illuminations, but he knew he would need the help of others.

Sally Mae Joseph joined the project in June to function as studio manager. She would also be one of the main scribes and lettering artists. Olivia Edwards joined the Scriptorium staff as production manager in the summer of 1999 and held this position until the spring of 2001 when she was succeeded by Rebecca Cherry, who remained production manager until 2007. And plans were laid to hire and train the scribes who would help Donald write the text. In the meantime, Donald and Vin Godier continued to lay out pages on the computer in preparation for the arrival of the scribes.

At this early stage, a new issue also arose, one that would complicate the project significantly. The contract specified that the translation selected for The Saint John's Bible was to be the responsibility of the client. When Saint John's selected the New Revised Standard Version (NRSV), this had serious implications for the design process. As I described in chapter 4, the NRSV has stringent formatting guidelines that must be followed. Although Donald was able to negotiate some aspects of the design with the NRSV, in many respects his ability to shape the text became restricted. Negotiations over formatting decisions began in the summer of 1999. This had a huge impact on production, as it again slowed the whole process down. This was not something Donald had banked on when he created his original schedule.

The experience of creating the first illumination had demonstrated the fact that Donald needed more detailed guidance from the Production Committee for the creation of the illuminations. At first the Production Committee, as representatives of the Saint John's community, felt responsible to directly supervise the artist, making sure he delivered to a tight schedule. This was not going to be a fruitful way to work, either for the committee or for Donald and his team.

The name of the committee was changed to the Committee on Illuminations and Text, which clarified its role as more of collaboration with the artist than as a supervisory body. They began to create the series of extensive briefs that would guide the illuminations from this point on.

By the opening days of 2000, the page size and main scripts had been finalized, and Donald was ready to train a team of scribes to join him. In February, Donald invited five calligraphers to take part in an intensive series of master classes. These were all highly skilled, professional scribes. At the end of the classes, just three scribes—Sally Mae Joseph, who worked permanently at the Scriptorium, Sue Hufton, and Brian Simpson, who worked at their own studios—joined the project and were ready to begin writing. Mark L'Argent had been hired by this time as a studio assistant and spent many hours preparing vellum for the scribes and curing goose wing feathers for quill pens. Sarah Harris took over Mark L'Argent's position in October 2002. She would stay on for many years, replacing Sally Mae as studio manager in the summer of 2005. She later became assistant artistic director of the Heritage Program in May 2008.

The writing begins

THE FIRST WORDS of The Saint John's Bible were penned on Ash Wednesday, March 8, 2000, in Donald's Scriptorium in Wales. A camera crew arrived and set up its lights and cameras. Donald wrote the opening of the Gospel according to John: "In the beginning was the Word." The filming of the first words marked yet another "beginning" to the project. That same month, *Newsweek* magazine dubbed the project "America's Book of Kells."

Now the scribes began writing their regular allotment of pages. They dispersed to their homes, scattered

Hazel Dolby's special treatment, *You Shall Love the Lord*, appears opposite Luke 9.

across Britain, and churned out page after page. At intervals, they would return to the Scriptorium for detailed critique and encouragement and to compare their writing. Each letter would often be stripped down to the bare bones of its structure, and there were always the regular "quill clinics." They worked together for two or three days and then returned home again to continue writing.

Donald remembers this period fondly. "We got into a rhythm working together in the same room. You heard nothing but the scratching of the pens against the vellum." He laughed as he remembered this: "Or you heard the scraping of a knife," indicating someone had made a mistake and was erasing a part of the text they'd written. The energy in the room could be intense and focused. "You heard breathing, or the creaking of a chair."

The scribes continued to write until September 2005. Their work surged ahead of the schedule for illuminations, and they moved from one volume to the next more quickly than Donald did.

As the scribes embarked on the writing, it became clear how hard the task was. "Consistent, lively, harmonious writing is the most difficult thing," Donald said. "It is harder than painting or creating an illumination. The biggest surprise was how little time in a week the scribes could devote to the writing. This was because not only did they have busy lives and other projects, but also it was due to the sheer difficulty of maintaining sustained, intense concentration for long periods of writing. People could only physically handle so many hours of writing on any given day."

Although the scribes worked steadily and dutifully, with tremendous care and attention to detail, their work went more slowly than had been anticipated.

Design

BY THE TIME the scribes started writing, the basic hierarchy governing the page was set. The book headings, with their strong blocks of color, divided the text into clear sections. The text script was well-defined (although it must be said that it evolved subtly over the years). The other scripts for poetry and notes, as well as the chapter numbers, had their fixed forms. The all-capital incipit script was used to mark the beginning of each book. Space was left for the drop-caps that mark the main divisions within each chapter.

In autumn 2000 Chris Tomlin traveled to Saint John's to begin studies for the animal and plant illustrations that populate the margins of many pages. In *Gospels and Acts*, these serve a decorative function and help balance the visual pace of the volume. Donald commented, "Many of the creatures depicted are native to Minnesota and link the volumes with the environment around the Abbey and University of Saint John's."

The first special treatments also appear in this volume. The design challenge was enormous, because the special treatments were part of the continuous text of the book. They therefore had to be placed correctly in the sequence of the text, and they had to respect the NRSV formatting guidelines. This constrained Donald's options as he laid out the text with Vin on the computer. He not only had to guess at the amount of space to be left for each special treatment but also had to worry about how the text would be placed on the page. The three separate special treatments that appear at the beginning of Luke's Gospel jockey for our attention, and Donald

The last book of the volume ends with a cosmic vision of the spread of the Christian faith to the "ends of the earth"—and beyond.

MARK

THE
SHORTER ENDING
OF MARK

[[And all that had been commanded them they told briefly to those around Peter. And afterward Jesus himself sent out through them, from east to west, the sacred and imperishable proclamation of eternal salvation.]]

THE
LONGER ENDING
OF MARK

9 [[Now after he rose early on the first day of the week, he appeared first to Mary Magdalene, from whom he had cast out seven demons. ¹⁰She went out and told those who had been with him, while they were mourning and weeping. ¹¹But when they heard that he was alive & had been seen by her, they would not believe it. After this he appeared in another ¹² form to two of them, as they were walking into the country. ¹³And they went back & told the rest, but ¹⁴ they did not believe them. Later he appeared to the eleven themselves as they were sitting at the table; and he upbraided them for their lack of faith and stubbornness, because they had not believed those who saw him after he had risen. ¹⁵And he said to them, "Go into all the world & proclaim the good news to the whole creation. ¹⁶The one who believes and is baptized will be saved; but the one who does not believe will be condemned. ¹⁷And these signs will accompany those who believe: by using my name they will cast out demons; they will speak in new tongues; ¹⁸they will pick up snakes in their hands, and if they drink any deadly thing, it will not hurt them; they will lay their hands on the sick, and they will recover." So then the Lord Jesus, after he had ¹⁹ spoken to them, was taken up into heaven and sat down at the right hand of God. ²⁰And they went out and proclaimed the good news everywhere, while the Lord worked with them & confirmed the message by the signs that accompanied it.]]

f Other ancient authorities add *Amen*
g Other ancient authorities add, in whole or in part, *And they excused themselves, saying, "This age of lawlessness and unbelief is under Satan, who does not allow the truth and power of God to prevail over the unclean things of the spirits. Therefore reveal your righteousness now"—thus they spoke to Christ. And Christ replied to them, "The term of years of Satan's power has been fulfilled, but other terrible things draw near. And for those who have sinned I was handed over to death, that they may return to the truth and sin no more, that they may inherit the spiritual and imperishable glory of righteousness that is in heaven."*
h Or gospel
i Other ancient authorities lack in their hands
k Other ancient authorities add Amen.

Modern biblical scholarship recognizes the fact that the Bible has come down to us with many variant texts. The NRSV includes footnotes that record these different readings. In Mark, which has two different endings, these textual variants are lengthy, producing an interesting layout dilemma: how to indicate these two alternative texts. Here, small frames contain the headings for each text, echoing the format of the main book headings.
A large illustration of monarch butterflies by Chris Tomlin fills the empty last column.

All the basic elements are in place in the rough
sketch. The design does not, however, tie in
to the text. In the final version text and image
overlap and become a subtly
integrated whole.

The use of rubber stamps allows patterns
to repeat and multiply across the page. The
fish are based on a Byzantine mosaic from
Tabgha in Galilee, identified by tradition as
the site of one of the miraculous feedings.
The spiral pattern of the Native American
basket suggests the exponential multiplication of loaves and fishes.

had little ability to rearrange their placement on the page. They had to be placed where they fell within the text.

Within this constraint, however, the special treatments still enliven the pages on which they appear and celebrate passages that have deep resonance within the liturgical and devotional life of the church. Hazel Dolby executed four special treatments in this volume, using her characteristic small painted capitals and subtle color. Sally Mae Joseph contributed four special treatments, including liturgically significant texts such as the *Magnificat* in Luke and Zechariah's prophecy.

Gospels and Acts is unique among the volumes in including "carpet pages." The term comes from art history and describes the elaborate decorative pages that punctuate some manuscripts made in Britain and Ireland in the period around the eighth century, such as the *Lindisfarne Gospels* and *Book of Kells*. Each book of *Gospels and Acts* opens with a full-page illumination on the verso, or left-side, page, and the text begins on the recto, or right-hand, page. All the other books in the other volumes begin wherever the previous book ends; the text flows continuously. This arrangement in *Gospels and Acts* causes some problems with layout, as the previous book may not finish on a right-side page, leaving a blank space at the end of the book. The inevitable show-through on the previous page also becomes a design issue.

Show-through can be ameliorated by painting an underlayer in light color, like a primer coat, before making the illumination. This effectively masks the dark colors that may be painted on top. But the problem of pacing is more serious. Matthew ends on the right side of the page, but there is a portion of the last column that is blank. The other three Gospels end with a full blank page.

The carpet pages were made by Sally Mae Joseph using stencils and rubber stamps. The patterns are often

6

He left that place and came whis home-town, and his disciples followed him. On the sabbath he began to teach in the synagogue, & many who heard him were astounded. They said, "Where did this man get all this? What is this wisdom that has been given to him? What deeds of power are being done by his hands? Is not this the carpenter, the son of Mary & brother of James and Joses & Judas & Simon, and are not his sisters here with us?" And they took offense at him. Then Jesus said to them, "Prophets are not without honor, except in their hometown, and among their own kin, and in their own house." And he could do no deed of power there, except that he laid his hands on a few sick people and cured them. And he was amazed at their unbelief.

Then he went about among the villages teaching. He called the twelve and began to send them out two by two, and gave them authority over the unclean spirits. He ordered them to take nothing for their journey except a staff; no bread, no bag, no money in their belts; but to wear sandals and not to put on two tunics. He said to them, "Wherever you enter a house, stay there until you leave the place. If any place will not welcome you and they refuse to hear you, as you leave, shake off the dust that is on your feet as a testimony against them." So they went out and proclaimed that all should repent. They cast out many demons, & anointed with oil many who were sick and cured them. King Herod heard of it, for Jesus' name had become known. Some were saying, "John the baptizer has been raised from the dead; and for this reason these powers are at work in him." But others said, "It is Elijah." And

others said, "It is a prophet, like one of the prophets of old." But when Herod heard of it, he said, "John, whom I beheaded, has been raised." For Herod himself had sent men who arrested John, bound him, and put him in prison on account of Herodias, his brother Philip's wife, because Herod had married her. For John had been telling Herod, "It is not lawful for you to have your brother's wife." And Herodias had a grudge against him, and wanted to kill him. But she could not, for Herod feared John, knowing that he was a righteous and holy man, and he protected him. When he heard him, he was greatly perplexed; and yet he liked to listen to him. But an opportunity came when Herod on his birthday gave a banquet for his courtiers and officers & for the leaders of Galilee. When his daughter Herodias came in & danced, she pleased Herod & his guests; and the king said to the girl, "Ask me for whatever you wish, and I will give it." And he solemnly swore to her, "Whatever you ask me, I will give you, even half of my kingdom." She went out and said to her mother, "What should I ask for?" She replied, "The head of John the baptizer." Immediately she rushed back to the king and requested, "I want you to give me at once the head of John the Baptist on a platter." The king was deeply grieved; yet out of regard for his oaths and for the guests, he did not want to refuse her. Immediately the king sent a soldier of the guard with orders to bring John's head. He went and beheaded him in the prison, brought his head on a platter, and gave it to the girl. Then the girl gave it to her mother. When his disciples heard about it, they came and took his body, and laid it in a tomb.

The apostles gathered around Jesus, and told him all that they had done and taught. He said to them, "Come away to a deserted place all by yourselves and rest a while." For many were coming and going, and they had no leisure even to eat. And they went away in the boat to a deserted place by themselves. Now many saw them going and recognized them, and they hurried there on foot from all the towns and arrived ahead of them. As he went ashore, he saw a great crowd; and he had compassion for them, because they were like sheep without a shepherd; and he began to teach them many

The miracle of the multiplication of loaves and fishes explodes into the margins of Mark 6 and 7.

things.³⁵ When it grew late, his disciples came to him & said, "This is a deserted place, and the hour is now very late; ³⁶ send them away so that they may go into the surrounding country and villages and buy something for themselves to eat."³⁷ But he answered them, "You give them something to eat." They said to him, "Are we to go and buy two hundred denarii worth of bread, and give it to them to eat?" ³⁸ And he said to them, "How many loaves have you? Go and see." When they had found out, they said, "Five, and two fish." ³⁹ Then he ordered them to get all the people to sit down in groups on the green grass. ⁴⁰ So they sat down in groups of hundreds and of fifties. ⁴¹ Taking the five loaves and the two fish, he looked up to heaven, and blessed & broke the loaves, and gave them to his disciples to set before the people; and he divided the two fish among them all. ⁴² And all ate and were filled; ⁴³ and they took up twelve baskets full of broken pieces and of the fish. ⁴⁴ Those who had eaten the loaves numbered

45 five thousand men. ▮ Immediately he made his disciples get into the boat & go on ahead to the other side, to Bethsaida, while he dismissed the crowd. ⁴⁶ After saying farewell to them, he went up on the

47 mountain to pray. ▮ When evening came, the boat was out on the sea, and he was alone on the land. ⁴⁸ When he saw that they were straining at the oars against an adverse wind, he came towards them early in the morning, walking on the sea. He intended to pass them by. ⁴⁹ But when they saw him walking on the sea, they thought it was a ghost and cried out; ⁵⁰ for they all saw him and were terrified. But immediately he spoke to them & said, "Take heart, it is I; do not be afraid." ⁵¹ Then he got into the boat

53 with them & the wind ceased. And they were utterly astounded, ⁵² for they did not understand about the loaves, but their hearts were hardened. ▮ When they had crossed over, they came to land at Gennesaret and moored the boat. ⁵⁴ When they got out of the boat, people at once recognized him, ⁵⁵ and rushed about that whole region and began to bring the sick on mats to wherever they heard he was. ⁵⁶ And wherever he went, into villages or cities or farms, they laid the sick in the marketplaces, and begged him that they might touch even the fringe of his cloak; and all who touched it were healed.

7

ow when the Pharisees and some of the scribes who had come from Jerusalem gathered around him, ² they noticed that some of his disciples were eating with defiled hands, that is, without washing them. ³ [For the Pharisees, and all the Jews, do not eat unless they thoroughly wash their hands, thus observing the tradition of the elders; ⁴ and they do not eat anything from the market unless they wash it; and there are also many other traditions that they observe, the washing of cups, pots, and bronze kettles.] ⁵ So the Pharisees and the scribes asked him, "Why do your disciples not live according to the tradition of the elders, but eat with defiled hands?" ⁶ He said to them, "Isaiah prophesied rightly about you hypocrites, as it is written,

'This people honors me with their lips,
    but their hearts are far from me;
7   in vain do they worship me,
        teaching human precepts as doctrines.'

⁸ You abandon the commandment of God & hold
9 to human tradition." ▮ Then he said to them, "You have a fine way of rejecting the commandment of God in order to keep your tradition! ¹⁰ For Moses said, 'Honor your father & your mother'; and, 'Whoever speaks evil of father or mother must surely die.' ¹¹ But you say that if anyone tells father or mother, 'Whatever support you might have had from me is Corban' [that is, an offering to God] – ¹² then you no longer permit doing anything for a father or mother; ¹³ thus making void the word of God through your tradition that you have handed on. And you do
14 many things like this." ▮ Then he called the crowd again and said to them, "Listen to me, all of you, and understand; ¹⁵ there is nothing outside a person

קרבן·

ᵃ The denarius was the usual
  day's wage for a laborer
ᵇ Meaning of Gk uncertain
ᶜ Other ancient authorities read
  and when they come from the
  marketplace, they do not eat unless
  they purify themselves
ᵈ Other ancient authorities add
  and beds
ᵉ Gk walk
ᶠ Gk lacks to God

slightly distressed, making a short abstract interlude between each of these books. Although visual references are made to the carpet pages in other volumes, they are never as elaborate as they are in this volume.

In this first volume, Donald invited his guest artists to create several of the illuminations. Thomas Ingmire began his first illuminations, *Beatitudes* and *I Am Sayings*, in 2001. Suzanne Moore began her first, *Last Judgment*, in 2001. And Aidan Hart began to work on illuminations as well, usually in concert with Donald.

The Loaves and Fishes

THIS ILLUMINATION includes two different stories—the feeding of the five thousand and the feeding of the four thousand—in a single image. The theological briefs suggested that these were variants of a single story and so Donald concentrated on the image of the multiplication of the loaves and fishes, the element common to both versions.

It was meant to be a rather small illumination. As Donald worked on it, however, it exploded into the margins, filling the edges of a whole spread.

"This isn't two halves," Donald said. "You have two stories, one is hot, the other is cold." But they are unified into a single unified composition. "It just grew. I worked with overlays and collage. The CIT had some visual suggestions—the fish, for instance. Michael sent me a postcard of a mosaic from Tabgha on the Sea of Galilee where the miracle was said to have taken place."

On the left he placed two fish and five loaves from one version of the story; on the right there are three fish and seven loaves.

A fifteenth-century Book of Hours from northern Europe shows a late medieval tradition of marginal illumination. Tiny vines and flecks of burnished gold spill out around the text. The *Loaves and Fishes* illumination is a modern echo of this ancient tradition. Gavin Hill Book of Hours. Gavin MS 2. Hill Museum & Manuscript Library, Saint John's University.

"What elements have you got?" he asked out loud. "Bits of loaves, fragments which start to float. Baskets to take up and pass on the remnants."

The basket designs are based on Native American patterns. "I'd been looking for baskets. I found some Native American baskets and I said to myself, 'This is sacred geometry!' Basketmakers in some North American traditions sing sacred songs as they make their baskets. I wanted them in there because they are American. But they were also like the abstract intellectual constructs of sacred geometry."

With these elements—baskets, fish, bread, two sides of the Sea of Galilee—the design began to lay itself out. "It speaks for itself. I did this organically." The images began to multiply across the margins of the page.

"This is all about love," he said. "These few fish and few loaves were given out, symbolically shared with the many. It was an act of giving, of loving. The basket shapes started to spin, a dizzy feeling. The baskets themselves have a geometrical shape. The arithmetic of love is exponential. One act of love begets another."

A design issue then led to the addition of the blue batons which interrupt the composition. "As these shapes are flowing around the page, it could be mushy. I needed something staccato to give the design fixed points. Dark blue batons which are placed at intervals represent obstacles to the flow. In a design sense, they create little eddies and in a moral sense they represent sins of commission, moments when our actions interrupt the flow of love. I also left blank spaces, representing times when we should act with love but don't; these would be sins of omission."

The finished illumination begins to take shape next to the complex sketch. The stages of making the final work are carefully considered as layer upon layer is added to the composition. Here the diagonal bands are hard and crisp. They will later be overpainted and interrupted. In the final version they recede into the background, creating a subtle armature within which the stories are placed.

The diagonal bands pick up the cosmic mandala theme which runs through a number of the illuminations.

The inscriptions in small capitals are added late in the process of making a finished illumination. Loosely indicated in white, they are written with great freedom.

A series of parables is tied to the story of Mary and Martha in the *Luke Anthology* opposite Luke 15.

younger of them said to his father, 'Father, give me
the share of the property that will belong to me.'
So he divided his property between them. [13] A few
days later the younger son gathered all he had &
traveled to a distant country, and there he squan-
dered his property in dissolute living. [14] When he
had spent everything, a severe famine took place
throughout that country, and he began to be in need.
[15] So he went and hired himself out to one of the
citizens of that country, who sent him to his fields
to feed the pigs. [16] He would gladly have filled him
self with the pods that the pigs were eating; and no
one gave him anything. [17] But when he came to him
self he said,' How many of my father's hired hands
have bread enough & to spare, but here I am dying
of hunger! [18] I will get up and go to my father, and
I will say to him,' Father, I have sinned against heaven
& before you; [19] I am no longer worthy to be called
your son ; treat me like one of your hired hands.'
[20] So he set off and went to his father. But while he
was still far off, his father saw him and was filled
with compassion; he ran and put his arms around
him and kissed him. [21] Then the son said to him,
'Father, I have sinned against heaven & before you;
I am no longer worthy to be called your son.' [22] But
the father said to his slaves, Quickly, bring out a
robe ~ the best one ~ and put it on him; put a ring
on his finger and sandals on his feet. [23] And get the
fatted calf and kill it, and let us eat and celebrate;
[24] for this son of mine was dead and is alive again;
he was lost and is found !' And they began to celebrate. [25] "Now his elder son was in the field; and
when he came & approached the house, he heard
music and dancing. [26] He called one of the slaves
and asked what was going on. [27] He replied,' Your
brother has come, and your father has killed the
fatted calf, because he has got him back safe and
sound.' [28] Then he became angry and refused to go
in. His father came out and began to plead with
him. [29] But he answered his father,' Listen! For all
these years I have been working like a slave for you,
and I have never disobeyed your command; yet you
have never given me even a young goat so that I might
celebrate with my friends. [30] But when this son of
yours came back, who has devoured your property
with prostitutes, you killed the fatted calf for him!'
[31] Then the father said to him,'Son, you are always
with me, and all that is mine is yours. [32] But we had
to celebrate & rejoice, because this brother of yours
was dead and has come to life; he was lost and has
been found .' "

j Other ancient authorities
read *filled his stomach*
with
k Other ancient authorities
add *Treat me like one of*
your hired servants
l Gk *he*

When he stepped back from the work, he realized he'd made something with a medieval precedent. "Then I thought, this is fifteenth-entury illumination—little bits of gold in the margins with that three-pronged leaf pattern. It's a cracking solution. They got it right. But I wasn't recreating an ancient thing. It could very easily have become a re-creation. I did this illumination in this way because of the logic of it." Almost by accident he had stumbled on a graphic solution which was centuries old and made it his own.

The Luke Anthology

THE *Luke Anthology* incorporates five parables and a story from the life of Jesus. The five parables—the lost coin, the lost sheep, the prodigal son, the good Samaritan, and Dives and Lazarus—appear on the left-hand page while Jesus appears on the right with Mary and Martha. Donald worked hard to blend all these tales into a single image.

"It was truly an anthology," Donald recounted. "How do you sum up Luke's Gospel? The brief alone ran to three pages of dense text—and I had to boil that down to a single page."

Donald also knew he would have to visually separate the parables from the narrative of Jesus with the two sisters. "Five parables, then a story about Jesus. They're quite different. It's a gear change." He solved that dilemma by separating parable and narrative onto two different pages. The whole composition is unified with strong diagonal lines. As he explained, "There is a lot going on and the onlooker has to hunt." It is an illumination which repays careful examination.

The themes of love and forgiveness run through all the parables. "These stories are about the power of God's love beyond human comprehension and what happens out of sheer love between human beings."

In the story of the prodigal son, in the lower left, the father carries the finest, brightest coat out to his penitent son. His gesture points upwards toward a golden image of the World Trade Center. The diagonal band holding these images leads the viewer's eye straight up to the gilded face of Christ.

"This parable is all about forgiveness. You're really challenged to overcome your anger. It's got to be really

The *Crucifixion* illumination slowly takes form in a series of variations. The photocopied reference of a late tenth-century crucifix is transformed into a splash of gold in the final drawing. Sketches like these were sent over the Internet from Wales to Minnesota for the comments of the Committee on Illumination and Text.

The Crucifixion is depicted opposite Luke 24.

difficult to forgive." Donald used the image of the Twin Towers as a modern expression of the challenge of forgiving evil. It is an example, he said, "representing the difficulty of achieving pure, unreasonable love."

The figures of father and son in the parable were painted by Aidan Hart in his traditional icon-painter's style. Donald reworked Aidan's image a bit, explaining, "The paint surface was a bit too coarse in finish. But I wanted that period look. It contrasts well with the Twin Towers. I wanted to express a sense of then-and-now, showing the relevance of these old stories in our contemporary world."

Donald painted in the prodigal son's pigs "after an image out of a children's pictorial encyclopedia I grew up with."

Sally Mae added some fragments of the recurring mandala motif which had appeared in the *Genealogy of Christ*. Donald explained, "The cosmic mandala fragments here on the right and the left do not signify Buddhism per se. They stand for the working of people's minds, trying to make sense of their experience." These motifs provide a thread which runs through the Bible, unifying the whole.

Martha and Mary, who stand on the right at the bottom, complete the composition and were finished by Donald while he was at Saint John's. Christ's words to Martha appear in gold above their heads. Donald said, "It's the punchline quote: 'There is need of only one thing.' For me, it is the love of God, the need to reach out to God."

The Crucifixion

THE DEATH OF JESUS is rendered with great directness. The crucified figure in raised and burnished gold is central to the composition. The cross is set at an angle, heightening the drama of the scene. To one side fragments of purple seem torn by the bright glory of the gold.

"The brief tells us that the curtain of the Temple was covered with astrological symbols," Donald said. The text in Luke says the Temple curtain was torn in two at the moment Jesus died. Here it tears into fragments. Above the cross a patch of sky suggests the "blue of enlightenment and the new order" breaking in. The crucifixion marks a transition from an old, hierarchical ritual order to a liberating freedom.

"I used a coarse bristly brush for the blue, applying direct, dry dabs of paint right onto something that's taken me weeks. That's just a need—I have to do it. You do a coarse brush stroke with brute energy, and this then calls forth a delicate counterpoint. There is the energy of attack with the delicate supporting of embellishment."

Surrounding the vibrant scene is a cool grey/blue border. This has medieval precedents: often a heavy Romanesque illustration will have a transitional, softer edge. Hard color gives way to softer color; it helps tie the illustration to the page on which it lies. In this case there was a practical reason for it as well.

"The writing on the page behind was disturbing the delicacy of anything I could add, so I needed to obliterate it. That's why I added the grey border. I broke that down by printing on it with *Broderie Anglaise:* English lace. It also brought in the recurring theme of textiles. I am always looking for links, visual metaphors linking each illumination to the others. For the torn curtain, I inked a piece of silk and printed it."

The Life of Paul

THE *Life of Paul* began as another anthology page, illustrating a series of scenes from the Acts of the Apostles. As it took shape, it became a unified image. The details of specific events dropped out—Donald didn't want to make what he calls "a comic strip" with seven little illustrations. Instead he opted for a broader treatment.

Paul's role as the Apostle to the Gentiles led him to found churches across the Mediterranean world and Donald chose to express this through the collage of urban images, both ancient and modern, which surround his portrait. A ship in the background evokes Paul's many preaching journeys. The text above his head, in gold, refers to his dramatic conversion to Christianity in a light-filled vision. The text under his feet describes his missionary calling to the far ends of the known world.

"So when the first sketch was almost completely executed by Aidan Hart the CIT balked, because at that point I had been struggling with the *Resurrection* scene for some time, and they hadn't seen much work from me for a while." Donald recalled, "They wanted to know, 'How much is Donald going to do in the book?' So the *Life of Paul* illumination became much more of a collaboration than I had first intended with Aidan, concentrating on his beautiful figure of St. Paul."

The initial sketch by Aidan Hart envisioned a very literal rendition of Paul's life drawn in a traditional iconographic style. Based closely on the theological brief, the design was rejected on stylistic grounds.

Aidan Hart's work is based on a strong sense of line. Clearly delineated figures contrast with solid backgrounds. Donald Jackson's work by contrast is informed by bold brushwork and a fluid relationship between figure and ground.

In a later version the narrative vignettes have been replaced with a more evocative rendering of cityscapes both ancient and modern. The story of Paul is told in a symbolic rather than literal fashion. Aidan Hart's precise painting is integrated into Donald Jackson's broader, more painterly style.

The final illumination was a collaboration between Aidan Hart and Donald Jackson. Here Aidan paints in the figure of Saint Paul.

The design went through three versions. "Aidan first, then I," said Donald, "Then Aidan and I together." Some of the earlier versions literally lie in layers under the paint of the sketch.

The buildings to Paul's left and right are apartment buildings which line Fifth Avenue in New York City. Above them, to the right, the jewel-like Stella Maris chapel, which overlooks Lake Sagatagan in Collegeville, makes a reference to Saint John's. Below these, black line drawings evoke the thousands of churches built through Christian history. Paul holds a little model of a church in his arms. He is wrapped in a Jewish prayer shawl, evoking his youth as a devout Pharisee.

Old and new combine once again to form a unified whole.

A liturgical celebration

IN SPRING 2001, Donald and Mabel came to Collegeville for a Saint John's Day Celebration, at which there would be the first public viewing in the United States of selected illuminations from *Gospels and Acts.* Donald remembers this as a pivotal moment in the project. A ceremony was held in the Abbey Church. Pages of the Bible were mounted on a specially made portable easel, and the pages were carried in procession and placed on the altar.

He said, "At that moment when I saw the *Crucifixion* illumination from Luke on the altar, and the gold shining and picking up the light, it changed for me. When the illumination was unveiled, there was an intake of breath from the congregation."

"On the one hand it was pure theater—I know. I helped orchestrate the detail of the unveiling. But at

The Life of Paul appears opposite Acts of the Apostles 15.

that moment in the Abbey Church, I realised it had a presence apart from me, that one of the people the image was speaking to was *me.*"

Seeing the image from across the room, he felt a particular calm. "That disconnection, the letting go of possession was important. The fear and pain of doing it was behind me. It now had a life of its own."

That awareness gave him a new sense that he was on the right track. "I don't normally come from a confident place. Fear of failure is never far away. But looking at that gilded page in the Abbey Church, I realized it did work. And I said to myself, 'You must be getting something right here.' It was reaching out, connecting—what I had always hoped for. The validation was coming from the work itself."

Steps along the way

BY THE SUMMER of 2001, it became clear that the deadlines would have to be readjusted. The work was taking significantly longer than had been planned. The contract was renegotiated, and the completion date was set back to March 2006.

Plans also began to be laid for a major exhibition that would open at the Minneapolis Institute of Arts and be presented at venues around the country. In November 2001, the Target Corporation announced its sponsorship of the national exhibition tour. This huge undertaking was orchestrated from Saint John's and would eventually take a selection of Bible pages and other displays to many cities around the United States and spawn several smaller shows that would show a smaller—or different—selection of pages from the manuscript.

In the summer of 2002, the BBC descended on the Scriptorium for ten days to film sequences for their documentary, *The Illuminator and a Bible for the 21st Century.* The BBC also traveled to Minnesota to film sequences at Saint John's. It was aired in Wales on Easter 2003 and later aired on over twenty-five PBS stations in the United States in 2003 and 2004, and it has been aired periodically ever since.

All of these activities brought The Saint John's Bible to a wider audience and generated intense interest in the project. But they also had a real cost in time and energy that affected production of the manuscript itself.

In Mark 3, the *Sower and the Seed* was executed by Aidan Hart with additions by Donald Jackson and Sally Mae Joseph.

Process questions

AS I DISCUSSED the history of the Bible project, certain questions nagged at me. Dates, facts, and figures are important. But other questions begged to be asked, especially in regard to this first volume.

I have often wondered why the project began with the *Gospels and Acts* volume. It is the most heavily illuminated of all seven volumes and therefore the most challenging. But it had to be produced while Donald was assembling his team, working out how to communicate with his client, and developing the script. In all, the selection of the most ambitious volume as the starting point for the project piled challenge upon challenge, an almost impossible task.

I asked Donald about this—wouldn't it have been easier to begin with a text-heavy book like the Historical Books, so he could work out the kinks in his system before embarking on more ambitious parts of the project?

"I always thought the simple answer was to do with Benedictine priorities. Remember we didn't know for sure at this point whether this project was going to run the full course. So they asked me to start with the volumes most important to them." He pointed out that there was always a promotional aspect to the project. In order to attract donors and excite the whole community about the project, it would have been a mistake to begin with one of the drier volumes. The project had to open with something spectacular.

As he thought about it, he said to me that he was, in fact, glad that he had started with the Gospels. "Starting with the Gospels actually helped me. I could engage with the words, with the meaning, and with the implications more easily for myself. Starting with the message of love and forgiveness that is so central to the Gospels helped me engage with the text and feel more confident that I would come up with ideas which could illuminate the message."

There is so much in the Bible that is challenging, even ugly. So much of the sacred text is devoted to war and human conflict. The Law in the Pentateuch is often beautiful, but in many parts it reflects a crueler era than our own, with different norms and values. Donald said, "If I'd started with the Historical Books, I don't think I could have engaged with the text at the required level of understanding or confidence that I could come up with visual interpretations that carried personal conviction. It also taught me that when I dug beneath the surface of the words and into myself I would always be sure of finding something to connect with and hopefully offer to others." The Gospels set the tone and gave him a perspective that helped as he and his team worked through the more difficult, less appealing books.

Artistic limits

ANOTHER QUESTION I had always wanted to ask him was about how the volume held together visually. With so many participants, so many styles, what would make the work cohere? The medieval scribes who made illuminated Bibles did not have to worry about this. Their style was set by the tradition in which they worked, and their color range was limited by the availability of pigments. Why, for instance, did he not set out a limited palette?

Donald considered this. "It became clear that what I needed to do was to constantly generate and maintain a high level of emotional and physical energy, a kind of fuel for action. It's physical as well as emotional energy."

He turned my question on its head. It was not about setting artificial limits. It was about entering into a certain kind of process: "How does an actor step onto the stage and play the same part every performance? They have to bring the same energy as if it was the first time they did it. So much of the preparation is internal. The marks themselves come from desperation and passion."

He made a musical comparison, one that would come up again and again: "I asked myself, what key do you play this in? What chord do we want to strike?"

I asked him, "So did you feel you had to set bounds?"

"No. I didn't think of it that way. The page itself is boundary enough and within my own competence of course."

The materials themselves helped define his approach. He said, "Gouache, casein paint, gold. That felt solid. Those materials and tools make work that have something of the silky tenacity of the best medieval work."

And as he worked, he tried to create the right atmosphere for all the artists. He said, "The structure was intended so that artists could do their work without looking at what others had done on the page before." And he returned to the musical metaphor: "It was intended that artists would be soloists who would play their instruments as if in an orchestral context. I thought it would be visually connected by me, by the conductor."

Seeing himself in that role, he gave the other artists a lot of room to express their own vision within the framework of the project. "I did have an idea that tools, quality, a common approach, choosing people who worked in a certain way—these things would unify the book. My illuminations usually came last anyway.

I often worked on folios which had several months of work on them already and of course I completed the books with book headings and chapter capitals. I chose the colors for these to complement the work of everyone else."

He acknowledged that my question was a valid one. It reflected certain attitudes we have about art and art making today.

"This is countercultural," he said. "I get a strong reaction when I talk to people working in the fine arts. The modern cliché is that of the individual in a garret creating his own unique vision. The tendency is to equate collaboration with compromise and direction with subjugation."

And he pointed to another medium where this communal approach is used.

"This is closer to the analogy of film. Each actor has a role to play, but we understand and accept that direction is aimed at bringing out and channeling the actors' gifts in the service of the director's vision of the whole (which is subject to change as the work progresses—just think of the cutting room floor). In our culture, we accept it in film."

The special treatment *Hear, O Israel*, created by Hazel Dolby, appears opposite Mark 13.

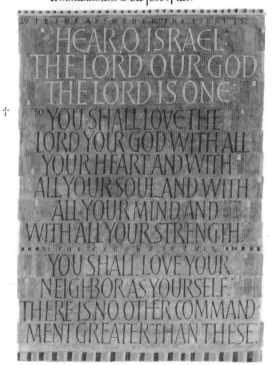

28 One of the scribes came near and heard them disputing with one another, and seeing that he answered them well, he asked him, "Which commandment is the first of all?"

29 JESUS ANSWERED THE FIRST IS,

HEAR, O ISRAEL:
THE LORD OUR GOD,
THE LORD IS ONE;
30 YOU SHALL LOVE THE
LORD YOUR GOD WITH ALL
YOUR HEART, AND WITH
ALL YOUR SOUL, AND WITH
ALL YOUR MIND, AND
WITH ALL YOUR STRENGTH.
31 THE SECOND IS THIS,
YOU SHALL LOVE YOUR
NEIGHBOR AS YOURSELF.
THERE IS NO OTHER COMMAND-
MENT GREATER THAN THESE."

sat down opposite the treasury, and watched the crowd putting money into the treasury. Many rich people put in large sums. 42 A poor widow came & put in two small copper coins, which are worth a penny. 43 Then he called his disciples and said to them, "Truly I tell you, this poor widow has put in more than all those who are contributing to the treasury. 44 For all of them have contributed out of their abundance; but she out of her poverty has put in everything she had, all she had to live on."

13

As he came out of the temple, one of his disciples said to him, "Look, Teacher, what large stones and what large buildings!" 2 Then Jesus asked him, "Do you see these great buildings? Not one stone will be left here upon another; all will be thrown down." 3 When he was sitting on the Mount of Olives opposite the temple, Peter, James, John, and Andrew asked him privately, 4 "Tell us, when will this be, and what will be the sign that all these things are about to be accomplished?" 5 Then Jesus began to say to them, "Beware that no one leads you astray. 6 Many will come in my name and say, 'I am he!' and they will lead many astray. 7 When you hear of wars and rumors of wars, do not be alarmed; this must take place, but the end is still to come. 8 For nation will rise against nation,

His approach suggested a very intimate relationship with his guest artists. "That means there has to be a level of trust. The idea of two people working on one image (as I did frequently with Aidan and Chris) is not part of our graphic arts tradition."

At the end of our conversation, he balked at setting artificial or theoretical limits to the work. "I'm not talking about the intellectual side of this," he said. "I'm talking about the making. Intellectual appraisal of the text and the briefs serves the intuition. That sparks the emotional energy behind the images. If an illumination doesn't start by meaning something to me, how can I expect it to mean something to anyone else?"

Completion

IN SEPTEMBER 2002 volume 1, *Gospels and Acts*, was completed. All scribal work and guest illuminations were done, and the pages were gathered at the Hendre.

One of the last tasks was the insertion of the drop capitals through the whole book. Donald does these in one go. As he pointed out to me, "This is another way the manuscript is unified—I get my colors and tools together and sit down to make all the drop caps."

The work at the very end was rapid and focused. The deadline loomed. "The *Road to Emmaus* [at the end of Luke] was actually finished at the Hendre while the car was outside waiting to take us to the airport."

Donald may complain sometimes of the pressure of working to deadline, but there is part of him that thrives under the tension of working to the very last moment.

The pages were packed up, and Donald and Mabel Jackson flew to Minnesota to present the finished volume to Saint John's University and Abbey. They were accompanied by Rebecca Cherry.

Four years after signing the first contract, the first volume was done. It has 132 pages of writing on thirty-three skins. There are twenty-seven illuminations, nine special treatments, seventeen marginal decorations, and one hundred eleven large capitals.

Donor Acknowledgment

In each volume, a small illumination acknowledges the donor who made the production of the volume possible. In *Gospels and Acts*, Gene and Mary Frey were recognized with a painting of a peacock butterfly opposite Acts 20. The family visited Donald and Mabel at their house and studio, and while they walked in the garden the Buddleia nearby was covered in peacock butterflies.

The *Creation* appears
opposite the beginning
of the book of Genesis.

CHAPTER 10

PENTATEUCH

Delivered August 2003

THE CREATION OF *Gospels and Acts* had been a rollercoaster ride as Donald got the project up and running and worked on the most ambitious volume of the project. Now he and his team settled into a different rhythm—the rhythm of the long-distance runner. Between 2002 and 2007, they would create one new volume each year, a steady and demanding pace.

Pentateuch is much less heavily illuminated than *Gospels and Acts*. Many pages are simply composed of continuous columns of text. The tone and the pacing of the volume is therefore much more reserved, more quiet, less frequently interrupted. The *Pentateuch* volume demonstrates the power of the writing itself to hold its own and provide visual interest. There is also much more writing: *Pentateuch* is twenty-five pages longer than the previous volume.

In the public exposure of The Saint John's Bible, the bright colors, gold, and bold compositions of the illuminations and other illustrative elements of the page often catch the public's imagination. These visual elements are each unique, so each one has its own story. But the Bible would not be what it is if it weren't for that steady undercurrent of pure writing. And in the *Pentateuch*, the writing comes to the fore. Donald commented to me, "The writing alone has the power to engage and has moved people to tears."

By now, of course, the three scribes and Donald had been writing for some time already, and their skills had grown; their style had matured. In October 2002, Donald held a second master class, once again inviting a group of skilled calligraphers to train and see if they would be able to join the project as scribes. From this class, two new calligraphers joined the team—Susie Leiper and Angela Swan. They were folded into the writing team and began to participate in the regular meetings of the scribes at the Scriptorium.

Another calligrapher to join in the project at this point was Izzy Pludwinski from Israel. He had already served as a consultant for the Hebrew portions of the project and had advised Donald on the Hebrew texts in *Gospels and Acts*. For *Pentateuch*, he flew to Wales to work in the Scriptorium, adding for the first time his own writing to the project.

All the volumes, with the exception of *Psalms*, have running heads in the upper corners of the spreads. In the books of the Old Testament and Apocrypha, these appear in English on the left page and in Hebrew or Greek on the right page, reflecting the language in which the books were composed and have come down to us. Izzy wrote all the Hebrew running heads in *Pentateuch* and later volumes. He also added the names of each book in Hebrew over the main book titles.

The book divisions in *Pentateuch* differ from those in *Gospels and Acts*. In the previous volume, each book had opened with a new spread, showing a full-page illumination on the left and the book title and opening of the text on the right-hand page. In *Pentateuch* each book title is placed within a column: where one book ends, the next book begins immediately with its title. There is no interruption in the continuous flow of text from one column to the next. This is the pattern Donald would follow in all subsequent volumes of the Bible (with the exception of *Psalms*, which is has a unique structure).

Another visual change that took place in *Pentateuch* was the dislodging of the special treatments from their position in the text. In *Gospels and Acts*, Donald had tried to keep the special treatments as part of the flow of text. This was very restrictive. The placement of the special treatments was entirely dependent on their position in the text, so their position on the page could not be visually adjusted. Furthermore, if they were considered an integral part of the text, they had to be perfectly legible; this constrained the graphic possibilities of the artists.

In *Pentateuch*, the main text was left uninterrupted. A passage selected for special treatment would appear as part of the main text. The passage would then be repeated elsewhere on the page in its more elaborate form. This move of the special treatments out of the main text would prove very liberating. The special treatments are still placed within the grid of the text column, but their placement on the page becomes flexible. Comparing the positioning of special treatments in this volume to those in *Gospels and Acts* shows that now Donald tended to place these elements at the top or bottom of a column, making for much cleaner, simpler page layout. The other benefit of removing the special treatments from the flow of the text was to allow much greater freedom in their graphic treatment; they didn't have to be immediately legible.

The nature of the illuminations changes somewhat in this volume as well. In *Gospels and Acts*, Donald found himself sometimes overwhelmed by the detail of the briefs provided him by the CIT. He often felt he had to somehow include everything in the brief within the space of an illumination. He refers to this as "ticking off the boxes." The resultant illuminations were often highly detailed, packing a great deal of imagery into a single composition. Donald says the breakthrough came in *Gospels and Acts* when he was doing the *Luke Anthology*. For the first time, members of the CIT indicated to him that he did not have to try to incorporate every idea they sent him; instead, he should draw from their briefs the inspiration he needed to create an image of his own.

Donald's illuminations in *Pentateuch* tend to have a somewhat simpler structure as a result. They become more unified as compositions. There is still plenty of detail, and the illuminations are still very rich. But there is a greater assuredness of scale and clearer structure to the illuminations of this volume. It is as though one can watch the artist and client growing into the process of making a Bible together.

Another shift in the illuminations in this volume is that they begin to refer back to earlier illuminations. This is a process that would become more frequent as the project continued. In the final illumination of the volume, the *Death of Moses*, the two tablets held by Moses refer directly to Thomas Ingmire's *Ten Commandments* illumination.

Because Donald and his guest artists were working without the framework of a fixed tradition of religious images, they had to develop their own iconography. This was not an explicit mandate; it was implicit in the task they had taken on. As they continued to work on the Bible, certain images emerged as visual themes that could be picked up and reused later on. This is a fascinating aspect of the project, mirroring the process by which the emerging Christian Church had begun to create and codify its own iconography in the fourth and fifth centuries.

The sketches for each illumination involve many weeks of careful preparation. The elements of the design are built up in collage. Here Donald Jackson uses an acetate overlay to position the large raven which floats over his composition.

The position and scale of the illuminations in this sketch are carefully balanced within the two-column design of the text pages. The illustrations break the tight bounds of the grid, engaging the marginal space.

The Creation

THE STORY OF THE CREATION in Genesis is told within a framework of counting. As each day of the first week passes, the writer repeats his refrain: "And there was evening and there was morning, the first [or second, or third, or fifth] day." Donald built the structure of his illumination around this ordered counting out of days. Each vertical strip presents a single day and small golden squares are arranged in sequences of the sacred number seven. "I wanted," Donald said, "to symbolize God's presence in nothingness as well as everythingness."

The imagery Donald selected for each day mixes contemporary sources and ancient ones to create a timeless retelling of the ancient story.

"I value those times the CIT and I can talk in person rather than just use the written word," Donald said. "The best ideas come out in discussion. It was their idea to use fractals."

These complex geometric equations create self-perpetuating patterns of ever-greater complexity. "The fractals make patterns which emerge from nothingness." Their fragmented shapes explode from the dark primordial void, expressed verbally at the bottom with the Hebrew words *tohu wabohu*—chaos.

"My assistant Mark collected images of enhanced fractals on the Internet and in books. I got printouts and chopped them up. I put them together with the birth of a star—the beginning of space and time. I find that the Genesis story fits a lot of science. It tells us about timelessness."

A long, thin gold line in the midst of the first day marks a moment: "And God said, 'Let there be light.'"

Garden of Eden

To illustrate the separation of land and sea, a satellite image of the Ganges delta was used. The sun and moon are represented in silver and platinum, respectively.

In the fifth day, for the creation of the creatures of the sea, Donald first tried a brightly colored fish. "The CIT said it reminded them of tropical fish in tanks," Donald remembered. "So I made an image of a young, flat fish. It is shown at a stage of its life when it is almost transparent. It has the vulnerability of a newly born fish and at the same time evokes a fossil. Although it is living, it looks like something ancient. I also used the same rubber stamp fish that I had used earlier in the *Loaves and Fishes* illumination."

For the creation of human beings on the sixth day, Donald evoked the most ancient representations of human beings. "I drew images from aboriginal rock paintings in Australia. Above them the huntress appears from an even earlier rock painting in Africa. It represents all of our beginnings."

The background of the sixth day is rendered in earthen tones, suggesting a volcanic landscape.

At the bottom of the sixth day small fragments of a snake imply the danger which awaits in the Garden of Eden. "Chris Tomlin painted the snake. It has been interesting to watch him modify his technique. He used to work from dark to light; since working with me, he has begun working the opposite way round—from light to dark, letting the vellum speak for itself when it seems right."

On the golden seventh day, the first sabbath, all is calm and gold and shimmering. "I used gold leaf on a very diluted acrylic base. You burnish on gold; and you can keep adding bits of gold and silver. I tinted the acrylic so it has a slightly sandy color, retaining the earthiness of the creation in the presence of God."

In order to unify the composition, elements from one day overlap and interpenetrate the other days.

"At the end," Donald said, "I took a deep breath and with a coarse brush smudged the raven right on top of the finished illumination. Wisps of paint suggest birds flying across the whole face of creation. Birds are these magical, mobile, extraterrestrial creatures."

The raven is a familiar bird around The Hendre. "I'm surrounded by ravens. Their vocabulary is more extensive than any birds I know. I have learned to recognize many of their calls.

"The raven is a messenger in the Bible. Ravens are dark, powerful, they have that strong wingbeat. Yet they seem to delight in tumbling acrobatics in the air. The raven represents power, continually flying, tireless, endless. It's taking us for a ride across space and time."

The Garden of Eden and Adam & Eve

TWO LINKED ILLUMINATIONS flank chapter 2 of Genesis. The first depicts the innocence of the Garden of Eden; the second, Adam and Eve, the parents of humankind.

Donald commented, "There are tiny echoes of the *Creation* scene at the top of the *Garden of Eden* illumination to suggest light and dark, the progression of day and night."

The illumination is full of color; animals surround the humans in the garden. "The whole point was teeming fecundity. There is a feeling of joy with bright colors and that amazing bright face of an ape."

Donald repeated some of the ancient cave painting images from the *Creation* illumination. "The huntress reappears. In a way I suppose she represents work while the family groups in the background dance, make music and play."

Human beings living in harmony, enjoying the innocent companionship of Eden are enveloped in the natural environment. "Surrounding them are poisonous bugs—American—damned exotic! There are little bits of the snake, a parrot and a harlequin shrimp, which is a predator. There is a fraction of it against a background of plankton. At the bottom is the teeming sea."

Donald asked Chris Tomlin to add the animal painting. "I laid in the background and Chris painted the parrot, snake, scarlet-faced monkey, harlequin shrimp and the locusts behind the parrot." Donald then painted in the finishing details. "For the most part, my painting is much more loose, so I pulled it together."

Trying to remember the order in which each element was added, Donald corrected himself. "I think he painted the parrot afterwards. There was a bit of to and fro. I painted the grass over the locust. Chris will always try to make the bugs the most important thing!"

A small fraction of a mandala arcs into the scene from the left side. "The Buddhist mandala bit is about the birth of intellect. Human beings in the garden are enjoying animal life, but it's not just mindless reveling in life. They are also thinking about what it means. People begin to make patterns."

The second illumination of the pair is a portrait of Adam and Eve.

"The quotation in the margin is from Second Corinthians 3:18. I use that as a kind of caption. Behind Eve is a platinum background, like a mirror, to refer to the quotation. God is within us when we look into the mirror. Eve and Adam are mirrors of us."

The images are based on photographs from Africa. "I was interested in the idea of nakedness. It is both sensual and innocent. There is the joy of nakedness, like the child's freedom at the beach or in the bath. I was looking at African photos, at adult people who rejoice in nakedness.

"I chose her because she was a deliciously mischievous girl, all bedecked with beautiful things. The story is also about the loss of innocence. She's sparky enough, someone you might want to get into trouble for. Adam is inspired by another photograph of a beautiful man looking pensive."

Adam and Eve

THAT CREEPS UPON THE GROUND OF EVERY KIND, AND GOD SAW THAT IT WAS GOOD. ⁂ THEN GOD SAID, 26 "LET US MAKE HUMANKIND IN OUR IMAGE, ACCORDING TO OUR LIKENESS: AND LET THEM HAVE DOMINION OVER THE FISH OF THE SEA, AND OVER THE BIRDS OF THE AIR, AND OVER THE CATTLE, AND OVER ALL THE WILD ANIMALS OF THE EARTH, AND OVER EVERY CREEPING THING THAT CREEPS UPON THE EARTH."

27 SO GOD CREATED HUMANKIND IN HIS IMAGE, IN THE IMAGE OF GOD HE CREATED THEM: MALE AND FEMALE HE CREATED THEM.

28 GOD BLESSED THEM, AND GOD SAID TO THEM, "BE FRUITFUL & MULTIPLY, AND FILL THE EARTH & SUBDUE IT; AND HAVE DOMINION OVER THE FISH OF THE SEA AND OVER THE BIRDS OF THE AIR AND OVER EVERY LIVING THING THAT MOVES UPON THE EARTH." 29 GOD SAID, "SEE, I HAVE GIVEN YOU EVERY PLANT YIELDING SEED THAT IS UPON THE FACE OF ALL THE EARTH, AND EVERY TREE WITH SEED IN ITS FRUIT: YOU SHALL HAVE THEM FOR FOOD. 30 AND TO EVERY BEAST OF THE EARTH, AND TO EVERY BIRD OF THE AIR, AND TO EVERYTHING THAT CREEPS ON THE EARTH, EVERYTHING THAT HAS THE BREATH OF LIFE, I HAVE GIVEN EVERY GREEN PLANT FOR FOOD." AND IT WAS SO. 31 GOD SAW EVERYTHING THAT HE HAD MADE, AND INDEED, IT WAS VERY GOOD. AND THERE WAS EVENING AND THERE WAS MORNING, THE SIXTH DAY.

FOR CREATION WAITS WITH EAGER LONGING FOR THE REVEALING OF THE CHILDREN OF GOD

2

THUS THE HEAVENS & THE EARTH WERE FINISHED, AND ALL THEIR MULTITUDE. 2 AND ON THE SEVENTH DAY GOD FINISHED THE WORK THAT HE HAD DONE, AND HE RESTED ON THE SEVENTH DAY FROM ALL THE WORK THAT HE HAD DONE.

3 SO GOD BLESSED THE SEVENTH DAY AND HALLOWED IT, BECAUSE ON IT GOD RESTED FROM ALL THE WORK THAT HE HAD DONE IN CREATION. ⁂ THESE ARE THE GENER4 ATIONS OF THE HEAVENS & THE EARTH WHEN THEY WERE CREATED

Using similar colors and repeated motifs, Donald Jackson ties the two illuminations together in his asymmetric composition.

4 ❧ In the day that the LORD God made the earth and
the heavens, 5 when no plant of the field was yet in
the earth & no herb of the field had yet sprung up
for the LORD God had not caused it to rain upon the
earth, and there was no one to till the ground ; 6 but
a stream would rise from the earth, and water the
whole face of the ground; 7 then the LORD God formed
man from the dust of the ground, and breathed into
his nostrils the breath of life; and the man became
a living being. 8 And the LORD God planted a garden
in Eden, in the east; and there he put the man whom
he had formed. 9 Out of the ground the LORD God
made to grow every tree that is pleasant to the sight
and good for food, the tree of life also in the midst
of the garden, and the tree of the knowledge of good
and evil. ❧ A river flows out of Eden to water the
10 garden, and from there it divides and becomes four
branches. 11 The name of the first is Pishon; it is the
one that flows around the whole land of Havilah,
where there is gold; 12 and the gold of that land is good;
bdellium & onyx stone are there. 13 The name of the
second river is Gihon; it is the one that flows around
the whole land of Cush. 14 The name of the third river
is Tigris, which flows east of Assyria. And the fourth
15 river is the Euphrates. ❧ The LORD God took the man
and put him in the garden of Eden to till it & keep
it. 16 And the LORD God commanded the man, "You
may freely eat of every tree of the garden ; 17 but of
the tree of the knowledge of good and evil you shall
not eat, for in the day that you eat of it you shall die."
18 ❧ Then the LORD God said, "It is not good that the
man should be alone; I will make him a helper as his
partner." 19 So out of the ground the LORD God formed
every animal of the field and every bird of the air,
and brought them to the man to see what he would
call them; and whatever the man called every living
creature, that was its name. 20 The man gave names
to all cattle, and to the birds of the air, and to every
animal of the field; but for the man there was not
found a helper as his partner. 21 So the LORD God
caused a deep sleep to fall upon the man, and he slept;
then he took one of his ribs and closed up its place
with flesh. 22 And the rib that the LORD God had tak-
en from the man he made into a woman & brought
her to the man. 23 Then the man said,

"This at last is bone of my bones
 and flesh of my flesh;
this one shall be called Woman,
 for out of Man this one was taken.

24 Therefore a man leaves his father and his mother
and clings to his wife, and they become one flesh.
25 And the man and his wife were both naked, and
were not ashamed .

בראשית

3

❧ N ow the serpent was more crafty than any
other wild animal that the LORD God
had made. He said to the woman, "Did
God say, 'You shall not eat from any tree in the garden'?"
2 The woman said to the serpent, "We may eat of
the fruit of the trees in the garden; 3 but God said,
'You shall not eat of the fruit of the tree that is in
the middle of the garden, nor shall you touch it, or
you shall die.'" 4 But the serpent said to the woman,
"You will not die; 5 for God knows that when you
eat of it your eyes will be opened, and you will be
like God, knowing good and evil." 6 So when the
woman saw that the tree was good for food, and
that it was a delight to the eyes, and that the tree
was to be desired to make one wise, she took of its
fruit & ate; and she also gave some to her husband
who was with her, and he ate. Then the eyes of both
were opened, and they knew that they were naked;

5 Or formed a man [Heb
  adam] of dust from the
  ground [Heb adamah]
h Or for Adam
i Heb ishshah
j Heb ish
k Or gods

*AND ALL
OF US
WITH
UNVEILED
FACES,
SEEING
THE
GLORY
OF
THE
LORD
AS
THOUGH
REFLECTED
IN A
MIRROR,
ARE
BEING
TRANS-
FORMED
INTO
THE
SAME
IMAGE
FROM
ONE
DEGREE
OF
GLORY
TO
ANOTHER;*

The harlequin shrimp acquires its many-colored coat at the expert hand of Chris Tomlin.

Chris Tomlin paints the detailed, natural-istic animal images in the *Garden of Eden*. Many of the illumina-tions are the work of many hands, working under Donald Jack-son's supervision.

Donald Jackson lifts his tracing paper to check a detail of the collage sketch underneath. The sketch's somber coloring will be considerably brightened in the finished illumination.

Tracing paper is used to transfer portions of the design from the rough sketch to the finished work. Donald Jackson keeps these sheets; as he works, designs sometimes need to be repeatedly transferred.

Adam and Eve have painted their bodies. "The first clothing was to paint oneself. On the right I added a pattern from a Peruvian cape of feathers. It is clothing of a kind, but it is also about status. The horizontal stripes are details of Middle Eastern textiles. There's a progression from painted skin, to 'primitive' stuff, to woven textiles. In our loss of innocence, we are one."

The coral snake is deadly poisonous. "The disturbing presence of the snake, fragmented, separates Adam and Eve. Once again, Chris painted the snakes with life-like detail."

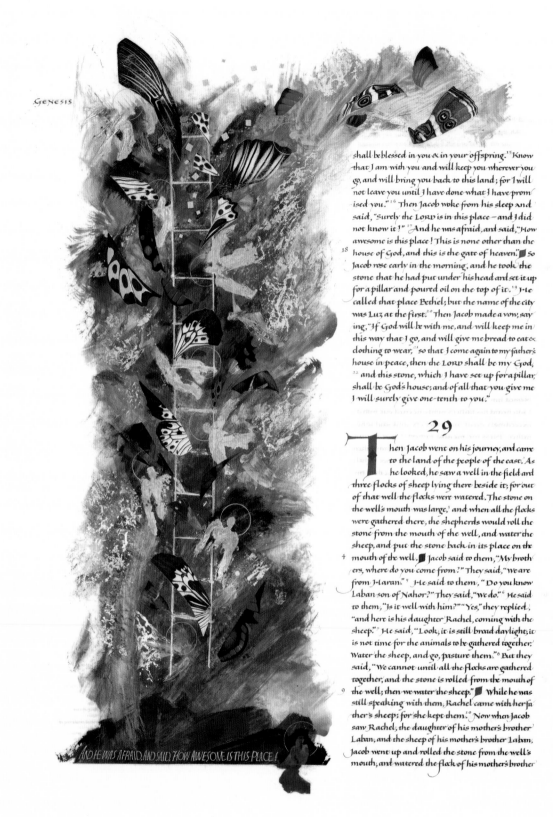

GENESIS

shall be blessed in you & in your offspring." Know that I am with you and will keep you wherever you go, and will bring you back to this land; for I will not leave you until I have done what I have promised you." [16] Then Jacob woke from his sleep and said, "Surely the LORD is in this place — and I did not know it!" And he was afraid, and said, "How awesome is this place! This is none other than the house of God, and this is the gate of heaven." So [18] Jacob rose early in the morning, and he took the stone that he had put under his head and set it up for a pillar and poured oil on the top of it. [19] He called that place Bethel; but the name of the city was Luz at the first. [20] Then Jacob made a vow, saying, "If God will be with me, and will keep me in this way that I go, and will give me bread to eat & clothing to wear, [21] so that I come again to my father's house in peace, then the LORD shall be my God, [22] and this stone, which I have set up for a pillar, shall be God's house; and of all that you give me I will surely give one-tenth to you."

29

Then Jacob went on his journey, and came to the land of the people of the east. As he looked, he saw a well in the field and three flocks of sheep lying there beside it; for out of that well the flocks were watered. The stone on the well's mouth was large, [3] and when all the flocks were gathered there, the shepherds would roll the stone from the mouth of the well, and water the sheep, and put the stone back in its place on the mouth of the well. [4] Jacob said to them, "My brothers, where do you come from?" They said, "We are from Haran." [5] He said to them, "Do you know Laban son of Nahor?" They said, "We do." [6] He said to them, "Is it well with him?" "Yes," they replied, "and here is his daughter Rachel, coming with the sheep." [7] He said, "Look, it is still broad daylight; it is not time for the animals to be gathered together. Water the sheep, and go, pasture them." [8] But they said, "We cannot until all the flocks are gathered together, and the stone is rolled from the mouth of the well; then we water the sheep." [9] While he was still speaking with them, Rachel came with her father's sheep; for she kept them. [10] Now when Jacob saw Rachel, the daughter of his mother's brother Laban, and the sheep of his mother's brother Laban, Jacob went up and rolled the stone from the well's mouth, and watered the flock of his mother's brother

AND HE WAS AFRAID, AND SAID, HOW AWESOME IS THIS PLACE!

Jacob's vision of angels descending and ascending a heavenly ladder spills out from a single column opposite Genesis 28.

Jacob's Ladder

"THIS STORY really moved me," Donald said. "I was familiar with it from childhood. I became powerfully affected by the sheer enormity of this vision—suddenly you are thrust into the midst of this incredibly awesome event. I wanted it to be surreal, shining things and light, with dawn about to break."

His original sketch caused some controversy when it was first seen by the CIT. Sally Mae recalled, "Oh, on that one, Donald really dug his heels in."

Donald agreed with her. "I'll show you the correspondence. It was complicated."

In the brief, the CIT had mentioned in passing a common monastic image from the Middle Ages—the Ladder of Perfection, depicting monks mounting upwards toward their heavenly goal as some fall to their doom. They compared this admonitory image to the Jacob story. In Donald's words, this inadvertently created a "red herring," a distraction from Jacob's vision.

The schema had also called for Jacob's vision to be tied to the story of Jacob wrestling with an angel. These two stories needed to be separated. Donald remarks, "I had to break free from my original instructions." He created a place on another page for a small picture of the wrestling Jacob.

More discussion ensued about the angels in the piece. Were some fallen angels and others angels of light? And what, the CIT wanted to know, were the butterfly wings? Were they some other class of angel?

Donald stuck to his guns about the butterflies. His conversation with the CIT clarified the awesome simplicity of the story. This was not about sorting the good from the bad; this was a moment when heaven and earth were momentarily joined and Jacob received his new name—Israel.

"I suppose I had a bee in my bonnet. I wanted to use butterflies as an analogy for angels," he said. "Ask yourself how you feel about a butterfly. Their enormous rarity! They are beautiful, full of grace, fragile and very mysterious in a funny kind of way. There is a subtext, too. You bat your eyelid and the

Layers of paint go down only to be scraped away. Using an erasing knife Donald Jackson removes one butterfly wing. Sometimes the knife or sandpaper are used to distress the surface, creating subtle gradations in contrast to areas of solid color.

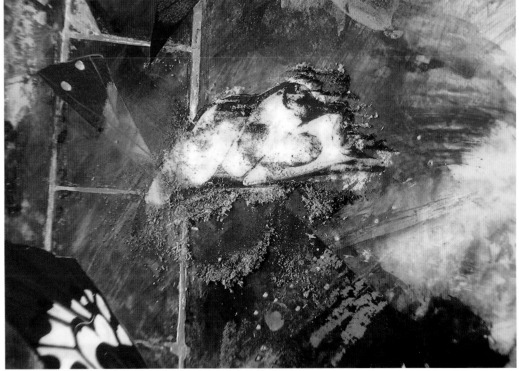

Donald Jackson carefully peels away a layer of frisket masking film. Spaces for butterfly wings were masked out while Donald used free vigorous brush-strokes to fill the background.

butterfly is gone. Now it's there, now it isn't." It was the perfect metaphor for the fleeting wonder of Jacob's vision.

"They have such a life-will," he continued. Their incredible fragility contrasts with the thousands of miles they travel on their yearly migrations. "I was determined to use super-realistic bits of butterfly wings. They appear against a lacy pattern of gold, a gossamer presence. The pattern is a textile print. I applied acrylic medium to a crocheted material."

Making the finished illumination carried its own challenges. "I thought this was relatively straightforward. I painted the background, masking off spaces with frisket for Chris to paint in the butterfly wings. He really went to town, working in exquisite detail with immense care. That's the danger of distance collaboration. If he'd been here while he was painting them, I would have realized there were one too many wings. As it was, I ended up having to scrape off some of his lovely work to regain the color balance of the whole."

The Ten Commandments

DONALD INVITED Thomas Ingmire to create several major illuminations for The Saint John's Bible, including this image from Exodus. Thomas was rather quiet as I interviewed him by phone. He thought carefully before answering questions and weighed his words before speaking.

"I said to Donald, 'I've always avoided illustrative things.' Donald has selected pieces for me to do which have lettering as their major feature. I had no direct contact with CIT; everything went through Donald.

"I do two or three really very sketchy sketches. Donald and I talk about it conceptually, we discuss a direction, then I do a detailed sketch. I also write an explanation of my ideas to Donald. They rewrite what I say and they submit it to the committee. So far the CIT has been really positive to my things. They liked this one right from the beginning."

In the brief, five different passages from Exodus were to be incorporated into a single illumination. Thomas said, "My first thought was, 'How do I make this into one image?' Any one of these stories could be the most important."

שמות

In the *Ten Commandments* illumination, a collage of scenes from Exodus is presented in a highly abstract form immediately before Exodus 20.

An early sketch by Thomas Ingmire sets out the bones of the design. Working in colored pencil he works out areas of light and dark and begins to bring his composition together.

A later sketch opts for dark tones. The final design would be much brighter.

The brief suggested that the story of the giving of the Ten Commandments represented a new creation, the gift of law bringing order to the chaos of human affairs. Thomas chose this as the principal image around which he grouped the others.

"The other passages were all miracles—evidence of God or God's power. Seeing them as miracles gave me one way to think of these four as one unit."

The four stories along the top of the composition are: the burning bush, the first Passover, the parting of the Red Sea, and Israel at Mount Sinai. Across these four stories Thomas has arrayed the voice of God speaking in gold letters.

"In so far as the structure of the page goes, the only gilding is within the top of the page where the miracles take place."

The bottom of the page contains the commandments themselves, overlapping and dissolving the colored background behind them. Thomas used typography for the letters.

"The CIT made reference to the Ten Commandments etched in tablets of stone. They described God's hand etching the tablets. I didn't feel the text could be written by hand; for me to write them calligraphically didn't seem right. I used the typeface Stone Sans. Was it semi-bold? I forget.

"That solved a lot of technical problems, too. It was an awkward skin. It had a surface like glass, and it was slimy. So the decision to use type solved a lot of problems.

"Another reason I thought of the possibility of using type was that I was in Bruges visiting Brodie Neuenschwander. We were going around town looking at things he had done. He'd made a piece on the wall of a hotel lobby. He'd done the thing in Photoshop and it was all executed in stencil." Thomas liked the stencil idea, so he used it.

"It's a complicated process. I discovered many ways to make mistakes. All the letters are pre-cut but there is a sheet of release paper. You roll out this paper and lay the stencil down and peel away the paper.

My first mistake: I didn't get the release paper flat, so there was a wrinkle. I had to start again. On the second try I positioned it wrong."

Eventually he mastered his technique. "It's a very precise, fine stencil. You get beautiful sharp lines with a stencil brush."

Conceptually Thomas found the text very engaging. "I was reading a book called *The Alphabet versus the Goddess*, by Leonard Shlain. He has a whole section on the Ten Commandments. He saw the commandments as the transforming of culture with the invention of the alphabet. It represented the first time the alphabet as we know it emerged. Before then we had pictograms. This new kind of writing must have seemed like wizardry or magic and was tied to a God who forbade graven images. So the background shows Egyptian motifs, gods, goddesses, society before the giving of the commandments. It is a kind of chaos, active in color contrasts. The alphabet comes over the top of it."

Thomas' other work often involves looking at the alphabet and thinking about the implications of this social construct of writing. He reflected, "It's interesting that this is an extension of things I've been developing in my own work. It's very hard to make that kind of connection."

Others have offered their own interpretations of his illumination. Thomas recalled, "Donald told me a rabbi saw it and had a whole different interpretation from mine. The illuminations have a life of their own."

Thomas also commented, "It's really a bit brighter than I'd like. Vellum gives everything this unbelievable richness and density. Paper absorbs more; it's more muted. On vellum it pops!"

Completion

IN AUGUST 2003 volume 2, *Pentateuch*, was completed. Donald and Mabel Jackson flew to Minnesota to present the finished volume to Saint John's University and Abbey. *Pentateuch* has 157 pages of writing on forty skins. There are eight interpretive illuminations, eight special treatments, seven marginal decorations, and 193 large capitals, of which 187 were written by Donald.

This sketch closely resembles the finished illumination. The tightly drawn menorah on the upper left would later become much more abstract and the piece would become more layered. The basic elements of the design have, however, been resolved.

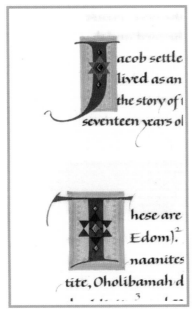

Donor Acknowledgment

In *Pentateuch*, the donors Jim and Theo Baustert were recognized with decorative capital letters for their forenames: J and T. These two letters mark the beginning of chapters 36 and 37 of Genesis—a happy accident that Donald took advantage of.

All the major visual themes for *Psalms* appear in the frontispiece. Broad, vigorous brushstrokes are contained within long vertical shapes which evoke open books. The skittish lines in gold, blue and black which pass across the page are the visual representation of chants sung by the monks of Saint John's. The vertical patterns represent sacred music from other world traditions interweaving with the Christian voices. Donald Jackson incorporated the text of Psalm 1 into the design of the frontispiece.

CHAPTER 11

PSALMS

Delivered April 2004

My tongue is like the pen of a ready scribe.

PSALM 45:1 (NRSV)

EMAIL is cold and quick. For two years digital messages passed back and forth between the Scriptorium in Wales and the CIT in Minnesota. Sketches were made and photographed; they whizzed over the wires and by satellite across the Atlantic with terse messages of explanation. Comments bounced back in icy, pixellated prose.

Donald is not cold. He is warm. He wants to read the nuances in your face as you talk. As the first two volumes were coming to completion, he wanted to reinvigorate his relationship with the committee.

"I insisted on a face-to-face meeting with the CIT," Donald remarked. "For the chemistry of it."

Through the making of the first two volumes, the relationship between artist and committee had sometimes been stormy but over time it had matured. The members of the CIT grew to understand Donald and his work; he learned how to digest and make use of the dense theological briefs. They all learned the limitations of long-distance communication. A single remark in the briefs could take on an importance it never would have had in a face-to-face conversation. It was hard to judge which ideas were crucial and which were simply suggestions.

Donald was given the briefs for the third volume, *Psalms*, in June 2002. The members of the committee were very proud of their work. By the time they wrote the brief, they had worked with Donald for several years. They knew his quirks and his strengths. They could see how his mind worked and what had sparked his imagination. And they could picture the kinds of solutions which might arise from their theological reflections.

The Psalms are not like the rest of the Bible. The Psalter is pure poetry, composed to be sung. The recitation of Psalms forms the core of the Benedictine hours of prayer. These were texts that every member of the monastic community knew intimately.

The CIT took the opportunity to devise a different kind of brief. The Psalms don't lend themselves to illustration; they are not narrative. So the members of the CIT decided to treat the book as a set of texts which would receive a more purely calligraphic treatment. Whatever illuminations might appear would be more abstract, tied to broad themes and they would serve to divide the text into sections. They felt sure that this text-based approach would please Donald and play to his strengths.

A meeting of minds

DONALD RECEIVED the brief for *Psalms* and began to work his way through it. There was a good deal of detail and one theme overlapped another. He wasn't sure how he could include all these ideas into his manuscript.

Donald Jackson examines sketches for the book of *Psalms*.

"There were so many different ideas. For instance, some of the psalms are written as acrostics; the first letter of each verse is a letter of the Hebrew alphabet. They thought I could do something with that.

"Then, every psalm is in a particular genre. Some psalms were half in one genre, half in another. Irene, who is a scholar of the Psalms, was big on genres. Other scholars would like this, she thought. Perhaps there was a way of differentiating each genre graphically.

"Then they wanted to highlight the penitential psalms. They also felt it was important to divide the text into five parts: the whole book of Psalms is broken into five books. They thought each of the five books should have a different tone," said Donald.

He wasn't sure how he could pull it off. Their wish list was too long. And he began to worry that it would throw the whole project out of schedule. Donald asked Sally Mae to work out how long it would take. She did; it was more time than they had.

"We worked out how long it would take to do all these things, and it simply didn't fit the schedule or the budget. Had I not insisted on meeting with them in person, we would have been driven mad."

Donald and the CIT sat down in September 2003 at Saint John's and began to go through the brief. Donald's fears were misplaced.

He recounted, "Nathanael said to me, 'I can see how this bothers you. You're reading this wish list as a to-do list in order of preference.' They weren't asking for anything like as much."

Back in the studio, Donald decided that the first and last psalms would receive special treatment but the rest of the text would remain relatively simple. The five book divisions were crucial but the different genres could be marked with small notations. Each book would be written in a slightly different hand, by a different scribe. A changing color scheme for the psalm numbers could also distinguish book from book.

The genres would be noted with small roman numerals, I–IX, and a key would be added to the marginal notes.

What had seemed daunting in a long, detailed brief was now much simpler. "We boiled it back down," Donald said. Face-to-face he knew what was really important to the committee and what could be relegated to secondary significance and what could be dropped altogether.

Working

DONALD CHOSE Sally Mae and Brian to write one book each. He would write a third. He engaged another calligrapher, not previously connected with the project, to write out a fourth. Where would the fifth scribe come from? There was no one available with the requisite skills and there was no time to train anyone. The writing of the psalms had to begin right away, so Donald decided to write two of the books. Then after the other scribes had begun writing, the extra scribe pulled out—he had too many work commitments. Sally Mae stepped into the breach and agreed to write the remaining book in addition to the one she'd already begun.

The books were divided up. Brian would write Book I (Psalms 1–41). Sally Mae would write Book II (Psalms 42–72) and Book V (Psalms 107–50). Donald would write Book III (Psalms 73–89) and Book IV (Psalms 90–106). Donald would do the illuminations at the beginning of each book, as well as the special treatment of Psalm 1. Sally would do the special treatment of Psalm 150.

Sally, Brian, and Donald each devised special scripts for the books they would write out. They agreed certain details would remain constant throughout the book, including psalm headings, the genre notations and the Amens.

Sally remembers, "I did Book V first, my first allocation. It was special to me. I had to develop a script different from the standard poetry hand which I'd been using for the prophets. So I played around. I gave a slope to it and gave it a distinctive feel."

Book V is full of psalms of praise. They are joyous and celebratory. They matched Sally's mood as she wrote in a script of her own devising. "I had the enjoyment of writing a script that was more natural to me," she said, "rather than emulating Donald's hand. I just loved writing the Psalms. I would go home elated. They are full of human feelings—they run the gamut. I would go home and read the Psalms after writing them all day."

Once Book V was complete, she turned her attention to Book II. Here she wanted to try another style of writing. "In Book II, I tried a very formal hand, a kind of angular Renaissance italic. I liked it, so I decided to use it. I did try some other variations, including one that was closer to the standard Bible hand, but I decided to base it on the Renaissance script in the end because it contrasted with Brian's and Donald's more fluid styles in the books which were on either side of it."

This script had its own character, with a very precise rhythm. She recalled, "It's all down to spacing between the letters, keeping the right pen angle and keeping the letters upright like soldiers marching across the page. It took a bit of getting used to but you haven't got weeks and months. You are actually practicing on the real thing. You can't live your life on a scrap of vellum. It's just like life: you have to live it to do it. You are learning as you write. Changes and variations happen. That's why I always start in the middle of the book, then go back to the beginning."

Brian and Donald, too, devised their new scripts. Brian's was close to the standard Bible poetry hand. Donald used a classic oval-based letterform in Book III. His script for Book IV had rounder shapes and more measured spacing between the letters and words. There is a family resemblance between their work, reflecting, perhaps, the fact that both of them trained with Irene Wellington at the Central School in London.

Sacred song

IN THE MEANTIME, Donald began to work out the illuminations. A large frontispiece would appear at the beginning of the whole volume and then smaller variations would mark the division between the other books.

Donald explained, "I walked away from the CIT meeting with the idea of using sound as a visual image. To that theme, I added the idea of using sacred music from different traditions."

The theme was perfect for a book of sacred song. "Johanna said to me that sound never stops. Once uttered, it reverberates through the universe forever. When you think about sacred music sounding out through the ages—that's something."

He continued, "There are no interpretations in the brief, so I had a great deal of freedom to define my theme. I wanted to use many chanting voices—Jewish, Buddhist, Native American, along with the sheer singing energy and power of

The book of Psalms evokes a long tradition of musical manuscripts. The square notes of this medieval Processional find a contemporary, abstracted echo in the gold squares which dance across each page of Saint John's *Psalms*. The manuscript shown here was made in Spain in 1541.

Processional. Dominican Rite. *Processionariu[m] secu[n]du[m] ordinem predicatoru[m].* Spain, 1541. Manuscript on vellum. Black leather binding over boards.
Kacmarcik Collection of Arca Artium, Saint John's University.

the Psalms themselves. In my design the voices of many traditions interweave with the Christian voice, which runs throughout the volume. The Saint John's Bible includes and respects those voices."

How was he to find a graphic means of expressing this idea? Donald began to explore computer programs which could translate sound into visual images. "By using two programs, we were able to obtain representations of the sound—you play a disk and it comes out as oscillations on the screen. I think they're called oscillographs."

Rebecca loaded CDs with different chants into the computer. Sarah, the studio assistant, sat in front of the screen with a digital camera. "We couldn't print out the moving images, so we had to sit and shoot away until we got an interesting pattern."

They played with different kinds of oscillations until they had a working set of images. Fragments of these wavy patterns of song were made into rubber stamps. The voices of monks at Saint John's provided the most important stamp. Running horizontally through the middle of every page, it became the unifying Christian voice which tied the volume together. On the frontispiece and at the opening of each book, the patterns of non-Christian voices were used. Placed vertically, they create a counterpoint to the Christian voices.

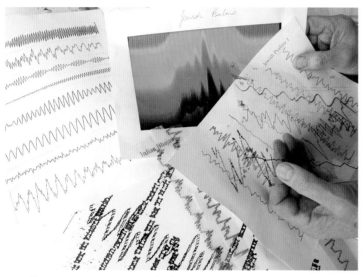

Using a computer program, sounds of sacred music from many cultures are transformed into oscillating patterns on the screen. These trembling lines were rendered as rubber stamps to be used in the illuminations.

Graphic renditions of sacred song from across the world provide a motif which appears on the frontispiece and book divisions of *Psalms*.

The monks at Saint John's.

Native American   Taoist   The *Adhan*, the Muslim call to prayer.

The key illumination in the volume was the two-page spread at the beginning of the book. All the rest of the book divisions would be constructed of details from this principal image.

"I did a sketch," he said. "It became five open books. They grew and I started to divide them up. Motifs like the menorah from Matthew's Gospel just crept back in."

The large opening spread was then sliced up. "Book II began with two sections, Book III with three sections and so on. It is a simple idea, but it works."

Throughout the volume rubber stamps and small golden squares and bars create a rising and falling rhythm, a counterpoint to the lines of writing, a visual leitmotif which ties the volume together visually.

Providence is the word you're looking for

THERE IS NEVER an uncluttered moment in the making of this Bible; even as Donald was buried in preparations for the *Psalms*, he continued to supervise scribes writing out the fourth and fifth volumes. His research, too, is ongoing. And in the process little accidents happen which move the project along.

Donald recounted, "I was at the British Museum looking at the whole period of art before Christ, the period of the growth of the Israelite nationhood. I especially wanted to look at Assyrian and Babylonian art. I was photographing chariot wheels and thinking about Ezekiel's visions of wheels within wheels." Although the vision described the wheels as "covered with eyes" Donald noted how sturdy and practical the Assyrian wheels were: no eyes, certainly.

A week later, he found himself at a wedding in France. "I met a man there. He was a professor of exegesis from Belgium. Suddenly there we were, in the middle of the French countryside, hammer and tongs into the design of Assyrian cartwheels. I told him my thoughts about the Assyrian and Babylonian sources for some of the biblical stories. I had a gut feeling that those visions were rooted in that sort of multicultural exposure.

"He said the description of chariot wheels with eyes in them was a mistranslation for 'brass studs' or 'brass nails.' When I thought about the photographs I'd taken, the wheels in them were covered with these little studs. Hearing him speak, I felt that little light bulb go off.

"Things just fall into place with this project. We don't even roll our eyes anymore. Like meeting an exegete who likes to talk about Assyrian chariot wheels."

Donald tried to characterize these odd coincidences once in a press conference. He was in Rome with a delegation from Saint John's to present the Pope with a facsimile of the first volume of the Bible. In front of the reporters, he struggled to find the right word to describe these unusual coincidences. Cardinal Pio Laghi, who was listening, smiled indulgently and said, "I think the word 'Providence' is what you're looking for."

Special treatments and happy accidents

THE VOLUME opens and closes with two special treatments in gold. Sally Mae tackled hers first.

"Donald saw Psalm 150 as being like the *Magnificat* from Luke," she said. "He wanted me to use that lettering. He saw it in gold. I thought about colored backgrounds again and played around with a few ideas. Nothing seemed to work. The Psalms pages had a voice of their own. So gold lettering on plain vellum was what the page needed."

She ended up with quite a calm composition. "But within that calmness there's a lot of movement, like tai-chi."

The large quantities of gesso she was using began to worry Donald. One of the ingredients of the mixture is white lead, a deadly poison which can be all too easily breathed in. Lead poisoning is a serious hazard any craft gilder must be attentive to.

"Mabel bought a dust buster, so I had to use it. My own little gesso hoover—it feels so bizarre hoovering the vellum!"

It is a wise precaution, nonetheless.

Donald turned to his special treatment for Psalm 1 and immediately ran into his own problem.

"We hit a major snag. I'm not sure how it happened. For some reason—it was probably my own fault—Vin had printed out all the psalm layouts starting on the wrong page. Instead of having a whole page to work with, I ended up with no place to put the special treatment of Psalm 1."

The writing had long been under way; there was no question of rearranging the layouts now. Donald would have to work with the space he had available.

"It left only half a column. Suddenly, I had to redesign the frontispiece to include the whole of Psalm 1."

Remarkably he was able to fit the whole of his text into the existing design. It was a beautiful solution to an ugly problem. But he wasn't out of trouble yet.

"Sara started to check it," he remembered. "Then she goes quiet. 'You've left out a full verse on the first psalm.'" Of all the places to make a mistake, this was about the worst Donald could imagine. Days of illumination could have gone down the tube.

He continued, "We're talking and she says, 'Wait, there's a space here.' And suddenly I see the text is missing where I've actually left a space. So I sketched out the missing verse in caps and then laid it over the gap. Sally had already gilded the small gold rectangles that spangle the frontispiece, so I had those shapes to contend with as well. Not only did the new tracing fit, but each space between the words corresponded exactly to where the small squares of gold had already been laid. There was only one little gold square in the way which I'd have to scrape off."

Grateful for his uncanny good fortune, he bent down to scrape off the single errant gold square.

"Sally had used a new technique we'd devised, using frisket to mask the areas of gilding. She had started to gild this rectangle, but she'd neglected to remove the frisket—so it just popped off when I touched it with my knife!"

Talk about good fortune. Or providence.

Too soon

DONALD GREW WISTFUL as he spoke of the *Psalms*. "It's hard for me to talk about them. The cooking time was so long on it, then it was taken away from me so fast."

The process of writing this volume had been grueling, unforgiving.

"It was preceded by four or five months of being tired. I got back from delivering the *Pentateuch* in September 2003. I was burned out from that trip—people, people, people. I didn't have energy and couldn't psych myself up. I needed to have time to recharge."

He was grateful for the support of his family and staff. "Oh, the brilliance of people—Sally, Mabel, Rebecca and Sarah. They all knew I would do it. I had to write two full books. It gave me so much respect for the calligraphy scribes. The people around me never wavered in their belief that I'd come up with the goods and deliver it on time."

After Christmas 2003, Donald worked seven days a week, every week until April 2004.

"That's how it got back on track. It was physically and emotionally demanding on top of everything."

And yet despite the tight schedule, he could still say, "To write the Psalms was just a beautiful experience because of the words themselves."

Completion

IN APRIL 2004 *Psalms* was completed. Donald and Mabel Jackson flew to Minnesota to present the finished volume to Saint John's University and Abbey. The third volume was done. It has eighty pages of writing on twenty-two skins. There are six illuminations, one special treatment, eighty-one marginal decorations, and 143 small capitals, of which 33 were written by Donald.

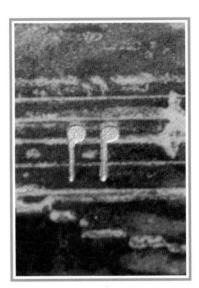

Donor Acknowledgment

Two musical notes "C" on the *Psalms Frontispiece* acknowledge the donor, Nicky Carpenter. This photograph has been taken from the printed Heritage Edition.

Donald Jackson's illumination *The Suffering Servant* appears between the fifty-second and fifty-third chapters of Isaiah.

CHAPTER 12

PROPHETS

Delivered April 2005

PROPHETS IS ONE of the longest volumes in The Saint John's Bible, clocking in at an astonishing 226 pages of writing. The scribes had continued with their page allotments so the work was well underway when Donald turned his attention to *Prophets* after returning from the delivery of *Psalms* in April 2004. Many outside forces now began to bear down on him and his team; it was not a peaceful time.

The planned exhibition at the Minneapolis Institute of Arts was now just a year away, and the plan was to deliver the *Prophets* volume at the same time as the opening in April 2005. The exhibition was to include pages from all three of the previously delivered volumes, and there was an enormous amount to prepare. Special cases were constructed in Minnesota to hold the vellum pages. A vast amount of information had to be collected to explain and document the work on show. Exhibition labels had to be created. Promotional material, logos, and press releases had to be prepared. And even though most of these tasks were in the hands of Saint John's and the curator and exhibition designer at the MIA, Donald and his staff were inevitably involved in the process.

I can speak from first-hand experience—the first edition of this book was prepared in this period. Although my own research and documentation had been ongoing for the previous four years, I still needed significant advice and input from Donald and his staff. Photos had to be collected and organized, and the text of the book itself was sent to Donald, who went carefully through it, correcting, annotating, and making suggestions. This inevitably pulled him away from his own production schedule.

The needs of the MIA were similar. I asked if the preparation for the exhibition was disruptive. He said, "I had a lot of help from Rebecca. I was grateful to have her and the other members of the staff who could help out."

And he told a funny story: "I asked the MIA curator of the exhibition, Jane Satkowski, where she was going to get information for the captioning. She was a medievalist. She said she would refer to the sources, as she always did. She was very thorough."

Donald was a little nonplussed. "I said, 'But you could just call me.' And she laughed and said, 'Oh I never thought of that. Of course, you're still alive!'"

As a result, much of the caption content for the MIA was supplied by the Scriptorium.

The exhibition was proof that there was a wide and enthusiastic audience for the Bible he and his scribes and artists were producing. From its starting venue at the MIA it would later travel to cities all over the United States. Donald, his team, and the people at Saint John's all had to get it right.

At the Scriptorium, other distractions intervened. The regular visits of the scribes were logistically difficult. Space was at a premium in the Scriptorium, and in order to accommodate all five of the scribes, Donald had to give up his drafting table. When the scribes were all there, Donald not only was called away from his own work on illuminations to sit and work with each calligrapher but also lost his own working area.

The book titles in *Prophets* reflect the languages of the original texts. The Hebrew title of Isaiah appears over the English title and was written by Izzy Pludwinski. Baruch, which comes down to us in Greek, has a corresponding Greek title.

It was decided that an addition should be built on to the building to allow for more space. The work began in August 2004. The Scriptorium was enveloped in the sounds and distractions of the building work. Although the plan was sound, the work dragged on and took much more of Donald's time than he had been led to believe it would.

The addition was finally linked to the main Scriptorium building in April 2005, while the team was in Minneapolis for the exhibition opening. And by that time, the scribes were getting close to finishing.

He lamented to me, "Builders being who they are—not to mention planning permissions and all that—by the time the building was finished, the writing was done."

In the midst of these distractions, it was becoming clear that the project as a whole had continued to lag behind the planned schedule.

Donald Jackson discusses the handling of chapter numbers with Sally Mae Joseph and Brian Simpson.

"This is when reality finally caught up with us," Donald said. "At this point, it was pointed out that in every volume to date, we were delivering 30 percent more illumination than was scheduled for."

Some of this was what is referred to in the business world as "mission creep," the inevitable enlarging of the scope of a project so it becomes much more ambitious than was it was first envisioned to be. Donald said, "The work was changing continually, but we had a fixed-price contract. Production wasn't reaching the levels we'd hoped. Why? A lot of it was the extras—the promotional events, the trips to openings of the traveling exhibition—that I was being asked to do. These actually added up to three and a half years of the first nine years of the project. So many things had to go through me, I became the bottleneck."

In January 2005, the contract was negotiated anew. The completion date was now set for July 2007 and the total cost revised upward to £2.2 million. It would not be the last time the contract would need to be revised.

All of these developments took a toll on everyone involved, but with the impending exhibition, the Bible project was about to make its biggest impression yet on the public stage. The exhibition would reach a vast new audience and break attendance records as some of the venues where it was exhibited. From outside, The Saint John's Bible was a huge success, the fulfillment of a grand dream. From within, it was a bit of a pressure cooker.

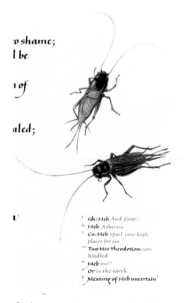

Crickets appear in a margin, painted by Chris Tomlin.

Design considerations

THE *Prophets* volume, like the *Psalms* volume that preceded it, presented some unique design challenges. The most important of these was the fact that much of the text in *Prophets* is in poetry rather than prose. This disturbed the natural organizing principle of having two strong columns of justified text to give structure to the pages. Instead, the columns are ragged, with changing line lengths on the right side and a series of varied indents on the left. The poetry script for *Prophets* was therefore modified and is slightly more heavy than the poetry script used in the more prose-dominated volumes of the Bible.

This threw off the balance of the page. In *Prophets* the chapter numbers appear in small squares of color.

The scribes at work in the Scriptorium.

The large amount of poetry in *Prophets* required adjustments to the format. The large drop-caps used in previous volumes do not appear here. The chapter numbers in small colored squares punctuate the page instead.

The new treatment for the chapter numbers punctuated the page with these bolder elements, saving it from devolving into an amorphous mass. Donald commented, "The strict protocol for the indenting of poetry and the sparseness of text did not allow for the accommodation of full-size, three-line drop caps. These large capitals provide strong visual punctuation in other volumes. This function was replaced by having colored rectangles as backgrounds for gilded chapter numbers instead."

Another feature of the volume is the use of a rubber stamp pattern of wings to decorate certain margins and fill small gaps in the text. This rubber stamp was made for the illumination of Isaiah's vision and became a leitmotif used throughout the book. Its recurrence provides another unifying element that helps tie the book together as a whole.

The illuminations in this volume all depict visionary experiences of the prophets, which lend themselves to the suggestive, collaged approach Donald favored throughout the Bible.

The Vision of Isaiah

The Vision of Isaiah depicts the moment when the prophet is called by God to deliver his message to the people of Israel. The prophet, confronted with the sight of God on his throne in the Holy of Holies of the temple flanked by the many-winged Seraphim, is profoundly aware of his inadequacy. An angel takes a coal from the altar and touches it to the prophet's mouth, a purifying action. He hears the call of God: "Whom shall I send?" To which the prophet replies, "Here am I. Send me."

In his layouts, Donald had created a space for illumination that spreads across two skins. It is narrow at its base and expands at the top. "There was such drama in the text, and it was full of sound," he said. "Beating wings. Horses' hooves." Donald made a gesture with hands to describe the feeling: his hands clasped in front of his body, bursting upward and outward. "The whole scene seemed to explode upwards."

There were many elements to work into the composition. The scene of the temple had to be suggested, along with the divine figure on his throne and the flanking cherubim. The words of the Seraphim—Holy, holy, holy—had to be included, in Hebrew, Latin, and Greek.

"This actually came rather easily," he said. "I just attacked it with a large brush."

The background is a lush violet blue with soft, brushy edges. The arched shapes along the top suggest an architectural framework. Various elements from descriptions of the temple appear, including ranks of lamps and small fragments of masonry rendered in thin gold lines.

Down the central axis, the divine figure is suggested with loose brush strokes; his head is silhouetted against a square of gold. Bits of rainbow pattern and sapphire make this region around the head sparkle

Donald shows the rubber stamps that he used to add the sinuous wing motifs to *The Vision of Isaiah.*

The Vision of Isaiah in progress. The free brushstrokes of the background are in place on the final vellum sheet. At each side, Donald Jackson's sketches provide a guide for the progressing work.

Thomas Ingmire's *Messianic Predictions* appear opposite Isaiah 10.

and symbolize the divine presence. As this illumination was actually made after the ones in Ezekiel, Donald picked up these images from those illuminations.

Two seraphim flank the figure of God. In the text, these are described as creatures with many wings. Donald found images of wings from Assyrian bas reliefs, traced them, and had them scanned. They were then manipulated on the computer to morph into curved, evocative shapes. The prototypes were made into rubber stamps.

At the base, he placed the slightly abstracted figure of the prophet, rather painfully being touched with the coal by and angel with golden tongs.

In the original sketch, Donald had placed the face of the prophet, looking upward toward the divine figure, and next to the words "Here am I."

The CIT balked at his treatment of this face. Donald reflected that removing it could actually improve the interpretation and make it more powerful. "By removing the face, and leaving just the words, it puts the viewer in the prophet's shoes." With the face in place, the story seems to be distant—a story about someone else, long ago. "Now the question is directly addressed to you or me. When we read those three short words, we are involved," he said. "We are forced to ask ourselves, 'Where do I stand?'"

The Vision of Isaiah. appears adjacent to Isaiah 6.

Ezekiel's Vision at the River Chebar

The images for this illumination are shown on pages 217 and 218.

THIS ILLUMINATION got more attention than was originally planned. "If you look at the brief," Donald said, "this was supposed to be a one-third-page illumination. In laying out the page, I gave it a generous third of the page. When I came to do it, I spread it out, even more, into the margins."

He made me laugh when he described what this illumination was meant to portray: "In this story God pulls out the fireworks, whiz-bang on your knees, be afraid! You have to believe in me. Here's a scroll: Eat these words, they must become part of you!"

In Ezekiel's vision, four great creatures surround the heavenly chariot: a lion, an eagle, an ox, and a figure like a human being. These figures were adopted by the early church as the traditional symbols of the four evangelists.

Donald said, "When I was nineteen years old, I drew images of the four evangelists." Back then, he had used the traditional, rather tame representations. Here, he wanted to evoke the mysterious, frightening nature of the vision. His research took him on a foray into ancient art. As he explained to the CIT,

"Instead of the blander images which one thinks of from the evangelist portraits of the Common Era, I went straight to the Assyrian, Babylonian, and Egyptian sources. For the human faces, I took my inspiration from a low relief portrait on a ceramic lid of a casket made, it is said, under Greek influence."

The result is an amorphous mass from which frightening faces loom. The animal figures blend with the textured background.

This image was also the origin of the rainbow motif that Donald would come to use increasingly as a symbol of the divine presence. The image comes directly from the text: "Like the bow in a cloud on a rainy day" (Ezek 1:28). Although there was some concern from the CIT that the rainbow might be interpreted as a contemporary political reference, they allowed Donald to use it. It would appear in many subsequent illuminations. It appears here behind the distant divine figure in the upper left corner of the illumination and again to the right as it approaches the tiny figure of the prophet.

Dancing in the margins are images of spinning wheels made with rubber stamps. These were based on Assyrian carvings as well. Their studs represent the "eyes" that the text describes on their rims.

"I love using rubber stamps," Donald said. "Although I sometimes retouch them a bit, they are very direct. You have to live with the imperfections of the impression. Those imperfections pick up on the instantaneous quality of the brush. They also share in the element of risk—commitment to the act."

The scroll the prophet is given to eat is described in the text as being written on two sides. Donald asked Izzy Pludwinski to provide him with text in Hebrew. He wrote it out on a piece of vellum, which he then twisted to see how the text would flow in three dimensions. He used these experiments to create the fragments of scroll that appear on various parts of the illumination. These lead the viewer's eye from the figure at the top left, across the fold, to the figure of the prophet who receives the scroll in the far right margin.

The Valley of Dry Bones

DONALD frankly struggled with the themes of this illumination. "It simply doesn't work for me," he said. "I struggled to get past the sheer implausibility of flesh growing on old, dead bones." But as he worked with the brief and read and reread the text, he reacted to the word *spirit*. In the passage, God promises to give the people his spirit, and they will live.

"Notice that there are no figures in the top part of the image," he said. The illumination is divided

The images for this illumination are shown on pages 220 and 221.

into distinct halves: at the bottom, literal images of genocide, environmental destruction, and war. At the top, abstract imagery represents the everlasting life of the spirit. By approaching the divine promise in terms of an abstraction, Donald escaped literalism. Nothing can negate the suffering depicted below, but perhaps there is a way forward, a better way.

When Donald speaks of this illumination, as I have heard him do several times, he describes a scene from his childhood. His father had a mechanic's workshop. It was grey and filthy, a place of machinery and toil. Donald did not like going there as a child. But he remembers seeing on the floor, in a puddle of oil, the rainbow sheen reflected on the surface. That, it seemed to him, was a perfect metaphor for what he was trying to depict here: in a scene of ugliness, a ray of hope.

Ezekiel's Vision at the River Chebar appears at Ezekiel 2.

Sketches for *Ezekiel's Vision* at the River Chebar emphasize the strange, frightening nature of the prophet's vision.

The scenes below were inspired by images "drawn from archive sources recorded in Armenia, Auschwitz, Rwanda, Iraq, and Cambodia." In his description of the illumination to the CIT, he wrote: "[I have] linked the images of wasted human life with the waste generated by our society by incorporating 'skeletons' from garbage tips and auto wreckers' yards. The latter serve as metaphors of our attitude to God's created earth. Even here, however, there is beauty in the rainbow reflections on an oil slick in a sordid and filthy puddle."

Along the bottom, thick black bars are meant to describe "the prisons in which we trap ourselves." Yet even here, the small gold squares suggest there are small glimpses of hope.

Above, against a gold- and rainbow-abstracted background, they become seven gold bars, a symbol of transformation.

of eyes all around. When the living creatures moved, the wheels moved beside them; and when the living creatures rose from the earth, the wheels rose. Wherever the spirit would go, they went, and the wheels rose along with them; for the spirit of the living creatures was in the wheels. When they moved, the others moved; when they stopped, the others stopped; and when they rose from the earth, the wheels rose along with them; for the spirit of the living creatures was in the wheels. Over the heads of the living creatures there was something like a dome, shining like crystal, spread out above their heads. Under the dome their wings were stretched out straight, one toward another; and each of the creatures had two wings covering its body. When they moved, I heard the sound of their wings like the sound of mighty waters, like the thunder of the Almighty, a sound of tumult like the sound of an army; when they stopped, they let down their wings. And there came a voice from above the dome over their heads; when they stopped, they let down their wings. And above the dome over their heads there was something like a throne, in appearance like sapphire; and seated above the likeness of a throne was something that seemed like a human form. Upward from what appeared like the loins I saw something like gleaming amber, something that looked like fire enclosed all around; and downward from what looked like the loins I saw something that looked like fire, and there was a splendor all around. Like the bow in a cloud on a rainy day, such was the appearance of the splendor all around. This was the appearance of the likeness of the glory of the LORD. When I saw it, I fell on my face, and I heard the voice of someone speaking.

2 He said to me: O mortal, stand up on your feet, and I will speak with you. And when he spoke to me, a spirit entered into me and set me on my feet; and I heard him speaking to me. He said to me, Mortal, I am sending you to the people of Israel, to a nation of rebels who have rebelled against me; they & their ancestors have transgressed against me to this very day. The descendants are impudent & stubborn. I am sending you to them, and you shall say to them, "Thus says the Lord GOD." Whether they hear or refuse to hear (for they are a rebellious house), they shall know that there has been a prophet among them. And you, O mortal, do not be afraid of them, and do not be afraid of their words, though briers & thorns surround you & you live among scorpions; do not be afraid of their words, and do not be dismayed at their looks, for they are a rebellious house. You shall speak my words to them, whether they hear or refuse to hear; for they are a rebellious house. But you, mortal, hear what I say to you; do not be rebellious like that rebellious house; open your mouth and eat what I give you. I looked, and a hand was stretched out to me, and a written scroll was in it. He spread it before me; it had writing on the front and on the back, and written on it were words of lamentation and mourning and woe.

Ezekiel's Vision at the River Chebar appears at Ezekiel 2.

Ezekiel's Vision of the Renewed Temple

JUST A FEW PAGES beyond the *Valley of Dry Bones* is *Ezekiel's Vision of the New Temple*. Here the promises of the dry bones passage come vividly to life in a restoration of the religious community. The image seems deceptively simple, with the strong centralized plan that dominates the page.

The text describes a vision in which the prophet is led around the rebuilt temple by an angel. They carry a measuring rod, and the whole story suggests a precise and literal description of a real building. From the temple emerges a river, a symbol of abundant life, swarming with healthy trees, birds, and fish.

The raw materials for the illumination *The Valley of Dry Bones* sit on Donald Jackson's table.

Donald was guided by the brief to evoke the tension between the literal, measurable aspect of the vision and the way it leads us to a vision of the unbounded, the indescribable. As the CIT pointed out, the exactitude of the description had led many to try to devise clear representations of this visionary temple. But the reconstructions of the plan always differed enormously from one another. "I read the text," he said, "and realized I was getting lost. You can't add up the numbers. But in losing the literal sense, you get where you're supposed to be. It's a verbal labyrinth: you must first lose yourself in order to find your way to God." Ultimately, this could not be reduced to a clear and measurable plan for an actual building.

Another aspect that Donald had to keep in mind was that this image needed to refer explicitly to a later image in the last volume: "I needed to be aware that this image would link to the illumination of the building of the New Temple in *Historical Books* and the New Jerusalem spread at the very end of Revelation, the last illumination in The Saint John's Bible."

The Internet provided a rich source of visual reference for the images of genocide and environmental degradation in *The Valley of Dry Bones*.

"The image of the plan of the temple came from a seventeenth-century Dutch engraving," he said. It was a hard-edged attempt to produce a literal plan. Donald reproduced it in three sizes, layering them one atop the other, so it seems to explode from the central altar of sacrifice. The result is a shimmering image against a kaleidoscopic rainbow background.

He used mixed media in this image. "The black line drawing of the temple was printed by a silkscreen," he explained. "We took a big risk. The background was completely painted in before it was taken to the silkscreen shop." Everyone was aware that many days of work were at stake if it went wrong. He said, "The woman at the silkscreen shop was white as a sheet. We did just one proof on a piece of vellum prepared exactly the same way as this sheet was. It was stretched on a board with staples and all."

"It had to be a one-shot," Donald said, "and it had to have a mechanical look." At the same time, the technique sits well with the hand-rendered elements on the page. As Donald explained, the silkscreen

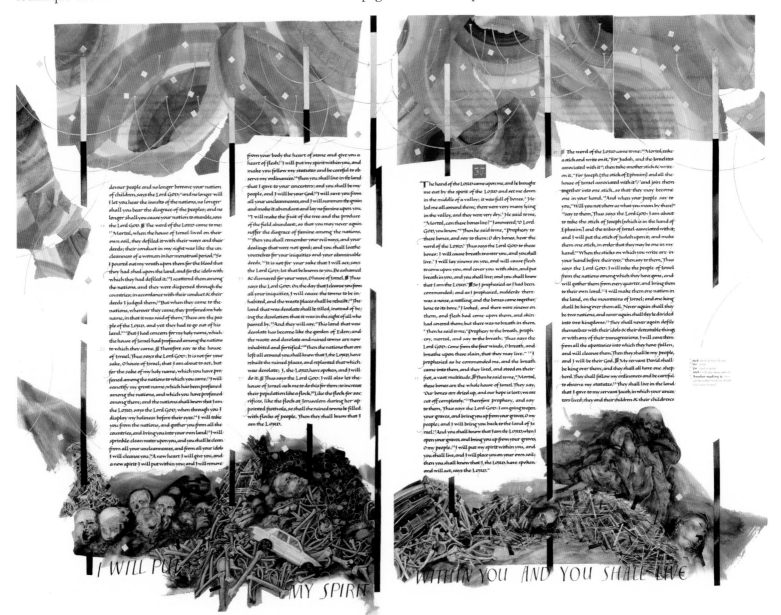

The Valley of Dry Bones appears at Ezekiel 36.

EZEKIEL

W

S

N

E

THE SPIRIT LIFTED ME UP
AND BROUGHT ME TO
THE INNER COURT:
AND THE GLORY OF
THE LORD FILLED
THE TEMPLE

*Ezekiel's Vision of the Renewed Temple appears oppo-
site Ezekiel 43 and provides an image of hope and
renewal after the more somber visions in the previous illuminations of the prophetic book. A fine gold
line traces a path inward, to the Holy of Holies at
the center of the temple.*

technique has a different feel than an engraving. "Silkscreen ink has a finish similar to calligraphy and painting, in that it sits slightly proud of the page surface, because it's like laying paint on the surface; it sits on top."

Once the silkscreen image was done, a golden line was drawn, suggesting a path through the temple diagram. It was not an easy feat. "The gold lines were put on after we did the silkscreening, with gold leaf on gum ammoniac. It was a real pain. Even though I had done successful tests beforehand, wherever the gum ammoniac lines intercepted, they flooded and the gold leaf tended to stick to everything. This meant a lot of cleaning up."

To begin with Donald was not entirely happy with the painting at the base of the image. He lamented, "It's very difficult to be fresh when you are executing an illumination from a sketch. I thought the piece pretty wooden at the bottom, but in retrospect I think it turned out pretty well." The scene depicted below shows the water of life pouring from the rebuilt temple, nourishing plants and animals. He used the rubber stamps from the *Loaves and Fishes* illumination in *Gospels and Acts*.

Completion

IN APRIL 2005, when Donald and his team arrived in Minneapolis for the opening of the exhibition Illuminating the Word at the MIA, volume 4, *Prophets*, was almost completed. A few loose ends still needed to be finished, but the work was mostly done. The *Prophets* volume has 226 pages of writing on fifty-seven skins. There are nine interpretive illuminations, eight special treatments, thirteen marginal decorations, and 257 small capitals.

The exhibition opening at the Minnesota Institute of Arts was a spectacular gala affair. Donald was accompanied by his regular staff at the Scriptorium—his wife Mabel, Rebecca Cherry, Sarah Harris, Sally Mae Joseph, and Vin Godier. The scribes Angela Swan, Susie Leiper, and Sue Hufton were there as well; Brian Simpson was unable to make the trip. The artists Hazel Dolby and Aidan Hart traveled from England, and Thomas Ingmire and Suzanne Moore, based in the United States, flew in to join the party. Diane Von Arx, who is based in Minnesota and joined the project in May 2004 as a guest artist, was also there. She designed the logo for the exhibition. I was there as well.

The excitement began at Saint John's in Collegeville with a series of receptions and then decamped to Minneapolis, where there was a gala dinner before the opening. Donald was rushed from one interview to the next and appeared on television and in the local papers. The Bible received a warm welcome; over sixty thousand people visited the exhibition in the course of its four-month run, making it one of the top three most successful exhibitions held at the MIA in the previous fifteen years.

Donor Acknowledgment

The donor acknowledgment in *Prophets* honors Tom Carpenter. The papaya tree is decorated with a quote from Ezekiel 47:12.

Wisdom Books opens with the full-page frontispiece to Job.

CHAPTER 13

WISDOM BOOKS

Delivered July 2006

RETURNING from the opening of the exhibition in Minneapolis, Donald and his team set to work on the next volume, *Wisdom Books*. Late 2005 and early 2006 was a time of transition at the Scriptorium. The building work was finished; they came home to find the addition had been connected to the existing building while they were in the States. But the changes were not just environmental. In September 2005, the scribes Sally Mae Joseph, Sue Hufton, Susan Leiper, Brian Simpson, and Angela Swan finished their writing allocations. Together, they had written an astonishing 96,781 lines. There remained 2,414 lines for Donald to complete on his own.

Sally Mae Joseph, Donald Jackson, and Sue Hufton examine pages of writing at the Scriptorium.

Sally Mae, who had been a daily presence in the Scriptorium as studio manager, left the Scriptorium on 29 April 2005. She continued to work on a freelance basis from home between May and August 2005 on script in *Wisdom Books* and special treatments in *Wisdom Books* and *Historical Books*. In June and December she came in to meet up with the visiting scribes for final script review and sign-off of scribes' text pages. She moved away, back to the southeast of England.

I asked Donald, "When the writing was finished, did it feel lonely? Suddenly you found yourself on your own, and the rhythm of visits by the scribes had stopped."

He answered, "No, not really. The fact is Susie, Sue, Brian, and Angela continued to come in to do bits and pieces—small things like chapter numbers, notes, or running heads. They had never been a part of the day-to-day production at the Scriptorium. Also Rebecca and Sarah, who took over from Sally Mae as studio manager, were still here coordinating and assisting me and the other artists."

Donald had other work for the scribes unrelated to the Bible. For much of his career, Donald has been a scribe to the Crown Office of the House of Lords, and he made his early fame through his hand-written and illuminated official documents for the Queen's signature. "We still had peerages to do," he said, "and the team, including Sarah, worked on them at home—so we were in regular contact."

He added, "As much as I enjoyed the scribes coming in every six weeks or so, it was always an additional challenge to support and encourage them in the best way I could. So as well as being a vital and rewarding part of the work, it often left me drained and distanced from my own 'doing' because it involved a different kind of emotional energy. I also had to give up my desk in the Scriptorium, so I experienced a feeling of relief that this stage of the work was complete."

Exhibitions and new ventures

IN JANUARY 2006, the exhibition that had opened at the MIA moved to the Joslyn Museum in Omaha, Nebraska, where it ran for six months and attracted sixty-eight thousand visitors. Donald flew in for the opening and took the opportunity to discuss another venture—the printed facsimile edition of the Bible.

Conversations about the facsimile had been ongoing since 2004. The intention was for Saint John's to produce the facsimile on their own without him, but Donald was inevitably involved to some extent. His

The loose brushstrokes that define the backgrounds of the illuminations are a recurrent motif throughout the Bible.

Sketches for *Creation, Fall, Passover, and Deliverance* show the way Donald Jackson effectively uses collage to build up his compositions.

The finished illumination of *Creation, Fall, Passover, and Deliverance* is full of visual quotations from earlier volumes of The Saint John's Bible. At this point in the creation of the manuscript, motifs emerge as part of a new iconography, unique to this Bible.

approval of the facsimile was crucial if they were to promote it as a faithful representation of the manuscript.

Up until this point, Carol Marrin had been working with European printers who specialized in facsimiles of medieval manuscripts. The results did not please Donald.

"It was a hard time," he said. "Carol was trying hard to get this done, and I kept having to tell them the consultation process wasn't working." Even though the facsimile project had been under discussion for some time, Donald still could not give his wholehearted approval of the samples he was seeing.

The Pillars of Wisdom appears in Proverbs.

By 2006 John Roberts Printing Company in Minneapolis had been selected as the probable printer for the project, and Saint John's had the advice of Dave Peterson, an expert printer, to guide them through the process.

On his trip to Minnesota and Nebraska in January 2006, Donald took the opportunity to sit down with Fr. Columba Stewart and Dave Peterson to review paper samples for the facsimile.

It was at about this time, in February 2006, that the facsimile project had acquired a name—the Heritage Edition. The name derived from the notion that the printed version was a "heritage" of the original manuscript.

As the Heritage Project grew, it acquired its own corporate structure, and Craig Bruner was appointed its director in 2006.

Between January and the fall of 2006 paper samples as well as printing and foil samples were produced by John Roberts, and these bounced back and forth between the Scriptorium and Collegeville.

The Bible project was growing in scope, as the traveling exhibition made its way around the United States, and the related printing and publishing ventures were becoming more ambitious. The operations of the Bible project became, by necessity, more formalized and more corporate. In February 2006, Liturgical Press, with its headquarters on the Saint John's University campus, entered a formal partnership with the Bible project for trade reproduction, cards, and other print projects for the Bible.

In February 2006 another exhibition of selected pages from the *Prophets* volume opened at the Victoria & Albert Museum in London. The attendance figures over the three-month run of the show totted up to seventy-five thousand.

All of this activity, as gratifying as it was, proved an interruption to the production schedule, and Donald worked hard to maintain his focus on the creation of the original manuscript. Work on the *Wisdom Books* had to continue apace.

Design considerations

Details of the layout of *Wisdom Books* reflect the textual peculiarities of the texts.

THE TEXT OF *Wisdom*, like the text of *Prophets*, is largely composed of poetry, so the same slightly heavier poetry script was continued in this volume. The chapter numbers, however, were not enclosed in small colored squares, as they were in the previous volume, but instead appear in this volume written in color.

Donald's approach to the illuminations began to change in *Wisdom*. By this time, he had created four volumes, and now he began to consciously reach back and draw motifs from his earlier work to incorporate in his new illuminations. In Wisdom of Solomon, chapter 13, for example, he produced a series of four images that were explicitly drawn from previous illuminations.

I asked him about his thought process. He said, "At the beginning, we were creating everything from scratch." The intention from the outset—perhaps not explicitly stated, but implicitly—was to avoid traditional iconography and create a new response to the biblical text. That meant at the beginning he had no body of symbols and images to draw from. By this stage, however, he had devised many visual devices, and he could begin to recombine them as he worked on his illuminations.

"You've had to create an entirely new iconography," I said to him. He liked that term. Yes. In the process of creating the Bible, he had begun to establish a body of symbols that he could use to evoke the theological ideas in the text.

Another development was an increasing integration of text and image. The frontispiece to Ecclesiastes and the *Seven Pillars of Wisdom* in Proverbs show a new interrelationship between the imagery and the text. These illuminations are not confined neatly within the space of the page but spill out across their respective spreads; the written text is shaped around the structure of the image. In previous illuminations, Donald had explored the use of margins and allowed his images to spill into empty spaces, but here the text and image are shaped together.

In the Song of Songs, Donald took this a step further. For the first time, an entire book within a volume received a distinct treatment, both in terms of its distinctive text script and in terms of ornament that fills every page with dancing color. Leafing through the whole volume, the viewer is struck by the Song as a distinctive, unique book.

The Woman of Valor appears at the end of Proverbs.

The Woman of Valor

THIS ILLUMINATION was executed by Hazel Dolby. It was originally intended to be a third page, but it turned into a half page. The brief for this illumination was long. The exegesis section of the brief emphasized the idea of the practical wisdom of the woman managing her household as a figure for the practical wisdom of the divine. "We see God as a housewife," the CIT had said.

Donald explained, "The free association section of the brief went on for almost two pages. Hazel found herself in the same situation I had often found myself, trying to tick all the boxes and cover all the ideas in the brief. Imagine if you're Hazel—what am I supposed to do with all of this?"

Donald encouraged her to boil it down, to capture the essence of what the CIT had suggested. She certainly shouldn't feel she needed to include every image and idea the brief proposed. Those were just her starting points, ideas to get her moving.

When she had resolved the broad strokes of the design, Donald sent it off to the CIT with these comments:

> In order to fine tune her ideas for this illumination from the many pencil sketches she worked on, Hazel looked at the role of African women in family life: the nurturing of children, plants, animals, the home and cooking. Also the role of women in the community: valued for their wisdom and practicality. [. . .] Hazel felt that the lettering needed to be strong but not heavy and still feminine, using the colours that the text suggested.

Sketches for *The Woman of Valor* in Hazel Dolby's studio.

Donald's role as artistic director put him in between the guest artists and the CIT. "Regarding the guest artists, I had the role of being the interpreter to the CIT," he said. "But I was also selling their work." He paused to reconsider. "No—*selling* is not the right word. I was a broker—that's better—between the artist and the CIT. I had learned early on that a single misplaced phrase in my CIT sketch submissions could cause a flurry of misunderstandings. I presented the artists' own words in a form which related directly to the brief and my understanding of the committee's requirements."

He also had to decide how best to work with each artist. "Hazel once told me, 'I'm not used to working with a client.'" And indeed that is true. Most of Hazel's work has been made as an independent artist, not as work for commission. When she has made things on commission, they have usually been pieces that have grown out her personal work.

Donald admired her tenaciousness. "It rattled her chain, this process. But she stuck with it. She fought her way through it. I like what she did."

He commented, "Choosing who did each illumination was like casting a play." And Hazel's work on this illumination meshed nicely both with the passage itself and with other illuminations. As Donald pointed out, *"The Woman of Valor* takes up on the textile theme that runs through the Bible."

It also picks up on a theme Hazel had worked with in her own work in the past, when she had explored Victorian quilts as a visual theme. Donald liked the way she knit the image into the structure of the page. "She added life to it by adding tassels to the bottom and very subtle flecks of gold," he said. "This saved it from being just a block on the page. It hasn't got hard edges (although in the cleaned-up version printed in the Trade Edition, the edges have been cleaned up, and seem quite hard)."

Ecclesiastes Frontispiece

THE FRONTISPIECE to Ecclesiastes explodes across the page, full of energy. The brief here was long—a full seven pages. Donald explained, "The original schema asked for three separate small quarter- or third-page interpretive illuminations, but they also gave me the option of hanging them into one composition."

The sketch for the frontispiece to Ecclesiastes stands above the table where the finished illumination is in its early stages.

The unity of text and image was made possible because Donald executed both on this spread. He said, "I had assigned myself the writing on these pages, so the text wasn't written when I started. I knew I would need more flexibility. The sketch and the arrangement of the text were done at the same time." This gave Donald much more freedom than he usually enjoyed to build a fluid composition.

In his notes to the CIT when he presented his sketch, he explained his visual reasoning:

[I] decided to set the whole in a dramatic fragmentary cosmic skyscape and used your wheel suggestion by using a diagram of the moon's phases, which is "spun" by the rubber stamp wings. [. . .] The bright colours represent life's joys whilst the moon's waxing and waning represent the ups and downs of our earthly life. There is also here a reference to the feminine in the 28-day cycle of the moon.

The raven refers to a story about Saint Benedict, in which a raven acts as a messenger. It also alludes to the saint's admonition to "keep death daily before your eyes." At Donald's home in the Hendre, ravens are a frequent visitor. The raven seemed to him a natural evocation of death.

He said, "There is a swirling motion, a sort of whirlpool carrying your eye." He used this vortex to suggest the nuanced worldview of the book. "The main theme of Ecclesiastes is that while life is linear and cyclical at the same time. All we have is the present moment."

Other elements of the composition bring out further complexities of his theme. "The butterfly wings, which were painted by Chris Tomlin, are there for the color but also for their flimsiness, suggesting the fleetingness of life. The butterfly also symbolizes the idea of metamorphosis." He did not leave these pristine. "There is also a sort of destruction going on. I scraped off parts of Chris' exquisite, precise painting. It evokes our own decay as we age."

And finally, a familiar image recurs: "The rainbow staves add a note of joy and exuberance and suggest God's presence in all of this."

In his preliminary sketches, the circle with the cycles of the moon was a dominant element. This was later toned down, as the raven became the most forceful image on the page.

Donald explained, "In the final execution, the writing was done first, to match what I had done in the sketch." Once the writing had been done, he masked out the area to be painted using Frisket so as to recreate the torn edges of the collaged sketch. He said, "With Frisket I could have the freedom of making free brush strokes without fear of paint spilling onto the text."

Chris Tomlin works on the butterfly wings that feature prominently in the illumination.

The frontispiece to Ecclesiastes.

Song of Songs

DONALD DID ALL THE WRITING in Song of Songs, because he felt his writing suited the emotional quality of the text. "In Song of Songs," he said, "The writing is my straight Italic."

His vision for the Song was more ambitious than had been envisioned in the schema. He said, "According to the budget, I had fifteen days to make this, from concept to sketch to execution. It was supposed to be just a third of a page." But there as no way he could let such a rich, evocative book be treated with such minimalism.

"The poem uses highly sexualized language to convey the intensity of our desire for our unity with God," he said. "Rumi and the Sufi mystics use the same device. The male lover is dying to get to his beloved, and she is eager for him."

Yet the desire described in the text is never consummated. Donald used direct language to describe

In the Song of Songs, the illuminations spill into the margins, unifying text and image.

Donald Jackson uses rubber stamps to create some of the motifs in the Song of Songs.

Gold is applied to details of the illuminations in the Song of Songs.

Donald Jackson at work on the special
treatment at the end of the Song of Songs.

this: "But they're not going to get it together. She's locked within her garden of desire. The goal is unattainable, but there is an intense longing inwards: God wants you and you want God."

Thinking of Rumi, Donald turned to the art of the Middle East. He said, "I picked on a geometric Islamic interlace as a motif. The dots join up, it's resolved, the affair is consummated. But I broke it into pieces. The two lovers are trying to achieve the unity the interlace suggests."

On the second page of the book, he created the one bold image, a garden of desire guarded by a red lock, covered with gold geometric patterns. "Only the boundaries are in place; the rest is incomplete. The parts are scattered across the page."

Reflecting on the theme of the poem, he said, "I suppose God is incomplete without us, and we, likewise, without him." And exploring the idea of attraction, of desire, he said, "I thought of this garden motif as being like a magnet surrounded by iron shavings." The iron shavings are drawn by the force of the magnet. Likewise, the visual elements sprinkled all across the spread begin to align like pieces of a puzzle, drawn to the lock.

On the second full spread, bold flower-like marks punctuate the margins. He explained, "What I wanted was to capture passion and risk. So I took a piece of lace, inked it with watercolor and pressed it down on the skin with the palm of my hand. Then I protected the text with Frisket, took a big brush and—splat! I turned the board upright, pressed the brush down and squeezed it, so the paint could dribble down the page of its own will. Also, I was trying to suggest both the masculine and the feminine elements in the text. The lace is feminine, the bold splatters masculine."

He also incorporated butterflies in this sequence of illuminations. "The butterflies on these pages are painted by Sarah; there wasn't time to turn to Chris Tomlin. And I added the butterfly next to the book title."

The Song of Songs ends with a lush special treatment. The bold letter forms are made with a great deal of pen manipulation, playing with thicks and thins in a novel way, he said: "I used a reed for this, dipping it into different colors. Sensuous to the touch, the reed gives you a softer line when you turn it on its edge than the quill does."

Just as he had completed the Song of Songs, he was invited to Cambridge University by Christopher de Hamel, the noted scholar of manuscripts and a long-time supporter of the Bible project. Donald told this anecdote: "It was the five hundredth anniversary of the founding of the Parker Library at Corpus Christi College, Cambridge. I had brought along pages from the Song of Songs with me. Christopher showed to the assembled guests the earliest, single-volume, portable Bible written in England. 'This was completed eight hundred years ago,' and pointing to my page he said, 'and this was finished on Thursday!'"

Mirror of Wisdom

THIS IS ARGUABLY one of the most striking illuminations in the whole Saint John's Bible. The face of a wise old crone gazes out at us from a silver and gold mirror. We see ourselves reflected, our image refracted through the figure of Wisdom. "This was also supposed to be a third-page illumination," Donald said. But it grew.

The brief was very short. Wisdom, it explained, is a semi-divine figure. The CIT directed that Wisdom is a reflection of the divine light, not the light itself. Donald commented, "The CIT had a much more Marian interpretation of the text than I did."

He reflected on the way we conceive of wisdom in our own society. "I considered how we used to think of old people as the wise ones," he said. "It's something we have lost in our society."

He put the image right in the center of the spread, going right across the gutter. The whole image glows with metal leaf. "I used both platinum and gold," he said, "suggesting both masculine and feminine aspects of God."

He surrounded the mirror with a rich border. He said, "I used an Islamic astronomical chart showing the phases of the moon—the same image I had tried to incorporate into the opening of Ecclesiastes and rejected. The moon image was reference to the menstrual cycle. The mirror is framed with symbols of the cosmos, linking this image to the *Seven Pillars of Wisdom*, Ecclesiastes, and the Cosmic Christ." He paused for a moment. "I have to say, I hate that term."

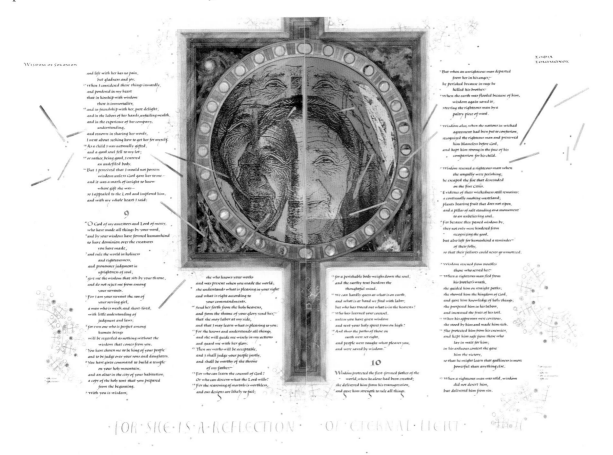

The Mirror of Wisdom appears in the Wisdom of Solomon.

The face was taken after a photograph of an old Palestinian woman. It was silkscreened, like the image of the temple in Ezekiel. The image is repeated, suggesting as though our own vantage point changes as we look back at her.

One technical problem presented itself: what to do with the part of the image that disappears into the gutter. He explained his solution: "The circle itself is not a perfect circle. Because it crosses the gutter of the spread, the middle part is slightly elongated, flattened at the top and bottom. This makes up for the fact that part of the center of the illumination will be lost in the folds of the book."

Angela Swan

WISDOM
IS
RADIANT
AND
UNFADING
AND SHE
IS EASILY
DISCERNED
BY THOSE
WHO
LOVE HER
AND IS
FOUND
BY THOSE
WHO
SEEK HER

Brian Simpson

To
fear the
Lord is
fullness of
wisdom
she
inebriates
mortals with
her fruits
she
fills their
whole house
with
desirable
goods
and their
storehouses
with her
produce

Sally Mae Joseph

friend disappears.

per,

lf and

ard against him.
lishes a mirror,
ome

nd take your place.
ght hand,
your own seat;
the

ave said.

r when he is bitten;
wild animals?
o associates

the other's sins.
ile,
not be there.
with his lips,
to

in his eyes,
unity he will never
blood.
u will find him

ll trip you up.
td

show his true face.

ts dirty,
with a proud person

Come to me
you who desire me
and eat your fill

For the memory
of me is sweeter
than honey
& the possession
of me sweeter than
the honeycomb

Susie Leiper

she
is a
reflection
of
eternal
light
a
spotless
mirror
of the
working
of
God.

and
an
image
of
his
goodness

to deprive an e
is to shed bl

When one builds
what do they ga
When one prays a
to whose voice r
If one washes afte
and touche
what has been g
So if one fasts fo
and goes again
who will listen to
And what has
humbling h

The one who ke
one who heeds t
an offering
The one who retu
offers choic
and one who gi
a thank off
To keep from wi
pleasing to
and to forsake
is an atone
Do not appear be
for all that you
of the comm
The offering of th
and its pleasin
the Most H
The sacrifice of
and it will nev
Be generous whe
and do not stir
With every gift s
and dedicate yo
Give to the Most
and as generous

Sue Hufton

LIKE·CASSIA·&·CAMEL'S·THORN·I·GAVE·FORTH·PERFUME·
AND·LIKE·CHOICE·MYRRH·I·SPREAD·MY·FRAGRANCE·LIKE·GALBANUM·ONYCHA·AND·STACTE·

I·TOOK·ROOT·IN·AN·HONORED·PEOPLE·I·GREW·TALL·LIKE·A·CEDAR·IN·LEBANON·

SIRACH

It is the moon that marks the changing seasons,
governing the times, their everlasting sign.
From the moon comes the sign for festal days,
a light that wanes when it
completes its course.
The new moon, as its name suggests,
renews itself;
how marvelous it is in this change,
a beacon to the hosts on high,
shining in the vault of the heavens!

The glory of the stars is the beauty of heaven;
a glittering array in the heights of the Lord.
On the orders of the Holy One they stand in
their appointed places;
they never relax in their watches.
Look at the rainbow, and praise
him who made it;
it is exceedingly beautiful in its brightness.
It encircles the sky with its glorious arc;
the hands of the Most High have
stretched it out.

By his command he sends the driving snow
and speeds the lightnings of his judgment.
Therefore the storehouses are opened,
and the clouds fly out like birds.
In his majesty he gives the clouds
their strength,
and the hailstones are broken in pieces.
The voice of his thunder rebukes the earth;
when he appears, the mountains shake.
At his will the south wind blows;
so do the storm from the north
and the whirlwind.
He scatters the snow like birds flying down,
and its descent is like locusts alighting.
The eye is dazzled by the beauty
of its whiteness,
and the mind is amazed as it falls.
He pours frost over the earth like salt,
and icicles form like pointed thorns.
The cold north wind blows,
and ice freezes on the water;
it settles on every pool of water,
and the water puts it on like a breastplate.
He consumes the mountains and
burns up the wilderness,
and withers the tender grass like fire.
A mist quickly heals all things;
the falling dew gives refreshment
from the heat.

By his plan he stilled the deep
and planted islands in it.
Those who sail the sea tell of its dangers,
and we marvel at what we hear.
In it are strange and marvelous creatures,
all kinds of living things, and huge
sea-monsters.
Because of him each of his
messengers succeeds,
and by his word all things hold together.
We could say more but could never say enough;
let the final word be: "He is the all."
Where can we find the strength to praise him?
For he is greater than all his works.
Awesome is the Lord and very great,
and marvelous is his power.
Glorify the Lord and exalt him as
much as you can;
for he surpasses even that.
When you exalt him, summon all your strength,
and do not grow weary, for you cannot
praise him enough.
Who has seen him and can describe him?
Or who can extol him as he is?
Many things greater than these lie hidden,
for I have seen but few of his works.
For the Lord has made all things,
and to the godly he has given wisdom.

HYMN IN HONOR OF OUR ANCESTORS

44

Let us now sing the praises of famous men,
our ancestors in their generations.
The Lord apportioned to them great glory,
his majesty from the beginning.
There were those who ruled in their kingdoms,
and made a name for themselves
by their valor;
those who gave counsel because
they were intelligent;
those who spoke in prophetic oracles;
those who led the people by their counsels
and by their knowledge of the people's lore;
they were wise in their words of instruction;
those who composed musical tunes,
or put verses in writing;
rich men endowed with resources,
living peacefully in their homes—
all these were honored in their generations,
and were the pride of their times.
Some of them have left behind a name,

Donald and Mabel Jackson commissioned the scribes to create special treatments in the Wisdom Books.

Special treatments

IT WAS AT THIS POINT in the *Wisdom Books* that Donald and Mabel decided to commission from each scribe a special treatment—their own unique act of patronage. The scribes' work had always been very controlled, following the set forms of the text and poetry scripts that they had written. They wanted to give the scribes a chance to add an example of their more expressive work. Donald said, "Each of the scribes were lettering artists in their own right, and we wanted to acknowledge that. Commissioning them to make special treatments was also a personal thank you for their contributions and a sign of respect for their work."

The scribes were given a list of passages from which to choose. These special treatments appear in the margins of text pages in the books of Job and Sirach, the first and last books in the volume.

Completion

IN SEPTEMBER 2006 volume 5, *Wisdom Books*, was completed. Carol Marrin traveled to Wales to collect it and deliver it to Saint John's. She was accompanied by her husband, K. C. Marrin, and Tim Ternes. The *Wisdom* volume has 133 pages of writing on thirty-three skins. There are eleven illuminations, ten special treatments, thirteen marginal decorations, and 157 small capitals.

Donor Acknowledgment
The donors Gerald and Henrietta Rauenhorst were acknowledged with a special treatment of a passage from Sirach 33.

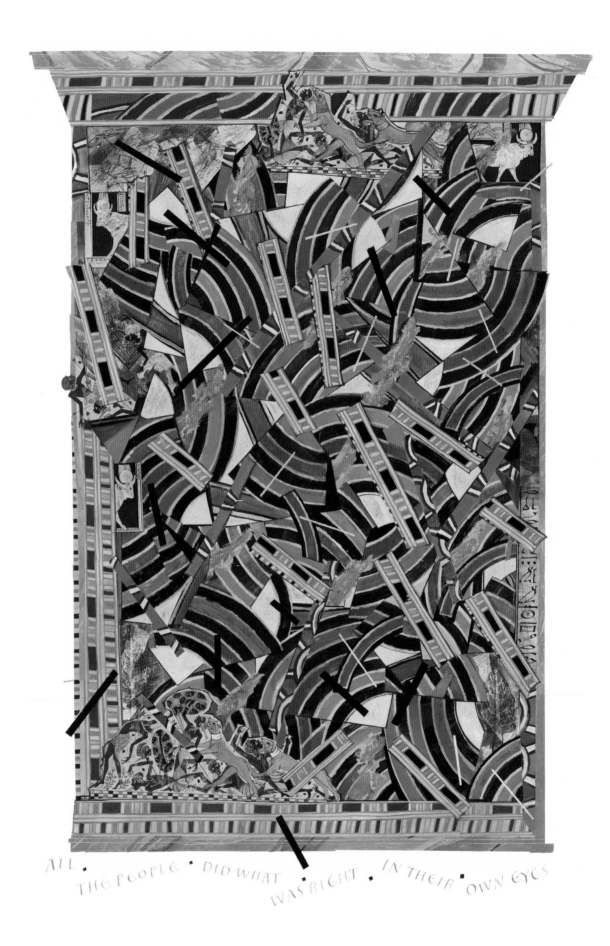

ALL · THE PEOPLE · DID WHAT · WAS RIGHT · IN THEIR · OWN EYES

The book of Judges culminates with the full-page *Judges Anthology*, which uses visual motifs that run through the illuminations in the book.

CHAPTER 14

HISTORICAL BOOKS

Delivered March 2010

DURING THE MAKING of the *Historical Books* volume, the project reached a very difficult period. It could even be said that it reached a crisis. Although Donald and the team had been steadily finishing one volume a year, for many reasons, they continued to fall behind the schedule that had been set. Continued funding came into question, raising the frightening specter that the project might not reach completion. At the same time, the planned Heritage Edition needed to be put into production. The launching of the Heritage Program was officially announced in the fall of 2006. Many decisions had to be made.

In the meantime, the Illuminating the Word exhibition continued to tour. It was not the only exhibition taking place. In September 2006, a separate exhibition of the *Prophets* volume was put on show at the Museum of Biblical Image & Art in New York. Donald flew to New York to give a talk. In October, the main exhibition moved to the Library of Congress in Washington, DC, and Donald traveled down to be part of that.

In Washington, Donald met with Fr. Columba Stewart. Donald said to me, "In the fall of 2006, things changed dramatically. Saint John's told me that unless they raised more money, they couldn't finish the project."

It was decided that the facsimile project, the Heritage Edition, would have to go forward in order to raise money to finish the original manuscript. Donald, however, was not to be directly involved in Heritage. Donald commented, "They said they would take care of the facsimile, and I was to concentrate solely on finishing the original manuscript."

In January 2007, the Illuminating the Word exhibition moved to Naples, Florida. Here tensions came to a head.

Donald was still indirectly involved with the printing process. His opinion was continually being sought on the prototype pages. "I didn't feel the process was working and that the results were unsatisfactory to me. I was getting upset, fearing that the spirit of the original might be lost."

The conversation was frank and to the point. Donald said, "We reached a pivotal point. I had registered disapproval of how the facsimile was going. They registered disapproval of my rate of production."

Donald, who had been traveling back and forth to promote the traveling exhibition, was impatient too. "The myth is: 'You are always behind schedule, always over budget.' The Myth is stronger than the math. But by the time we reached year nine, in 2007, we looked back at our work records, and fully *three and a half* years out of the nine were spent on agreed billable extras."

Time spent on publicity, traveling to exhibitions, giving lectures and press interviews all represented time that was taken from the production schedule. And although his extra trips and promotional activities had been budgeted for in terms of money, they had never been properly reflected in the production schedule. No one had fully allowed for a concurrent rolling exhibition schedule. He said. "I had always felt I was under-delivering."

Donald Jackson uses silk to brush off excess gold from the frisket stencil in the gilding process.

Luckily, Brother Dietrich asked Dan Whalen, a member of the University Board of Regents, to help. Donald recalled, "He was a businessman. He saw that the original fixed-price contract was no longer suited to a project like this. And he negotiated like a businessman. Turning to each side, he asked: What do *you* need? He broke the impasse and put the wheels back on the project!"

It was a learning moment both for him and for his client. He commented, "It has to be said that if we had tried to set up the original contracts differently, there would never have been a Bible. Saint John's wanted to know what the project would cost. By having a fixed number, that was the only way they could have signed the contract."

He acknowledges that he had never anticipated all the difficulties of managing such a huge undertaking. "I had also underestimated just how long the project would take. I never realized how much of my time it would take to gather and direct a team of artists, scribes, and support staff, for instance."

Saint John's complaint about Donald's production rate was on the table. Now he threw down the gauntlet over the way the facsimile was being made. "I had become the fly in the ointment," he said. "They were experiencing my comments as negative and unhelpful. And no one wants to hear that."

With all the issues now out and in the open, Donald and his client were able to start with a clean slate. For the next five months, negotiations would continue for the final, definitive contract. In fact, it would result in two separate contracts: one to finish the original and another to supervise the facsimile. He would be artistic director of *both* projects. "Now I was to be paid for the Heritage Edition as a separate job," he said. "And every day dedicated to the Heritage Edition was added to the completion date of the original." This meant that the trade was even; Donald was given an extra production day to make up for each day he spent working on the Heritage Edition.

In February 2007 meetings were held at John Roberts Printing Company to define Donald's involvement and decide how to proceed with the printing of the Heritage Edition. People from John Roberts, Saint John's, and the Scriptorium were part of the conversation. Donald's two consultants, John Parfitt and Michael Gullick, were also there. Later, in May, another set of meetings took place in Minnesota, where Donald hammered out issues regarding the printing with John Roberts, McIntosh Embossing, and Cal Sixta at Colormax, who would provide the digital files.

In July 2007, the new contracts were signed. The completion date for the original manuscript was set for the end of 2010, with the provision that days spent on Heritage would be added to the end of the manuscript production deadline. Donald was formally appointed artistic director of the Heritage Program. The two projects would proceed in tandem.

Printing

THE PRINTING of the Heritage Edition now became intertwined with the making of the manuscript. The full story of the making of the Heritage Edition appears in chapter 19, but it is germane to our story to note some of the major events that marked milestones in the printing process, because they inevitably had an impact on the flow of work on the manuscript.

In July 2007, Dave Peterson and Mike Nordberg from John Roberts Printers and Dave McIntosh from McIntosh Embossing visited the Scriptorium with Craig Bruner, Heritage Program director. They reviewed the proofs of the first litho-printed pages from *Wisdom Books*. At the same time, prototype bindings for the Heritage books were prepared in London under the supervision of Michael Gullick. The

The *Joshua Anthology* illumination is protected with sheets of paper as Donald Jackson paints in a detail.

printing of the *Wisdom Books* began in August that year. Donald, John Parfitt, and Sarah Harris were on press to sign off on every page, this time comparing them with the original vellum folios. This visit would set a pattern for the printing. Afterward, Donald and Michael Gullick flew to Phoenix, Arizona, with Craig Bruner, the director of the Heritage Program, to open detailed discussions on revised binding specifications with Roswell Bookbinders, who would later be engaged to bind the edition, working from prototype constructions designed by Habib Dingle and Donald.

At this crucial juncture, in September 2007, Dave Peterson, who had first acted as a print consultant for Saint John's on the Bible project and who became manager of the Heritage Printing Program for the John Roberts Company, died suddenly. He would never see the Heritage Edition in print, but he had seen the project through to the point where it could go forward with confidence. Kelly Bortz replaced him as print coordinator of the project on behalf of John Roberts.

By October, the *Wisdom* volume of the Heritage Edition was printed. Donald, John Parfitt, and Sarah Harris were on hand to see the work completed.

In April 2008, Donald and Mabel Jackson, Abbot John Klassen, Br. Dietrich Reinhart, and Gerald Raeunhorst traveled to Rome to present two copies of the Heritage Edition *Wisdom Books* to Pope Benedict XVI. Both were specially hand-bound in the United Kingdom, one by Lester Capon and one by Habib Dingle.

The *Prophets* volume went through prepress in Minnesota in May 2008. John Parfitt and Sarah Harris were present for this process. Donald joined them in July to oversee the printing.

In September 2008, Donald was diagnosed with congestive heart disease and was unable to travel for the next six months or so.

In November, printer's proofs for the *Psalms* volume were taken to Mobile, Alabama, because the original pages were there as part of the traveling exhibition. The John Roberts team, Craig Bruner, John Parfitt, and Sarah Harris were there. *Psalms* went to press in February 2009 in Minnesota; John Parfitt and Sarah Harris were there.

The *Pentateuch* went into prepress in August 2009 and was printed in September and October of that year. Donald and Sarah Harris supervised the prepress. John Parfitt joined them for the printing.

In 2009, 80 percent of the *Historical Books* manuscript was delivered. This section of the *Historical* volume went into prepress in March 2010, under the guidance of John Parfitt and Sarah Harris.

Exhibitions and milestones

WHILE THE PRINTING of the Heritage Edition continued, the traveling exhibition, Illuminating the Word, continued to tour. There were supplemental exhibitions of Bible pages as well.

In October 2007, the project manager Rebecca Cherry left the Scriptorium. Rachel Collard took on the role of project manager from 2008 until 2009. She was then replaced by Jane Grayer.

The Bible project also lost two key supporters at Saint John's. In July 2008, Carol Marrin retired. And in December, the president of Saint John's University, Br. Dietrich Reinhart, OSB, died. Carol had been with the project in one capacity or another since its outset. As executive director, she had shepherded it through many ups and downs. And Br. Dietrich had been instrumental in making the Bible happen. It was his initial enthusiasm that had propelled the Bible from an idea to fruition. The loss of these two crucial people was a tremendously sad moment for the project. But by now the project had achieved a level of institutional maturity that allowed it to move forward. The Bible and the Heritage Program were now much more

Many of the book titles in *Historical Books* have wide frames. The labeling above the English titles reflect the Hebrew or Greek titles of the original texts.

Donald Jackson at work in
the Scriptorium. On the
wall in front of him, the
pages from the book of
Judges show the layouts in
progress. The illuminations
in Judges are small and unified in style, punctuating the
text at intervals. Passages
from the text appear in the
margins, giving variety and
lending visual interest to the
otherwise plain rows of text
columns.

corporate in their approach; the project was less personal than it had been in the earlier, formative years.

The traveling exhibition continued to make its way across North America. It was on display at the Phoenix Art Museum from December 2007 through March 2008. It moved on to the Winnipeg Art Museum in Manitoba in April 2008. From there it went to the Tacoma Art Museum in Washington in July. The final venue for the traveling exhibition was the Mobile Museum of Art in Alabama, where it opened in October. This finally brought the touring exhibition to a close, and all the pages returned to Saint John's.

In addition to this, six folios were exhibited with the Dead Sea scrolls in an exhibition that traveled to San Diego, California; Milwaukee, Wisconsin; and Saint Paul, Minnesota, between June 2007 and March 2010.

Another exhibition took place at the Walters Art Museum in Baltimore, Maryland. Titled "The Saint John's Bible: A Modern Vision though Medieval Methods," it ran from February through May 2009.

Design considerations

ALL OF THIS exhibition history and the printing of the Heritage Edition has detracted from my narrative about the making of the manuscript. But that's indicative of how the project was developing. It had become a much larger enterprise than it ever had been before, and somehow Donald had to return to the basic verities of creating the original.

With the *Historical Books*, Donald's graphic approach continued to evolve. This volume is the largest of the seven volumes of the Bible, with 269 pages of writing. In a Roman Catholic Bible, the historical books are all grouped together, telling the whole sweep of the history of the Israelites in one collection. (Protestant Bibles, by contrast, move the later books into the Apocrypha, breaking the continuity of the narrative.) The story begins where the Pentateuch leaves off, with the entry of the Israelites into the Promised Land. In Joshua, the conquest of the Land of Canaan is described, followed by the period of loose confederation in Judges. The first unification of the tribes of Israel under the kingship of Saul is followed by the reigns of David and Solomon, after which the kingdom is divided. A long period of strife and decline ends with the destruction of the Northern Kingdom by the Assyrians and, not long after, the destruction of Jerusalem by the Babylonians, who carry the people into captivity. The remaining books describe the ongoing struggle of the Jews to maintain their traditions while dominated by the great empires of late antiquity.

With relatively few illuminations planned for this volume, Donald faced a unique challenge to graphically express this wide sweep of history. In this volume, he suggested using marginal inscriptions pulled from the text to drive the narrative along. At the beginning of the volume, almost every spread has a passage written in free blue capitals in the left or right margin highlighting some important event in the unfolding tale. Donald said, "The marginal texts pull the reader along with the flow of the text. I asked the CIT for enough quotations to choose appropriate themes to carry the story through."

The illuminations also are slightly different in this volume. In Joshua and Judges, the illuminations have a unified graphic effect, employing the same color palette and repeating motifs. This consistency of style contrasts to his more eclectic approach in the earlier volumes of the manuscript.

In Joshua and Judges, Donald said, "I wanted to give the illuminations an Egyptian theme." The text is full of references to the backsliding of the people as they endure the hardships of entering and conquering the land. They are torn between the promise of the new and the old certainties of their lives in Egypt. Their allegiance to their new God is constantly tested and strained, and they experience a longing for the old gods.

In this volume, Chris Tomlin's marginal illustrations reflect the violence of the text.

Graphically, these illuminations draw on a consistent visual tension. Donald explained, "The constant element is a basic contrast: bold brushwork against highly controlled detail. The urgency of a splash contrasted with detailed work." He added, "That sensibility is rooted in my looking at medieval manuscripts. Detail is added to a very bold composition. In the Spanish Beatus manuscripts, for instance, the page is often organized into three bold bands of color, on top of which are painted highly detailed figures."

This graphic language helped Donald work with stories that are often challenging. He said, "What's brilliant about the Bible as a document is that it gets you angry. It stirs you like a spoon in a pot. For example the story of Saul. I think he was rather hard done by."

I asked whether these violent stories from the *Historical Books* were hard to work with. "Yes. There is so much death and fighting. You see the dark side of people." On the other hand, there is a vivid reality to these stories; this is human history, in all its ugliness and beauty.

He devised a color scheme to suggest some of the grappling for power that is described in the *Historical Books*. He said, "The main theme of the *Historical Books* is a nation struggling to reconcile different centers of power. I used different colors to suggest these centers of power. Purple is used for the kings, and green for the priests. Gold and silver represent the power of God."

As the *Historical Books* become more violent, and more full of strife, Donald chose a new approach for the marginal illustrations by Chris Tomlin. Where the earlier volumes had featured insects and plants from the environment around Saint John's, now we find spiders and dueling scorpions. The violence of the human story is reflected in the predatory behaviors of the creatures that populate the margin.

Joshua Anthology

THE *Joshua Anthology* pulls together in one image the sweep of the Israelites into the land of Canaan under the leadership of Joshua. The whole composition is set within an architectural frame; elements of the composition burst out of the edges of the frame.

Donald said, "This was a turning point. The sketch I had given to the CIT differed radically from the image I eventually produced. There was a full year between making the sketch and actually creating the illumination."

He remarked, "It seemed that the CIT had begun to feel more comfortable with my freedom. By this volume, the CIT gave me more latitude. They trusted me."

Another shift was taking place in Donald's imagery. "By the *Historical Books,*" he said, "I was beginning to draw design elements from the earlier volumes." The Saint John's Bible does not rely heavily on traditional Christian iconography; many of the images and symbols used in the manuscript are new to the Christian tradition. But here, in the *Historical Books,* Donald began drawing from the symbolic repertory he and his fellow artists had created and began cycling those images into the new illuminations. The book, like the Bible text itself, began to rhyme with itself. Visual elements echoing Thomas Ingmire's *Ten Commandments* flutter through the landscape, accompanying the Israelites on their mission of conquest.

Donald said, "The CIT said the physical setting was important—especially the two mountains, Mount Gerizim and Mount Ebal." The action, therefore, takes place on a plain between the two mountains.

Donald said, "The basic theme was the stress between the past and the future." As the Israelites enter the Promised Land, they carry with them powerful memories of Egypt. "It was apparent how exotic and powerful Egypt was," Donald remarked. The pull on the Israelites to go backward was strong.

The image is meant to be read from left to right. On the left are the scarab beetle, the Eye of Horus, an idol in the form of a bull, and the sphinxlike faces of lions. Egyptian decorative patterns frame the work along the left and bottom. All of these images represent the attraction of Egypt and its ancient culture. To the left and top, these give way to great washes of gold and color—a less defined but more glorious future.

Donald Jackson at work on the
Joshua Anthology.

Two sketches for the *Joshua Anthology* show the evolution of the design.

The *Joshua Anthology* appears opposite Joshua 3.

Illuminations in Joshua and Judges

THE *Joshua Anthology* sets the tone for a series of small illuminations that runs through the books of Joshua and Judges. The series ends with another full-page illumination at the end of Judges. The color palette and Egyptian border patterns are uniform through the series.

In the first small vignette, opposite Joshua 4, the text "Choose whom you will serve" is illustrated with the figure of the Eye of Horus, which competes with the Hebrew menorah. The people's loyalties lie in doubt—will they follow their own God or will they stray into the worship of other gods? Donald pointed out that the text was also related to a monk's vows.

Describing the following vignettes, Donald said, "There was such a clear relationship to our present day—to the human condition that we share with the writers of these stories, the loss of ideals, the constant backsliding."

In Judges 9 the trees talk to the brambles, asking them to rule. Donald said, "Well, that's what happens when you put the military in charge!"

In Judges 20, there is a painting of a child running from rockets, a reference to the present-day conflict in the Middle East. It is juxtaposed to scenes of battle triumphs taken from Egyptian temples. "I'm making a biblical point," he said. "The conflict is still going on."

There are two kinds of marginal texts. Near each vignette is a text that refers to the images portrayed. In the upper margins are further texts that comment on the conflict described in the text.

The final full-page illumination, full of fractured Egyptian decorative motifs and images of people being torn to pieces by animals, is an icon of conflict. The closing text of Judges explains that the entire period described in the book was one in which the people continually fell from grace "and did what was right in their own eyes."

Small illuminations in a unified style are used through Joshua and Judges. Above, an illumination from Judges. To the right, a spread from Joshua.

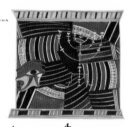

Ruth

THE TWO-PART ILLUMINATION in Ruth was made by Suzanne Moore. Donald said, "That is, I think, my favorite of Suzanne's illuminations. She stretched herself there. To represent the relationship between Ruth and Naomi, she couldn't get away from figuration."

On the left-hand page, Ruth and her mother-in-law Naomi are shown embracing. On the right, Ruth is shown as the gleaner—a pivotal moment in the story, in which the widowed Ruth is shown kindness by her kinsman Boaz.

Suzanne described the gleaner in notes that Donald sent to the CIT: "I plan to use the same fabric treatment [as the one used in the first illumination], and patterns at the bottom of her hem cascading down will create various 'Star of David' designs."

The symbolism is very subtle: the stars of David emerge from the freely rendered swashes of her garment, and are executed in fine lines of gold. One has to hunt for them. Suzanne continued: Ruth "will provide the 'seed' for the future king, and so I wanted to suggest her stature, even working as one gathering after the gleaners. Having her look up into the optical center of the page, brings her 'up' into the page. She carries an expansive basket of abundance and promise."

This illumination stands out from Suzanne's others in its representational character. Her familiar visual vocabulary of arcs and abstract areas of color are harnessed to the problem of rendering the human form.

Elisha and the Six Miracles

IN HIS SKETCH PROPOSALS to the CIT, this illumination was presented as a part of a sequence of images meant to be considered together. Once again, we see here Donald's growing tendency in this volume to create unified groups of images that employ similar colors and motifs. The sequence begins in 1 Kings with *The Sound of Silence*, depicting Elijah's mountaintop encounter with God. It continues with Elijah's ascent to heaven in a fiery chariot and Elisha's assumption of the mantle of the prophet. It culminates with this illumination, *Elisha and the Six Miracles*.

These stories are scattered through chapters 2–6 of 2 Kings. Donald said, "It seemed to me the five stories boiled down to five essential themes: hunger, poverty, death, disease, and loss." Elisha is shown against a background divided into vertical strips. In the strips that flank the prophet, symbols referring to each of the five miracles are placed.

Donald's comments to the CIT explain that they can be read from left to right: "loaves and fishes imagery [taken directly from *Gospels and Acts*]; flowing jars of oil; the child rising from his couch under the shadow of Elisha's mantle; the microscopic bacteria design used in the *Son of Man* illumination (for Naaman's leprosy) and *Peter's Confession*; and the axe head in the water." Here we can see Donald reviving images from previously executed illuminations.

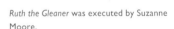

Ruth the Gleaner was executed by Suzanne Moore.

Donald Jackson and Aidan Hart work together on *Elisha and the Six Miracles*.

Donald Jackson compares the magnified research image of the leprosy virus against his painted interpretation.

The gilding at the top of the images, executed in great brushstrokes of gold, represent "both the concept of the gateway upwards to heavenly mansions and also the idea of portals through which the love and power of God may flow down to his prophet and his people on earth and ours to him in heaven."

Donald explained that he chose to work with Aidan on this illumination "to bring a self-conscious element of antiquity to the stories (a tradition used in some medieval manuscript illuminations) as well as bringing a recognisable flavour of the art of the Eastern Church. I asked Aidan to make sketches which allow the background to show through the figure of the prophet so that he may appear to be literally a part of the events portrayed."

Elisha is shown with bits of mantle—the small black and striped bands depicted on the lower parts of his clothing.

Donald invited Aidan to come to the Scriptorium so they could work on the image together. This was different from the way they had collaborated on the figure in Paul's *Life*, which Aidan had painted at home. Donald explained, "We worked side by side, positioning and repositioning Aidan's sketches of the prophet over my painted and gilded backgrounds. Then Aidan set to work painting the figure of Elisha, creating the wonderfully translucent effect I had hoped for."

Another motif that Donald wove in from an earlier illumination were the three colors, picked up from the *Death of Saul*, to indicate the presence of different forces vying for power. Green represents the priests; purple, the power of kingship; and gold, God.

Elisha and the Six Miracles appears adjacent to 2 Kings 6.

Esther

THE PORTRAIT of Esther has a strongly psychological dimension. Donald said, "I split her face in two parts, because she is such a mixed character in the story. She is very ambivalent." On one side, we can see brightly tinctured images of the luxury of the Persian court; on the other, we see chromatically more somber images of the queen's Jewish heritage. The simple menorah in gold stands out against the dark background.

"This is a woman who is resisting the luxuries of the royal court," Donald said. "So on one side we see the woman of wealth, on the other the woman who willingly puts away her fine things and covers herself humbly when she appeals to God to appeal for guidance on how to save her people."

The face was directly based on a portrait by Gustav Klimt. Donald remarked, "The reference to Klimt is quite on purpose. For the luxurious woman, I quoted his portrait of a wealthy young wife of a Fin-de-Siecle Viennese merchant prince."

Completion

IN JULY 2009 80 percent of *Historical Books*, volume 6, was completed. Tim Ternes and Linda Orzechowski traveled to Wales to collect the originals and take them to Saint John's. The remaining pages were completed in July 2010, and Sarah Harris and John Parfitt traveled to Minnesota to deliver the remaining pages. The *Historical* volume has 269 pages of writing on sixty-nine skins. There are twenty-four illuminations, three special treatments, seven marginal decorations, 306 large capitals, and three small capitals.

The portrait of Esther.

Donor Acknowledgment

For the donors Dan and Katharine Whalen, the initial capitals *D* and *K* in I Chronicles 13 and 14 were specially decorated. A chameleon that appears at the end of 2 Maccabees 15 has a *W* on his back.

The illumination in progress.

The opening of Revelation.

The
REV
ELA
TION
to John

HE REVELATION OF JESUS
CHRIST WHICH GOD GAVE HIM
TO SHOW HIS SERVANTS WHAT
MUST SOON TAKE PLACE; HE
MADE IT KNOWN BY SENDING
HIS ANGEL TO HIS SERVANT
JOHN, WHO TESTIFIED TO
THE WORD OF GOD & TO THE
TESTIMONY OF JESUS CHRIST,
EVEN TO ALL THAT HE SAW.
BLESSED IS THE ONE WHO
READS ALOUD THE WORDS OF
THE PROPHECY, AND BLESSED
ARE THOSE WHO HEAR AND
WHO KEEP WHAT IS WRITTEN
IN IT; FOR THE TIME IS NEAR.

John to the seven churches that are in Asia: Grace
to you & peace from him who is and who was and
who is to come, and from the seven spirits who are
before his throne, and from Jesus Christ, the faithful witness, the firstborn of the dead, and the ruler
of the kings of the earth. To him who loves us and
freed us from our sins by his blood, and made us
to be a kingdom, priests serving his God & Father,
to him be glory & dominion forever & ever. Amen.
Look! He is coming with the clouds;
        every eye will see him,
    even those who pierced him;
        and on his account all the tribes of the earth will wail.
So it is to be. Amen.

RSB
Rev 1:7

a Gk slaves
b Gk and he made
c Gk slave
d Other ancient authorities
   read washed
e Gk priests to
f Or testimony to Jesus
g Or in the Spirit
h Or deny my faith
i Gk slaves
j Or to shepherd

8 "I am the Alpha & the Omega," says the Lord God,
who is & who was & who is to come, the Almighty.

9 I, John, your brother who share with you in Jesus
the persecution and the kingdom and the patient
endurance, was on the island called Patmos because
of the word of God and the testimony of Jesus. I
was in the spirit on the Lord's day & I heard behind
me a loud voice like a trumpet saying, "Write in
a book what you see & send it to the seven churches,
to Ephesus, to Smyrna, to Pergamum, to Thyatira,
to Sardis, to Philadelphia & to Laodicea." Then I
turned to see whose voice it was that spoke to me,
and on turning I saw seven golden lampstands, &
in the midst of the lampstands I saw one like the Son
of Man, clothed with a long robe & with a golden
sash across his chest. His head and his hair were
white as white wool, white as snow; his eyes were
like a flame of fire, his feet were like burnished
bronze, refined as in a furnace, and his voice was
like the sound of many waters. In his right hand
he held seven stars, and from his mouth came a sharp,
two-edged sword, and his face was like the sun shining with full force. When I saw him, I fell at his
feet as though dead. But he placed his right hand
on me, saying, "Do not be afraid; I am the first and
the last, and the living one. I was dead, and see,
I am alive forever and ever; and I have the keys of
Death & of Hades. Now write what you have seen,
what is, and what is to take place after this. As for
the mystery of the seven stars that you saw in my
right hand, and the seven golden lampstands: the
seven stars are the angels of the seven churches, and
the seven lampstands are the seven churches.

2

To the angel of the church in Ephesus write:
These are the words of him who holds the
seven stars in his right hand, who walks
among the seven golden lampstands: I know your
works, your toil & your patient endurance. I know
that you cannot tolerate evildoers; you have tested
those who claim to be apostles but are not, & have
found them to be false. I also know that you are
enduring patiently and bearing up for the sake of
my name, and that you have not grown weary. But
I have this against you, that you have abandoned
the love you had at first. Remember then from what
you have fallen; repent, and do the works you did
at first. If not, I will come to you & remove your
lampstand from its place, unless you repent. Yet
this is to your credit: you hate the works of the Nic-
olaitans, which I also hate. Let anyone who has an
ear listen to what the spirit is saying to the churches.

CHAPTER 15

LETTERS AND REVELATION

Delivered May 2011

T LAST, twelve years after signing the original contract to produce the Bible, Donald embarked on the last volume. It took him just over one year to bring it—and the manuscript project—to completion.

The text of the letters had been completed by the scribes long before and awaited the additions of special treatments, interpretive illuminations, chapter headings, and drop capitals. But all of Revelation was reserved for Donald, including both text and illumination. It would be his final artistic statement for the project, and it was planned as the unified work of a single hand.

As in other volumes, the format and structure of the text dictated adjustments to the graphic system of the Bible. The letters are unusual in being, so many of them, short. This created a different rhythm to the pages; in the later letters, sometimes this necessitated placing as many as three of the large book headings on a single spread. With so many interruptions in the text, other page elements, such as the drop caps, had to be adjusted accordingly.

The verbal tone of the letters is also more intimate than most of the other texts in the Bible. They are presented as personal communications between the writer and a specific community or individual. This suggested a less magisterial visual treatment would be appropriate.

Because the letters contain so many key passages that are important in Christian thought and the church's liturgy, the CIT requested more special treatments for this volume, further interrupting the text and making the pages more complex.

Every preceding volume in the manuscript, with the exception of the *Psalms*, begins an opening passage in the Incipit Script. *Letters and Revelation* does not. Donald explains, "I didn't use the Incipit Script for the beginning of Romans [the first letter in the volume], because Romans is more conversational. The tone would be wrong." It was an instinctive choice; as Donald says, "I am not a slave to convention." And, true to his approach through the Bible, he was willing to break the established pattern to suit the moment. So the text of Romans begins with a book heading and a drop capital and slides immediately into the standard Bible Script.

From the beginning of the volume, the drop capitals also stick out. They are more geometric than many of the drop capitals used in earlier volumes. This addresses the problem of unifying a text that is frequently interrupted. In this volume, a single pattern is used for the drop capitals. Functioning like a typeface, the letterforms have the same structure through the whole volume. They do change in color, but their shapes remain consistent. While in previous volumes the lush, playful, and wildly varied drop capitals served to enliven long passages of continuous text, here they have been quieted, tamed. To use one of Donald's favorite analogies, they have had the volume turned down.

Another change in this volume involved the lettering in the book headings. In previous volumes, Donald had used a brush for the lettering. Now he used both brush and quill. The freely-written Italic script in the

Donald Jackson applying a rubber stamp to *The New Jerusalem.*
The stamp was so large that it had to be mounted on a curved support and gently rolled onto the illumination.

Many of the letters in the New Testament are very short, leading to spreads with multiple book headings.
Ornament fills the empty spaces at the bottom of these pages.

The letters in the New Testament were given many special treatments, such as the one shown here at the end of 2 Thessalonians.

headings of the letters was made with a quill. The shell gold he had been using up until this point had been slightly coarse-grained, and so it did not flow freely from the pen. But now Donald persuaded the maker in France to grind the gold powder much more finely. He sent them a fifty-year-old tablet of shell gold that had belonged to Irene Wellington, a mid-century English scribe who had been his teacher. They were able to match the fine grinding. He said, "Using that was literally like writing with liquid gold."

Special treatments

HAZEL, Thomas, Suzanne, and Donald all have special treatments in this volume. Donald also produced special treatments using a variant of the Incipit Script in shades of warm blue, purple, or rusty red. He explained, "I simply did the special treatments where there was the least money to spend on them." For these, he used a fairly uniform style.

Yet, although the basic script in Donald's special treatments is consistent, the scale and details vary.

An illustration by Chris Tomlin fills a gap before the beginning of Colossians.

In *Letters and Revelation,* many special treatments punctuate the text, written in a fairly uniform style.

NOW BEFORE FAITH CAME
WE WERE IMPRISONED
& GUARDED UNDER THE
LAW UNTIL FAITH WOULD
BE REVEALED. THEREFORE
THE LAW WAS OUR
DISCIPLINARIAN UNTIL
CHRIST CAME, SO THAT WE
MIGHT BE JUSTIFIED BY
FAITH. BUT NOW THAT
FAITH HAS COME, WE ARE
NO LONGER SUBJECT TO A
DISCIPLINARIAN, FOR IN
CHRIST JESUS YOU ARE
ALL CHILDREN OF GOD
THROUGH FAITH. AS MANY
OF YOU AS WERE BAPTIZED
INTO CHRIST HAVE
CLOTHED YOURSELVES
WITH CHRIST. THERE IS NO
LONGER JEW OR GREEK,
THERE IS NO LONGER
SLAVE OR FREE, THERE IS
NO LONGER MALE AND
FEMALE; FOR ALL OF YOU
ARE ONE IN CHRIST JESUS.
AND IF YOU BELONG TO
CHRIST, THEN YOU ARE
ABRAHAM'S OFFSPRING,
HEIRS ACCORDING
TO THE PROMISE.

A special treatment from Galatians.

This is a perfect example of the way calligraphic "styles," in the hand of a master, are not procrustean beds, chopping the letters into rigidly consistent patterns. Instead, letters can be massaged to fit their context; only a skilled eye might notice the difference.

The special treatment Donald made in 2 Thessalonians did, however, receive a unique treatment. The letters are decidedly angular. Donald explained, "They were written with a reed. The writing looks purposely a little ragged, a little primitive, as if I were actually writing a letter." In this passage, the ink is slightly watery, so it varies in tone as the ink puddles at the end of the strokes. It's meant to evoke the quality of these intimate letters written by people without power or influence so long ago.

Milestones

THE PRODUCTION for the Heritage Edition continued in the period when Donald was finishing this last volume. In July 2010 the first half of *Historical Books* were printed at John Roberts in Minnesota. Very sadly, Carol Marrin died on 27 May 2011, just as the manuscript reached completion.

The scribes' signatures

IN THIS VOLUME, Donald chose to make one spread a kind of signature for all six scribes. This appears in 1 Corinthians, chapters 9, 10, and 11. The four columns on the spread were divided into six portions. Each scribe who had worked on the book wrote an allotted number of lines: it is the only place in the Bible where you can see the writing of all six scribes on one spread.

Each scribe also designed a small cypher of their initials, which appear in the little row of squares in the bottom right of the spread.

Revelation

DONALD DID ALL of Revelation by himself—both the writing and illumination. This gave him much more control than he had had through the rest of the manuscript. It was the last book to be written, and it had to close the making of the manuscript with an appropriately strong statement.

He enjoyed having the luxury of being more free with the layout. In all the previous volumes, he had needed to accommodate the work of the team, laying out pages sometimes years before the illuminations would be executed. Now he could really think of illuminations and text as a graphic whole. He said, "I could shift stuff around. For instance, I was able to shift the text so the New Jerusalem illumination could appear where I wanted it. This was also the case with the final Amen."

He made a small concertina-format dummy of the book and considered it as a whole. This also allowed him to plan for technical problems. He said, "It allowed me to plan some illuminations across spreads and avoid having them on two different skins."

"Almost all the motifs here had been used before," Donald said. The long process of creating the manuscript had given him a rich body of symbols with which to work. Of the seventeen pages in Revelation, only four lack illuminations, and the pages are richly ornamented with marginal designs and texts as well.

The Woman and the Dragon

THIS TREMENDOUSLY COMPLEX illumination depicts the great cosmic battle recounted in Revelation 12. Donald rendered it in two parts: a long upright rectangle on the right-hand side of one page, and a continuation on the next page.

He said, "There was so much to include in this illumination. I wrote it all down in my notebook to boil it down to discrete moments." The result was "like a storyboard for a little movie." The characters are a woman "clothed in the sun with the moon at her feet," a terrible dragon, the child she bears, Michael and his angels, and the dark angels of the dragon.

His notes to the CIT give a brief overview of the scenes:

- She appears (in heaven)
- He appears (in heaven)
- Child snatched away and taken to God
- She flees
- The Devil is vanquished toward the earth by St. Michael
- The Devil makes war on earth and pursues the woman
- She is flown to safety by the two wings of a great eagle

Gold behind the woman's head suggests the sun. Donald described how he did the moon: "In the loop of the snake, which is a visual quotation from the *Garden of Eden* illumination in Genesis, the figure of the moon appears. It has been made with gold leaf and holographic foil. This is an innovation that grew out of the making of the Heritage Edition. Holographic foil had been used in the stamping process to make certain images shimmer. Now, the printed book was beginning to affect the creation of the original manuscript—an interesting reversal of the expected process."

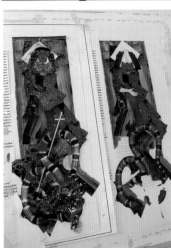

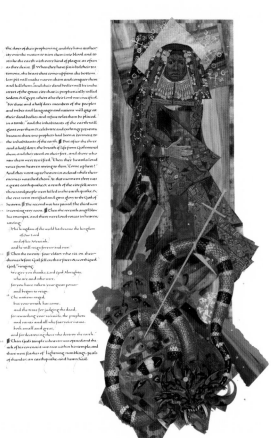

The Woman and the Dragon in process.

The Woman and the Dragon appears at Revelation 10.

9

Am I not free? Am I not an apostle? Have I not seen Jesus our Lord? Are you not my work in the Lord? [2] If I am not an apostle to others, at least I am to you; for you are the seal [3] of my apostleship in the Lord. This is my defense to those who would examine me. [4] Do we not have the right to our food and drink? [5] Do we not have the right to be accompanied by a believing wife, as do the other apostles and the brothers of the Lord and Cephas? [6] Or is it only Barnabas & I who have no right to refrain from working for a living? [7] Who at any time pays the expenses for doing military service? Who plants a vineyard and does not eat any of its fruit? Or who tends a flock and does not get [8] any of its milk? Do I say this on human authority? Does not the law also say the same? [9] For it is written in the law of Moses, "You shall not muzzle an ox while it is treading out the grain." Is it for oxen that God is concerned? [10] Or does he not speak entirely for our sake? It was indeed written for our sake, for whoever plows should plow in hope and whoever threshes should thresh in hope of a share in the crop. [11] If we have sown spiritual good among you, is it too much if we reap your material benefits? [12] If others share this rightful claim on you, do not we still more? Nevertheless, we have not made use of this right, but we endure anything rather than put an obstacle in the way of the gospel of Christ. [13] Do you not know that those who are employed in the temple service get their food from the temple, and those who serve at the altar share in what is sacrificed on the altar? [14] In the same way, the Lord commanded that those who proclaim the gospel should get their living by the gospel. [15] But I have made no use of any of these rights, nor am I writing this so that they may be applied in my case. Indeed, I would rather die than that—no one will deprive me of my ground for boasting! [16] If I proclaim the gospel, this gives me no ground for boasting, for an obligation is laid on me, and woe to me if I do not proclaim the gospel! [17] For if I do this of my own will, I have a reward; but if not of my own will, I am entrusted with a commission. [18] What then is my reward? Just this: that in my proclamation I may make the gospel free of charge, so as not to make [19] full use of my rights in the gospel. For though I am free with respect to all, I have made myself a slave to all, so that I might win more of them. [20] To the Jews I became as a Jew, in order to win Jews. To those under the law I became as one under the law [though I myself am not under the law] so that I might win those under the law. [21] To those outside the law I became as one outside the law [though I am not free from God's law but am under Christ's law] so that I might win those outside the law. [22] To the weak I became weak, so that I might win the weak. I have become all things to all people, that I might by all means save some. [23] I do it all for the sake of the gospel, so that I may share in its blessings. Do you not [24] know that in a race the runners all compete, but only one receives the prize? Run in such a way that you may win it. [25] Athletes exercise self-control in all things; they do it to receive a perishable wreath, but we an imperishable one. [26] So I do not run aimlessly, nor do I box as though beating the air; [27] but I punish my body and enslave it, so that after proclaiming to others I myself should not be disqualified.

10

I do not want you to be unaware, brothers and sisters, that our ancestors were all under the cloud, and all passed through the sea, and all were baptized into Moses in the cloud and in the sea, [3] and all ate the same spiritual food, [4] and all drank the same spiritual drink. For they drank from the spiritual rock that followed them, and the rock was Christ. [5] Nevertheless, God was not pleased with most of them, and they were struck down in the wilderness. [6] Now these things occurred as examples for us, so that we might not desire evil as they did. [7] Do not become idolaters as some of them did; as it is written, "The people sat down to eat and drink, and they rose up to play." [8] We must not indulge in sexual immorality as some of them did, and twenty-three thousand fell in a single day. [9] We must not put Christ to the test, as some of them did, and were destroyed by serpents. [10] And do not complain as some of them did, and were destroyed by the destroyer. [11] These things happened to them to serve as an example, and they were written down to instruct us, on whom the ends of the ages have come. [12] So if you think you are standing, watch out that you do not fall. [13] No testing has overtaken you that is not common to everyone. God is faithful, & he will not let you be tested beyond your strength, but with the testing he will also provide the way out so [14] that you may be able to endure it. Therefore, my dear friends, flee from the worship of idols. [15] I speak as to sensible people; judge for yourselves what I say. [16] The cup of blessing that we bless, is it not a sharing in the blood of Christ? The bread that we break, is it not a sharing in the body of Christ? [17] Because there is one bread, we who are many are one body, for we all partake of the one bread. [18] Consider the people of Israel; are not those who eat the sacrifices partners in the altar? [19] What do I imply then? That food sacrificed to idols is anything, or that an idol is anything? [20] No, I imply that what pagans sac-

RSB
I Cor 9:27

[1] Gk: a sister as wife
[2] Gk: brethren
[3] Other ancient authorities read: the Lord
[4] Gk: my beloved
[5] Gk: Israel according to the flesh

This spread from I Corinthians was used as a signature page for all the scribes. Each scribe wrote a portion of the text, and the slight variation in their hands can be observed. At the bottom, small squares contain their initials.

rifice, they sacrifice to demons and not to God. I do not want you to be partners with demons. 21 You cannot drink the cup of the Lord and the cup of demons. You cannot partake of the table of the Lord and the table of demons. 22 Or are we provoking the Lord to
23 jealousy? Are we stronger than he? ▌"All things are lawful," but not all things are beneficial. "All things are lawful," but not all things build up. 24 Do not seek your own advantage, but that of the other. 25 Eat whatever is sold in the meat market without raising any question on the ground of conscience, 26 for "the earth and its fullness are the Lord's." 27 If an unbeliever invites you to a meal and you are disposed to go, eat whatever is set before you without raising any question on the ground of conscience. 28 But if someone says to you, "This has been offered in sacrifice," then do not eat it, out of consideration for the one who informed you, & for the sake of conscience— 29 I mean the other's conscience, not your own. For why should my liberty be subject to the judgment of someone else's conscience? 30 If I partake with thankfulness, why should I be denounced because of that for which
31 I give thanks? ▌ So, whether you eat or drink, or whatever you do, do everything for the glory of God. 32 Give no offense to Jews or to Greeks or to the church of God, 33 just as I try to please everyone in everything I do, not seeking my own advantage, but that of many, so that they may be saved. 1 Be imitators
11 of me, as I am of Christ.

2 ▌ I commend you because you remember me in everything & maintain the traditions just as I handed them on to you. 3 But I want you to understand that Christ is the head of every man, and the husband is the head of his wife, and God is the head of Christ. 4 Any man who prays or prophesies with something on his head disgraces his head, 5 but any woman who prays or prophesies with her head unveiled disgraces her head - it is one and the same thing as having her head shaved. 6 For if a woman will not veil herself, then she should cut off her hair; but if it is disgraceful for a woman to have her hair cut off or to be shaved, she should wear a veil. 7 For a man ought not to have his head veiled, since he is the image & reflection of God; but woman is the reflection of man. 8 Indeed, man was not made from woman, but woman from man. 9 Neither was man created for the sake of woman, but woman for the sake of man. 10 For this reason a woman ought to have a symbol of authority on her head, because of the angels. 11 Nevertheless, in the Lord woman is not independent of man or man independent of woman. 12 For just as woman came from man, so man comes through woman; but all things come from God. 13 Judge for yourselves: is

it proper for a woman to pray to God with her head unveiled? 14 Does not nature itself teach you that if a man wears long hair, it is degrading to him, 15 but if a woman has long hair, it is her glory? For her hair is given to her for a covering. 16 But if anyone is disposed to be contentious - we have no such custom, nor do the churches of God. ▌ Now in the follow-
17 ing instructions I do not commend you, because when you come together it is not for the better but for the worse. 18 For, to begin with, when you come together as a church, I hear that there are divisions among you; and to some extent I believe it. 19 Indeed, there have to be factions among you, for only so will it become clear who among you are genuine. 20 When you come together, it is not really to eat the Lord's supper. 21 For when the time comes to eat, each of you goes ahead with your own supper, and one goes hungry and another becomes drunk. 22 What! Do you not have homes to eat and drink in? Or do you show contempt for the church of God & humiliate those who have nothing? What should I say to you? Should I commend you? In this matter I do not com-
23 mend you! ▌ For I received from the Lord what I also handed on to you, that the Lord Jesus on the night when he was betrayed took a loaf of bread, 24 and when he had given thanks, he broke it and said, "This is my body that is for you. Do this in remembrance of me." 25 In the same way he took the cup also, after supper, saying, "This cup is the new covenant in my blood. Do this, as often as you drink this bread & drink the cup, you proclaim the Lord's death until he comes. ▌ Whoever, therefore, eats the
27 bread or drinks the cup of the Lord in an unworthy manner will be answerable for the body and blood of the Lord. 28 Examine yourselves, and only then eat of the bread and drink of the cup. 29 For all who eat and drink without discerning the body, eat & drink judgment against themselves. 30 For this reason many of you are weak and ill, and some have died. 31 But if we judged ourselves, we would not be judged. 32 But when we are judged by the Lord, we are disciplined so that we may not be condemned along
33 with the world. ▌ So then, my brothers and sisters, when you come together to eat, wait for one another. 34 If you are hungry, eat at home, so that when you come together, it will not be for your condemnation. About the other things I will give instructions when I come.

y The same Greek word means man & husband
= Or head of the woman
a-b
c Or glory
Gk lacks a symbol of
d Or have freedom of choice regarding her head
e Other ancient authorities read is broken for
f Other ancient authorities add in an unworthy manner.
g Other ancient authorities read the Lord's body
h Gk fallen asleep
i Or When we are judged, we are being disciplined by the Lord
j Gk brothers

it, in remembrance of me." 26 For as often as you eat

When writing out this portion of the text, Donald Jackson accidentally omitted a line. The small scroll drawn at the bottom contains the missing line; a cord ties it to its intended place in the column above.

AFTER THIS I LOOKED & THERE WAS A GREAT MULTITUDE THAT NO ONE COULD COUNT, FROM EVERY NATION, FROM ALL TRIBES & PEOPLES AND LANGUAGES, STANDING BEFORE THE THRONE & BEFORE THE LAMB,

The New Jerusalem spreads across two
pages near the end of Revelation.

[16]The city lies foursquare; its length the same as its width; and he measured the city with his rod, fifteen hundred miles; its length & width & height are equal.[17] He also measured its wall one hundred forty-four cubits by human measurement, which the angel was using.[18] The wall is built of jasper while the city is pure gold, clear as glass.[19] The foundations of the wall of the city are adorned with every jewel; the first was jasper, the second sapphire, the third agate, the fourth emerald,[20] the fifth onyx, the sixth carnelian, the seventh chrysolite, the eighth beryl, the ninth topaz, the tenth chrysoprase, the eleventh jacinth, the twelfth amethyst.[21] And the twelve gates are twelve pearls, each of the gates is a single pearl, and the street of the city is pure gold, transparent as glass.[22] I saw no temple in the city, for its temple is the Lord God the Almighty and the Lamb.[23] And the city has no need of sun or moon to shine on it, for the glory of God is its light, and its lamp is the Lamb.[24] The nations will walk by its light, and the kings of the earth will bring their glory into it.[25] Its gates will never be shut by day – and there will be no night there.[26] People will bring into it the glory & the honor of the nations.[27] But nothing unclean will enter it, nor anyone who practices abomination or falsehood, but only those who are written in the Lamb's book of life.

d Gk. twelve thousand
   stadia
e That is, almost seventy-five
   yards

Donald Jackson adds gilding to *The New Jerusalem*.

He offered this interpretation of his treatment of the dragon: "I created a set of masks for the seven-headed monster that threatens the woman. I had the idea that if you take off the mask, a person's face is revealed. In the end, the devil is us; we blame evil on the devil, but if we take off the devil's mask, we find ourselves."

Donald had wanted Aidan Hart to paint the woman's face, but in the end, he did it himself. "I borrowed Aidan's technique of beginning with a dark under-painting and adding light to build form." His wife, Mabel, served as the hand model for the woman's hand.

Donald used the page turn to good effect. He said, "Then there is a break in the story: you have to turn the page. The monster has come to earth, and the woman flies away. This is represented with the wings that appear in margin." The wings come directly from the stamps used in the *Prophets* volume. He added praying mantises to represent the devil's servants, wreaking havoc on earth; these crawl out of the illumination to inhabit the margins of the page.

New Jerusalem

AT THE VERY END of the book, Donald created a very deliberate pacing of images to evoke the climax to the story told in the book. The pages containing chapters 18–21 are very simple and unadorned. But in the right margin appear the words "Behold I make all things new."

The show-through on this page is very pronounced: you can see a large dark rectangle showing through from the next page. This sets up an expectation that something is about to be revealed. Donald said, "You turn the page and blam! All the instruments are playing loud."

His colors are in a high key. He explained, "I was thinking of strong bands of color. And I had in my mind the powerful illuminations produced in the Carolingian era and in the Spanish Beatus manuscripts."

Still, he had moments of self-doubt. He said, "I was struggling because I was fighting against the image becoming kitschy, with happy families looking into the sunset."

He played with many ideas, but opted to keep this illumination fairly simple. "I did try to use crowd images from the Baptism of Christ illumination: tiny figures seen in the distance. But this illumination did not need impressionistic figures."

Along the bottom, tiny squares break up the hard edges of the illumination. Donald explained, "The tiny squares at the bottom are a quotation from Hazel Dolby's illumination in Nehemiah. Hazel came to the rescue here!"

"The tree of life in the lower right corner was a big thrill to do," Donald said. "I made it with a single

impression of a rubber stamp. I had to put it down in one go. The stamp was so big, it had to be affixed to a curved wooden support. I had to ink it then roll it exactly in place, in one shot across the background I had painted in. That's the kind of risk I love to take when a complicated piece is almost finished."

If you look closely, you will see that there are twelve pearls, twelve gates, and twelve fruits on the tree, picking up the strong numerological symbolism of the passage.

The Final Amen and Final Mark

THE WRITING of the first word of the manuscript had been treated as a special event, on Ash Wednesday, March 8, 2000. Now, more than eleven years later, the manuscript was finished. The final word—"Amen"—was written on May 9, 2011.

In June 2011 volume 7, *Letters and Revelation*, was completed. Donald Jackson, Mabel Jackson, and Sarah Harris delivered the final volume to Saint John's University. The *Letters and Revelation* volume has ninety-four pages of writing on twenty-seven skins. There are nine interpretive illuminations, twenty-one special treatments, eight marginal decorations, and 131 large capitals.

Donald also considered the moment when the last volume would be received by the Abbey and University, marking the completion of the manuscript project. He wanted to give the Saint John's community the role of formally marking the moment. He said, "I painted two gold crosses in shell gold at the foot of the New Jerusalem spread, and the abbot, John Klassen, OSB, and the president of the University, Fr. Robert Koopmann, burnished them brightly at the altar of the Abbey Church as a symbolic last mark in The Saint John's Bible."

Donor Acknowledgment

At 2 Corinthians 7, the capital S was decorated for Steve and Barbara Slaggie. Their first initials are marked with another S intertwined for Steve and a bee for Barbara.

The closing words of the New Testament receive a special treatment. Note how the style of this special treatment matches the book heading of Revelation (shown at the beginning of this chapter).

PART 3

ARTISTS, SCRIPTS, & PRINTERS

Part 3 examines specific issues about the making of The Saint John's Bible. As the Bible has toured in public exhibitions, certain questions have regularly arisen. Audiences have wanted to know more about the artists and scribes who helped Donald Jackson and contributed their efforts to bring the Bible to fruition. Calligraphers have wanted to know more about the scripts used in the Bible. And others have wondered about how the delicate vellum pages were mounted in their custom-made display cases. The following chapters answer some of these questions.

In addition, the creation of the printed Heritage Edition has radically changed the nature of the Bible project. The final chapter offers a brief account of how the Heritage Edition came to be and how it relates to the making of the manuscript.

CHAPTER 16

COLLABORATION: ARTISTS AND CALLIGRAPHERS

ONE OF THE MOST intriguing aspects of the making of The Saint John's Bible has been the collaborative aspect of the project. Some collaborations follow set patterns. In well-established art forms like the cinema or theater, the role of each participant is carefully defined within a fixed hierarchy; everyone knows what part he or she plays. In the high medieval scriptoria this was true as well. Scribes and illuminators worked within a system that was well established. The ruling of the pages might be the work of an assistant; the text was written by professional scribes; rubricators added headings and versal capitals at the beginnings of chapters or other subdivisions of the text; and one group of illuminators might add decorative ornaments in the margins, while the more elaborate representational images might be added by dedicated masters of painting.

All the artists and scribes have careers outside the Bible project. This piece of Donald Jackson's writing was made with a steel brush on paper. Detail from the *Lord of the Rings* series, 1988.

In other art forms, collaborations are the result of a process of negotiation, as the different players invent ways of working with one another. As we have seen in earlier chapters of this book, Donald Jackson and Saint John's developed a pattern that worked for both artist and client over a period of several years. The task was not easy for either party, but, with time, Donald and his client allowed the relationship to evolve and find an equilibrium.

In his relationship with the scribes and illuminators whom he invited to join the project, Donald also had to search for ways to work collaboratively. He could not fall back on a set, traditional division of labor. The medieval scriptorium is dead; its patterns of work are foreign to contemporary artists and calligraphers. And though Donald often uses the metaphor of the conductor to describe his role, it remains a metaphor: the artists and scribes who joined him were not trained in the musical conservatories or accustomed to the hierarchies of the orchestra.

Donald's artistic collaborators fell into two basic divisions: scribes and illuminators. The scribes were responsible for writing the bulk of the text, following the layouts devised by Donald and Vin Godier. Their work was largely a matter of craft: accurately and efficiently writing out the columns of text using carefully defined scripts. Good technique and consistency were the heart of their practice. The individual personalities of the scribes and their work was subsumed by the task at hand.

The Minneapolis Institute of Arts

At the opening of the first Bible exhibition at the Minneapolis Institute of Arts in 2005, most of Donald Jackson's team assembled for the opening. For this group portrait, the photographs of the missing team members were mounted on sticks so they could be included (They are marked with asterisks here). From left to right:

Thomas Ingmire, *artist*
Mabel Jackson, *Donald's wife and partner*
Chris Tomlin,* *natural history artist*
Donald Jackson, *artistic director*
Rebecca Cherry, *project manager*
Vin Godier, *computer consultant*
Izzy Pludwinski,* *Hebrew scribe*
Sally Sargeant,* *proofreader*
Aidan Hart, *artist*
Sarah Harris, *studio assistant*
Suzanne Moore, *artist*
Sue Hufton, *scribe*
Christopher Calderhead, *documentarian*
Sally Mae Joseph, *studio manager, scribe, artist*
Hazel Dolby, *artist*
Brian Simpson,* *scribe*
Angela Swan, *scribe*
Susie Leiper, *scribe*

At the time this group portrait was taken, Diane Von Arx had not yet joined the production team of the Bible.

The illuminators, by contrast, were called on to create illustrations for the Bible, and their unique personalities and artistic decisions came to the fore.

The division between the two types of collaboration were not always hard and fast. The special treatments in the Bible are a kind of hybrid of calligraphy and illumination. They are meant to be legible texts, but they involve color and composition in a way that allows for a degree of creative response. These were executed by artists in each category.

Donald had a slightly different working relationship with each of his collaborators, but there were certain patterns to his interactions. With the scribes, he fell naturally into the role of the master teacher. Throughout his career, he has employed scribes in his workshop, working with them on an apprenticeship system. The scribes fell naturally into this familiar pattern, and their initial work with Donald was much like a master class. All the scribes were already fully fledged professional calligraphers before they joined the project, but the craft nature of their work meant that their work with Donald was organized along the lines of an atelier under a master artist. Because the scribes were working on the same basic task and trying to keep their writing consistent, they had a strong identity as a group, working alongside Donald.

The illuminators, by contrast, produced their individual contributions largely on their own, in their own studios. They were given a great deal of autonomy in devising artistic solutions to the design problems with which they were presented. Donald guided their work and provided important feedback; he also took on the important task of communicating their ideas to Saint John's, passing their sketches on to the CIT, and relaying the CIT's comments back to the artists. For the illuminators, a great freedom of personal expression was a guiding principle.

Each of Donald's collaborators has brought a special contribution to the project, and we introduce them in this chapter. I sent each one a questionnaire by e-mail and then conducted interviews by telephone. I have chosen to present them as a single group, and they are presented here in alphabetical order.

Hazel Dolby Illuminations and Special Treatments

BORN IN London, Hazel Dolby attended Camberwell School of Art in the early 1960s. She said, "Donald Jackson was teaching there at the time." She added, laughing, "I don't remember him at all, much to his disgust!"

She enjoyed the incredible diversity of the classes she was taking. She said, "The most important classes—and they have stood me in good stead—were the life drawing classes."

The school day was long. "We were there from nine in the morning until five in the evening, and we had a compulsory lettering class in the evenings." The lettering class, it should be said, was not taught by Donald.

As a student she found lettering "incredibly boring. I didn't see the point of it." Transfer lettering like Letraset had just come on the market, and the traditional drawn lettering she was being taught seemed stodgy, dull, and old-fashioned. Her interest in calligraphy and lettering would come much later.

After receiving her National Diploma in Design in Illustration, she began a long career teaching in secondary schools. After stints in Brixton, South London, and a Comprehensive School, she found herself at Esher College. When she arrived it was a boys' grammar school, and while she was there it made the transition into a sixth-form college, which is loosely equivalent to the higher grades of an American high school. She taught painting, print making, textile design, drawing, and photography.

"When I chose to teach photography," she said, "I knew absolutely nothing about it. That's what you do when you're twenty-six! I did a crash course one weekend, and then we were off and running. We made pinhole cameras and I piled my whole class into a minibus. We went to Hampton Court and shot with our pinhole cameras. Our work made it into the *Guardian* because of a competition. We won!"

She thrived in the creative atmosphere of the school. "It was exciting to be around young people so full of energy. Many of our students went on to do amazing things. Quite a few of them went on to study at art school and have successful careers in the arts."

In late 1980s, she decided to pursue calligraphy. At a weekend course she met the calligrapher Ann Hechle, who gave a lecture on the work of Irene Wellington. Hazel was fascinated with what she saw. She decided to begin taking evening courses. In one evening class taught by Sue Hufton, she was encouraged to start from the beginning, to take a methodical approach to lettering.

As a result, she enrolled in the program run by Ann Camp at the Roehampton Institute. "I got into Roehampton with samples of skeleton Roman capitals and the Foundational Hand that I had taught myself. In my interview with Ann Camp, she showed me everything I had done wrong. Ann was incredibly rigorous, and I'm grateful for that."

Originally intending to stay just one year at Roehampton, she ended up staying for five years, and she earned an Advanced Diploma in Calligraphy. The education was much more formal and analytical than what she had received at Camberwell. "At Camberwell, it just seeped in through your pores. The training at Roehampon was far more systematic."

Hazel was elected to Fellowship in the Society of Scribes and Illuminators in 1991.

In her work since then, she has focused on drawn and painted lettering more than on edged-pen writing. Quite a bit of her work has been three dimensional. She has worked with papier mache to create pots that she has covered with painted designs and inscriptions. Out of that grew a long exploration with blocks of various shapes. Color and texture are key elements of this work.

"I'm mostly motivated by themes," she said. And in her work, she has explored aspects of seascape, gardens, and pottery. In one commission she was inspired by women's quilting from the nineteenth century. That project provided imagery that she then used in The Saint John's Bible in the *Woman of Valor* illumination in Proverbs.

In her teaching since leaving Roehampton, she has concentrated on explorations of color theory. This has influenced her own work, which is characterized by an exploration of color theory and drawn and painted letterforms.

She came to the Bible project during the making of the first volume, *Gospels and Acts*. She remembered, "Sally [Mae Joseph] put in a good word for me with Donald. There were four special treatments needed."

Work in progress in Hazel Dolby's studio.

Hazel was invited to the Scriptorium, where she worked on ideas under Donald's supervision. It was a period of testing the waters both for Donald and for Hazel. "After I had done three special treatments, I think Donald trusted me."

After that initial visit to the Scriptorium, Hazel generally worked on her special treatments and illuminations at her home studio in Hampshire. Briefs were sent to her by post, and telephone conversations with Donald provided an opportunity to discuss the progress of each of her contributions. Donald would talk her through each brief and offer interpretations of the text. "And then" she said, "I had to just get on with it."

"Donald is eagle-eyed," she said. "He notices little, tiny, subtle things. You needed to be on your toes."

The Bible has been a challenging project for her. "These are texts I wouldn't necessarily choose, and sometimes I'm not even sure I completely understand them. But you have to be engaged, or you can't do anything. I had to get immersed and find a key that was relevant to me. It could take a long time, but fortunately I usually had the briefs well ahead of time so I was able to mull them over. Sometimes I went down blind alleys until I found what felt right for me, Donald, and the Saint John's team."

In the first four special treatments she did, she was directed by Donald fairly tightly. In the subsequent volumes, she had more freedom to explore each illumination on her own, with feedback from Donald as the work went on.

Working on vellum was initially a challenge. "I had very little experience of the material," she remarked. "I was more used to working with materials such as papier mache and handmade papers." She also was concerned that, compared to some of the other artists, she had less confidence with raised and burnished gold. She opted to use shell gold and flat gold instead, media with which she was more familiar.

Her work on the Bible pushed her to work outside of her normal comfort zone, both in terms of materials and subject matter. But what comes through all her work on the Bible is her keen sense of composition and a lush color sensibility.

Aidan Hart Illuminations

AIDAN HART is a trained iconographer who works within the carefully defined traditions of Orthodox Christianity. Most of his commissioned work has been panel icons, but he has also worked in fresco, mosaic, painted illuminations on vellum, and carved wood and stone.

He told me, "I have three studios: a barn and two buildings in the back garden. One of the garden studios is for painting, the other and the barn are used for more messy operations like woodworking and stone carving."

He has recently taken on an assistant, and when he needs further help he asks some of his students.

Aidan was not originally from an Orthodox background. He said to me, "I was born in London. My parents were from New Zealand, where we returned when I was one year old."

In New Zealand he took a degree in literature and a diploma in education, and then worked as a professional sculptor. It was in 1983 that he joined the Orthodox Church. The two monks in New Zealand through whom he was received encouraged him to travel more widely because the Orthodox Church in New Zealand is a very young community and they felt he should have a broader experience of Orthodoxy.

He entered the monastic life and spent twelve years as a *rasophore*, a rank roughly equivalent to a novice monk in the Western tradition. After some years with a monk in Wales he was sent for further training to Mount Athos for eighteen months. In 1993 he moved to Shropshire to live as a hermit. With the help of donors he bought twenty acres of land and a derelict cottage to convert into a hermitage.

He said, "The property had a ruined two-up two-down cottage. With the help of friends and my parents—who came over from New Zealand for five months—the first job was to restore the cottage so I had somewhere to live. There was also a stone barn. Half of that I converted into a chapel and frescoed the interior. Then I turned an old stone pigsty into guest quarters. [He laughs]. It sounds terrible—'You'll be staying in the pigsty,' I would tell guests. But it was probably the warmest place on the property. I also planted five thousand native trees."

An interior view of the Monastery of Saint Anthony and Saint Cuthbert, Shropshire, England. The frescoes, icons, oak icon screen, and furniture were all made by Aidan Hart.

He was living at the Hermitage when he first met Donald around 1998.

I asked him about his approach to icon painting and about the teachers who had influenced him. He responded, "On Athos I lived at the monastery of Iviron (I had studied modern Greek five years earlier). The abbot of Iviron was Fr. Vasileios. He had not studied art formally, although he knew the great iconographer Leonid Ouspensky. What most affected me was his approach to life in general, the way he linked art to theology and the life of prayer. One of Fr. Vasileios' sayings was 'There is an imperfect perfection and a perfect imperfection.' In this way he often warned against rigid conceptions of perfection, and overworking art."

The abbot's way of life often challenged Aidan when his approach to the religious life was too cerebral: "Fr. Vasileios spoke from the heart. And by heart I don't just mean the emotions but rather the spiritual center of a person. I would sometimes ask him a question, and my question would sometimes be from the brain, and so I would expect a rationalistic answer. But he would give an answer from the heart, not the head. This would initially throw me off balance, but gradually I would see that the reply helped me to see differently and the question answered itself."

He thrived in the prayerful atmosphere of the monastery. He commented, "In Orthodox monasticism, prayer is at the heart of the life. It is demanding. The services are long. But their sublime beauty and asceticism capture the imagination."

I asked him how his experience of Saint John's compared to the Orthodox monasteries he had lived in. He responded, "I've only been to Saint John's once, and then very briefly, but it struck me that Roman Catholic monasticism has often felt the need to do active service in the world. The Roman Catholic tradition is very good at getting out there in the world, getting its feet dirty, educating people, taking care of the poor and the sick. The struggle then is to ensure that the daily life of prayer remains at the heart of the monastery and is not eclipsed by practical demands. It has been a blessing to have an ongoing relationship with the monastery through the numerous icons they have since commissioned from me."

I asked him about the current resurgence of interest in icons within many Western faith communities. He said, "I think it's because an icon is not just about the subject matter. It's also about how the subject matter is depicted. Icons show the world transfigured, radiant with the presence of God. You could say it's about the style—not that there is only one way of painting icons; there are many styles in fact."

He began to explore the nature of the icon with me. "I think it's that icons are painted in a paradisiacal way. As human beings we are made for paradise. We are made in the image of God, and we naturally look at the world in that way, even if we don't know it or have forgotten how. When we see icons, they resonate with our very nature. They speak to our nostalgia for a paradisiacal way of seeing."

It took him time, however, to appreciate icons. "My first experience of icons was negative: I didn't like them," he said. "I had been trained in a representational, naturalistic style."

I was struck by his holistic approach to the art of painting icons. "I use egg tempera for my icons. I don't use oils. There were some interesting experiments with oil in nineteenth-century Greece and Russia, but the results weren't good. I think it's to do with the fact that because oil dries very slowly there is a tendency to blend and over-refine an image."

He prefers materials that are natural and local. He said, "I like the idea of using natural materials. Painting icons is an ecological act and transfiguring. The iconographer makes the natural materials even more articulate in the praise of God. And all materials have a history that is evoked when you use them. When I paint using eggs from my neighbor's garden I think of the neighbors and the chickens running around."

Does he use acrylics? "No. What do they make me think of? The factory where the chemicals were made."

His training was largely self-guided, and he has looked at icons carefully for all his adult life. He explained, "I have quite a scientific mind and have learned primarily from a close study of good icons. You can learn a lot just by observing and analysing icons, or even good detailed photographic reproductions. Observing that way you see how they were actually made. Sometimes my observations contradict the common received wisdom. I also talk to art conservators who use scientific methods and technology to examine icons. Using things like spectrometers they can tell precisely what pigments were used."

He does not describe himself, however, as being self-taught. "I would have loved to have studied under a master," he said, "but I didn't have that opportunity. Instead, I organized my own course of study. I've gleaned a lot from talking to icon painters and exploring the technical, scientific side of the practice as well as its theology. I have tried to embody these two aspects of the icon tradition in my recent book, *Techniques of Icon and Wall Painting*."

When he first met Donald he had just completed a series of paintings on vellum for an exhibition in New Zealand. "The choice of illumination over wooden panels was purely practical," he said. "It was less expensive to ship the lightweight skins to NZ than heavy wooden icons. It was sort of providence really. I just happened to have been working on vellum, and I showed those to Donald."

Donald asked if he would like to work on the Bible project, and Aidan said yes.

Like the other artists, Aidan grew into his collaboration with Donald. "In the first volume, *Gospels and Acts*, I recall I was given five or six illustrations to do. Donald gave me the briefs and showed me the size and location for each one. The *Sower* was the first illustration I worked on. I did pencil sketches, then Donald and the committee at Saint John's made comments, and then I went ahead and finished them."

As the project progressed, the working method shifted. Usually Donald would produce a design and ask Aidan to contribute figurative elements.

I asked why the working pattern changed, and Aidan responded, "I think there were two reasons. Saint John's wanted a more contemporary illustration style; I think they saw my work as too traditional. But I also think it was about consistency, making the book hold together. With this new approach the illuminations were more obviously related to Donald Jackson's hand."

I asked if there was any ego involved in that for him. He replied, "No. If you are working on a building everyone has their job: one person makes the door, another does the brickwork, and so on. I love the fact that The Saint John's Bible is created by a community, not just by an individual." He explained that since we are created in the image of the Holy Trinity we are most in God's image when we are operating as a community. Collaborating in this way felt comfortable, theologically sound.

He added, "Being a communal project there was give and take. I said if I thought a suggestion wouldn't work aesthetically or was not theologically sound."

He appreciated Donald's approach to the project: "Donald has an instinctive sense of the meaning of the stories he's illuminating in the Bible. He distills each one to its essence. Donald is humble in the way he tries to serve the text he's interpreting. Even though he is not a church attender and is not formally trained as a theologian, I find his images are theologically and spiritually insightful."

I remarked that perhaps Donald's approach reflects his origins in the calligraphy world, rather than a fine art training. It's a different sensibility. Aidan concurred: "Yes, perhaps so. It's interesting. What's going on in the graphic design schools is probably more akin to making icons than what happens in the art schools, where it's so often about disembodied ideas and ego, and few techniques are taught."

He expanded on that thought, saying, "The commercial graphic design world is akin to the world of the iconographer in that both are fulfilling a clearly defined function. These functions are different, but both try to mediate between the viewer and the message. I love the fact that the word *art* comes from the Latin word *artis*, to fitly join together. The very word *art* suggests this joining subject and viewer and not being purely for its own sake.

"In iconography the icon mediates between two worlds: the heavenly and the mundane." Laughing, he added: "Graphic designers mediate between the product and the buyer, but the aim of finding the best aesthetic way of attracting the viewer to the object is the same with icons and advertising."

He commented, "Although they are iconographic in style I wouldn't call my images in the Bible 'icons' as such. They are more illuminations or illustrations."

What is the distinction, I asked. "A panel icon is primarily designed for veneration, to be kissed, to be prayed in front of, and to be a place of encounter with the person depicted. Illuminations, on the other hand, are there primarily to give theological insight. We live in a literate age, so we can read the stories. We don't need the pictures to tell us the stories. But the way illuminations tell the story can initiate the viewer into a deeper way of seeing. The highest role of the illustrations is to provide a theological insight into the Scriptures. Good illumination is like a commentary: it goes beyond the merely didactic."

I asked him how the project had affected him spiritually.

He answered: "I found that researching each image was a very rich experience. An icon is not just a copy of an old image; the iconographer needs to enter into the theology of that particular subject and so paint it with understanding. Take, for example, the full page image of Saint Paul in the book of Acts which Donald and I painted. In my research for this image I realised that the heart of Saint Paul's missionary labours was his life of prayer, his mysticism, his experience of Christ. After he had his conversion on the Road to Damascus he retired to the desert. He lived the life of a monk. And it was only when God called him forth that he set out on his missionary journeys."

Apart from working outside the classic icon tradition, Aidan found the project opened him to some new techniques. He said, "Sometimes for the Bible I have worked in monochrome—that's a change for me. The face of the Son of Man in *Prophets*, for instance is painted only with blue and white."

And working with Donald he made connections between this project and some aspects of the classic icon tradition. "Donald likes contrasts," he said. Perhaps that's one reason Donald enjoyed combining Aidan's work with his own in one image. "You look at his work and there are the messy parts and the tidy parts, spontaneous brush strokes and deliberate strokes. But by messy I don't mean sloppy; they are still controlled. It's that perfect imperfection that Fr. Vasileios used to talk about."

Aidan tied this to work of a thousand years ago: "At Saint Catherine's monastery in Sinai, some of the tenth- and eleventh-century icons were painted with very fluid backgrounds. No sense there that everything's regular, straight and 'perfect.' The faces might be rendered more carefully, but the backgrounds were freer in execution. Not everything is in control. It appears that the painter had a sense of urgency, was under divine power, and had to get it down on the surface of the painting before the inspiration passed."

He added, "I would love to get to that place of freedom. The wonderful thing about working with Donald is learning and seeing those places where he lets loose and lets happenstance take over."

Sue Hufton Scribe

SUE HUFTON said to me that the greatest value of The Saint John's Bible is that "people feel part of it—the awe and excitement with which people react to it. They want to know details; it involves them."

She recounted to me how she had gone to Japan and had shared her work on the Bible. "I was warned," she said, "that people would not be particularly interested in The Saint John's Bible because Japan is not a Christian culture, but they were fascinated. They were really listening." In her experience, it has been a project that crosses cultural boundaries.

Sue was born in Worcester and moved often as a child. The eight years she lived in Clapham, London, as an adult was the longest time she has ever spent in one place. That experience may account for her no-nonsense practicality: "It gave me the ability to be uprooted and move elsewhere and get on with it."

She went to Southlands College, a Methodist college that formed part of the Roehampton Institute, where she earned a BEd degree in preparation for teaching at primary level. As part of her course, she studied art.

"In our second and third years," she said, "we had to specialize. I was going to do textiles, but I was told I had to look at other departments."

This is when she first met Ann Camp. "I walked in and I saw big handmade books. Something inside me said, 'You have to take this chance now.'"

Ironically, in the first year she failed her calligraphy module. This proved a fortuitous setback. "If I hadn't failed," she said, "I would have done bookbinding the following year, but I had to retake calligraphy."

She ended by staying on for a fourth year for the honors degree, which enabled her to pursue her calligraphy more deeply. Ann Camp backed her. It was the first year that Ann's diploma course was running, and Sue was the only undergraduate in a class of diploma students.

After college, she spent three years teaching in a primary school, but she decided she wanted to return to Roehampton for the one-year certificate in calligraphy. Her husband, Rob, was at the time a market research manager, and he supported her through the diploma. (Rob would later become a Methodist minister).

A piece by Sue Hufton. The text is from *In Parenthesis* by David Jones, painted with a pointed brush and white acrylic ink onto very dark green Nepalese handmade tissue which was mounted over a board and waxed. The red lines were made of twisted Nepalese tissue. The piece is about twenty-four inches wide.

In the end, she spent three years as a full-time student in the advanced diploma program.

After this, using a grant from the Crafts Council, she studied for one year under the letter cutter Tom Perkins, where she learned to work in drawn lettering and letter carving in stone.

She said, "That's when I learned how to live and work in one place, with kids around—and that it wasn't easy. Tom and [his wife, the calligrapher] Gaynor Goffe were incredibly generous. They would share their experience and skills with anybody. If a stranger rang and asked for help, they would down tools. It's an important thing to share what you know."

She contrasted this with much of the calligraphy world, where she said there is a sense of "protectiveness," an occasional unwillingness to share methods and techniques.

At the end of that period with Tom and Gaynor, she had her first son, Joe. "Ann Camp was pushing me to apply for Fellowship [in the Society of Scribes and Illuminators]. She, and I, knew if I didn't do it then, I would never do it."

Six months pregnant, she felt under tremendous pressure to prepare work for her Fellowship application. She said to herself, "I'm never going to be ready, but I just have to get on with it." She commented that she brought the same spirit to her Bible pages. "For me," she said, "that's quite liberating." She was elected a Fellow of the Society in 1987.

As her children grew, she never gave up working. Her commissioned work has given her the chance to explore her own ideas. She has not done much in the way of certificates and envelopes—the sort of bread-and-butter work that sustains many calligraphers. Instead, her work has involved more creative projects. Her style is exquisite, with letterforms pared to their beautiful essence.

Sue found her work on the Bible surprisingly liberating: "When I was writing text for the Bible project it was the most freedom I've ever experienced [in my work], even though it was the mostly tightly controlled thing I had ever done. That was not something I expected at all."

When she was invited to join the first group of scribes to train (and perhaps be selected for) the Bible project, she balked at first. She thought, "It's too big. I can't go to Wales for a month. And I hadn't been writing much. I can paint, carve, draw letters . . ." She doubted whether she had it in her to do such a demanding calligraphic project.

When she got to the Scriptorium in Wales, those inner voices of doubt continued. But she reflected that Donald had asked her to join the project; he had confidence in her.

As she worked at the Scriptorium in those opening weeks, it became clear to her that writing—actually doing calligraphy—was not really the problem. Her block was a result of having trained with a metal pen. She said, "I remember at Roehampton, other students would wax poetic about the pleasure of writing. I didn't know what they were talking about. But writing with the quill is a completely different experience. When I started writing with a quill on vellum, I realized I had never experienced such delight."

Sue reflected on the way writing the text related to her Christian faith. She said, "As far as I know, I was the only one of the scribes who was a regular churchgoer." Yet when she talks about the Bible project with other Christians, she often feels a sense of disconnect: "I think a lot of people who are Christians talk to me as if writing the text was a conversion experience. This project produces very personal reactions—all valid. It's not about getting an expected reaction."

For her, the experience of writing the Bible "is not a holy thing. It's a mystical experience as anything else is. It was only a spiritual experience in the context of life."

By e-mail, she sent me some thoughts about how writing the Bible had affected her life of faith:

> Being closely involved with the Scriptures showed me that it is a very human document and that taking passages out of context and reading small parts at a time, whilst it has a value in the context of worship, is actually to devalue the text. What I found very valuable and eye-opening was to write out whole chunks and the befores and afters of familiar passages. It is about people, their stories, experiences, reactions, and emotions and therefore in some ways that demystified the Bible for me but at the same time gave it even more relevance and value. The human condition changes very little, the relevance of the Old Testament [OT] was a complete surprise to me. When I returned to writing the New Testament [NT] and passages (in the *Letters*) that I would have said are at the foundation of my faith, I found my reaction to them was that they lacked the warmth, humanity, and realism of the OT chunks I had been writing.
>
> That realization, I think, may have shifted my faith more than I thought as I look back on the last ten years. My viewpoint is wider as a result of those years intimately involved with the OT, whereas before I'd seen the OT as a collection of stories that I'd known from childhood and largely in the shadow of and simply a precursor to the NT and not as relevant to me. Now I see them as actually more relevant and, despite the wars and blood and gore depicted in the stories, bravely and clearly say things that acknowledge the realities of life and yet how life can be underpinned by a huge amount of hope and capacity for redemption and renewal. In contrast the writing in the NT felt monochrome after the colour and life of the OT. Very surprising.

It was hard for Sue to part with the project. "The last passage I wrote," she said, "was in *Letters*. It helped; I felt very sad. I was a kind of bereavement. The shape of my working week changed. I no longer had this framework."

The text, Jude 24–25, "was like a benediction on the work we had done."

Thomas Ingmire Illuminations and Special Treatments

BASED IN San Francisco, Thomas Ingmire has carved out a unique position in the world of American calligraphy. A much sought-after teacher, he brings a thoughtful, intellectual approach to his work. Soft spoken, with a wry intelligence and self-deprecating humor, he has brought his calligraphy into a deep conversation with the world of fine art.

Trained as a landscape architect, he studied calligraphy and illumination with Donald Jackson when Donald spent a year teaching in California in 1976–77. The two have been friends and colleagues ever since.

In my interview with Thomas, I was struck that he was the only member of the team who expressed ambivalence about the project. It's not that he was critical, or didn't believe in the project, but he was willing to step back and to look at the project without needing to present it in rosy, glowing terms. I also felt that, as a calligrapher with an international reputation in his own right, Thomas could approach the project and his work with Donald on rather more equal terms than some of the other members of the team.

He recalled his earliest involvement in calligraphy: "At the beginning I treated calligraphy as a hobby. Living in San Francisco, with Chinatown so close . . . I looked a lot at Chinese, Japanese, and Arabic calligraphy. And in my reading about Arabic calligraphy I saw how they just worked with letters and pushed them. So from very early on, I did very little illustration."

This visual/verbal book by Thomas Ingmire is entitled *CROSSROAD*. The text is by Federico García Lorca, and it measures 8 x 8 inches. UCLA Young Research Library, Special Collections.

In his early career, he decided to call his studio the Scriptorium Saint Francis. I asked him why. "Scriptorium Saint Francis started in 1974 or 1975, a year or two after I studied with Donald," he said. "I was living on Tuscany Alley. I lived near a poet / lawyer who send out poems with a request for money donations. He would write 'City of Saint Francis' on the return envelopes. One day while browsing through a neighborhood bookstore I found a book on the Life of St. Francis and was reminded that he had lived in Tuscany. My studio name seemed fated."

He continued, "At that time I was making small printed books. I did a book of Shakespeare Sonnets and printed one thousand. After ten years, I still had 950! They were five dollars a piece."

Very quickly, he started to teach calligraphy and began to establish a reputation as a teacher. He remarked, "I didn't like commercial work. I never really pursued it. Most of the things I did were commissioned things."

Unlike many calligraphers who have tried to earn a living through their work, Thomas didn't seek out the wedding invitations, certificates, logos, or editorial work that can provide a steady stream of work. "I was pretty entrenched in the teaching," he says.

He has been particularly interested in creating a modern calligraphy for our own time, informed by the tradition, but willing to go further, to experiment with novel letterforms and push the limits of legibility. He said, "Donald pushed me to do more modern work."

He made several forays into showing his work with galleries. This at first seemed promising, but he eventually soured on selling his work in that way. He had a number of gallery shows. He said, "Economically, while it was a good way to get your name out, I do better selling things through my teaching contacts, on my own. The gallery scene is a pretty strange world. They started telling me what kind of work to do, setting price points, and so on."

The galleries wanted to promote his work as "Fine Art"; he was content to refer to it as calligraphy. He has experienced firsthand the problem that Western calligraphy has when it tries to cross over into the art world. "I don't avoid the word calligraphy," he says, "but it does carry baggage. Once people see my work, that's all that matters."

In any case, "It didn't last. The art crash of 1989 killed that off."

In 1989, Michael Gullick published a monograph of his work called *Words of Risk: The Art of Thomas Ingmire*. Thomas has also published a book titled *Codici1*, which describes his research into creating a modern Western calligraphy.

He said, "Life drawing has influenced my calligraphy a great deal." He has studied with Eleanor Dickson and incorporated ideas from her teaching into his approach to calligraphy.

He explained, "In her classes, Eleanor discussed using line and composition as a way of expressing the emotion of the model and particularly our own feelings about the model. She would have us interact with them, talk to them. These classes were in her own studio in San Francisco. During my first year of study with Eleanor, my drawings weren't great by any means, but I would return to my studio and apply the ideas to my calligraphy. That experience changed everything about my work."

He has sent his own students to study with her.

I asked Thomas how The Saint John's Bible tied into his work. He responded, "That's been one of the biggest problems: it hasn't fit into my most current interests in calligraphy. It does tie into my work from the 1980s. The work was more painterly then. I tried to look at calligraphy as shape, line, composition, and color. But it's not like my current work for a long time."

Of his current work he said, "The things I've been doing in my teaching are more about abstracting letters. But the Bible asks for legibility." So the project forced him into a different way of working.

He clearly had the experience needed to tackle his illuminations and special treatments. He said, "Vellum is not what I work on at all these days, but I've certainly worked on vellum enough."

At times he had doubts about the project. As he recalled: "I thought to myself at times, 'Oh man why am I doing this?' The work in so many ways was both technically and conceptually challenging."

Quite honestly, he appreciated the project as a good paying job. "There's a little bit of calligraphy mercenary in there. Sometimes it's been my only paying work."

But he has no regrets. He said, "I'm happy I did it. I am quite aware that it has been a privilege and an honor to be involved in this work. And having the opportunity to work with Donald was probably the greatest gift. Besides, it was impossible to say no to him."

Donald chose illuminations for Thomas that he thought played to his interest in more expressive lettering. Some of the briefs, however, called for a more direct illustrative treatment, but he said, "Illustration would have been a big challenge and too removed from my work."

He actually gave some of these assignments back to Donald, who did them himself. He recounted, "When I saw Donald in Minnesota in September 2009, we met with the CIT. There were a couple of illuminations I'd turned back to him, and what he did was amazing."

Sally Mae Joseph Scribe, Special Treatments, Carpet Pages, and Occasional Ornaments

SALLY MAE's role as a participating artist and scribe was shaped by her role as studio manager at the Scriptorium in the initial years of the project. She moved to Wales to take the position, and she worked with Donald on a daily basis, unlike the other artists and scribes.

She was born in Kingston-upon-Thames. She said, "I didn't come from an artistic family. My father was a garage mechanic, but he always did DIY projects at home. I used to spend time with him and from an early age he encouraged me to use his tools." This gave her a lifelong affinity for working with her hands, making things. She added, "In calligraphy and bookbinding, the feel for tools came from my Dad."

She married young and started a family. Once the children had started school, she decided to take an evening drawing class. "The teacher told me to go to the British Museum and draw the objects. I'd never done anything like that; it was an incredible adventure."

As she wandered into the British Library (which at the time was housed within the museum) she saw a medieval manuscript; the gold and the black ink immediately spoke to her. "I told a friend who had been to art school, and she said, 'That's calligraphy.'"

A memorial stone for Charles Wesley for a public garden in Marylebone, London. Welsh slate, designed and carved by Sally Mae Joseph and Sue Hufton, 2007.

Sally Mae then enrolled in calligraphy evening classes, and eventually took the calligraphy O level and A level, as well an art O level.

A full year at the Reigate School of Art and Design followed, where she studied calligraphy and heraldic painting under Anthony Wood. Then it was on to the Roehampton Institute to study under Ann Camp. She earned a diploma in four years as a part-time student.

She thrived in the intense atmosphere of the Roehampton course. "I reveled in it. I lapped it up. And when I was there, the people I had around me were amazing." Hazel Dolby, Denis Brown, Diana Stetson were all students with her at the time. "The vast majority of them are still working calligraphers," she said. "They are at the top of the field." She particularly enjoyed working with Gaynor Goffe, who was teaching with Ann Camp at the time. "Gaynor was a huge influence," she said.

In 1991, she was elected a Fellow of the Society of Scribes and Illuminators.

"After that, I set myself up as a self-employed lettering artist," Sally Mae said. She also took on one day a week as an instructor at Roehampton, where she taught italic handwriting in the mornings and gilding in the afternoons. She also made two instructional videos, "Gilding for Calligraphers" and "Modern Gilding for Calligraphers."

As a freelancer, she did all manner commissions. "What pleased me most," she commented, "was commissioned work for people. I loved working with clients. I was a jobbing calligrapher."

She said she had always had a "fantasy" of working with Donald Jackson after she left Roehampton. One day, after he had been commissioned to create The Saint John's Bible, Sally Mae saw a picture in the *Telegraph* of the *Genealogy* page from *Gospels and Acts*. "I wrote him a congratulatory letter, and added: 'If you ever need the services of a humble scribe . . .'"

Donald picked up the phone and called her. It was a fortuitous moment. Recently divorced and setting herself up on her own, she was open for new possibilities. Her friend, the lettering artist Lieve Cornil, said to her, "You can't say no!"

She went up to Wales for a weekend with Donald and Mabel. She said, "A week later I arrived with my suitcase." The first few months were a transitional period. With one daughter still living at home, Sally Mae split her time between the Scriptorium in Wales and her home in Guildford. Once her daughter was ready to go off to university, Sally Mae moved to Tal-y-coed, a village near the Hendre, and became involved full time on the Bible project.

When she arrived, Donald was beginning the process of gearing up to produce the Bible. "I was sort of like the secretary to start off with. I worked on every aspect of the project in those early days, getting everything set up for a good nine months to a year before I was doing any writing."

Her time with the project was a completely immersive experience. "I was there from nine to six, five days a week, for six years," she said. In that time, in addition to managerial responsibilities, she was one of the first set of scribes to begin writing the text. She also created special treatments and worked on the carpet pages in *Gospels and Acts*.

"I loved the teamwork," she said.

Once the scribes had finished writing the text, she left the project and returned to the Southeast of England, where she again took up her freelance career.

As she reflected on her experience writing the Bible, she recalled, "I said to Donald once, 'This is just like writing the ten o'clock news. It's the same thing then as now.'"

Susie Leiper Scribe

SUSIE LEIPER was born in Glasgow. Her mother taught art and design and her father was a banker. At university in St. Andrews she read French language and literature. Later she received an MA from the Courtauld Institute of Art in London. Then she landed a job at British Museum Publications and for much of her career has been involved in publishing.

After that, things got really interesting. "My husband and I went to Hong Kong in 1980," she said. "I found a job with a monthly Oriental art magazine called *Orientations*. The new editor, Hin-cheung Lovell, wanted to make it more academic and less of a travel magazine."

She thrived in her new environment. "It was wonderful living in Hong Kong at the time. Everything was cheap; we were able to travel all over Asia."

In Hong Kong, she first began to study Western calligraphy with Derick Pao. "He had just that summer gone to the first international calligraphy conference in Minnesota and had studied with Donald Jackson. In his evening classes, I learned to use double pencils and studied the Foundational Hand."

Pao would later on arrange for Donald's traveling exhibition, Painting with Words, to come to Hong Kong.

Susie continued, "In 1986, we returned to Edinburgh. I was pregnant, so there was no time for calligraphy." The hiatus was short-lived. "In 1992, I took calligraphy evening courses at Edinburgh College of Art. My teachers were David Lang and Michael Ashley."

At the time, she was still working as a freelance editor for the British Museum. All of her projects were on Chinese themes. Then, in 1996, she was commissioned by National Museums of Scotland to write a book on the history of the Scotland-China trade. This made her realize that being the author of a book, rather than the editor, was much more creative. But it was with calligraphy that she felt she really wanted to be creative.

Susie Leiper, *What is an artist book?* Temporary wall painted during exhibition by The Artist Book Group. Visitors' definitions of the artist book were painted on the wall, then overpainted with the character 拆 chai (destroy). Patriothall Gallery, Edinburgh, 2012

Her calligraphy training began to deepen when she took a weekend course with Margaret Daubney at West Dean in Sussex. She subsequently applied to the Advanced Training Scheme of the Society of Scribes and Illuminators and was accepted. From then on, she began to take her calligraphy much more seriously.

She also explored other calligraphic traditions. She said, "In 2001, with the ATS done, our whole family went for six months to Hong Kong. I studied Chinese calligraphy and painting. I became a bit of a hermit, just writing, painting, making Chinese-style books." She paused and added, "I didn't think a Westerner could really become a Chinese calligrapher unless they completely immersed themselves in it." She knew the limits of her ability, and her high standards meant that she could study Chinese writing without the delusion that she would eventually attain full mastery.

Her involvement with The Saint John's Bible began with a phone call from Sally Mae Joseph. Sally Mae explained that Donald was looking to add a second group to the team of scribes who had begun writing out the Bible pages. Susie said, "She asked me to come and visit the Scriptorium. Sally Mae and I had always got on well—that's so important."

Susie explained, "I was one of twenty or so people who were invited. Many others had turned the invitation down. In my life, when there's a wee gap, something lands in it."

"I went for a day in Wales to look at the project," she went on. "Then I acquainted myself with the script over the summer."

In September, she went back for five weeks of training. She said, "We had one week in Wales; one week home; the third week in Wales; then back home for a week; and then a final week in Wales. It's the most difficult thing I've done in my life."

This training period was a time of testing. "It was almost like a competition," she said. "At the end of week five, it was like going to the schoolmaster's study. Donald called each of us in individually. He said, 'I think you will one day write some beautiful pages.' But he also said, 'You're not good enough yet,' and, 'I trust you.'"

The project was daunting. "It took quite a while to settle down into the script," she said. Angela Swan and I were the second team to join the scribes."

Of Donald, she said, "I'm terrified of him because I want to do my best. I still ask myself 'Would I show this to Donald Jackson?' If not, I know it's not good enough."

But the experience was nonetheless incredibly positive. "We had such fun at the scribes' meetings. It wasn't just work."

Now she works full time as a calligrapher and painter, exhibiting regularly, especially in Edinburgh.

Her work includes commissioned projects as well as her own, personal work. Her time working on the Bible has had a major effect on her own calligraphic practice. She said, "My work on the Bible has made my other work easier. Donald once said to me: 'After this, you'll have a newfound freedom.' It's true. I have more confidence."

She added, "It's made me believe in copying precisely [as a way of learning]. That's what Chinese calligraphers do."

Did the project have a spiritual component, I asked her. She responded, "I'm not a religious person, but in being totally focused, lost in the work, the writing can be meditation. Donald says this as well."

Suzanne Moore Illuminations

SUZANNE comes from a family of inventive engineers and architects. Two of her brothers and a nephew work at the Jet Propulsion Laboratory. "My dad had a heating business," she said, "and then he transitioned to be a steam fitter in institutional settings. He taught me how to do electrical rewiring when I was eight."

She recalls from her childhood, "There was always a pad of scratch paper in the kitchen. When we were explaining an idea or a project we were imagining, my dad would say: 'Here: Draw it.'"

Throughout school her aptitudes were high in math and science, but when she went to college, she majored in French with an art minor. She said, "I wonder what I would have done if I'd had a female model of a scientist."

But that was the path not taken. In college, she said, "I had an Estonian professor of art, Tiit Raid, who cultivated students. He said I should think about the BFA program. I said, 'I'm not an art major—I just don't see it.'"

But she followed his advice. "Without his enormous encouragement, I would never have done it," she said. "The BFA program was new, but because I hadn't majored in art, in two years I had to recoup four years of work. I then did a fifth-year certificate in art education.

"When I was doing the certificate program, I met Sister Alice Rita Keegan at St. Bede's, a Benedictine priory. She had done a thesis on Benedictine manuscripts, and she became my first teacher. She rarely picked up a pen for demonstration but described the lettering process as I wrote."

Suzanne began to attend meetings of the Colleagues of Calligraphy, the Minnesota calligraphy group. This exposed her to the wider world of calligraphy. "Thomas Ingmire was one of the first lecturers I saw. I had a two-week class with Ieuan Rees on Foundational Hand and drawn Romans. I had no idea what I was doing, but it was an eye-opener. I studied all the time. I was trying painted letters as well as pen calligraphy."

A manuscript book by Suzanne Moore. The text is from Lucretius' *De rerum natura*, "On the Nature of Things." The pages are layered monoprints on Rives BFK with acrylic, gouache, 23k gold and freehand gold tooling.

She attended the first international calligraphy conference. That is when she made the decision to move from Pigeon Falls, Wisconsin, to San Francisco to study with Thomas Ingmire.

She laughed and said, "I was so mousy and so in the shadows; so it was bold."

"I sold a quilt collection and cashed in my retirement from the university where I was working," she said. "I treated my time with Thomas as if it were an MFA program. That was in 1981. He let me join his two-year class midway through. He rented a space on Pier 49 in San Francisco. There were eight students in the class, and we met once a month. We were doing assignments that you could spend days or weeks completing. I worked full-time, practicing, reading, and exploring. Thomas was generous to trade extra one-on-one critiques for assistance in his studio.

"San Francisco was my Walden Pond," she said. "My life in Wisconsin had been very busy, with full-time work at the university and a stream of guests at our restored seventeen-room farmhouse."

Thomas suggested she take a bookbinding class, and their mutual friend, Stella Patri, proclaimed, "If you want the best, see Don Glaister." "That's when I met Don, a design bookbinder." Don would become her second husband, and they would embark on a creative life together.

The rich book arts community in the Pioneer Valley lured them to Massachusetts, where they lived for fifteen years. Suzanne's work as a manuscript book artist grew and flourished, with collaborations, individual projects, and teaching. A move to Tuscaloosa offered Don a professorship in the book arts MFA program at the University of Alabama.

In 2000, Suzanne took a job with American Greetings as art director of the lettering design group, where she worked for five years. It was the kind of compromise artists often make to earn a decent living. She said, "I'm really proud of a lot of my time at American Greetings." But she had her doubts. "This is a great salary. But I asked myself, 'Man, why can I *not* love this job?'"

Her role was to develop a creative team—the talented lettering artists—to add more illustration and new product development to their repertoire, while also producing hand lettering designs and calligraphic fonts. She had very little creative time of her own. "I approached the job more like a small agency, repping the twelve people in my group. I spent 80 percent of my time as an art director and about 20 percent managing my team." Finally, she had to ask herself: "Am I going to be a maker? Or a facilitator of other artists creating and making things?"

While she was experiencing these doubts, Donald Jackson called and invited her to work on The Saint John's Bible.

Suzanne asked Donald why he had chosen her. As she remembers, "He talked about my book *Tracing Magic Lines*, which was the third manuscript she had made in a series on the Cherokee syllabary. "He said he remembered the way it felt." That was twenty years before the invitation came to work on The Saint John's Bible, and during that time Suzanne had been working full-time making manuscript books and occasionally teaching.

As she discussed that book with him, he asked her, "Whatever possessed you to put scarlet next to pistachio? How many layouts did you do?"

And she said, "None. This is it."

Donald was taken aback. Suzanne explained her method: "I do a lot of preliminary work to find out how a technique is going to work, writing samples, layout, and painting. It's not cost effective to do multiple complete roughs of an entire book."

That method, of course, would not work for The Saint John's Bible, with its multiple layers of sketches and approvals. But Suzanne was eager to take the opportunity to work on the project.

Having worked as an art director herself, she appreciated Donald's role as the creative director. She said, "Donald has an eye for the whole, a *vision* for the Bible project. But he's also aware of what the CIT would approve. I was actually surprised by the breadth of what the CIT would accept."

She continued, "Donald is honest. I asked for that specifically. In collaborations, the more honest you can be, the better. I said to him, 'I want you to be honest all the time,' and he agreed."

She said, "Donald had the perfect approach as creative director. His vision and ideas are stunning, even at a distance. He pushes when he needs to, and he makes you move forward when it's time. Sometimes he suggests things, and other times he says, 'I'm confident you'll figure it out.'"

She was only able to visit the Scriptorium once, as she continued to be employed at American Greetings. All the work was done long-distance.

"I would get up really early," she said, "and talk to Donald before going to work at American Greetings." She added, "I wouldn't have been able to keep my job at American Greetings without the Bible. I had to drop all the concerns and distractions when I got into my studio to work on the Bible."

Donald could be demanding. She remembered, "When I worked on the *Choose Life* illumination, I sent it off to the UK. Donald called and said, 'This isn't making it.' It was very wimpy; my work did not fit into the context, impact, and scale of other works in the volume. He gave me three choices: stand by it, let him fix it, or take it back."

She made the decision to take it back and rework it. "I sanded it, gessoed it, then used rubber stamps of Futura type to render the text. You can see through to the earlier layer: the words 'blessings' and 'choose life' in thirty different languages is under and bordering the text."

As she worked on the Bible, she reflected on the difficulty of working at a distance. "What I tried to do was look at enough of the others' work so I could make links. I was concerned that the book—and my work—would be too disparate. I was concerned that the scale and the paint techniques were so different: How would it hold together as one work?" She added, "In the end, the rhythm of the lettering, and paired with the artists' varying approaches and interpretations, came together in the seven volumes in a musical way: harmonizing, complementing and sparking off of one another to create a unified and unexpected whole. A true collaboration."

Izzy Pludwinski Hebrew Scribe

IZZY PLUDWINSKI is a calligrapher who lives and works in Jerusalem. He first became involved with the Bible project when Donald was sourcing vellum and visited several parchmenters in Israel. Although Donald eventually settled on an English supplier of vellum, he continued to use Izzy as a resource. For the first volume, Izzy pointed Donald to samples of Hebrew that could be used for the relatively small number of Hebrew and Aramaic words and phrases in *Gospels and Acts*. Subsequently, Donald asked Izzy to come to Wales to add Hebrew running heads and book headings to the volumes of the Old Testament.

Raised in Brooklyn, Izzy studied at Bar Ilan University in Israel. "I began by studying chemistry and ended up by graduating in psychology."

After college, he went back to Brooklyn and was teaching chemistry. Restless in his twenties, he was struck by a line from a Billy Joel song that spoke to deeply to him: "When will you write your masterpiece?"

He said, "One day at *shul* I saw a poster with an enlarged letter *yud*, and it pointed to one tiny mark on the lower left of the letter. The message on the poster was that if a Torah scroll was written with just one *yud* lacking this tiny flick of the pen, then the entire Torah would be invalid."

He was fascinated with the intricacy and the inner meanings of the Hebrew letters, and wanted to learn to become a Hebrew scribe. "But I was a long-haired, jeans wearing guy," he said, "and I couldn't find anyone within the ultra-orthodox world that would be willing to teach me."

Eventually he found himself in a class at the Ninety-Second Street Y in Manhattan which gave him his first foundation in Hebrew calligraphy. "But we wrote with Osmiroid pens," he said, "whereas Torah letters can only be written beautifully with a quill. Besides, kosher ink does not flow well through a fountain pen."

Back in Jerusalem, he took private classes with a master Hebrew scribe. "After three months, I wrote

Izzy Pludwinski's accordion book *Man Must Renew Himself Constantly 2*.
The text is by Rebbe Nachman. The text was set on alternating panels in Izzy's Hebrew font Shir followed by a rendering in brush-made abstracted Hebrew. Depending on the angle at which the book is viewed, one can see only the abstract or the typographic text.

out the book of Esther." Esther is a good practice book for a beginning scribe, because the divine name never appears in the text, so the strict rules that guide the writing of that word do not apply.

He eventually was recognized as a sofer STaM, a scribe qualified to write the sacred texts of Judaism for ritual use. These include the Torah as well as *mezzuzot*, the small scrolls attached to the doors of observant Jewish homes, and *t'fillin*, the phylacteries wrapped around arm and forehead for Jewish times of prayer.

"Early on," he said, "I was interested in the mystical shapes of the Hebrew letters. Later I was exposed to a more universalistic reading of the Torah, and the idea of creativity being tied to the divine spark. At the same time, I was exposed to the wider world of calligraphy, which was full of creativity and expression."

After some time practicing his craft in Hebrew, he decided to explore roman-alphabet calligraphy. He enrolled at the Roehampton Institute, where he received a certificate in calligraphy and bookbinding.

Roehampton gave him a broader view of calligraphy. To this day, he works in both traditional styles and with more experimental, gestural forms. He has also explored typeface design and has printed limited edition books.

I asked him how he felt about the Bible project, and he said, frankly, "It was a job—a high prestige job, but still a job." He quickly added, "The great thing was being with Donald and the other calligraphers."

When he was asked to formally join the project as a scribe, he had to consider it carefully. He said, "My first question was a religious question. It's not simple thing for a nice Jewish boy to write a Christian Bible."

He consulted a rabbi and asked, "Should I be beautifying something whose beliefs don't jibe with my beliefs?"

After explaining to the rabbi that he was only working on the Jewish testament, the rabbi gave him encouragement: "The rabbi said, 'You should do this and make it as beautiful as possible.'"

Izzy also said, "For me, the importance of the Hebrew writing is it points to the fact that this is a translation. If you want to come as close to the original as possible, then you have to look at the Hebrew text."

Once his qualms were eased, he joined the project with enthusiasm. He said, "You don't want schlumpy Hebrew there."

"I sent many samples to Donald," he said. "It was amazing how much freedom Donald gave me. He involved me in the decision-making process and took my opinions to heart."

Izzy chose a Sephardi script. "Ashkenazi," he said, "seemed too stylized. The form and weight of the English text made me choose Sephardi."

He took some risks. He said, "I chose a script I wasn't comfortable writing small." This would make the project quite challenging. "I had some rough days."

He also struggled with the fact that his writing was not in continuous lines of text, as he was simply adding headings. "There's absolutely no rhythm when you're writing one word at a time." Still, he persevered, and his writing can be seen in all the books of the Bible that have come down to us from the Hebrew.

He was impressed with Donald's approach to problem solving. "He has an ability to cut through to the essence of things," Izzy said. "He's interested in the thing itself. He rethought every problem from scratch: what's the right thing to do?"

Brian Simpson

BRIAN SIMPSON was born and bred in Leicester and has lived there his whole life. Leicester was a major printing center, and his working career centered on the printing trade.

"I was apprenticed to a graphic commercial artist," he said. "In the 1950s, before Letraset had come on the market, there was lots of hand lettering. I produced drawn lettering for reproduction."

During his National Service in the Royal Ordinance Corps in Aldershot near London he took evening classes in calligraphy at the Central School two days a week.

Painted lettering by Brian Simpson.

He said, "I was a typographer for many years. At the end of my career, the last four or five years or so, the computer came in. For most of my working life, artwork was all hand drawn. Now you push a button. I miss that hands-on quality."

He worked for a large printing company for fifteen years. "My layouts tended to be neat and tidy," said, "rather than free and adventurous."

While working in printing, calligraphy assignments cropped up regularly. Donald, who knew him, occasionally sent him overflow projects.

Brian said, "When The Saint John's Bible came up, I'd been retired for about a year or so, and then a call came from Donald. These things are meant to be."

Brian reflected on his work on the Bible. "We were part of a team, under Donald Jackson, under his direction. We had to match what he was giving us to do. The members of the team were so different, and comparing work when we met together at the Scriptorium was very important."

He said the consistency of the work was invaluable: "This was five years of solid writing." That steady pace made for much greater consistency.

"It was harder than I thought it would be," he said. "Even Donald thought a week of practice would do when he first trained us." But the script was not so easy. "The Bible script looks like an upright italic, but it's not."

Handling the inevitable scribal errors was a challenge. "Sometimes we would miss a whole line out. Two or three times at the beginning we'd erase and rewrite the whole column. I came close to putting a hole in the page when scraping my writing off. We had to confess all when we got to the Scriptorium!"

"I hadn't used quills so much," Brain said. "I remember spending three weeks struggling to master the tool. It wasn't square cut, the quill; it was cut at a very subtle angle. If you didn't get the angle right, it was very hard to replicate the script."

When he was writing the Psalms, he enjoyed the freedom of working with a ragged right margin. By contrast, "The main Bible script is justified, which made for less-free writing. You were always watching to make sure the line would not run long or short."

Brian also wrote all the chapter numbers and the small crosses in the margin indicating texts related to the Rule of Saint Benedict. He said, "It's not so comfortable to do the chapter numbers, but you get into the swing of it. They're full of subtleties. I did sheets and sheets of numbers. The 8 is the one we all hated."

These chapter numbers also changed from volume to volume. "In the *Psalms*, the chapter numbers were in color. In *Prophets*, they were made with shell gold on a square of color. The gold went down easier on reds, purples, and browns. With some of the blues, it brought the blue up, so these had to be retouched."

Working mostly at home, he would have to collect his finished pages for the regular scribal meetings at the Scriptorium. "Rolling your work when done was always a bit intimidating," he said. "To carry the sheets back and forth the vellum was put on a roller, covered in bubble wrap and paper."

He thinks of his time on the project with real fondness. "Finishing it was quite a wrench," he said. "I miss the others. We formed a close-knit team. It's a shame it had to end."

He remembered the excitement "the first time we put pages together and it looked like a book." And he appreciated working with Donald. He said in closing, "Donald has an ability to draw out more than you thought you had in you."

Angela Swan Scribe

ANGELA SWAN was born in London. When she was nine, her family moved back to her father's hometown, Cheltenham in Gloucestershire. She stayed there until 1985, when she returned to London to study at the Roehampton Institute.

I asked her how she came to calligraphy.

"I started by taking an informal calligraphy class. My teacher, a silversmith by trade, was, I think, self-taught in calligraphy. He was so inspiring and enthusiastic. He had a fine strong italic hand."

A friend later introduced her to Alex O'Sullivan, a professional calligrapher in Cheltenham. "He gave me such a lot of his time," she said. "He was so kind, generous and encouraging."

O'Sullivan had been a student of Dorothy Mahoney, who had been a student of Edward Johnston, and so he was connected to the professional world of English calligraphy. "He encouraged me to get a portfolio together and apply to [the full-time calligraphy course at] Roehampton. He really pushed me."

She took her portfolio up to London and had an interview with Ann Camp, who ran the calligraphy program at Roehampton. "It was exciting and a bit scary to have an interview with Ann Camp. I was thrilled when she said yes and offered me a place in the course."

When she was at her interview, she first encountered Sue Hufton, who was a student at Roehampton at the time. I remarked to her how interesting it is that so many of us have connections that stretch back that far.

She laughed and replied, "Given the number of people on the planet, calligraphers are a small bunch! We're a tight family."

A family tree by Angela Swan.

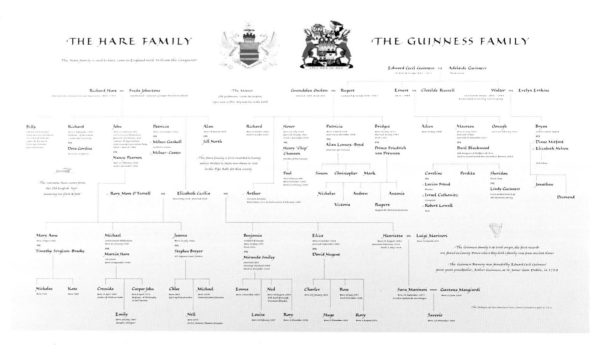

She said, "The tutors at Roehampton—Ann [Camp], Gaynor [Goffe], and Tom [Perkins]—gave us so much." In her first year, she also took the bookbinding component of the course with Jen Lindsay. "Bookbinding helped me really look at the detail," she said. "Things had to be perfect to the millimeter."

After three years at Roehampton, she earned an advanced diploma in calligraphy. As her time on the course was winding up, she landed an extraordinary opportunity. Gaynor Goffe facilitated her move to Wales to become Donald Jackson's assistant.

Gaynor had worked under Donald some years before. Now Donald was looking for a new assistant.

Angela said, "Donald asked Gaynor if anyone was leaving Roehampton, and she put me forward as a candidate."

Angela worked for Donald for three years, from 1988 until 1991. At the time, Donald had a thriving business, the Calligraphy Centre. She said, "It was very commercial in those days. We were doing a lot of certificates for big clients. There was also a lot of work for reproduction. I also had the opportunity to work on more creative projects and even some of the Peerage Patents for the Crown Office."

She said, "It was a steep learning curve. When I first went there, I was the only assistant."

At the same time, Donald's exhibition, Painting with Words, was traveling around the world. Angela said, "He would disappear for weeks at a time and I was left manning the studio. I was trying figure out how to run his workshop. It was a baptism by fire!"

In the process, Angela learned a lot about the business side of running a calligraphy studio. She said, "At college we could take a long time on a single project. Working for Donald in his studio was quite different: you had to get it done and get it out the door. It was much more in the real world."

After she left Donald's studio, she stayed in Wales and set up her own independent practice. Being nearby—she lives only about ten miles from the Hendre—she stayed in contact with Donald and his wife Mabel. She lives in a small cottage in the countryside outside Abergavenny, with a free-standing studio that looks west toward the Black Mountains. The studio is built on the site of a garage that had fallen into disrepair. Donald encouraged her to build a new studio on the site. "It's a wonderful part of the world," she said. "I watch the sun go down over the mountains. I wouldn't be living here if I hadn't been part of Donald's studio."

When the Bible project got under way, she thought to herself, "Oh, it would be lovely to be part of that." She added, "I think it was Mabel who first said to me that Donald was going to need more scribes."

Angela was invited to join the second group of scribes who were trying out for the project. She said, "Of course, I was friends with Sally Mae from Roehampton. After Donald asked me to join the second group, Sally brought me some samples of the Bible script and some quills."

She was able to examine the script and practice a bit before going down to the Scriptorium. The training session was "exciting and daunting. It was like having your senses, your mind, and your eye-hand coordination stretched in ways you didn't think they could be stretched." She added, "They were very, very full-on days. I felt very lucky to be part of that."

She said, "We didn't really know how many people were going to be invited to join the project. Every time I looked around me I thought, 'I don't know if it's going to be me.'" But she succeeded. At the end of this second training session, she and Susie Leiper were invited to join the team of scribes.

She said the Bible Script was very tricky: "It's hard to pin it down, it's such a complex script."

She also found working with quills a deep challenge. "How it feels is really down to the quill," she said. "A quill might be working one evening, and the next morning the writing might come out a different weight, because the quill had dried out."

Some days could be frustrating. "I remember days when I hardly got any lines written at all because I was up and down from my table cutting and recutting the quill." On other days, everything ran smoothly. "I had some very good quills," she said. "One quill lasted for twenty-four pages. Of course, I had to recut it, but that quill worked really well for me. It sat in my hand well, held its edge and didn't go soggy. The quills varied so much."

She also found the vellum surface quite variable. She said, "I liked writing on the hair side best. When the quill was working well on hair side of the vellum, it felt like the quill and vellum were natural partners."

Of working with Donald, she said, "He is such an inspiring figure. I think there are many talented and skillful calligraphers and artists, but he's got that charisma as well. I don't think anyone else could have pulled all the artists and scribes together."

She commented, "Sometimes when we're sitting around or working Donald will start to talk, and you don't know where he's going. The depth and breadth of his thought process is amazing. I find him such a fascinating person. I'm immensely fond of him—that genius, energy, and creativity. Plus the impish sense of humour, of course!"

There were times when she was working on the project that she would have moments of self-doubt. When that happened, she said, "Donald was always wonderful. He would say to me, 'I've invited you to be here, so that means you are good enough.' He is very kind."

She said that working on the project had given her more self-confidence. "It's encouraged me to take on more ambitious work," she remarked. "I've accepted complex commissions like family trees that I wouldn't have taken on if I hadn't done the Bible."

Chris Tomlin Natural History Illustrations

LIKE Aidan Hart, Chris Tomlin came to the project from outside of the calligraphy community. He said, "It was Olivia [Donald's assistant] who found me. She got in contact with the Illustration Department's secretary at the Royal College of Art, and she gave her a brief outline of what the project was. I was studying for a master's degree natural history illustration at the college."

Several students were invited to send samples of their work to the Scriptorium for the illustrations of plants, animals, and insects that Donald envisioned in the margins of the manuscript.

Chris said, "There were about five or six of us who sent in work. I could see that my style of illustration was more what Donald was looking for. The others were more interested in large creatures—elephants and tigers—whereas I have always had a particular interest in the creatures that most people won't notice. I've always been interested in lots of detail, small subjects like plants and insects, the more realistic the better."

He continued, "I did a sample for Donald, two actually, and he paid for them. I got a letter inviting me to [the Scriptorium in] Monmouth. I still didn't know if it was a go. Donald is big on that—getting to meet. Will it be a good fit?"

Donald told Chris what the project was about. "It was my first job leaving the college, and I thought, 'Wow, if it starts like this . . .' Donald said the manuscript would last perhaps a thousand years. I was sold on it instantly."

Some aspects of the project were new to Chris. "I'd heard of vellum," he said, "but that was about it. I always worked on more traditional surfaces such as stretched paper or board. Donald gave lots of advice on how to work on it." He learned about the effects of temperature and humidity on material.

"I actually found it was better than working on paper; if you want to remove something, you just scratch it off."

The transition to the new support was not difficult. He said, "In a way I didn't have to adjust my practice that much. The fine little hairs on the surface of the vellum sometimes impede the brush and paint flow."

In his work, much of which is intended for reproduction, he is accustomed to many media—oil, gouache, watercolor, acrylic. He said, "It's much better to use all these mediums rather than just specialize in one."

For the Bible, he started off using acrylic. "The blue dragonfly was done in acrylic," he said. "The swallowtail butterflies were acrylic as were the monarch butterflies on milkweed. I checked with Donald that acrylic was okay, and he said yes."

Chris Tomlin's mixed media illustration of a great white shark *(Carcharodon carcharias)* hunting a brown fur seal *(Arctocephalus pusillus)*.

In the Bible, he also worked in gouache and watercolor. Each medium has its own particular qualities. He said, "Acrylic, gouache, and watercolor can be used very thinly; like this they can all look very similar, but when used thickly, unlike the other two, acrylic forms a solid, shiny surface and can be much harder to remove if a mistake is made, so I had to be very careful when using it. I decided quite early on in the project that watercolor and gouache were the preferred media as their textures were more complimentary to the vellum."

In addition to the marginal illustrations, Chris collaborated with Donald on several of the interpretive illuminations.

He said, "Donald would give me the concept and let me think about it. He might show me a full-color rough draft. For instance, he would paint a snake in on the rough and then say, 'Could you paint this in detail?' Then I would often come down to the Scriptorium and work for four or five days at a time."

Donald and Chris would work in turns. Chris said, "He had already worked on his section of the painting, leaving my sections blank; I would then add my part."

I asked Chris what he used for reference material. He responded, "For this type of work, you really are only as good as your reference. You want people to actually think it is an insect sitting on the page. I like to work directly from an actual specimen whenever possible."

For exotic animals, such as snakes and macaws, Chis would work from photographic references. He also went to Saint John's to study the local flora and fauna.

He said, "You get a real feeling of wilderness in North America, in Minnesota. I like the fact that you feel like you could wander off. You really can get away from people." He added, laughing, "You also get bigger animals like bear and moose."

Chris and Donald formed a good friendship. "I really liked Donald's company," he said. "I looked forward to going to the Scriptorium to see him as much as doing the artwork. He taught me a lot of things as well. His artwork and style were very different to mine."

He commented, "Donald's attention to detail in the roughs was a lot stricter than mine at the outset. He would keep trying different placements of one illustration and keep moving things around." He laughed and said, "It was amazing how much Donald would tinker with the rough!"

Chris said, "Donald actually says I taught him things as well. I think the mark of a good artist is someone who is open to change, constantly looking at what they're doing. If you're an artist of any merit, you should always strive to learn more and improve."

"I treated Donald as a mentor," Chris said. "We talked a lot about artwork in the studio, but actually we talked about anything and everything. He was great fun to talk to in general. It wasn't unusual for us to chat when we were both working. I remember fondly that there would often be a really long pause—minutes sometimes—before Donald would reply to something I had said, as he was concentrating so hard!

"I was really sad when it finished," he said, in closing, "because it spanned such a long part of my life—over ten years. At the final party for the creative team, it felt like it was the end. But it's not really; the artwork is eternal."

Diane von Arx

DIANE VON ARX has the bright, direct demeanor of native Midwesterner. She told me, "I was the second oldest of nine. I grew up on a struggling small dairy farm with twenty-five head of cows."

She said, "Much of my artistic talent comes from my mom. She did a lot of designing, cutting, and painting of wooden miniatures, creating little collections."

Early on, she showed an interest in lettering. "I also had a Speedball Textbook in high school. I used to make what I called 'ribbon names' for friends in school. I was drawing thick/thin letters rather than using a chisel edge tool, and I wasn't familiar with the word *calligraphy*."

A school counselor told her about an art school in LaCrosse, Wisconsin, the local big city. She recalled, "Later on I found out my aunt had said to my mother, 'Why are you letting her go to art school? You can't make a living at that!' It was a gift that my mother never shared that with me at the time.

"Bill Jefferson ran the school, the Jefferson School of Commercial Art. It was an accredited school that offered a two-year degree."

Jefferson was a working illustrator. Diane said, "He had the Northwest Airlines account. He would make full-color illustrations of the interiors of planes. He also knew about advertising and marketing."

His teaching style was strict. She remembered, "He'd say 'Get some glasses—you're not looking at what's there.' I felt he expected great things of me. He said I should go to Chicago or Boston. 'Don't settle!' he would say."

These lessons have stayed with her. "I won't let [my own] students just get by. The best gift anyone can give you is to have high expectations. Donald Jackson is like that."

She took herself to Minneapolis and showed her portfolio. "I found a job and worked for eight and a half years at Harry Hauck & Associates, a package design studio. Harry too set high standards and instilled a strong work ethic."

She said, "We did a lot of work for General Mills. My boss was a graduate of the Minneapolis School of Fine Arts (Now MCAD). He paid half the fees if we wanted to study in the evenings."

Diane von Arx: i carry your heart by e. e. cummings. From the collection of Casey and the late Carol Marrin, commissioned by Casey for his wife Carol. The piece is on stretched calfskin vellum with stamps, gold leaf, gouache, and stick ink.

During her time at the studio, she did lettering for the first Count Chocula, Frankenberry, and Boo Berry cereal packages.

As a founding member of the Colleagues of Calligraphy, she was exposed to the calligraphic tradition. She recalled, "I met Donald Jackson in 1977 when he was teaching a workshop. Jo White invited him to Minnesota. When Donald was teaching we hung on his every word. I had no clue there was so much to calligraphy. We were lucky; we had a lot of big guns coming through early in our calligraphic training."

In 1977 she quit the studio and began freelancing so she could take workshops during the day. Her old boss gave her lettering work, and she was also teaching four days a week.

She said, "I could never have survived on just calligraphy in those days. It was supplemented with a lot of graphic design, expressive lettering, and corporate identity work. Now there is more calligraphy than there was back then."

She has continued to work as a professional calligrapher ever since. She does a wide range of work. "I do all of it," she said, "certificates, addressing envelopes, headings, custom wedding invitations. I like doing corporate documents, such as board retirements for clients such as General Mills. I also do graphics that are painted on walls." Some of these mural projects are made using custom vinyl lettering.

She first became involved in the Bible project in 2004. She said, "At the end of 2004 Donald asked me to do titling for the Illuminating the Word exhibition at the Minneapolis Institute of Arts. He didn't have time to do it. He asked through Carol Marrin, then the director of The Saint John's Bible project."

After that, she was asked to contribute special treatments to the *Wisdom* volume of the Bible. She said, "I didn't get to wade in. I had to jump in." She worked directly with Donald. As she explained, "The CIT did not need to approve the special treatments."

She began by going to the Scriptorium one June, where she did layouts under Donald's supervision. She said, "In July, they sent my layouts back with notes. I asked Donald about the deadline. 'We have time,' he said. I'm a graphic designer. I want to hear, 'Tuesday at five.'"

Like many of the others, she had to learn how best to work with Donald. She said, "I work fast. I would get sketches done, photograph or scan them, and e-mail them to Donald. Then we would have a phone conversation of about an hour or so, and he'd send the sketches back with comments."

She began to feel frustrated. She thought to herself, "He's micromanaging my serifs." But then, around Thanksgiving, she and Donald spoke on the phone. "He said to me, 'I'm willing to help you as long as you need input.' And I thought, 'Oh my God, he isn't going to tell me when I'm ready to work on the vellum, *I* have to decide."

The next challenge was to transfer the rough draft to the finished vellum page.

"And then the horror set in because I had to put it on vellum," she said. "I had a great deal of retouching experience from my days in packaging. I would have to fix a Cheerios package to take out a deal flag on the front of the box. It had to be good enough to photograph. I know I can fix things, so I was confident."

On the other hand, when working on the vellum, she was adding her special treatments to pages the scribes had already written on. "That was frightening," she said. "I didn't want to deface others' work. I have tremendous respect for the scribes. There's no messing around for them."

Reflecting on her time working on the project, she said, "I'm pleased with what I did in the Bible. It represents the quality of my work: a farm girl made it to the city."

to them & said, "Take heart, it is I; (
Peter answered him, "Lord, if it is
me to come to you on the water."29
So Peter got out of the boat, starter
water, & came toward Jesus.30 But
the strong wind, he became frighte
ning to sink, he cried out, "Lord, so
immediately reached out his hand
saying to him, "You of little faith, wh
32 When they got into the boat, t
33 And those in the boat worship
"Truly you are the Son of God."
crossed over, they came to land
35 After the people of that place re

D SAW THA
THERE W
WAS MORI
Y. AND
ITERS BRIN
ING CRE

GOOD
AT THE
HAND
OF GOD,

friendship aright, for as they
are, so are their neighbors also.

My child, from your youth
choose discipline, and when
you have gray hair you will
still find wisdom.
Come to her like one who plows
and sows, and wait for her good
harvest. For when you cultivate
her you will toil but little, and
soon you will eat of her produce.
She seems very harsh to the
undisciplined; fools cannot
remain with her. She will be
like a heavy stone to test them.

The many different kinds of writing in The Saint John's Bible fulfill different functions. Some are practical scripts used to write large portions of text. Others are more playful and decorative.

CHAPTER 17

THE SCRIPTS OF
THE SAINT JOHN'S BIBLE

T HE SAINT JOHN'S BIBLE is at its heart a calligraphers' project. In public exhibitions, however, the illuminations, which are so bold and colorful, so varied, and so open to different interpretations, often take center stage. The writing, by contrast, continues page by page, unobtrusive and consistent, seemingly playing a supporting role.

One reason that the lettering receives less attention than the illuminations is that its ethos is different. Rather than calling attention to itself, it is a servant, in that classic sense in which calligraphers often invoke about themselves as "servants of the text." And the audience for the calligraphy is narrower than the audience for the illustrations. It takes a well-trained eye to appreciate the skill and craft that make the writing work.

This chapter looks at the scripts of The Saint John's Bible from a calligrapher's perspective. This suggests the question, of course, as to what scripts make up the repertoire of the Bible, because there are so many different scripts used in the project.

If you look through the pages of The Saint John's Bible, you will find an almost endless variety of letterforms, made with different techniques and using different styles. I think these break down into two broad categories.

One category can be referred to as the "expressive scripts." The special treatments fall into this category, as do letterforms integrated into the interpretive illuminations. Here, the scribes and artists have wide latitude to select and customize their letterforms to suit a specific context. There is no need or desire to make them consistent from one application to the next. Take, for instance the typographic forms used by Thomas Ingmire in his *Ten Commandments* illumination. These were produced with a mechanical stencil technique, and they were chosen to suit the needs of that particular illumination. Another example is the pointed italic used by Sally Mae Joseph for the special treatment of the *Magnificat* text in Luke. Written in gesso and gilded, these letterforms create a composition that celebrates the text and makes it stand out from the surrounding columns of writing.

The other category is what I call the "craft scripts." These are the scripts used for writing the main texts of the Bible. They have set forms that are used consistently through the Bible. They are workhorse scripts, but what fine horses they are! These are the main focus of this chapter.

Some scripts are used for continuous passages of text. The most important of the craft scripts is the one used to write prose passages in the text. Referred to by Donald and his scribes as the Bible Script, it is the dominant style used in the Bible. The Poetry Script, slightly smaller and more delicate than the Bible Script, is used, as the name suggests, to write passages of poetry. In the *Psalms* volume, a variety of Italics is used for the main text. In addition to these scripts, there are the massed capitals, which are used at the beginning and end of some books. These are slightly less regular, more playful, and exist in several variant forms. They are referred to as Incipit Scripts.

Other scripts are used for headings and to divide the texts according to the hierarchy Donald has established. These include the Titling Script used for the names of each book. Built-up Versals are used as drop caps to mark major divisions of the text. Although the basic technique used to write them is consistent from volume to volume, they vary strikingly in form.

The final craft script I will consider is what I refer to as the "Pull-Quote" Script, which is used for marginal texts and as an accompaniment to illuminations.

Donald described the two types of scripts thusly: "The craft scripts are like threads in a weaving of a cloth. The expressive scripts are more like applique. They function as highlights."

The popular misconception of calligraphic "style"

BEFORE EMBARKING on an analysis of the various craft scripts, it's important, I think, to be clear about the nature of the writing in The Saint John's Bible. As I described in chapter 4 of part 1, this set of manuscript volumes is the product of a team of very expert scribes, well versed in the practice of calligraphy. Each of the scribes has moved beyond the simple categories that guide novice and intermediate calligraphers as they learn their craft. Donald's team was composed of scribes who had internalized the basics of letterform and were ready to push the boundaries.

What do I mean by this? Simply stated, many beginning calligraphers have a very literal view that there are fixed rules that guide the writing of individual scripts. As they seek to master the various historical and contemporary scripts, students make hard distinctions between one script and another. This is only natural—learning to distinguish between a Gothic and a Carolingian script, for example, does entail simplifying and codifying the basic construction of each script. Students will parrot simple guidelines and interpret them as hard-and-fast distinctions. They will say things like, "Italic is written using a 45-degree pen angle," assuming that this is an eternally valid description of the Italic Hand. It is not. (And, it should be said, students will repeat this common directive even when looking at a sample that is patently written using a different pen angle.)

Students who are trying to achieve consistency in their letter formation and to develop even rhythm and spacing need these simple ways of examining their writing. But more advanced calligraphers know that these formulas are just a starting point, and once the basic principles of a script are understood, one can begin to push the parameters. Really expert writing is free and full of subtle deviations from the norm.

Looking at the scripts of The Saint John's Bible is also a lot like looking at a medieval manuscript. Written by multiple hands over a period of many years, the writing in The Saint John's Bible has an amazing consistency. The color and texture of the written lines remains fairly constant from Genesis to Revelation. But if you really look closely, if you examine an individual page in detail, you will immediately see that, while the gestalt of the script remains consistent, it is full of variations.

Medieval manuscripts were the same. Produced in workshop conditions by trained scribes, they are also full of inconsistencies. In fact, art historians will look closely at the scripts of large medieval manuscripts and discern the writing of different scribes, identifying small tics and personal habits that distinguish one scribe from the next. When modern scribes study medieval writing, they make selections from what they see and try to achieve some of the qualities of the original.

So when we speak of studying the scripts in The Saint John's Bible, we are not talking about mastering a set of perfectly defined ideal scripts. No—we are looking at samples of the writing and trying to understand how we can produce something like them. I mentioned in chapter 4 that Donald never provided the scribes with an exemplar to copy; there is no perfect prototype.

Trying to learn the scripts of The Saint John's Bible is like learning to dance by watching Barishnakov. There is much to appreciate, much to glean, from looking. But if one is to dance at that level, one must make one's own dance, drawing on what one has learned.

Willful obscurantism?

AS I WRITE this, I find I am falling into the same habits of speech the scribes used, as if the Bible scripts were simply impossible to describe. I quoted Sally Mae Joseph in chapter 4 as saying, "No pen angle, no *x*-height, no exemplars. At the end of the day I had to throw that all out the window."

Some readers may be chafing at all of my caveats. At the end of the day, it is possible to say quite a few things about the Bible scripts, but it's important to see these as observations rather than as fixed rules.

One final observation: By refusing to give the scribes an exemplar, by refusing to overly define the scripts, Donald was pushing them to move beyond the basic mechanics of the writing. A conductor does the same thing with an orchestra. He taps the music stand with his baton; the orchestra stops, and he says, "Now . . . galloping," or "push through to the end of the phrase." The conductor does not want to focus on mechanics; he wants to engage his musicians at the level of feeling. Donald's scribes were all fully fledged professionals; they knew instinctively about pen angle and slope and weight. Donald's intent was to make them trust their instincts and think of the deeper structure that makes writing sing.

When the scribes would meet together at the Scriptorium and present their finished pages, Donald would go over each scribe's pages and go through the whole alphabet, looking at their *a*'s, *b*'s, *c*'s, and so on through the whole alphabet. He would discuss which letters weren't working. He commented, "The common denominator was: If you're not enjoying it, you're not going to get it right."

Scale and materials

IN STUDYING the scripts, it is important to bear in mind certain qualities of the original. The main text script, usually referred to simply as Bible Script, was written with a quill on vellum at an extremely small size. Writing the script larger, or with metal pen on paper, will alter the quality of the writing. While it is possible to write a similar script in this way, many small details of the letters' construction will be hard—or impossible—to achieve.

Suzie Leiper made this sample of writing for a classroom demonstration. Because it was made in a larger size than the actual Bible Script, and because a different pen was used, it should not be considered an exemplar. It does, however, give a good sense of the basic features of the Bible Script.

The quill is a uniquely supple and responsive tool. Ink flow can be quite generous, allowing the writer to turn the tool on its corner without interrupting the stream of ink. The quill is also very responsive to pressure; pushing very slightly will subtly widen the stroke. The writer can also change his or her angle of attack, using just part of the tip to make marks on the page. A quill also tends to have a slight curvature, which can create a gently scooped shape at the end of thick strokes. Metal nibs, by contrast, tend to be more rigid and mechanical; the nib is more likely to give a writer a mark of fixed width, and it is harder to turn the pen on its corner and keep the ink flowing.

Changes in scale can also affect the look of the letters. There is a balance of thick and thin strokes in the Bible Script that have a certain proportion; if these letters are written at a larger size, the balance on thick strokes to the thin strokes at the ends of the letters may well be thrown off.

It is crucial to be sensitive to these issues of scale and materials when trying to write the scripts of the Bible. The further one deviates from the original, the more likely the writing will take on a character different from the sample.

Bible script

SEVERAL OF the scribes have tried teaching the Bible Script in workshops. Sue Hufton and Suzie Leiper shared with me some of their thoughts about the experience.

Sue Hufton

MY TEACHING of an SJB workshop may follow this rough outline:

First I show people the pages of script and talk about how it was developed and our experience of working on it as a team guided by Donald. Then by looking at the pages and copies of the pages I show people how it changed as time went on.

We look at how the quill has influenced the script, and I give each person a quill to use to write the script. I think it is quite difficult to get a close resemblance with a metal nib; the character of the script changes a lot when written with a metal nib.

We talk about the key points to consider when designing a script, relating that to the SJB script and what we had to continually watch and work at as we wrote—how the internal and external spaces balance, how the strokes and shapes relate.

What they realise pretty early on is that it is a difficult script to learn and write successfully. It is not easy to copy. Then they realise that there is more to it than meets the eye, as they begin analysing the script and learn to see how the forms relate.

I don't find it an easy script to unpack and have only really taken the route of encouraging people to copy it and help them individually. Exactly how we learn it, I guess!

Susie Leiper

A DIFFICULT one this! I have taught one or two huge one-day workshops, and two weekends and given a "demonstration" in Hong Kong. Each of these experiences confirmed for me exactly why it took us scribes SO long to master the script—and even then have our off days.

The attachments are written with a 3.5 Zig felt pen, as I found that was a visible way to try and explain the letterforms and gave students something to look at.

But I took pains to insist that it wasn't an exemplar, that any attempt to write the SJB script was an organic process, really just a practice of writing, and that we all wrote somewhat differently. I did not teach with quills.

I would then stress three keys:

1 Horizontal emphasis across, to create linearity
2 Strong upright verticals
3 Knitting the script: i.e., touching letterforms, keeping top line level, very little word space.

Looking at a sample of the writing from *Gospels and Acts,* we can examine some of the features of the script. I have chosen to work from one fine example of the script rather than making broad generalizations. Still less do I want to create an exemplar with all the letters of the alphabet carefully selected and presented; to do so would fly directly in the face of Donald's stated intention not to define the script in that way. Instead, we can observe and glean as much as we can while recognizing that the script is the product of a living workshop practice. All the remarks below are based on a careful examination of this one sample of the writing.

I will also use the technical terminology of calligraphy here without lengthy explanation. This is an advanced script, not intended for beginners, so a basic familiarity with the terminology of calligraphy is assumed in the observations that follow.

The dominant pen angle in our sample is about 25 degrees. As we will see, the angle is not rigid, and there are various places where the pen is manipulated. The x-height—the height of the small letters such as *a, o,* or *m*—is a little under three nib widths. The ascenders, such as *l* or *h,* are double the x-height, while the descenders are somewhat longer.

Looking at individual letters, we can begin to see some characteristics of the construction of the script. First, consider the arches in letters such as *n* or *h.* Each of these letters begins with an upright straight stroke; the second stroke begins with an arched stroke, which then turns to become a straight downstroke. The shape of this arch is distinctive. Looking at the underside of the stroke: we see a symmetrical, shallow arc. Looking at the top, however, we see the top shape is slightly weighted to the right side. The *h, n,* and *m,* then, create a series of gently undulating curves running along the tops of the small letters, along the x-height.

Several other letters also have parts that draw the eye along the top of the small letters. The top stroke of the *c,* for instance, is a very flat, horizontal stroke. The crossbars of *t* and *f* are long and frequently tie to letters that follow. The small horizontal stroke at the top of the *g* is made right up at the x-height line.

The small curved entrance strokes on the left sides of *n, m,* and *r* also draw the eye along the top of the small letters. At the bottom, the left-hand straight strokes have no serifs; the weight is along the top.

The tail of the small *r* makes an interesting contrast to the arches of the *n* and *m.* It could have been made as a small segment of the same kind of arch; instead, it arcs in the opposite direction, creating a distinctive pointed top. This allows the *r* to be tied to following letters without losing its distinct shape as a separate letter.

Letters that have bowls—*a, b, d, p,* and *q*—reveal a distinctive quality of the Bible Script. In many calligraphic hands, such as a classic Italic, a *p* and *d* can be turned upside down to reveal that they have essentially the same shape of bowl. In this script, however, the shapes of the bowls are quite different. The *b* and *p,* which branch from the first vertical stroke, take their cue from the *n* and *m:* they have shallow arched tops, which are quite round. By contrast, the *a, d,* and *q* all have asymmetrical bowls. They seem to partake more of the Italic than of the Roman. The arch at the bottom of the *u* has a similarly cursive form. The *u* in Bible Script is definitely not an inverted *n.*

This is one of the key qualities of the Bible Script. The top half of the small letters has a stately, rounded rhythm, with gently curved arches and many horizontal elements. The bottom half of the same letters, by contrast, has a more dynamic, cursive rhythm.

One way to see the difference in these two rhythmic patterns is to take a sheet of paper and place it over a line of the writing. Place it horizontally along the middle of the small letters, hiding the bottom of the line of writing. You will see clearly the rhythm of the top. Now do the reverse: cover the top of the line. The feeling is radically different. Along the bottom, many of the vertical strokes curve markedly as they reach the baseline, and the pen twists upward in anticipation of the next letter. The undulating, asymmetrical curvature of the bowls further underscores the cursive quality of the bottom of the line. The lack of serifs on many downstrokes creates a more open quality along the baseline.

Looking closely at the writing, you can sense the feel of the pen in the writer's hand; very deliberate marks at the top speed up at the bottom, and many letters end in a flick upward of the pen once it reaches the baseline. These tiny, fine flicks are particularly pronounced at the ends of words, and they are often quite free at the end of lines, where they enliven the negative space of the margins.

The shape of the vertical downstrokes varies widely, depending both on the individual letter and on the context of the letter in a word. The first downstroke on the *n* and *h* both end sharply with no added serif. The first two strokes of the *m* do the same. The final strokes of these letters end differently, with a small curve and a springing thin stroke. The *i* is often made with a very straight stroke that terminates

The detailed description of the Bible Script in this chapter was based on a careful examination of this passage of writing from Matthew 14. The writing is by Brian Simpson.

at the bottom with a small curved exit stroke; sometimes, when the context suggests it, the whole *i* takes on a curved shape, echoing the rounder form of the *t*. The final vertical downstroke of *a* and *d* curve distinctly to the right before they hit the baseline; this opens up the tiny triangle of white that separates the bowl from the straight stroke at the baseline.

Some letters have very distinctive, even unusual, shapes. The *p*, for instance, begins with a clear serif at the top of its first, vertical stroke. This stroke goes above the x-height. At the bottom of this stroke, the pen is flicked to the left, creating a fine, thin serif. This long upright stroke often has a subtle curvature. Where the bowl meets the baseline, the horizontal stroke goes across the upright. In places where there are two *p*'s in a row, the two descenders receive distinct treatment; the left-hand *p* has a flicked, rounded flourish at the base of its descender, whereas the following *p* is more chaste, with a simple, straight descender. Double *f*'s do the same.

The *f* is both an ascender and a descender. At its bottom, it ends with a sharp edge rather than having an arched shape, as it does at the top. This echoes the visual decisions taken with the rest of the script; as in the *m* or *n*, the emphasis remains at the top.

The *w* is made with three heavy strokes, a cursive mannerism. The *y* ends with a fine, thin tail made with the corner of the pen. The *g* is made with a relatively large top that is the same height as an *o*; its tail emerges from the top a sharp, angular turn that echoes the sharp tail of the *r*. The tail is an open shape with a wide aperture.

Another sample from Matthew 14. Note how the second line of verse 35 is adjusted to contain more text than the line above. Such subtle adjustments reflect the expertise of the scribes working on the project.

The *o* in the script is a bit of an outlier. It is an upright oval. When compared to the *a* or *d*, it seems a little narrower than one might expect; the latter are quite wide. In terms of how it sits with the other letters, however, it works.

All of these observations only begin to unpack the complexity of the Bible Script. Context informed many decisions made by the scribes as they wrote their page allotments. Because the text is justified on both sides, and certain lines had to be squeezed in, the Bible Script has been used in a malleable way. When a line required it, the script needed to be slightly condensed or expanded. Frequently, letters overlap, a practice referred to in medieval manuscripts as "biting the bow." In addition, ampersands sometimes take the place of the word *and*.

The capital letters in Bible Script are very wide, and they vary somewhat, just as the minuscule does. Some letters, such as *S, C,* or *O*, are basically larger versions of the minuscule forms. Letters with straight downstrokes, such as *F, H,* or *I,* often have tiny flicked serifs or flourishes at the bottom left. The letters *B, D,* and *P* have complex shapes at the top left, where the bowl is attached below the top of the first upright stroke. The horizontal crossbars on *A* and *H* are not perfectly straight; they take on a decorative zigzag shape, a combination of thick and thin, rather than a flat horizontal line. Finally, small decorative diamonds are frequently added to the center of vertical downstrokes.

⟨ 8 *This people honors me with their lips,*
but their hearts are far from me;

9 *in vain do they worship me,*
teaching human precepts as doctrines.'"

This passage from Matthew 15 shows the distinctive script used for poetry in *Gospels and Acts.*

The Poetry scripts

THE Poetry Script that appears in the first volumes is a lighter, smaller variant of the main Bible Script. Because it is written on the same baselines as the main script, the proportion of the interlinear space is relatively larger. The ascenders and descenders have a little more room to play and are proportionally longer.

In the *Wisdom* and *Prophets* volumes, a different Poetry Script was used. These volumes contain a high proportion of verse, so entire pages had to be written in the Poetry Script. It is slightly larger and heavier than the earlier Poetry Script, giving it more weight on the page.

The form of the second Poetry Script is a fairly straightforward Italic. It has just a hint of lean—just a few degrees. One echo of the Bible Script can be found in the shape of the *p*, but other letters, like *g*, have a standard Italic form. The *f* has arches on both top and bottom.

Psalms scripts

As DESCRIBED in chapter 11, the *Psalms* volume is divided into five books, based on current scholarship about the way the book was assembled in antiquity. Each book was written by one scribe in a distinctive script.

This passage from Job 3 demonstrates the way the Poetry Scripts evolved. In *Wisdom Books*, the text is heavy with poetry, requiring a slightly more robust script than was used in volumes where the poetry alternates with long passages in prose.

A selection of passages from *Psalms*, showing the work of different scribes. The headings for all the psalms were written by Brian Simpson. A different color is used for each book.

Psalm 12

To the leader: according to The Sheminith.
A Psalm of David.

Help, O Lord, for there is no longer
anyone who is godly;
the faithful have disappeared

Book I · Brian Simpson

Psalm 50

A Psalm of Asaph.

The mighty one, God the LORD,
speaks and summons the earth
from the rising of the sun to its setting.
2 Out of Zion, the perfection of beauty,

Book II · Sally Mae Joseph

Psalm 87

Of the Korahites. A Psalm. A Song.

On the holy mount stands the city he founded;
2 the LORD loves the gates of Zion
more than all the dwellings of Jacob.
3 Glorious things are spoken of you,

Book III · Donald Jackson

Psalm 94

O LORD, you God of vengeance,
you God of vengeance, shine forth!
2 Rise up, O judge of the earth;
give to the proud what they deserve!
3 O LORD, how long shall the wicked,

Book IV · Donald Jackson

Psalm 122

A Song of Ascents. Of David.

I was glad when they said to me,
"Let us go to the house of the LORD!"
2 Our feet are standing
within your gates, O Jerusalem.

Book V · Sally Mae Joseph

Book 1

Written by Brian Simpson, the script in book 1 is a variant of the Poetry Script used in *Wisdom* and *Prophets*.

Book 2

This script, written by Sally Mae Joseph, was inspired by the work of the Renaissance scribe Palatino. It is an upright Italic with a fairly angular, deep-branching arch structure. The letters do not join—a common feature of Italian Humanist-era writing—which gives the page an almost typographic quality.

Book 3

Donald Jackson wrote this book in his formal Italic hand. The interlinear spacing is fairly tight, and occasionally the descenders from one line are in danger of colliding with the ascenders from the line below. In the hands of a less skilled scribe, this would cause serious problems; in Donald's hands, the ascenders and descenders are modified to avoid problems.

Book 4

The script here, written by Donald Jackson, is also Italic. The texture of the script is wider and more extended than the writing in the previous book.

Book 5

The final book of *Psalms* was written by Sally Mae Joseph in a script developed from the Poetry Script used in the *Prophets* and *Wisdom* volumes. In contrast to the upright character of the script in book 2, this writing has a very pronounced lean and contains many cursive joining strokes.

THE LIGHT WAS GOOD; AND GOD SEPARATED THE LIGHT FROM THE DARKNESS. GOD CALLED THE LIGHT DAY, AND THE DARKNESS HE CALLED NIGHT. AND THERE WAS EVENING AND THERE WAS MORNING, THE FIRST DAY. AND GOD SAID, "LET THERE BE A DOME IN THE MIDST

The Incipit Script shown here comes from Genesis 1.

Incipit script

THE Incipit Script is used to mark the beginning of important books; it appears at the beginning of each Gospel, except for Luke, and at the beginning of each volume, except for *Psalms* and *Letters and Revelation*.

The term *incipit* comes from the study of medieval manuscripts. In medieval books the start of a text was often marked with a phrase, such as INCIPIT EVANGELIUM SECUNDUM MARCUM, or HERE BEGINS THE GOSPEL ACCORDING TO MARK, and the page would receive extra ornamentation. Donald pulled from this tradition, marking the beginning of important components of The Saint John's Bible with a block of massed capitals.

Because the texts in Incipit Script were written by Donald Jackson alone, the script itself did not need to be carefully regularized, as it would have been if it had been written by a team of scribes. Its most forceful characteristic is, in fact, its playfulness. The letterforms are distinctly varied, and Donald used variant letters (the two forms of *E* and *T*, rounded and straight, stand out in this regard). Many letters are tied together, sharing a stroke. And the letters are often adjusted to suit the context of the word in which they appear.

The two samples shown here come from the first chapters of Genesis and Job. They were written several years apart, and each has its own character while clearly belonging to the same basic script. The Genesis text is the more formal of the two. The Job text emphasizes the gestural play of the pen, and the strokes often have somewhat rougher edges; the shapes, while still very much under the control of the scribe, show much looser handling.

The script is based on a round *O* and has some strong affinities to Uncial, although it is *sui generis*. The contrast of thick and thin is very pronounced. Many horizontal strokes are made with fine, thin lines, terminating in a slight swelling or an added serif.

The pen handling is very fluid; the pen is frequently turned, and it really does not make sense to define the script according to a fixed pen angle. The pen angle varies depending on the stroke being made. In addition, the corner of the nib is frequently used to make fine lines. This is especially obvious with the left-hand stroke of *A, N,* and *M.*

The structure of the *A* is unusual and casts light on some of the distinctive qualities of this script. The top of the letter is rather mannered, with a flat top. It's the construction of this top that finds echoes elsewhere in the writing. The left-hand stroke begins with a distinct wedged-shape serif; the rest of the stroke, made with the corner of the pen, is a fine, thin line. This left-hand stroke as only nominally attached to the flat top, and the stroke that connects it to the thick right-hand stroke, is made in a variety of ways. Sometimes the flat top is a relatively thick stroke that abuts the serif on the left. At other times, a thin connecting stroke is written at a diagonal. The fluidity of the form reflects the playful, experimental quality that runs through the writing.

In addition, the *A* demonstrates how many of the letters have been "exploded." All the strokes in a letter may not connect but approach one another without touching or just kissing. These broken forms are particularly prominent in the *N, M,* and *K.*

The way the pen leaves the page at the ends of many strokes is also telling. The tail of the *R,* for instance, solves a typical calligraphic dilemma: the ordinary pen angle can result in a clubby, squared-off end, losing the fine, thin termination that makes inscriptional Roman capital *R*'s so elegant. Here, Donald twists the pen onto its right corner as he draws the nib off the page. This twist results in a fine, pointed end, but it often does not lift off evenly and cleanly: as the pen leaves the page, it produces a broken stroke. The gesture is clean, but the form itself is complex, like the leave of a dry brush in East Asian calligraphy.

At the end of many upright strokes, the pen is also twisted slightly. Sometimes, the shape is refined with an extra stroke of the pen at the end, as Donald "corners" the pen and shapes the stroke to his satisfaction.

Diagonal straight strokes often have distinctly curved contours. The upright straight strokes are often ornamented with small diamonds that project from the center of the form. These diamonds find an echo in the shape of the crossbar of the *H,* which is not a straight stroke but rather zigzags across the space between the uprights.

The *S* varies quite a bit. It is, on the whole, quite a narrow letter. Sometimes, it takes a standard *S*-shape, which tends to break the top and bottom guidelines. Other *S*'s have additional curves at top and bottom, creating a letter that slaloms back and forth with complex curves.

The tops of the bowls of *D, B, R,* and *P* spring with a branching stroke pulling out of the left-hand upright stroke. This is one of the features of the script that echo Uncial forms.

THERE WAS ONCE A MAN
IN THE LAND OF UZ
WHOSE NAME WAS JOB.
THAT MAN WAS BLAMELESS
AND UPRIGHT, ONE WHO
FEARED GOD AND TURNED
AWAY FROM EVIL. THERE WERE

The Incipit Script shown here comes from Job 1.

The *D* is particularly interesting. It is often tied to a preceding letter. This is particularly true of the common word AND. When this ligature is made, Donald makes the bowl in a single stroke that ends with a fine line at its bottom. Stand-alone *D*'s, by contrast, have some weight at the bottom of the bowl. By suppressing this weight when the *D* is tied to a preceding letter, Donald avoids awkward collisions of two thick strokes.

The *G*, which is rendered as a kind of spiral shape, demonstrates the use of variable pressure. In the small shape at the center of the letter, the width of the pen is not brought into contact with the page, leaving a stroke of slightly lighter weight than that of the larger, *C*-shaped strokes.

All of these observations could easily mislead an inexperienced scribe. If these variations and idiosyncrasies were mimicked mindlessly, the result would be a sorry mish-mash. In Donald's hands, these function to create a coherence of texture, to knit the line of writing together as a whole. Careful examination of the script shows that each decision to vary a letterform relies on its context within the line of writing.

The Versals throughout The Saint John's Bible are distinctly playful and varied.

A gain he enter
was there wl
watched hir
cure him on the sabba

N ow a certai
any, the vill
Martha.[2]
ed the Lord with perfu

B ut on the first
they came to th
they had prep
rolled away from the to

S o now, Israel,
ordinances that
so that you ma

T he LORI
mand th
you enter

MY

W hen
Kin
us,

T hen the Lc
ark, you an
seen that
me in this generatio

X ou are c
must n
forelock

A gain h
was th
watch
cure him on the s

B ut God r
animals
were with
a wind blow over th

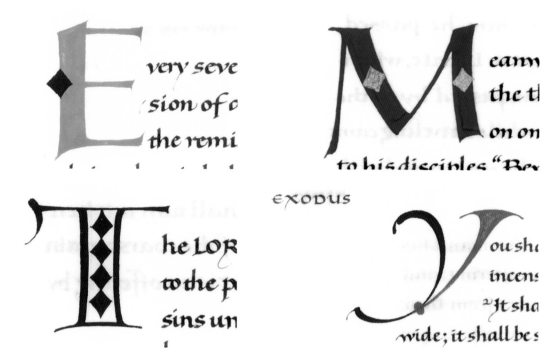

EXODUS

Versals

THE VERSALS that function as drop caps throughout the Bible take on a dizzying variety of shapes and approaches. In the text-heavy volumes, they often provide the only punctuations of unexpected color and variety of form on many spreads. They were entirely written by Donald.

Donald's basic method for making versals is to take an edged pen and draw the contours, which are then filled in. The fluidity of Donald's line is striking; these really do have the quality of *writing* even though they are made of built-up forms.

On the other hand, it doesn't do to generalize. Simply by looking at the selection we show here, one can see that many different techniques and tools have been used.

In *Letters and Revelation*, Donald chose a much more restrained, more angular letterform for the versals. He describes these versals as functioning like a typeface. The text of that volume is much more frequently interrupted; many of the books are shorter, and many more of their component texts were chosen for special treatment. The result was a series of very complex, even busy pages. As a result, Donald turned the volume down on the versals, opting for a less visually varied style.

In *Letters and Revelation*, Donald Jackson chose a more typographic, geometric treatment for the Versals.

Other ancient authorities read was out on the sea
Other ancient authorities read the wind
Other ancient authorities read commanded, saying
Or is an offering
Other ancient authorities add or the mother
Other ancient authorities read law; others commandment
Other ancient authorities lack of the blind

die.⁵ But you say that whoever tells father or mother, 'whatever support you might have had from me is given to God', then that person need not honor the father. ⁶ So, for the sake of your tradition, you make void the word of God.⁷ You hypocrites! Isaiah prophesied rightly about you when he said:

⁸ 'This people honors me with their lips,

but their hearts are far from me;

⁹ in vain do they worship me,

The notes in The Saint John's Bible are written at an incredibly small size, and two distinct scripts are used.

Notes

THE NOTES in the margins employ two different scripts. The black explanations are written in a running Roman hand; note the use of the two-story minuscule *a*. The alternative readings are written in a red italic.

Non-Western scripts

BOOK TITLES and running heads in the Hebrew Scriptures were written in Hebrew by Izzy Pludwinski. He used a Sephardic script.

In the books from the Apocrypha, which have come down to us in Greek, running heads in Greek Uncials are used.

Hebrew headings and running heads in the Old Testament were written by Izzy Pludwinski.

Hebrew headings for the *Pentateuch*.

בראשית

שמות

ויקרא

במדבר

דברים

אסתר

ΕΣΘΗΡ

A heading from Esther, showing the mix of Greek and Hebrew, reflecting the original languages of the Biblical texts.

Large marginal scripts

THERE IS A CLASS of scripts in the Bible that straddles the distinction between craft and expressive scripts. Starting with the first volume, *Gospels and Acts*, Donald often incorporated writing into the composition of some of the illuminations. This writing could take many forms. As the project continued, however, a manner of writing emerged that lent itself to the task of placing a text adjacent to an image. In *Historical Books*, these marginal inscriptions took on a greater importance as Donald added texts in the margins without illustrations.

I refer to these in the plural—large marginal scripts—because, though they bear a family resemblance, they follow a less fixed pattern than the craft scripts of the Bible. Their scale varies according to the context, and the letters can be spaced out or packed together. Sometimes the letters are tall and condensed; at other times they are wider.

The most obvious characteristic of these scripts is that they do not sit on a horizontal baseline; they dance in space. The uprights are also not rigidly vertical but lean back and forth. This allows the writing to become a pictorial element and makes it stand apart from the more formal writing of the text of the Bible.

Looking at the example from Joshua, we see how the all-capital script creates a delicate pattern in the margin. Some aspects of the script hark back to the Incipit Script: notice how the letters *A, N, M,* and *W* have components that do not join. In contrast to the Incipit Script, this writing has very minimal serifs; there is just a slight swelling at the end of some strokes. The rounded capital *E* here has a thick middle bar; the pen has been turned to 90 degrees. Donald also plays with the weight of the thick strokes; some are quite thick, while others are narrower. These thicker strokes were made by double-stroking. The variations in color were added with a brush.

The texts used in the margins are not tied to a baseline. They have free-flowing, dynamic compositions that contrast to the regularity and uniformity of the main columns of text.

The marginal scripts create delicate textures; their compositions are open at the edges. They engage the white space around them. Unlike the rectilinear composition of the main crafts scripts, these more fluid compositions play with the space around them.

Expressive scripts

THE MAIN AIM of this chapter has been to dissect the craft scripts of The Saint John's Bible. The craft scripts can be analyzed with the classic terminology of calligraphy practice, because they are meant to have a consistent, regular style. The expressive scripts, by contrast, are, by definition, irregular: each piece has been made specifically for its context, and there is no need to regularize the script.

In this gallery, we show a selection of expressive scripts.

Another sample of a large marginal script.

The Saint John's Bible is full of expressive writing. Each of these treatments of text was custom-designed by the artist or scribe to reflect the meaning of the words and to respond to their placement within the composition of the page.

CHAPTER 18

THE HANDLING OF THE BIBLE

ONCE THE MANUSCRIPT PAGES leave the Scriptorium, they still have to be handled with exquisite care. Vellum is a durable material; the many surviving medieval manuscripts attest to that. But it is only durable under certain conditions. Once they are bound into a book, all vellum needs is a consistent temperature and humidity. The binding holds the pages snug and safe.

The Bible pages came out of the Scriptorium unbound, and as they have traveled for exhibitions, they remain in the form of loose, individual sheets. As of this writing, they are still not bound, and there is some debate as to what form the eventual binding will take.

I interviewed Tim Ternes, the executive director of the Bible project since 2008, to find out how Saint John's handles the delicate folios. He described two trips to Wales he made to pick up finished pages of the Bible. On the first trip, he accompanied Carol Marrin, who was then executive director, and her husband, K.C. Marrin. They collected the *Wisdom* volume. On the second trip, once he had taken over as director, he went with Linda Orzechowski to collect the first part of *Historical Books*. On other visits, Donald and Mabel, or Sarah Harris, had taken pages to Saint John's themselves to present them to their client.

The transfer

THE HANDING OVER of the pages has elements of both a ceremonial unveiling and a formal release of the materials to the client. Donald's skills as a communicator come into play, and the representatives from Saint John's examine and accept the work that has been finished.

Tim told me, "Sarah generally stores the pages while they are at the Scriptorium in flat file drawers in the lower level of the Scriptorium. By the time we arrived for that first visit the pages had been placed in their travel cases." These are custom-made cases that were designed with minimum clearance for the pages, so they are held snug. Once packed, each case weighs about ninety pounds. On Tim's second visit, Donald had set up an easel board, so he could present the pages in an upright position, which made it far easier to examine them.

The folios are arranged in their gatherings, anticipating their placement in the bound manuscript.

Every page is examined by the representatives of the client. Tim said, "Donald doesn't just show us the illuminations. We also look at the pages of plain text."

The handing over is also an occasion for storytelling. On each visit, Donald regaled the group with stories about how each illumination was made. Tim says, "We videotaped some of these presentations." The archives of the project have a rich trove of this kind of documentation of the process.

Once the presentation is over and the stories have been told, the Saint John's team goes systematically through the delivered pages. There is a formal legal document that details what should appear on every page, and the team examines the folios to make sure that the manuscript has been delivered according to the terms of the contract. They make sure that the acceptance document corresponds precisely to the folios they have in front of them. Tim underscored what a great responsibility this could be. "We have to document that we are taking exactly what we say we're taking."

The cases are then carefully packed for travel to Minnesota. Layers of glassine and neoprene, a synthetic, chemically stable rubber sheet, protect the folios and prevent them from rubbing against one another in transit. In addition, packs of Rhapid Gel are added. These have been previously hydrated to 70 percent humidity; they maintain the interior of the case at a steady 50 percent humidity. This is particularly important because vellum is so sensitive to moisture.

On Tim's two visits to pick up Bible folios, a courier has come to pick them up and drive them back to London.

The day assigned to air travel from London to Minneapolis is always long. The logistics of boarding are complicated, and customs has to be handled correctly.

"We use an agent to handle this kind of thing," Tim said to me. The airline also must be notified, and special arrangements are made for bringing the travel cases on board. Needless to say, one does not check these boxes in as if they were ordinary luggage.

When arriving at the airport, Tim and his team are met by their agent and taken to business class check-in. From there, they are escorted through security. In a private room, the case is laid out. "We are asked many questions," Tim said, "and we have to unpack the whole case." The box is wanded with a metal detector and examined to make sure it contains nothing dangerous. The case is then repacked with care.

Tim laughed when he said, "The first members of the public to see the pages are the airport customs officers!"

Once they have been cleared, they take the boxes to the waiting area. At boarding, they are the first ones to get on the plane. The airline staff has been warned, and they have a letter from the chief pilot saying they are allowed to bring the cases into the first-class cabin. The cases are stowed in a little rest behind the cockpit. On one occasion, before 9/11, the rolled pages were actually stowed on the flight deck at the side of the pilot's seat.

On landing, the Saint John's team are the last to leave the plane.

U.S. Customs carefully declare the value of the folios. Tim explained, "We have to make it clear that this is a new manuscript and not an antiquarian item." In addition, each folio has to be declared as separate works of art. "If we declared the pages as a single whole manuscript, its value would be above the limit."

When the folios arrive at Saint John's, they are placed in a vault deep under the library. "We need to give them a rest," Tim said. "They take time to acclimate."

The pages are then presented to the members of the CIT. They too examine each and every page. "This is the ceremonial acceptance," Tim explained. The pages are then shown to members of the community, including those who work at the Hill Museum and Manuscript Library (HMML), Liturgical Press, and the library staff. They are not yet ready, however, for any large public display.

Imaging

BEFORE ANYTHING else happens, the pages go through imaging. Tim explained to me that this has two functions. First, it allows reproductions to be made. Pages can be shown on the project's web site, and the images are used for all the printed iterations of the Bible, from promotional literature to the Trade Edition.

These images also provide the raw data for the making of the Heritage Edition. Second, Tim said, "It's a security issue. Having high-resolution images means that if the original is ever damaged in any way the Scriptorium could create a matching replacement."

Wayne Torborg is in charge of this important step. He works in a basement studio in the Science Center on the university campus. In the early days, the scanning of each page was made by a digital capture that operated something like a photocopier or scanner; the capture device moved slowly down the page, taking the high-resolution image. This caused some technical problems, as the vellum sometimes shifted during the course of the digital capture. More recently, new technology has allowed Wayne to capture the image in a single shot.

The digital files are saved and stored at three separate locations. After each folio is scanned, it is returned to the vault.

Display

IN THE EARLIEST DAYS of the project, the few public displays of Bible pages were tightly managed events. The earliest completed pages were not put out for extended display but were shown briefly in the context of a ceremony or public lecture. When Donald and Mabel showed the earliest illuminations from the *Gospels and Acts* in the spring of 2001, they constructed a portable easel, and the illuminations were not covered in glass. They were attended at all times by people charged with their care. The folios are strong enough to

The beautifully constructed display cases both protect the vellum pages of the manuscript and present them as though they were in a bound book.

stand this kind of treatment for a single evening, but they cannot be displayed in this way for any extended period of time. Variations of humidity and the simple safety of the pages dictated that some kind of case or frame be created so they could be shown to the public at large.

For the Illuminating the Word exhibition at the Minneapolis Institute of Arts (MIA) in 2005, a solution was devised for how to display the manuscript in public.

Many museums will display individual vellum leaves in simple frames, floating the sheet between two mats. The frames can have glass on both front and back to allow the viewer to see both sides of the manuscript page. Donald was firm that he did not want to display the Bible pages flat on a wall; this was a book, and the pages should look like they come from a book.

Technically, this was tricky. In a bound book, the folios are folded down the middle and nested. The sewing runs through the folds in the nested section of folios, holding the pages in place. Once opened, book pages have a gentle curvature.

But the folios of this manuscript will not be folded until they are bound as books. In addition, because vellum shrinks and expands, depending on humidity, they have to be attached to some kind of support to keep them from curling at the edges or being damaged in the course of display. In addition, the folios have not been trimmed to their final size; they will only be trimmed once they are ready to be bound. This is actually helpful, because it leaves an extra margin, allowing the edges to be used to attach the vellum to its support.

The solution was to make deep wooden cases. Each case is designed to display a single spread from the manuscript. The cases were made by Metropolitan Frame in Minneapolis and measure 48 x 48 x 36 inches. The MIA mounted the first batch of folios for the opening of the exhibition. Since then, mounting has been done at Saint John's by Tim Ternes and Linda Orzechowski.

Forms are cut out of 100 percent cotton mat board, and this is shaped to receive the vellum folios.

Because the folios are not yet folded, they have to be carefully positioned. Sometimes the spread being shown is made on a single sheet of vellum. This happens with folios that will be at the center of each nest of folded folios in the bound book. In this case, a clear acrylic rod is placed vertically down the folio, where the fold will be, pushing the sheet down in the center. The supports push the pages up on either side of the clear rod, gently encouraging the folio to take the shape of an opened book.

Other spreads in the manuscript appear on separate folios. In this case, each folio is gently curved back, and the two sheets are positioned touching each other down the middle of the spread, just as they would if sewn together as a book.

The entire construction is carefully screwed together with mounting brackets; once everything is in position, it must not move.

It is a complex and detailed procedure. It takes the HMML team about twenty hours to assemble one case.

The most difficult thing is that the cases need to be scrupulously clean. Once the folios are mounted at Saint John's, they must survive travel without being opened again or interfered with in any way. The tiniest speck of dust that could be dislodged in transit could not only mar the display but also damage the manuscript.

Tim said, "To make sure there is no dust, when you drill holes, you have to screw the screws in, then take them out again, then vacuum the interior, then screw everything together again. We do it, undo it, clean, then do it again."

After he and Linda have completed assembling a case, Tim says they "pound it to make sure nothing falls out. We pound, shake, rattle, and then open the box up and clean it again."

Once the box is assembled and fully cleaned, hydration panels are added in the back to keep the humidity constant inside. The final step is to iron the case shut with a barrier film that impedes any moisture from reaching the interior of the case. Hygrometers inside the cases allow the humidity level to be monitored. Tim told me, "They work well. They hardly lose any humidity at all."

Storage

THE EXHIBITION that opened at the MIA in 2005 traveled all over the United States. As it traveled, the cases were left just as they had been when they were first made. It took two full semis to move the exhibition from one venue to the next.

When the cases came back to Saint John's, they were disassembled, and the folios were stored in the vault. This allowed the vellum folios to relax and lie flat under climate-controlled conditions.

When new displays need to be created, they have to start again and remount the selected folios.

Binding

AS OF this writing, the design of the binding has not been finalized. The traditional solution for preserving the manuscript volumes for posterity would be to bind them permanently between oak boards. This, indeed, was Donald's vision at the beginning of the project. While this solution would be one way to protect the pages, it would mean that there could never again be a comprehensive display of the original pages of the Saint John's Bible, since it would only be possible to have a maximum of seven spreads open at one time.

Another solution that has been discussed is to devise a form of binding that could allow the volumes to be occasionally disassembled. They would still function as bound books, and most of the time they would remain in their bindings. Such a binding structure would, however, allow selected folios to be removed. This would grant Saint John's a measure of flexibility; the volumes could be used and displayed as bound books, but exhibitions could also be held in which many pages from a volume were displayed individually. The techniques to make such a book do exist.

It remains to be seen what the final solution to the binding will be.

CHAPTER 19

THE HERITAGE EDITION

A FRIEND of mine from Chicago phoned me up one day and said, "I just saw The Saint John's Bible." I was a little surprised. I hadn't heard that the manuscript had traveled to Chicago, so I asked her some questions: Where did you see it? Was it shown in display cases? Was it bound?

Yes, she said. It was bound in a beautiful leather cover.

"Ah, I see. You saw the Heritage Edition," I said.

"Yes. And it was beautiful."

That brief exchange raised an interesting and perplexing question for me. What *is* The Saint John's Bible?

In the centuries before mechanical reproduction, each manuscript book was unique. It existed in just one copy, written by one or more human beings, and carefully preserved in a library. The great manuscripts we have inherited from the past have names—the *Book of Kells*, the Grandval Bible, the Codex Sinaiticus, *The Lindisfarne Gospels,* the Book of Durrow. We value them because they are original works; we can see the mark of the hand on them. They are as precious as paintings by Titian or van Gogh.

The printed Heritage Edition has allowed The Saint John's Bible to reach a much wider audience. At a celebration held at St. Martin-in-the-Fields in London on September 28, 2010, images from the Bible were projected on the east wall of the church to the accompaniment of music. Three volumes of the Heritage Edition appear at the bottom, standing before the altar.

And when we look at reproductions, even fine actual-size facsimiles, we are always aware that we are looking at a copy, not at the work of art itself.

But for the last five hundred years, we have lived with printed books. We may go to a great library and look at a Gutenberg Bible and appreciate seeing the real object. Yet it's quite a different mind-set we bring to this looking. Our language gives us away—"The Morgan Library has a Gutenberg Bible." Note the indefinite article. It is "a" Gutenberg Bible, not "the" Gutenberg Bible. We have seen one of *many* originals that were made. And when we say we have seen a *copy* of a famous edition, we are well aware that each book exists as one example from a group of identical printed books.

By contrast, when we say, "I have only seen the Mona Lisa in reproduction," we are indicating that we must suspend our judgment to some extent. We have not, in fact, seen the real thing, and we can only make tentative statements about it until we have actually seen it in the flesh. The copy is lesser than the original. But with printed books, the copy *is* the original. An edition exists only in multiples.

Why am I making these distinctions? Why does this matter? It matters because most contemporary people simply assume that a book exists as an edition, and if they think about The Saint John's Bible this way, they will be missing something that is crucial to the project.

In the case of The Saint John's Bible, we have an original manuscript book that was not made as a prototype for a printed edition. If it had been intended for that purpose, it would have been made quite differently. But the manuscript has now been reproduced in print, and that creates an entirely new and different work. Indeed, the effort of reproducing the Bible has posed enormous challenges, precisely because of the unique nature of the manuscript itself. In fact, if one compares page by page the printed versions against the original manuscript, one sees that they are not exactly the same. The printed versions, because they reproduced in a different medium from the original, must always be interpretations, not perfect copies.

This chapter tells the story of transforming the manuscript into printed versions, focusing mostly on the most complex problem, the printing of the Heritage Edition. These printed editions are, in essence, separate projects that grew out of the production of the manuscript. The original is a work of art with its own integrity, and if you want to see The Saint John's Bible, you need to see the manuscript itself, in the flesh—quite literally!

As projects that derived from the original manuscript, the printed versions of the Bible posed complicated technical problems. They are similar to the original, but, in the end, they are works in their own right.

First forays into print

I SAT ONE DAY in 2004 in Carol Marrin's office in the basement of HMML. Carol was executive director of the Bible project at the time. In her office there were framed prints of Bible pages on the walls, and on a table in one corner of the office were sets of printing samples of facsimiles of historical manuscripts made by European printers.

We discussed Saint John's strategy for printing images from the Bible.

"We can't cheapen the Bible by bringing out lots of inexpensive greeting cards or posters early on," she said to me. "We have to maintain the value of the printed reproductions." She reflected that if Saint John's concentrated first on producing beautiful archival-quality prints and editions, then later on they might make less expensive versions available. But if they started at the low end, there would be no way to climb back up and offer the higher-end reproductions.

The earliest reproductions were full-size prints of selected illuminations made by the giclee process. The very first illumination, the *Genealogy of Christ*, was offered as a full-seized giclee print soon after it was completed. The giclee process produces an image from a digital photograph of an illumination or Bible page using an inkjet technology. It can be used for large-scale prints, and both the paper and ink are archival. In addition to producing a high-quality print, the giclee technique has the benefit that prints are made one at a time; they can be printed on demand. This removes the need to invest in making a large run of prints on a press and keeps overhead and inventory costs down.

The volumes of the printed Heritage Edition are bound in tooled leather with metal clasps. The volume shown here is *Historical Books*.

A single copy of *Gospels and Acts* was made for presentation to Pope John Paul II using the giclee technique in 2004. This was a one-off project, made possible by the relative ease of giclee printing. The bound book was presented to the Pope at a public audience in St. Peter's Square in Rome on May 26, 2004. It was presented by Donald and Mabel Jackson, Saint John's Abbot John Klassen, OSB, and Saint John's University President Dietrich Reinhart, OSB.

The Saint John's Bible web site also offers giclee prints of all of the pages of the Bible, allowing the public to buy frameable, archival prints to hang on a wall.

Some greeting cards have been produced using Bible illuminations. But prints and cards are one thing. What about books? From the very beginning of the project, there was a clear demand for some kind of facsimile of each volume showing every page, bound as a book. Thus the so-called Trade Edition was born.

The Trade Edition is a reproduction of each volume of the manuscript as a separate, bound book. It is smaller than the manuscript, and it differs from the original in some other important ways. The Trade Edition measures 10 x 15¼ inches. This is not only distinctly smaller than the original but also slightly out of proportion; the margins are not exactly the same as those of the manuscript. Each page of the Bible was digitally photographed, and the pages were reproduced on coated paper in a simple four-color printing process. No gold foil or stamping was used. (I will explain some of these printing terms in more detail in a moment, when we turn to the Heritage Edition).

The Trade Edition was meant to be an accessible, affordable printed version of the Bible for a popular audience. It is still a large book and demands ample space on a bookshelf. No one, however, would confuse it with the original manuscript.

The most striking difference between the Trade Edition and the original is the fact that the images in this printed version have been significantly cleaned up. Remember that show-through is a fundamental quality of a manuscript on vellum; the skins, being slightly translucent, allow one to see a faint image of the writing or illuminations on the other side of each page. This show-through has been completely removed from the Trade Edition.

This makes perfect sense: show-through can be distracting, and the pages could look muddy and confusing if the show-through were maintained. Also, since the Trade Edition is smaller, it was important that the text not break up. The digital images of the original were therefore heavily manipulated using computer editing software to blast out the background, clean up the edges of the writing, and beef up the finest strokes so they didn't disappear.

Perhaps this makes it sound like a violence has been done to the original. To some extent, the Trade Edition is not perfectly faithful to the manuscript. But the changes had to be made to create

Layers of magenta and cyan (left and center) combined with yellow and black can create a vast spectrum of colors.

a smaller scale version that would function as a readable book. And anyone who has worked with photomechanical reproduction knows that there are many judgment calls to be made when capturing a digital image. By slightly adjusting the exposure at the time of the digital capture, or shifting the color balance or degree of contrast in the digital files, the lines of writing can be made slightly heavier or lighter in weight. It requires great sensitivity to know how the image should be processed to make a workable printed book.

The first volume of the Trade Edition—*Gospels and Acts*—was published in concert with the opening of the traveling exhibition, Illuminating the Word, at the MIA in 2005. As Donald and his team finished each volume of the manuscript, they were digitally imaged and printed as volumes of the Trade Edition. This printed version of The Saint John's Bible has proved enormously popular with the public.

All the early printing efforts were made by Saint John's, with relatively little input from Donald Jackson. He had plenty on his plate just working on the original manuscript.

The Heritage Edition

THE BIGGEST PRINTING CHALLENGE still lay ahead: how could Saint John's create a full-scale reproduction of The Saint John's Bible in book form that retained all the detail and lushness of the original manuscript?

From the very beginning of the project, there had been some idea of creating a full-size facsimile, and even the first contract between Donald and Saint John's had included terms between the artist and client should such a printed edition be made. As I described in the chapter on the *Historical Books* volume of the manuscript, this proved a matter of contention between Donald and Saint John's.

Donald Jackson's notes on the digital proofs indicate the subtle color changes needed to blend litho and gold foil printing techniques.

The benefits of producing a full-scale reproduction were obvious to all: it would make the Bible available to a much wider audience. The one great limitation of the original manuscript is its singularity. The delicate Bible pages must be handled carefully and can be in only one place at a time. If the book is bound traditionally, then only a very limited selection of openings can be shown. A printed reproduction allows people to experience the book through another medium. Even if it is not the manuscript itself, it feels very much like the original.

In the fall of 2006, Saint John's launched the Heritage Program to produce fine-art quality, full-size reproductions of The Saint John's Bible. The term "reproduction" is carefully chosen. The Heritage Edition is not a perfect facsimile; it is not a perfect copy of the manuscript. Instead, this set of printed books is an *interpretation* of the manuscript in the form of a printed book. The distinction is important, because in order to evoke the quality of the original, many small adjustments and technical challenges had to be addressed.

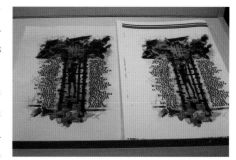

A printed sheet from the Heritage Edition lies next to the original illumination from the manuscript.

Craig Bruner took the helm as director of operations, and the Heritage Program would take on a corporate life of its own, distinct from the production of the manuscript.

With the launching of the Heritage Edition, The Saint John's Bible entered a more frankly commercial phase. Many of the events surrounding the production of the original manuscript were liturgical in nature, or took place within the Saint John's community, or involved exhibitions at museums. The focus was on the religious, liturgical, and cultural importance of the manuscript. With the Heritage Edition, Saint John's had a luxury product to sell. It was beautiful, it was artistic, but it was clearly a collector's item. It would certainly appeal to institutions.

The name "Heritage Edition" suggests the commercial nature of the enterprise. The program aims to create a limited edition of 360 copies on the finest paper using archival inks and metal foils. It is divided into several distinct categories:

A conversation takes place during the proofing of the *Wisdom Books* volume.

The Apostles Edition—twelve sets—is reserved for new major donors to the Heritage Edition. These donors funded the startup costs of the Heritage Edition.

The Prophets Edition—twelve sets—is reserved for major donors who increased their giving or gave major gifts to *The Saint John's Bible* and/or the Heritage Edition.

The Patriarchs Edition—twelve sets—is made up only of the Old Testament books, and is designed for major donors from faiths that may not recognize the New Testament.

Finally, the *Heritage Edition* itself—299 sets—is open to any subscriber. It started at $115,000 in pre-publication, and the price has risen to $165,000 over a period of five years. Twenty-five sets of the Old Testament Heritage Edition are designed for subscribers who may not recognize the New Testament.

Donald Jackson became artistic director of the Heritage Program in March 2007. This was defined as a role distinct from his work on the original manuscript. Bringing Donald in for a supervisory role had two benefits. For one thing, he could ensure the Heritage Edition lived up to his expectations and did justice to the work he had done with his team of scribes and artists. This was a responsibility he felt keenly. "I am not just watching out for my own work," he said to me. "I am looking after all the artists who worked on the project."

The other benefit of having Donald as artistic director was that he could approve changes. As a living artist, he could guide the way the manuscript was reinterpreted in print. This key input shaped the making of the Heritage Edition.

Donald was also helped through the process of making the Heritage Edition by his studio manager, Sarah Harris. By the time the Heritage Edition went into production, she had been with at the Scriptorium for five years. She accompanied him as he began his regular trips to the printers and embossers in Minnesota and eventually began to take on more and more responsibilities. By the time the last printed volumes were being prepared, she would actually go ahead of him and preapprove as many of the pages as she could, saving the more complex images for Donald. She also spent around three months hand-finishing the foiled sheets at the end of the production process for nine illuminations in *Historical Books* and *Gospels and Acts*.

Transformation

When a work of art is reinterpreted in a new medium, it changes. Think, for instance, of the watching a telecast of a live opera. As enjoyable as it may be to watch *Don Giovanni* broadcast from a famous opera house in Europe, the experience is strangely flat. If you have good sound on your TV, the aural qualities of the opera remain powerful. But the visual experience is stilted. The medium of television demands cuts from one camera to the other. Close-ups of faces become more important. But these effects—so crucial to making effective television—cannot be fully achieved when broadcasting a staged opera. A broadcast of a live performance cannot evoke the experience of sitting in the audience. Those who sit in the opera house lose themselves in the performance; those who watch at home are always reminded that they are one step away from the full experience.

The problem of turning a manuscript book into a printed piece is similar. Many aspects of the original cannot be reproduced. If the printed version is to have any of the life of the original, it will have to render it using means unique to printing.

Several challenges needed to be solved. How do you evoke the qualities of vellum using ink on paper? How do you re-create the gold and metal leaf of the original? How do you ensure color fidelity? How do you deal with the issue of show-through? And how do you re-create the three dimensionality of the original pages?

In May 2007, Donald went to Minnesota and had meetings with the John Roberts Company, the printer; McIntosh Embossing, who would be in charge of foil stamping; and Cal Sixta at Colormax, who would be creating the digital color files.

Wisdom Books at the printer.
From left to right:
John Eirich, *pressman*
Dave Peterson, *Vice President for Business Development*
Sarah Harris, *printing consultant*
Scott Zorn, *head pressman*
Donald Jackson, *artistic director*
John Parfitt, *printing consultant*

The prepress stage was time consuming and exacting, far more so than the actual printing. Donald provided a list of all the stages the images had to go through before the job went on press:

1. Digital proofs created and first-stage color corrections by John Roberts. They also reviewed raw original files (original digital capture) to look for any lost details and show-through element.
2. Make first-stage color corrections on screen.
3. Review digital proofs against original pages.
4. Make decisions on show-through and modify or remove according to a formula established by John Roberts and the Scriptorium team.
5. Decisions on interpretation of gold—gold litho or gold foil. Also any special colors that may be needed to support the four standard-process colors are decided at this point.
6. Creating artwork for foil and embossing dies; sometimes these had to be retouched or re-created by hand.
7. Modifying litho background colors (behind foil).
8. Several reviews of digital proofs for color correction and modification of above. Approval and sign-off of these digital proofs.
9. Digital proofs are profiled for ink density (stochastic process) to take into account the custom paper surface.
10. Plates are made.

Donald Jackson's approval signature on a proof sheet.

Only after these stages are complete can the printing actually begin. After the first printed sheets of each page come off the press, they are inspected, and fine adjustments to the color are made before they are signed off by a member of the Scriptorium team before the print run can begin.

The Heritage Edition was printed using offset lithography on a sophisticated Heidelberg XL-105 press.

The basics of offset lithography are simple. A full-color image is printed by separating the colors into four printing plates, corresponding to the four standard inks: Cyan (a light, bright blue), Magenta (a rich pink), Yellow, and Black. Combining these four inks creates a vast spectrum of fully composed colors. The term "offset" refers to the fact that the press uses large rollers: one roller picks up ink, and as it rolls against the plate, ink is transferred (or offset) onto the plate. Sheets are fed through the press, picking up each color as they pass through each set of rollers. They are spit out at the far end, in full color, having received the impression of each of the four printing inks. That's the basic principle.

John Roberts' Heidelberg machines take this to an extremely high level of sophistication. The inks used are special fast-drying UV inks; the sheets emerge at the far end of the press fully dry. In addition to the four standard inks, custom inks can also be used, which give a much richer tone to selected colors. The press is also completely computerized, allowing for tight control over the quality of the printing.

Offset litho can reproduce a beautiful full-color image. But it can't print gold. In the original manuscript, Donald used many kinds of gold, and the only way to mimic this is to use foil stamping. As a result, the sheets for the Heritage Edition had to pass through two quite distinct processes: litho first and then the stamping with metal foils. Using these two basic techniques, the printers had to work with Donald to make the Heritage Edition.

The Devil in the details

I ASKED Donald to walk me through the process. As he spoke, it was striking how similar our conversation was to the conversations we had had about making the original manuscript. Donald and the printers and embossers had to invent techniques on the fly, improvising their way page by page through the project and solving problems as they encountered them.

The first concern was that the techniques they chose be archival quality. "Obviously, the Heritage Edition had to be made to last," Donald said. "In February 2007 I had a meeting with the art director of the Trade Edition, Eric Madsen, and my consultants, Michael Gullick and John Parfitt, a printer specializing in facsimile editions, who had created the facsimile of the Domesday Book."

Their first concern was the paper. "We decided on a Monadnock paper. But the weights and colors of the samples we were shown were not quite right for our project. We wanted a paper that looked and felt beautiful as a paper in its own right, not an imitation of vellum."

Donald Jackson worked closely with the craftspeople at McIntosh Embossing to develop ways of stamping and embossing sections of metallic and other foils on the printed pages to evoke the finishes in the original manuscript.

The Monadnock paper mill is in New Hampshire and has been in operation since 1819.

The four men debated with the John Roberts team what qualities they were looking for in a paper. The show-through, which had been removed from the Trade Edition, immediately became an issue. In this edition, some degree of show-through was necessary, or the pages would look nothing like the original. Perhaps they should print on a thin paper, so that show-through occurred naturally.

This sparked an interesting debate. In the printing industry, show-through is generally considered a major faux-pas. But perhaps in this case, it would echo the translucency of the vellum. As they discussed it, they realized it wouldn't work. "It would be a nightmare for registration," Donald said. "We would always be anxious if the two sides of the printed sheet aligned properly." To do it right would require printing to the tight specs used for currency, where both sides of a banknote align to the micron—not an option for such a large-format project.

Then they discussed actually printing the show-through. Would this have integrity, they wondered? Donald decided that, yes, this was the only way to proceed.

Monadnock was therefore asked to produce a custom sheet that allowed only minimal show-through but not so thick it wouldn't fold easily. It is an uncoated 100 percent cotton sheet with absolutely no additives. Donald said, "Monadnock's 100 percent 'American Cotton' is beautiful and takes ink well." It would cause some anxiety for John Roberts, however. Donald pointed out, "The uncoated paper was not what the printers regularly used when they printed with their fast-drying ultraviolet ink." But through much experimentation, the printers were able to master the new paper.

With the problem of the paper solved, Donald had to return to the question of how to render the show-through. "When I got the job of being the art director I realized what a marvelous thing it was to have digital control over subtleties," Donald said. This degree of control allowed the team to create a highly sophisticated solution to the problem of the show-through.

He continued, "In the original manuscript, the viewers accept the show-through as a natural aspect of the object in front of them. In the printed version, however, if you just print the show-through as in the original image capture of a vellum page, it is too distracting and powerful; remove it and you have a dead page. So you just have to hint at the show-through."

He explained, "In prepress, we manipulated the show-through and we could 'play' God: we could make it just the right strength." By tinkering with the levels of the show-through, they were able to lighten or darken those elements on every single page.

In many places, they removed elements that were distracting. The show-through of drop caps, chapter numbers, and some book titles were simply erased.

"This is an example of where art direction can play with the original," Donald said. Instead of slavishly reproducing the images of the manuscript pages, they could be manipulated on screen to capture the spirit of the original, not just its surface.

While making these adjustments in prepress, Donald and his technical experts made constant reference to the manuscript itself. "John Parfitt had told us you can never work off a photo alone. You must have access to the original. As we were working we always had the originals there for comparison. So John Roberts created a special climate-controlled environment so the vellum pages could be kept stable."

Gold

AFTER LITHO PRINTING the Heritage Edition, the next challenge was how to reproduce the gold that is used throughout the original manuscript. "Gold could have been the biggest pitfall," Donald said. "One false step and it looks like a cheap greeting card. But this was meant to be 'fine art' edition. We had to get it right, and it was a challenge that was worth taking."

One of the reasons gold is used in illuminated manuscripts is that it functions very differently from ink and pigment on the page. However bright the colors are in a manuscript, they never do what gold does: they do not dance with the play of light across the surface. Gold is alive because it is always changing. When we stand in front of a page with gold, even our slightest movements make us perceive the gold differently. Now it is dark, now it is light. Now it sparkles.

In the original manuscript, there are three basic kinds of gold: raised and burnished gold, gold leaf on an acrylic medium, and shell gold. In addition to gold, occasionally a platinum and palladium leaf is used. How do these work in the manuscript?

Raised and burnished gold is made by laying a base of gesso on the page and applying gold leaf. Because the gesso is applied as a fluid paste, it is three-dimensional: it stands slightly proud of the page when dry. When gold is laid on this medium, it can be burnished to a high sheen. It literally looks like solid metal. The dimensionality of the gesso means that it catches the light on all its surfaces, so it always has highlights and shadows.

For a flatter tone, gold leaf can be applied on an acrylic medium. Donald told me, "This starts with a matte finish, but you can burnish it to bring out the sheen. The acrylic medium is very stable. But it can cause its own problems, because it doesn't let the vellum breathe, like the old medieval media did."

Powder gold, also called shell gold, is ground gold suspended in a binding medium. It is used as a paint. Because it is made of tiny granules of pure metal, it never takes the high, polished sheen of gold leaf. But it can be burnished as well, so that it sparkles.

In the Trade Edition, the gold was not given any special treatment, other than selective clear varnish. Each page was simply reproduced from a high-resolution digital photograph. Gold is a flat color; raised and burnished gold shows its highlights. But a printed photograph of the gold is not alive to the light. It is static and unchanging. In the Heritage Edition, gold foil restores it to life.

"In the printing and foil stamping process what you're trying to do is imitate the burnish of the original," Donald said. "We were able to use different varieties of gold foil—bright gold, matte gold, and true matte, which is dead flat." This gave them a range of tones.

To illustrate his techniques, he talked about specific illuminations. "In the background of the *Joshua Frontispiece* in the original manuscript, I painted bands of pink, orange, and a blue-green underneath. With those rainbow tints in place, I then put the gold down, and I distressed it so the underlying colors could show through very subtly. But how do I interpret that in reproduction?"

Stamped gold foil is impressed onto the page with a custom die. This causes a series of problems. The gold, for one, is flat. It has distinct, hard edges, and there is a tiny ridge along the edge of the area covered in gold, which is visually distracting. Working with his team of foil stampers, Donald improvised a series of solutions to break up these flat areas of gold.

"The pressure of hot foil stamping can crush the paper's naturally matte surface on both sides of the sheet, special care was taken to avoid this."

In some places, in addition to gold stamping, embossing was used to give the gold area some dimensionality, just like the raised and burnished gold in the original. Because embossing is pressed right into the page, it leaves an indentation on the reverse of the page. As a result, Donald tried to avoid embossing areas in the margins of the pages where the slight indentations could look unsightly.

The embossing used in the *Psalms* left small dimples on the reverse side of the pages. In most cases, this was not a problem, as the shapes were small and sprinkled unevenly across each spread.

"You can't always emboss large areas deeply, especially if the impression is in the margin, because it leaves a hollow impression on the reverse of the sheet" he said. So going page by page through the manuscript, they had to judge where embossing could be positioned and where it could not.

Another way to get gold foil to imitate gold in the manuscript is to texture it in one way or another. By placing a small piece of silk over parts of the stamping die, the flat texture could be broken up in certain areas. Where the die was not covered, it would produce a smooth surface; where it was covered, it would be slightly textured. This mimicked the feel of light catching different parts of an area of gold leaf with different degrees of reflection.

"You can texture the gold with silk; it gives the impression of shadows. It's very nice. It can mirror the spirit of the original. But the silk would wear out. We ran through all my best vintage Liberty of London silk handkerchiefs," Donald recalls. "Instead, we sometimes chose to texture the surface of the metal die itself."

A plate for foil stamping lies atop a stack of printed sheets.

They also discovered that the foil could be slightly distressed by hand after it was applied, revealing in some place a hint of the underlying litho printing. This was a technique he had first employed in making the original manuscript. He now tried it on the printed version. "What gradually followed, in the *Historical Books*, was that I experimented with my well-worn piece of ScotchBrite and gently rubbed off the foil in places. This softened the hard edge of the foil impression and allowed the background color to show through."

But if the underlayer of litho printing is thus exposed, what color should it be?

"The nice bright photograph of gold printed in litho underneath becomes a nasty yellow that clashes with the metal foil."

It was natural for the printer to want the page to look beautiful when it came off the press. So the first color corrections would always render the printed gold in lovely light and dark shades of yellow.

Donald explained, "I discovered that, unless you print the litho gold 'wrong,' it won't blend well against foil. That turning point was first reached when we were printing the *Creation*. We underprinted a dark peach color."

It looked dreadful straight off the press. But once the gold foil had been applied with a textured die allowing the color to show through, it looked spectacular.

"In the manuscript illumination of *Death of Saul*, there is a vertical sheet of gold with color under it. I began by painting a layer of acrylic medium, tinted orange and green. I laid the gold. Then I made scratch marks and distressed it with ScotchBrite so some of the background showed through. Finally, I painted over it."

This technique created an image in the original in which gold leaf and painted color were beautifully blended into a composition with few hard edges.

Heat and pressure bond the gold foil to the litho-printed page.

"In the Heritage Edition, we printed this image with a scratched gold die over color and Sarah hand-finished it by distressing the foil with the ScotchBrite pad to allow the background color to blend with the gold just like on the original."

Other technical difficulties presented themselves. Donald said, "To make things more complicated, heat stamping makes the gold spread slightly, making registration difficult. In fact, it is impossible at the end of the day to exactly re-create paint over gold through the printing process. But with experimentation and the superb skills of the foil stampers, we were able to catch the spirit of the original using a mixture of traditional and unorthodox techniques.

"In *Wisdom Woman*, we actually did print litho on top of gold foil. I actually liked the effect. But litho ink can pull off particles of foil and transfer it to the rollers and blankets on the printing press, causing problems with spoilage and extra cleaning time, so we had to abandon that technique elsewhere."

Donald was also able to mix different kinds of foil in one image, necessitating several passes through the stamping press. He explained, "You can mix colors and brightnesses of foil, vary heat and pressure, texture the dies and impress the image with silk."

The volumes of the Heritage Edition were carefully sewn by hand.

As Donald learned more and more, watching the foil stamping in process, he saw that many variations could be achieved, and the pressmen at McIntosh's enjoyed the experimentation. It was a real collaboration between craftspeople in different media.

Wrapping things up

MATCHING THE COLORS of the original involved not only careful color correction of the digital images but also the use of custom inks. Donald said, "Two special colors, an electric ultramarine and a bright orange, were frequently called for in addition to the four standard printing inks. In much of Thomas Ingmire's work, for instance, we had to add a special black plate because he often works black-on-black, and we needed a double hit of black to create the extra depth."

A final feature of the original that Donald worked hard to mimic was the dimensionality of the vellum page. Vellum does not lie perfectly flat, ever. Nor does it curve perfectly smoothly. There is always a little play to the page, which gives variety and reflection to the gold.

Donald explained, "In the *Crucifixion* illumination Sarah worked her way through around seven hundred printed sheets, hand-debossing the foil, molding the paper with her thumb against a soft support as well as distressing the edges of the foil stamps."

The process of working with the printing staff and embossers was invigorating. Pressmen often dread the appearance of a client on the printing floor—only trouble can ensue. But Donald's approach intrigued the skilled workers, and he created an atmosphere of collaboration. "The printers got it right in the end," he said. And he added, "One of the pressmen even asked to bring members of his family down to the press, because he was so proud of what he was doing on the Heritage Edition."

A detail of the binding taken during production.

A printed original

SO WHAT IS The Saint John's Bible? Is it a singular manuscript, or is it a printed edition? In the end, it is both.

The manuscript has its own life. It will continue to be displayed, and it will be used in the liturgical life of the Abbey.

In the end, the Heritage Edition will be seen by many more people than the manuscript will. It makes The Saint John's Bible available to the widest possible audience. And because it is not a cold reproduction but a carefully devised and crafted interpretation of the original, it has an integrity of its own. So maybe when my friend tells me she has seen The Saint John's Bible, and the version she has seen is the Heritage Edition, maybe, just maybe, she is absolutely spot-on.

A custom-designed viewing stand and cabinet allows the volumes of the Heritage Edition to be both properly stored and displayed. These stands are made by the Saint John's Abbey Woodshop.

Each volume of the Heritage Edition is protected by its own drop-back box.

EPILOGUE

A CLOSING REFLECTION ON THE SAINT JOHN'S BIBLE

THESE PAST 15 YEARS of documenting the making of The Saint John's Bible have been an incredible privelege. I have had access to Donald Jackson and the Scriptorium; I have been able to touch the actual pages of the Bible; I have had long and rich conversations with the many people who have made the project happen, both at Saint John's and on Donald's team. Now that the manuscript is finished, The Saint John's Bible takes on a life of its own, and all of us who have been so intimately involved in the project can perhaps step back and reflect on what has been achieved.

In this book I have served as a reporter, recounting as faithfully I could how the Bible was made, using the information that all the participants in the project gave me. In this final chapter, I want to say some things from the viewpoint of a commentator, to share some of my own thoughts about the significance of the project and ways that audiences might begin to approach and interpret The Saint John's Bible.

The fact is, The Saint John's Bible is absolutely unique. In my six years as editor of the quarterly magazine *Letter Arts Review,* I have not encountered any other project that can match the Bible in terms of the resources expended on it, the number of artists and scribes collaborating on it, the time devoted to it, or media and gallery attention that has been lavished on it. There is no other contemporary calligraphic project I can think of that compares in terms of its size and scope. It is also a distinctly religious object, which doesn't fit neatly into the categories of contemporary fine art, and this also makes it stand apart.

Artist and audience

ONE OF THE DANGERS of interviewing artists about their work is the inherent suggestion that it is the artists themselves who determine the interpretation of their own work. In the case of The Saint John's Bible, with its often new and frequently ambiguous imagery, there is a temptation to think that Donald and his artists will simply explain the work, or provide a definitive reading of the work from the artists who made it. To do this is to approach the work from the most reductive point of view; it places the artist in the uncomfortable position of ultimate arbitrator of the significance of the work at hand.

The process of looking at new and unfamiliar work is complex. As viewers, we begin with our first reaction, the feeling we have in our gut. If we are moved to examine the work more closely, we may well want to know more about the artist's process and thoughts. But then we usually need to step back and ask ourselves what the work means to us and to the world in which we live.

I think of the interviews and artists' remarks in this book as fulfilling the second part of that process. Donald and the other artists have shared a great deal of their thinking in these interviews. That is good raw material to use as background when we go back and look afresh at the illuminations. But the artists' words are not a straightjacket; they open up possibilities to look at the illuminations. They do not close down the conversation by providing all the answers; in fact, they can only begin that conversation.

The illuminations have been used in small groups all over the world in the context of Bible-studies. Just as the illuminations were produced through a process of rumination that involved both the CIT and the artists, so they now serve to open further exploration of the biblical text and its significance. In the end, the interpretation of The Saint John's Bible can only emerge in the interplay between the art and its viewers, and I suspect there will never be any single definitive reading of the book. If it continues to engage new audiences, it will speak in new ways, and probably interpretations will emerge that would surprise even the artists themselves.

Art and its orthodoxies

THE SAINT JOHN'S BIBLE is not simply a work of art; it is explicitly a work of religious art, produced out of the experience of a specific religious community. As such, it doesn't fit neatly into the categories of contemporary art. In particular, it does not exhibit the kind of detachment and irony that is so much a part of the contemporary art scene. An unapologetic work of religious art challenges some of the orthodoxies that govern the larger art world. Despite this, it has successfully been exhibited at museums of fine art around the country, and has attracted enthusiastic audiences. It has been able to achieve a cross-over that much contemporary religious art has not been able to do.

In art museums spread across the middle of the United States, in regions where religiosity is more taken for granted as a part of daily life, the project has met with record-breaking attendance. In the more secular Northeast, it has tended to be exhibited at venues that specialize in religious work, such as the Museum of Biblical Art in New York, or at venues that have large collections of historic manuscripts, such as the Library of Congress.

One could lament the tension that exists in our society between religiously engaged artwork and the more mainstream expressions of contemporary art; one could critique the fine art world for being resistant to a work with an explicitly religious message. I think this would be a mistake. The fine art of any period in history reflects specific historical developments. Art is, after all, a conversation. To some extent, The Saint John's Bible is an interloper in the conversation going on right now within the fine arts; the Bible's earnestness, its overt religiosity, is out of sync with the fine art of our times. There's nothing to be done with that but to note it as a fact.

Because The Saint John's Bible is explicitly a work of religious art, it asks to be approached as such. I mentioned Bible studies above; they are one classic way "in," if you like. The Saint John's Bible takes the biblical text seriously as the foundational Christian document; its illuminations, special treatments, and calligraphy explore the text with a high degree of reverence. That is its natural context. If one is a Christian, the manuscript opens new approaches to the classic texts of the faith. The fact that the illuminations of The Saint John's Bible are rendered in a recognizably contemporary style will add to a sense of freshness and creativity; it will confirm the Christian's belief that theirs is a living, vibrant tradition.

For non-Christians, The Saint John's Bible may be somewhat more challenging. It can be viewed purely as a modern expression of craft, and enjoyed as a unique handmade book. Or one might step back and appreciate the fact that this is the product of a specific religious culture; even if one is not a participant in this culture, one can suspend one's disbelief and enter into the spirit of this Bible. Perhaps, at the most extreme, The Saint John's Bible can be seen as a provocation: why is this forthright religious object not playing the game of irony that is so much a part of the contemporary art scene? What are we to make of a work that expresses its commitments so directly?

A contemporary Christian art

AS A WORK OF RELIGIOUS ART, The Saint John's Bible raises interesting questions about the nature of Christian art in our own period. I use the term "Christian art" as a purely descriptive term—art made for liturgical or devotional purposes within a Christian community. What does this Bible say about the kind of art that appeals to a contemporary Christian sensibility?

In the Roman Catholic tradition, the different periods of art reflect changes in both theology and piety. In this sense, the Western, Roman Catholic tradition differs from that of the Orthodox, who have a more explicit theology of art, and whose icons carry a weight of authority that art in Western Christendom never had. Orthodox icons have a more stable form; the iconographer is in service to a highly defined tradition. Within the Roman Catholic tradition, art has been more experimental, changing radically over the centuries. Artworks from the High Middle Ages reflect the systematizing sureties of Scholasticism. Many of the stained glass programs in the great cathedrals function almost as diagrams of the faith, displaying the whole scope of the Old and New Testaments as a logical outflowing of a unified divine plan. By contrast, the art of Renaissance in Italy emphasizes the human dimension of sacred story, with Jesus and the saints inhabiting recognizable physical space; this later degenerates into the worldly excesses of Mannerism. In reaction, the art of the Counter-Reformation reemphasizes the key doctrines of the faith while creating vast panoramas laden with ecstatic emotion. In the huge ceiling frescoes of Baroque churches the majesty and power of God burst into the human world, saints and angels swirling around images of the Holy Trinity, or Jesus, or the Blessed Virgin.

The twentieth century, not particularly known for its religious art, was actually a time of exciting experimentation for Christian imagery, and produced masterworks such as Matisse's chapel at Vence and Le Corbusier's church at Ronchamp. By the beginning of the last century, older traditions seemed to have lost their vigor; it was hard to imagine a way of making a straightforward devotional image that would be aesthetically convincing. Such traditional representations were largely left to the realm of the church suppliers—plaster saints still spoke to the devotional lives of the people, to some extent, but it was hard to engage them as serious works of art. In response, artists working on church commissions experimented with new forms including varying degrees of abstraction. What the twentieth century was not able to produce, however, was a coherent movement within Christian art. The old verities had passed away, but no new consensus took their place.

So what does The Saint John's Bible say about Christian art in our own time? The first thing one probably observes is that the illuminations employ very few of the traditional symbols from earlier Christian art. The cross is certainly used, as are the menorah and the Star of David. The figures produced by Aidan Hart make a clear gesture toward the iconographic traditions of Orthodoxy. And the figures of Jesus and John the Baptist are comfortably within the conventions of Christian art. Otherwise, the imagery and symbolism of The Saint John's Bible are quite novel. A large black bird wings its way across the creation illumination at the beginning of Genesis—an entirely new image, unique to this Bible. Strands of DNA, musical chants rendered as patterns of sound from a computer, images of contemporary violence and despair—all of these are new. This suggests that The Saint John's Bible is responding to a hunger for fresh imagery, a desire to respond to the text, not by falling back on tradition, but by favoring novel, creative expressions.

The second observation one might make is that the images in The Saint John's Bible are frequently ambiguous. They do not suggest a single, unified reading. Instead, they are products of individuals meditating on and chewing over the text, and they invite a personal response from the viewer. They embody the process by which they were created. The briefs produced by the CIT were purposely open-ended, suggesting many directions for the illuminators to ponder. The artists themselves were then invited to explore the dimensions of the text that spoke to them, with the CIT brief as a resource. Their visual responses, then, were examined by the CIT in a process of discussion and negotiation.

By emphasizing the personal, creative, and even idiosyncratic readings of the text, the illuminations in The Saint John's Bible reflect a powerful strain in contemporary Christian piety. The illuminated passages are not presented as texts with a single, authoritative message. Instead, the makers of the Bible treat them as texts that inspire multiple readings, that speak to each of us on an individual level. This could reflect a retreat from doctrinal certainty; it could equally signal a deeply held belief in the inspired nature of the Biblical text, in which there is an ongoing process of revelation as generations of Christians read, ponder, and respond.

Another interesting aspect of the illumination program in the Bible is the refusal to give the cycle of illuminations an over-arching structure. There is no grand scheme here linking one part of the Bible to another, as one would find in a medieval Bible. The makers could have chosen to use full-page illuminations as markers of some larger narrative running through the book, or they could have carefully calibrated the treatment of related themes so that parallels could be drawn. Instead, each illumination is treated largely on its own, with highly focused, individualized attention.

Although there are certainly themes that run through the images, and visual quotations that link certain illuminations to others, there is no attempt to create a single unified vision for the book as a whole. Perhaps this reflects the scholarly approach of the CIT, which draws from modern Biblical criticism in a way that makes it hard to view the entire Bible as a unified text. The illuminations suggest a close reading of each particular text within its own historical and theological context. As an artifact, then, The Saint John's Bible reflects a very contemporary way of reading the Bible.

Finally, the illuminations of The Saint John's Bible reflect new concerns within Christian theology and piety. The emphasis on the environment and on the role of the feminine make this a distinctly twenty-first century Bible. Some of the strongest illuminations, at least in my view, are those which explore the roles of women and female figures in the biblical text. This is a new dimension in what has often been a highly patriarchal tradition, and because these images reflect new dimensions of biblical scholarship and concern, they do not have to wrestle with long-established iconographic traditions. One of the illuminations I find most powerful is the *Mirror of Wisdom*; the wise old crone, staring back at us, is one of the most surprising and effective images in the whole book.

The invention of a unique iconography

As I have followed Donald Jackson and his team through the process of making The Saint John's Bible, I have been fascinated by the emergence of recurrent symbolic motifs in the illuminations. Donald could not rely on a tradition to guide him in the creation of the illuminations. Even when he incorporated the work of Aidan Hart, so firmly rooted in the Orthodox tradition, Donald had to be careful to adapt it to a new context, less firmly tied to specific iconographic conventions. Donald and the other illuminators had to discover new symbols and new ways of representing ancient stories.

If you look at the volumes in the order in which they were produced, you can trace a gradual emergence of symbolic devices that appear again and again. The small rainbow bars, and, more generally, rainbow background hues that evoke the divine presence are but one example. In the *Historical Books,* there is a striking unity of tonality, as Donald uses a specific palette in a series of illuminations. By contrast, in the first volume to be completed, *Gospels and Acts,* there is a much greater variety of approaches, as Donald and the illuminators felt their way into the project.

What I find so interesting about this progression is that it was an organic process. It's not that Donald suddenly began to impose a system on the project several years in. Instead, the images that began to emerge from the process worked, they spoke to specific dimension of the text. As the project continued, these provided a body of evocative symbols and motifs from which to draw.

In this way, The Saint John's Bible actually echoes the process by which traditional Christian iconography developed. When the early Church emerged from persecution and became more established in the fourth century, it began to have permanent buildings and to create works of art. In those early years, Christians had no obvious visual language from which to draw. Only slowly did a recognizable Christian iconography establish itself. Some of the early symbols, such as the fish, dropped out of the tradition (only to be revived in this century by Evangelical Christians). Other conventions, such as the bearded Jesus, the halo, or the Virgin's blue dress, emerged and became standard, codified motifs.

Early Christians drew from many sources, many of them not explicitly religious in their own day. To take one simple example, the early Christian basilica was not in fact based on the pattern of the temples of Greece and Rome; instead, it drew from the secular basilicas which were gathering places in the centers of Roman cities.

In a similar way, in seeking new images to incorporate into their illuminations, Donald and the other artists have drawn from a whole range of contemporary and historical references. And so, in looking at The Saint John's Bible, I would prompt you to look closely and see how Donald and the others were able to create a new iconography, to trace the emergence of new motifs. Look for the visual echoes from volume to volume. They are there.

Writing and reading

BY NOW I wonder if you see that I have fallen into a trap. It's a common trap when it comes to talking about The Saint John's Bible. I have only been talking about the pictures. I have said nothing about the writing.

This book is fundamentally about the act of writing. Most of the pages of the manuscript have no illuminations or special treatments at all. If you go through the volumes, you will see page after page of plain writing. It is tempting to pass over these pages, to move on to the more immediately appealing illustrations. But to do this is to miss out on one of the most special parts of the Bible. This is a book. It is meant not just to be looked at, but to be read.

It is not entirely easy to read hand-written text; we are not accustomed to reading from a manuscript. In addition, some of the scripts, such as the incipit scripts at the beginning of many of the volumes, actively slow reading down. The large page size also impedes quick legibility. And yet, if one stops and makes the effort, the Bible is highly legible.

Two dimensions of The Saint John's Bible emerge when one reads the text. First of all, the texts of the

Bible were produced in societies of limited literacy. They were very often read aloud. Indeed, reading aloud was the norm all across the western world until the advent of printing. In reading from The Saint John's Bible, reading aloud slows the process down, and creates a different experience of the text. Reading aloud makes for a more thoughtful, ruminative relationship to the words. The practice ties the reader to the long history of how the Bible has traditionally been read. It also, of course, slows the reading down to a pace that is appropriate for a handwritten text, one that is not so quickly deciphered.

The second dimension that emerges when one actually reads the text is that one becomes keenly aware that these words have been written by another human being. There is a direct human-to-human transmission of these ancient words. The writing changes from line to line and page to page; there is a personality that underlies the writing of each scribe. One might even detect when a scribe hit his or her stride in the writing, or when they had a particularly challenging day at the writing board. There are small imperfections, but there are also delightful details, as when the pen lifts quickly off the end of a line with a graceful and subtle flourish. These are things that we can only really observe when we actually read the text.

Within Judaism, the tradition of reading aloud from a handwritten Torah has survived; in the Christian tradition, it has largely gone by the wayside. The Saint John's Bible allows us to recapture this deeply humane, meaningful way of transmitting the sacred texts.

In conclusion

THE SAINT JOHN'S BIBLE was the brainchild of one man, Donald Jackson, who doggedly pursued his vision until he had found a patron willing to take the risk of creating the most ambitious calligraphic project of our time. Now that it is finished, it takes its place in the liturgical and communal life of Saint John's Abbey and University. But like all great works of art, it is not limited to one specific community. It belongs to all of us.

MICHAEL PATELLA, OSB, SSD, is both professor of New Testament at the School of Theology·Seminary of Saint John's University, Collegeville, Minnesota, and seminary rector. In addition to serving as chair of the Committee on Illumination and Text (CIT) for The Saint John's Bible, he has written The Death of Jesus: The Diabolical Force and the Ministering Angel (Paris: Gabalda, 1999); The Gospel according to Luke, New Collegeville Bible Commentary Series (Collegeville, MN: Liturgical Press, 2005); The Lord of the Cosmos: Mithras, Paul, and the Gospel of Mark (New York: T&T Clark, 2006); Angels and Demons: A Christian Primer of the Spiritual World (Collegeville, MN: Liturgical Press, 2012); and Word and Image: The Hermeneutics of The Saint John's Bible (Collegeville, MN: Liturgical Press, 2013). He has been a frequent contributor to The Bible Today and is a member of the Catholic Biblical Association.

SUSAN WOOD, SCL, is a professor of theology at Marquette University, Milwaukee, Wisconsin. She taught in both the theology department and School of Theology at Saint John's University for twelve years and was the associate dean of the School of Theology for five years. She earned her bachelor's degree at Saint Mary College in Leavenworth, Kansas; her master's degree at Middlebury College, Middlebury, Vermont; and her doctorate degree at Marquette University, Milwaukee, Wisconsin.

COLUMBA STEWART, OSB, is the executive director of the Hill Museum and Manuscript Library (HMML), the home of The Saint John's Bible, where he has developed HMML's projects of manuscript digitization in the Middle East. Having served on the CIT and as curator of special collections before becoming director of HMML, he often speaks about how The Saint John's Bible expresses the vision for the book arts and religious culture at Saint John's University. Father Columba has published extensively on monastic topics and is a professor of monastic studies at Saint John's School of Theology. He received his bachelor's degree in history and literature from Harvard College, his master's degree in religious studies from Yale University, and his doctorate in theology from the University of Oxford.

IRENE NOWELL, OSB, is a Benedictine from Mount St. Scholastica in Atchison, Kansas. She is an adjunct professor of Scripture for the School of Theology at Saint John's University. Sister Irene received her bachelor's degree in music from Mount St. Scholastica College in Kansas and master's degrees in German and theology from The Catholic University of America and Saint John's University. She holds a doctorate in biblical studies from The Catholic University of America.

JOHANNA BECKER, OSB (1921–2012), a Benedictine potter, teacher, art historian, and Orientalist, combined these in the different facets of her work. As a teacher in the art department of the College of Saint Benedict and Saint John's University, she taught both studio classes (primarily ceramics) and art history, focusing in later years on the arts of Asia. As a specialist in Asian ceramics, particularly those of seventeenth-century Japan, she did connoisseurship for public and private museums, published a book, Karatsu Ware, and wrote and lectured worldwide. Her art history classes benefitted from the years she lived in Japan and her time spent in the majority of Asian countries as an art researcher. Sister Johanna held a bachelor of fine arts degree from the University of Colorado, a master of fine arts degree in studio art from Ohio State University, and a doctorate in art history from the University of Michigan. She was a member of the Monastery of Saint Benedict, St. Joseph, Minnesota.

NATHANAEL HAUSER, OSB, is an artist who works in egg tempera, enamel, calligraphy, and mosaic. While teaching art history as an associate professor at Saint John's University, he also taught calligraphy and the theology and practice of icon painting. Father Nathanael has undertaken commissions for churches, monastic communities, and private collections, creating icons, enameled crosses, calligraphy books, reliquaries, and Christmas crèches. His work and papers have been exhibited and presented in the United States and Rome, Italy. Father Nathanael received his bachelor's degree in philosophy from St. John's Seminary College in Camarillo, California. He received his STB from the Pontificio Ateneo di Sant'Anselmo, Rome, and his doctorate in classical and medieval art and archeology from the University of Minnesota.

ALAN REED, OSB, is the curator of art collections at the Hill Museum and Manuscript Library. Brother Alan previously taught design and drawing in the joint art department of Saint John's University and the College of St. Benedict for twenty-five years and, toward the end of that time, was chair of the department for six years. He has a bachelor of arts degree from Saint John's University in studio art, a master of art education from the Rhode Island School of Design, and a master of fine art from the University of Chicago in studio art and art theory.

ELLEN JOYCE teaches medieval history at Beloit College in Beloit, Wisconsin. Her research interests are in the role of visions and dreams in medieval monastic culture. She also has a passion for the study of illuminated manuscripts and their production and often teaches courses on topics related to books and their readers in the Middle Ages. She served on the CIT while she was employed at the Hill Museum and Manuscript Library and teaching at Saint John's University. Dr. Joyce received her master's and doctoral degrees from the Centre for Medieval Studies at the University of Toronto and her undergraduate degree in humanities from Yale University.

ROSANNE KELLER (1938–2012) was a sculptor whose work is on permanent display throughout the United States and the United Kingdom. In 1993 she was commissioned to create a ceramic Buddha and eight ritual vessels for the private meditation room of His Holiness, the Dalai Lama. Her sculpture can be seen at St. Deiniol's Library and St. Bueno's Jesuit Retreat Center in Wales; Saint John's University and the St. Cloud Children's Home in Minnesota; Exeter Cathedral; Taize, France; and on the campus of Texas Woman's University. She published a book on pilgrimage, Pilgrim in Time, and a novel, A Summer All Her Own, as well as texts for literacy programs.

DAVID PAUL LANGE, OSB, a monk, artist, and teacher, has been a member of the art department of Saint John's University and the College of Saint Benedict since 2001. He has a bachelor's degree from Saint Olaf College in philosophy and a master of fine arts in studio art from the University of Southern Illinois at Edwardsville. A sculptor by training, Brother David Paul also teaches modern contemporary art history and theory, drawing, and foundations.

BROTHER SIMON-HÒA PHAN is an associate professor of art at Saint John's University. He holds a bachelor of arts in philosophy from Saint John's Seminary, Camarillo, a bachelor of arts in religious studies from Louvain, a bachelor of fine arts in painting from the Maryland Institute, and a master of fine arts in film and video from California Institute of the Arts. A member of the CIT since 2008, he served as artist advisor for the Bible Project.

Other members of the broader Saint John's community, including Susan Brix, Jerome Tupa, OSB, and David Cotter, OSB, have served at various times on the Committee on Illumination and Text.

Bible Project Director
>Valerie Kolarik (1999)
>Carol Marrin (2000–2008)
>Tim Ternes (2008–present)

Bible Project Leader
>Michael Bush (2010–present)

GOSPELS & ACTS

Interpretive illuminations, incipits and special treatments in this volume are the work of Donald Jackson, except:

CHAPTER	ILLUSTRATION	ARTIST	NOTES
MATTHEW			
1	Decoration facing Frontispiece	Donald Jackson (DJ)	With contributions from SMJ
5	Sermon on the Mount	Thomas Ingmire	
9	The Calming of the Storm	Suzanne Moore	
14	Middle-Eastern Arabesque	Andrew Jamieson (AJ)	
22	"You shall love the Lord"	Hazel Dolby	
24	Last Judgement	Suzanne Moore	
28	Carpet Page	Sally Mae Joseph (SMJ)	
MARK			
1	Decoration	Aidan Hart (AH)	
3	Sower and the Seed	Aidan Hart	With contributions from DJ, SMJ
5	Two Cures	Aidan Hart	With contributions from DJ, SMJ
10	Transfiguration	Donald Jackson	In collaboration with AH
11	"Listen to Him"	Sally Mae Joseph	
13	"Hear O Israel"	Hazel Dolby	
16	Carpet Page	Sally Mae Joseph	
LUKE			
1	Magnificat	Sally Mae Joseph	
2	Gloria in Excelsis	Sally Mae Joseph	
2	Nunc Dimitiis	Hazel Dolby	
9	"You shall love the Lord"	Hazel Dolby	
15	Luke Anthology	Donald Jackson	With contributions from SMJ, AH
24	Decoration	Sally Mae Joseph	
24	Carpet Page - Tree of Life	Sally Mae Joseph	
JOHN			
6	"I am" sayings	Thomas Ingmire	
7	Woman taken in Adultery	Aidan Hart	With contributions from DJ, SMJ
21	Decoration	Sally Mae Joseph	
21	Carpet Page	Sally Mae Joseph	
ACTS			
2	Decoration	Sally Mae Joseph	
5	Life in the Community	Aidan Hart	In collaboration with DJ
15	The Life of Saint Paul	Donald Jackson	In collab. with AH, contributions from AJ
27	"To the ends of the earth"	Donald Jackson	With contributions from SMJ, AJ
28	"You will be my witness"	Donald Jackson	With contributions from AJ

Scribes: Sue Hufton, Donald Jackson, Sally Mae Joseph & Brian Simpson
Hebrew Script: Christopher Calderhead (Notes), Donald Jackson, Izzy Pludwinski (Consultant)
Natural History Illustrations: Chris Tomlin
Computer Graphics: Vin Godier

PENTATEUCH

Interpretive illuminations, incipits and special treatments in this volume are the work of Donald Jackson, except:

CHAPTER	ILLUSTRATION	ARTIST
	GENESIS	
2	Garden of Eden	Donald Jackson (DJ) With contributions from Chris Tomlin (CT)
3	Adam & Eve	Donald Jackson With contributions from CT
29	Jacob's Ladder	Donald Jackson In collaboration with CT
34	Jacob's Dream	Donald Jackson With contributions from CT
50	Carpet Page	Sally Mae Joseph (SMJ)
	EXODUS	
19	Ten Commandments	Thomas Ingmire
	LEVITICUS	
19:2	"You shall be holy"	Sally Mae Joseph
19:18	"You shall not take vengeance"	Sally Mae Joseph
19:34	"The alien who resides"	Sally Mae Joseph
	NUMBERS	
6:24	"The Lord bless you"	Suzanne Moore
20:12	"You did not trust"	Thomas Ingmire
21:8	"Make a poisonous serpent"	Thomas Ingmire
	DEUTERONOMY	
6:4-5	"Hear O Israel"	Hazel Dolby
30:19-20	"Choose life"	Suzanne Moore
33	Death of Moses	Donald Jackson (In collaboration with AH)
34	Menorah decoration	Sally Mae Joseph (contributions from SMJ)

Scribes: Sue Hufton, Donald Jackson, Sally Mae Joseph & Brian Simpson
Hebrew Script: Donald Jackson, Izzy Pludwinski (Consultant & Scribe)
Natural History illustrations: Chris Tomlin / Computer Graphics: Vin Godier

PSALMS

The Frontispiece and all book headings in this volume are the work of Donald Jackson.

Psalms 1–41	Book I	Brian Simpson
Psalms 42–72	Book II	Sally Mae Joseph
Psalms 73–89	Book III	Donald Jackson
Psalms 90–106	Book IV	Donald Jackson
Psalms 107–150	Book V	Sally Mae Joseph
Psalm 150	"Praise the Lord"	Sally Mae Joseph
Psalms 6, 32, 38, 51, 102, 130, 143	Penitential Psalms	Donald Jackson

Raised & burnished gilding throughout: Sally Mae Joseph
Psalm Numbers: Brian Simpson / Computer Graphics: Vin Godier

PROPHETS

All incipits, marginals, book headings, capital letters, and decorations in this volume are the work by Donald Jackson, except:

CHAPTER	ILLUSTRATION	ARTIST
	ISAIAH	
1	Carpet Page	Donald Jackson and Sally Mae Joseph
1:16-17	"Wash Yourselves"	Sally Mae Joseph
2:4	"He Shall Judge"	Sally Mae Joseph
6:1-13	Isaiah's Vision	Donald Jackson
7, 9, 11	Messianic Predictions	Thomas Ingmire
30	Scarab Beetle	Chris Tomlin
40:1-5	"Comfort, O Comfort"	Sally Mae Joseph
49:1-4	"Listen to Me"	Sally Mae Joseph
52:13–53:12	Suffering Servant	Donald Jackson
60:1-3	"Arise, Shine"	Sally Mae Joseph
66:3-13	"As a Mother Comforts Her Child"	Thomas Ingmire
	JEREMIAH	
1:4-10	"Now the Word of God"	Sally Mae Joseph
17	Field Crickets	Chris Tomlin
35	Cicada	Chris Tomlin
	LAMENTATIONS	
5	Carpet Design	Donald Jackson and Sally Mae Joseph
	BARUCH	
6	Carpet Design	Donald Jackson and Sally Mae Joseph
	EZEKIEL	
1–3	Ezekiel's Vision	Donald Jackson
22	Black Fly	Chris Tomlin
37:1-14	Valley of the Dry Bones	Donald Jackson
40:1-48	Ezekiel's Vision of the New Temple	Donald Jackson
47	Papaya Tree	Sally Mae Joseph
	DANIEL	
7:9-14	Vision of the Son of Man	Donald Jackson, with contribution from Aidan Hart
	AMOS	
2	Carpet Design	Donald Jackson and Sally Mae Joseph
3–4	Demands of Social Justice	Suzanne Moore
9	Carpet Design	Donald Jackson and Sally Mae Joseph
	MICAH	
6:8	"He Has Told You, O Mortal"	Sally Mae Joseph
	HAGGAI	
2	Carpet Design	Donald Jackson and Sally Mae Joseph

ZECHARIAH

9:9	Messianic Prediction/Rejoice!	
		Hazel Dolby
14	Carpet Design	Donald Jackson and Sally Mae Joseph

MALACHI

4	Carpet Page	Donald Jackson and Sally Mae Joseph

Scribes: Donald Jackson, Sally Mae Joseph (poetry), Brian Simpson (poetry), Sue Hufton (text), Susie Leiper (text)

Hebrew Script: Izzy Pludwinski, Donald Jackson

Chapter Numbers: Numbers by Brian Simpson with colored squares by Sally Mae Joseph

Computer Graphics: Vin Godier, Sarah Harris

WISDOM BOOKS

All incipits, marginals, book headings, and decorations in this volume are the work by Donald Jackson, except:

CHAPTER	ILLUSTRATION	ARTIST
	JOB	
1–2	Job Frontispiece	Donald Jackson
15	"Wisdom Is Radiant" (Wisdom of Solomon 6:12)	Angela Swan
19:25	"For I Know That My Redeemer Lives"	Diane M. von Arx
38:1–42:6	Out of the Whirlwind — "Where Were You"	Thomas Ingmire
38:1–42:6	Out of the Whirlwind — "I Am the Lord"	Thomas Ingmire
42:7-17	He Will Wipe Every Tear	Thomas Ingmire
	PROVERBS	
1:7-8	"The Fear of the Lord"	Thomas Ingmire
8:22-31 and 9:1-6	The Pillars of Wisdom	Donald Jackson
31:10-31	Hymn to a Virtuous Woman	Hazel Dolby
	ECCLESIASTES	
1–12	Ecclesiastes Frontispiece	Donald Jackson, with contribution from Chris Tomlin
11:1	"Send out Your Bread upon the Waters"	Diane M. von Arx
	THE SONG OF SOLOMON	
1–2	Decoration	Donald Jackson
4:1-15	Love and Song of Solomon	Donald Jackson
6:3	"I Am My Beloved's"	Donald Jackson, butterflies by Sarah Harris
8:6-7	"Set Me a Seal"	Donald Jackson
	THE WISDOM OF SOLOMON	
1:16–2:24	Let Us Lie in Wait	Thomas Ingmire
4:7-9	"But the Righteous, though They Die"	Sally Mae Joseph
6:12-18	"Wisdom Is Radiant"	Sally Mae Joseph
7	Correction Bumblebee	Bee by Chris Tomlin, pulley system by Sarah Harris
7:22-30	Wisdom Woman	Donald Jackson
10:1–11:4	Creation, Fall, Passover, and Deliverance	Donald Jackson

SIRACH

Scribes: Donald Jackson, Sally Mae Joseph (poetry), Brian Simpson (poetry), Sue Hufton (text), Susie Leiper (text), Angela Swan (text)

Hebrew Script: Izzy Pludwinski, Donald Jackson / Capital Letters: Donald Jackson, Brian Simpson

Chapter Numbers: Brian Simpson / Computer Graphics: Vin Godier, Sarah Harris

HISTORICAL BOOKS

All incipits, marginals, book headings, capital letters, and decorations in this volume are the work by Donald Jackson, except:

CHAPTER	ILLUSTRATION	ARTIST

JOSHUA

JUDGES

JUDITH

16 Monarch Butterfly Being Eaten by a Whip Spider   Chris Tomlin

ESTHER

5:1-14 Esther   Donald Jackson

1 MACCABEES

4 Gold Beetle and Silver Beetle   Chris Tomlin

11 Glasswing Butterfly and Black Widow Spider   Chris Tomlin

2 MACCABEES

7 Painted Lady Butterfly and Caterpillars   Chris Tomlin

12:42-45 "And They Turned to Supplication"   Sally Mae Joseph

15 Chameleon   Chris Tomlin

Scribes: Sue Hufton, Susie Leiper, Angela Swan, Sally Mae Joseph, Brian Simpson
Hebrew Script: Izzy Pludwinski, Donald Jackson / Chapter Numbers: Brian Simpson
Computer graphics: Vin Godier, Sarah Harris

LETTERS & REVELATION

All incipits, marginals, book headings, capital letters and decorations in this volume are the work by Donald Jackson, except:

CHAPTER	ILLUSTRATION	ARTIST
	ROMANS	
1	Carpet Page	Donald Jackson
4:3	"For What Does the Scripture Say"	Donald Jackson
4:16-17	"For This Reason"	Donald Jackson
5	"Therefore, since We Are Justified"	Donald Jackson
6:22-23	"But Now That You Have Been Freed from Sin"	Thomas Ingmire
8:1-39	Fulfilment of Creation	Thomas Ingmire
11:17-24	"But if Some of the Branches"	Donald Jackson
	1 CORINTHIANS	
2–3	Nemoptera Bipennis Insect	Chris Tomlin
11	Scribes Signature Bar	Sally Mae Joseph, Angela Swan, Sue Hufton, Brian Simpson, Susie Leiper, Donald Jackson
11:23-26	"For I Received from the Lord"	Thomas Ingmire
13:1-13	"If I Speak in the Tongues of Mortals"	Thomas Ingmire
15:56-58	"The Sting of Death Is Sin"	Hazel Dolby
15:50-58	At the Last Trumpet — "We Will Be Changed"	Hazel Dolby
	2 CORINTHIANS	
7	Bee	Chris Tomlin
	GALATIANS	
3:23-29	"Now before Faith" and Comma Butterfly and butterfly Chris Tomlin	Special treatment Donald Jackson

EPHESIANS

4:4-6	"There Is One Body and One Spirit"	Hazel Dolby
5:8, 14	"For Once You Were Darkness"	Hazel Dolby

PHILIPPIANS

2:5-11	"And Every Tongue Should Confess"	Suzanne Moore

COLOSSIANS

1	Common Blue Butterfly on Buddleia Flowers	Chris Tomlin
1:15-20	"He Is the Image of the Invisible God"	Donald Jackson

1 THESSALONIANS

4:16-18	"For the Lord Himself"	Donald Jackson

2 THESSALONIANS

3:10	"For Even When We Were with You"	Donald Jackson

HEBREWS

1 and 3	Dragonflies on Yorkshire Fog Grass	Chris Tomlin
8:10	"This Is the Covenant"	Suzanne Moore
11:1	"Now Faith Is the Assurance"	Donald Jackson

JAMES

2:14-17	"What Good Is It, My Brothers and Sisters"	Donald Jackson
3:17-18	"But the Wisdom from above Is First Pure"	Donald Jackson
5:13-16	"Are Any among You Suffering"	Donald Jackson

1 PETER

3:18–4:11	Harrowing of Hell	Donald Jackson

1 JOHN

4:7-12	"Beloved, Let Us Love One Another"	Donald Jackson

REVELATION

1:12-20	Incipit and Son of Man Illumination	Donald Jackson
2:1–3:22	Seven Churches	Donald Jackson
6:1-8	Four Horsemen of the Apocalypse	Donald Jackson
12:1-17	Woman and the Dragon	Donald Jackson with contribution by Chris Tomlin
12:1-17	Down to Earth	Donald Jackson
21:5	"See I Am Making All Things New"	Donald Jackson
21:1–22:5	Alpha and Omega — The New Jerusalem	Donald Jackson
22:20-21	"The One Who Testifies . . . Amen"	Donald Jackson

Scribes: Donald Jackson, Sue Hufton, Susie Leiper, Angela Swan, Sally Mae Joseph, Brian Simpson
Chapter Numbers: Brian Simpson
Computer Graphics: Vin Godier, Sarah Harris

ACKNOWLEDG-
MENTS

IT IS FOUR YEARS since I began to write *Illuminating the Word: The Making of The Saint John's Bible*. Many people have helped with the research and production of this book, and I am grateful to all of them.

Donald Jackson opened the Scriptorium to me and sat for many hours of interviews. He put his staff at my disposal and gave me intimate access to the project as it unfolded. He shared his hopes, dreams and frustrations about the project and trusted me to tell this story. I could never have written the book without his help.

Mabel Jackson has always been a thoughtful and generous host. On my many trips to Wales, she made me feel at home and made sure I had everything I needed to do my work. Her quiet dedication to the project is often expressed behind the scenes and it is invaluable.

Sally Mae Joseph provided me an insider's view of the workings of the Scriptorium. I value her friendship more than I can express.

Other members of the Scriptorium team helped me collect reference material, make photocopies and pull out pages of the manuscript for me to see. Early in my involvement, Mark L'Argent and Olivia Edwards aided the research. In more recent years, Rebecca Cherry has fielded many of my phone calls and an alarmingly large flow of e-mail.

Jo White was the person who first suggested I should be the one to write this book. She made the introductions and helped me with details of my contract.

Saint John's Abbey provided me a place to work on many visits to Collegeville. The resources of the monastery and university were made available with great generosity. The staff at the Hill Monastic Manuscript Library was particularly helpful.

The monks at Saint John's welcomed me as a guest several times within the monastic enclosure. Their hospitality reminded me that the monastery is not simply a big institution—it is their home.

The leaders of the abbey and university took time out of very busy schedules to grant me interviews. I am grateful to Abbot John Klassen, OSB, and President Dietrich Reinhart, OSB, for giving me their time and supporting the writing of this book.

While I was living in England, my boss, the Reverend Andrew McKearney, gave me great flexibility to arrange short trips to Wales in order to do my research.

Betsy Jennings Powell—who has no background in calligraphy—read the entire typescript as a favor to me. Her careful attention to detail and sensitive comments on the text helped me make the book as accessible as possible to the general reader.

Fact-checking and proofreading by Margaret Arnold, Daniel Durken, OSB, Donald Jackson, Sally Mae Joseph, Carol Marrin, Mary Schaffer and John Taylor helped purge the text of errors. Any mistakes which remain are entirely my own.

Margaret Arnold and Wayne Torborg helped sort through many hundreds of images as we prepared the book. Wayne's expertise with digital imagery proved invaluable in sorting the wheat from the chaff.

All of those who sat for interviews, either in person or by telephone, were extremely generous with their time and their insights into the project. I hope I have captured not only their words but the spirit of our conversations.

Finally I owe a debt of gratitude to Carol Marrin, director of the Bible Project. Carol's enormous efficiency and her willingness to embark on the huge learning curve of putting this book together have been an inspiration. I have relied on her good humor and deep common sense throughout my work.

CHRISTOPHER CALDERHEAD, 2005

MOST OF THE first edition of *Illuminating the Word* was written while I was living in Cambridge, England. This edition has been written after I relocated to New York City. When I wrote the chapters for part 1 of this book, I had the privilege of visiting Donald Jackson's Scriptorium many times and watched the makers of the Bible at work. Since then, I have seen the project from the other side, spending time at Saint John's Abbey in Minnesota and visiting the touring exhibitions of the Bible in places as far-flung as Texas, Florida, and Washington, DC. I have watched the Bible project grow into a vast public enterprise, and I have participated in some of the events around the traveling exhibitions.

The research for the new chapters of this book was carried out largely by phone, e-mail, and Internet-based teleconferencing. In many ways, it has felt like a more solitary enterprise this time around.

I do want, however, to add some new thanks to those who helped me put this second edition together. Donald Jackson has once again made himself readily available for interviews and has provided rich feedback on the drafts of each chapter. His assistant, Sarah Harris, has been invaluable in assembling material, consulting the archives, and providing anything I needed to bring the new edition to fruition. I am deeply in her debt.

All the artists and scribes were very generous with their time as I conducted interviews with them.

I want to thank Tim Ternes for providing invaluable support. I have always appreciated his good humor and efficiency.

Lauren L. Murphy at Liturgical Press did a very thorough job copyediting the text and incorporating changes and additions to the drafts. This has been a complex jigsaw puzzle to put together, and she has brought a keen eye for detail to the project.

Finally, I want to thank Jerry Kelly, who designed both editions of this book. He has been an invaluable partner in the process. I'm not sure I would have made it through without him.

CHRISTOPHER CALDERHEAD, 2014

PRODUCTION CREDITS

Editor: *Christopher Calderhead*
Copy Editor: *Lauren L. Murphy*
Production Manager: *Colleen Stiller*
Designer: *Jerry Kelly*